The Bloody
Road to Tunis

For Mary and Launa

The Bloody Road to Tunis

Destruction of the Axis Forces
in North Africa:
November 1942 – May 1943

David Rolf

With a Foreword by
Major-General Julian Thompson

Frontline Books, London

The Bloody Road to Tunis

A Greenhill Book

First published in 2001 by Greenhill Books, Lionel Leventhal Limited
www.greenhillbooks.com

This paperback edition published in 2015 by

Frontline Books
an imprint of Pen & Sword Bookws Ltd,
47 Church Street, Barnsley, S. Yorkshire, S70 2AS
For more information on our books, please visit
www.frontline-books.com, email info@frontline-books.com
or write to us at the above address.

ISBN: 978-1-84832-783-2

CIP data records for this title are available from the British Library

Edited and designed by Donald Sommerville
Printed and bound by CPI Group (UK) Ltd, Croydon, CR0 4YY

Contents

List of Maps

Acknowledgements

The author wishes to thank the authors, publishers and copyright holders of quotations used in the text and listed in the Notes at the end of each chapter. The *Trustees of the Liddell Hart Centre for Military Archives* kindly granted permission to quote from a number of papers in their collection; specific details of these are given in the appropriate Notes and in the Bibliography. In a few other cases it was not possible to trace the copyright holder and any inadvertent infringement is regretted.

The author also wishes to place on record his appreciation of the work of John Richards, who drew the maps, and of Grace Horton, who compiled the index.

List of Illustrations

illustrations appear on pages 97–112

The following images were kindly supplied by the Imperial War Museum (IWM), London, and by the US National Archives and Records Administration (NARA), Washington, DC. Individual images are credited to the appropriate institution in the reference codes, which are listed below in parentheses.

1. Marshall and Eisenhower (NARA III SC 175179).
2. Rommel (Author's collection).
3. Alexander and Montgomery (IWM BM 17320).
4. De Guingand (IWM E 22000).
5. Paratroops en route to Tunisia (IWM NA 127).
6. American landings at Surcouf (IWM NA 30).
7. Anderson, Allfrey and Evelegh (IWM BNA 3089).
8. Fredendall on board Bitish aircraft carrier (IWM A 13895).
9. Giraud, Roosevelt, de Gaulle and Churchill at Casablanca (IWM NA 478).
10. Shattered gun turret of a German Mk III at Bou Arada (IWM NA 526).
11. SAS patrol (IWM E 21337).
12. Leclerc and Montgomery (IWM E 21955).
13. RAF Bostons over Tunisia (IWM CNA 475).
14. German Tiger tank (IWM BH 18334XP).
15. American soldiers crossing the Kasserine Pass (NARA III SC 167571).
16. Cameraman filming advance on Kasserine (IWM NA 848).
17. Bogged Valentine tank at Wadi Zigzaou (IWM NA 1348).
18. Patton (NARA III SC 171646).
19. German POW at Gafsa (NARA III SC 171124).
20. Coningham and Broadhurst (IWM CM 4260).
21. Freyberg (IWM BM 403).
22. Leese (IWM BNA 16880).
23. Allied troops in Gafsa (NARA III SC 175520)
24. Gurkhas at Medenine (IWM NA 1096).
25. Captured German 88mm gun at Enfidaville (IWM NA 2055).
26. Black Watch soldier at Gabès Gap (IWM NA 1846).
27. Lancashire Fusiliers (IWM NA 2126).
28. Stretcher bearers on Longstop Hill (IWM NA 2237).
29. Horrocks (IWM E 16462).
30. American patrol in Bizerte (IWM NA 2735).
31. Crowds in Tunis cheer Churchill tank (IWM NA 2880).
32. Von Arnim leaves plane at Algiers (IWM NA 2812).
33. Von Sponeck with Freyberg and Keightley at Bou Ficha (IWM NA 2817).
34. Montgomery with von Liebenstein and Messe (IWM NA 2891).

Foreword

The Tunisian campaign of 1942–43 failed to meet the objectives originally set for it by the Allies: to take Tunis by Christmas 1942, and trap Rommel in Libya. Instead, it took six months of some of the bloodiest fighting experienced by the Western Allies in the Second World War, before General Sir Harold Alexander could signal to Winston Churchill: 'It is my duty to report that the Tunisian campaign is over. All enemy resistance has ceased. We are masters of the North African shores.'

In his aptly titled *The Bloody Road to Tunis*, David Rolf makes it clear why the earlier hopes for quick victory were dashed. Perhaps the most fundamental error committed by the Allied planners, not for the first nor last time in the Second World War, was underestimating the Germans' speed of reaction – in this case to the combined US and British invasion of North Africa on 8 November 1942. A distinguished British soldier with much battle experience said of another battle, in another theatre: 'Time and again, however empty of Germans and peaceful the scene appeared to be, if you touched them in an area important to them, their reaction was swift and violent.' He was referring to the astonishing ability of the German forces, the Army especially, regardless of the punishment they might have taken, to be 'quicker on the draw', in the tactical and operational sense than most of their opponents. Nowhere was this more brilliantly demonstrated than in their lightning reinforcement of Tunisia by air and sea, and the ruthlessness with which they dealt with the French, snuffing out any attempts at resistance; few and feeble though these were under a dithering and divided leadership.

David Rolf has meticulously researched both Allied and German documents in order to present the reader with a balanced picture of the campaign. His clear exposition of the terrain is excellent, an aspect that is too often ignored, or brushed over, by authors of works of military history. The logistic difficulties faced by both sides are also given due weight, again important for the effect this was to have on the manner in which each side was to handle the campaign.

Although not sub-titled as a study in command, the author has provided many fascinating insights into this aspect at all levels, from Eisenhower, the Allied commander-in-chief, to junior non-commissioned officers. For me this is one of the most compelling features of the book. Many of the vivid passages which relate the experiences of commanders, especially at the lower level, are taken from unpublished sources in Britain, the United States and Germany.

There have of course been many books in which Eisenhower's character and military genius, or lack of it, have been discussed. Comment has ranged from uncritical hero-worship to denigration. When one examines Eisenhower's unremarkable military record, including a total lack of warfighting experience, it is a tribute to the perspicacity of General Marshall, the US Army Chief of Staff, that he summoned him to his staff in Washington immediately after America entered the war. Eisenhower's appointment as Commanding General of all American forces in the European Theater of Operations followed a few months later. Marshall was not infallible, as demonstrated by the early fall from grace of some of his other selections for high command when exposed to the crucible of battle, including Fredendall in Tunisia and Lucas in Italy. But Marshall's choice of Eisenhower was inspired. David Rolf's discussion of Eisenhower's faults and strengths is even-handed and perceptive. A generalissimo rather than a general, a committee chairman of genius, more than any other commander, Eisenhower was responsible for providing the glue which held together the US and British forces first in North Africa and later in Europe. As a supreme commander, the post he was eventually, in Alanbrooke's words, pushed 'up into', he excelled. As a field commander he was not a success — as events would show when he assumed personal command of all land operations in North-West Europe. This failing was evident early in the Tunisian campaign. Responsibility for the American disaster at Kasserine ultimately rests with Eisenhower for sanctioning, by default, the thinly spread deployment of the US II Corps. After a personal visit before the German attack at Kasserine, he expressed dismay at the dispositions, but did nothing, possibly lacking the experience to correct the flaws in the layout, and the confidence to 'grip' and 'sort out' the commanders responsible.

Commanders often make mistakes in their first battle, and those that remain in post and are promoted, are the ones who have learned from their mistakes, while avoiding being sacked, killed or being taken prisoner. The Americans had a great deal of learning to do in a very short space of time, and one of the consequences of the hard and protracted fighting in North Africa was to 'blood' the US Army. As battle pitilessly seeks out the weaknesses in human beings, so it finds the flaws and cracks in military organisations. Among those thus exposed were poor training, faulty tactics, inept leadership at all levels, and perhaps above all lack of what Napoleon called 'the first quality of a soldier: fortitude in enduring fatigue and hardship'. American soldiers, despite being the products of a comfortable society, commanded by officers with little or no battle experience, learned very quickly indeed. The basis for the performance of battle-hardened outfits such as the 1st Infantry Division ('The Big Red One') in Europe was laid in the misery of the wet, cold, scrub-covered mountains of Tunisia, fighting crack German formations.

The British were not immune to making mistakes either, with less excuse. Anderson, the commander of British First Army, which initially included the US II Corps, was uninspiring, slow, and tactless. With greater drive, and more imaginative use of the parachute troops at his disposal, both British and American, the Allies might, just, have reached Tunis before the German build-up stopped the advance in its tracks, leading to the grinding slog that ensued.

Alexander was brought in from his post as Commander-in-Chief Middle East to take charge of the mess as deputy C-in-C to Eisenhower. He ended up taking command of British First and Eighth Armies with all American and French ground forces under his newly formed 18th Army Group. Although his arrival brought considerable improvement on the muddle he inherited, the Allied armies in North Africa still suffered from a lack of firm control and direction from the top.

David Rolf also pays due regard to the indispensable contribution of the air forces and navies to Allied success in the campaign, and the daring, but ultimately fruitless, efforts by German and Italian air and sea transports to supply the Axis armies. He quotes the ferocious signal from Admiral Cunningham, the Allied Naval Force commander, to his ships attacking the vessels attempting to evacuate the Axis troops; 'Sink, burn and destroy. Let nothing pass.' For now was Cunningham's opportunity to exact revenge for the agony of the Royal Navy and British Army during the evacuation of Greece and Crete two years earlier under the lash of the Luftwaffe.

Axis prisoners taken at the end of the Tunisian campaign outnumbered those at Stalingrad earlier in the year. It was a crushing defeat for Hitler and Mussolini. There are those who argue that the invasion of North Africa and subsequent campaign were unnecessary. It is hard to see how Montgomery could have cleared the North African coast single-handed, without the pressure exerted on the Axis forces by the opening up of another front. The experience gained in the landings, the first Allied combined operation of such magnitude, was to be invaluable in those that followed; as were the formulation and testing under battle conditions of all the arrangements and organisation for staffing and commanding a huge military enterprise involving the armed forces of two nations. Finally, and it cannot be said too often, the foundations of the dash and spirit that the US Army was to show in Sicily, Italy, France and Germany, were laid on the bloody road to Tunis.

Julian Thompson

Major-General
Visiting Professor,
Department of War Studies
King's College, London

Preface

The struggle for Tunisia was a furnace in which British and Americans, from the top brass to the humblest soldier, learned how to live, fight and die together. To discover how the Allied fighting machine was forged, from the tentative floundering of the British First Army and US II Corps in the mud and rain of northern Tunisia to Montgomery's Eighth Army, far away in the burning sands of Libya, I have turned not only to official papers but especially to the letters, diaries and accounts of men who were there. They experienced the fighting at first-hand or bore the enormous stress of directing battles in which one false move could bring disaster.

In doing so I have been mindful of a remark made by General T.J. Conway who, as a young man, fought in Tunisia: 'You know, one of the matters seems to me not really discussed... [in] unit histories or the history of war, is again the question of personality... I think it's a core element which again, is largely neglected.' I hope this is something fully brought out in these pages. Time and again, I have been struck by the good humour, comradeship and limitless courage of the troops, irrespective of nationality, who were caught up in the struggle. Their common humanity lit up the sombre events which this book relates.

While researching archive collections in Britain, America and Germany, I have received much help and assistance from many people. In particular, Jürgen Seibel again accompanied me to the Bundesarchiv-Militärarchiv where his fluency in English and German enabled me to work quickly and efficiently through the German documents. He also translated other material into English, read part of my manuscript, and made a number of important comments. Angie Gibbs also kindly helped with some of the early research and commented perceptively on several draft chapters.

In London, Philip Reed, formerly Deputy Keeper of Documents at the Imperial War Museum and now Curator of the Cabinet War Rooms, was once more outstandingly helpful in directing me to the Museum's extensive manuscript collections. I am grateful also to Roderick Suddaby, Keeper of Documents, and Conrad Wood of the Museum's Department of Sound Recordings, who provided me with invaluable guidance.

At the Churchill Archives Centre, Elizabeth Bennett and her staff were unfailingly helpful, as was Patricia Methven and staff at the Liddell Hart Centre for Military Archives. My frequent requests for information when working at the Public Record Office and libraries of the Universities of Cambridge and Birmingham invariably met with professionalism and courtesy. I am the fortunate recipient of an Honorary Research Fellowship in the Department of Modern History at the University of Birmingham and a Research Associateship at

University College, Worcester. Both have offered me valuable opportunities to discuss my research with fellow historians.

In the United States I enjoyed researching in the Eisenhower Library and was particularly helped by Herb Pankratz. I also appreciated working at the George C. Marshall Research Library, where my task was made much easier by the fact that, exceptionally, I was allowed to read and photocopy sections of the Marshall Papers which at that time were in process of cataloguing and publication.

Returning to Washington, I was a regular visitor to the US National Archives at Suitland, MD (relocated in 1993 to Archive II at College Park, MD), where staff did their best with somewhat inadequate resources to guide me through the complexities of its filing system. In contrast, the Manuscript Division, Library of Congress, provided superb working conditions and I was particularly grateful to staff there for persisting until they secured access for me to the Patton Papers. Finally, my visit to the United States Army Military History Institute was rewarded by a splendid range of papers and associated material. The Archivist-Historian, Dr. Richard J. Sommers, introduced me to David A. Keough who possessed an encyclopaedic knowledge of the files I found most useful and Pamela Cheney also went out of her way to be helpful.

In staying in various places I met with a great deal of kindness from many people. With his considerable knowledge of the various archives, Samuel W. Mitcham was a friendly guide and sent me a copy of a German manuscript I was unable to obtain. Edward L. Field and I discussed common interests in military history and he located for me a copy of 1st Armored Division's *Battle History*.

I benefited considerably from advice offered by Carlo D'Este when I met him in London before visiting the US archives. Professor Neville Brown, now a Senior Research Associate in the University of Oxford and Associate Fellow of OCEES, was a supportive colleague – particularly when I was away from my University duties at Birmingham – and Colonel R.J. Gibson, who served with 4th Indian Division in World War II, has been immensely encouraging as well as providing insights from his own experiences.

My thanks are also due to my publisher, Lionel Leventhal, and my editors, Donald Sommerville and Catherine Stuart, who saved me from many inadvertent mistakes. Nevertheless, for such omissions and mistakes that still remain, I am solely responsible.

Dr Mark Thurston assisted with technical aspects of preparing a final manuscript, while my wife and daughter have had to put up with my absences when I have been exploring various archives. I hope they think it has all been worthwhile.

Note on Language

British and American spellings have been maintained, especially in direct quotations and official titles. Thus, British 7th Armoured Division but US 1st Armored Division; British honour but US Medal of Honor and so on.

PART ONE

Armour for Tunis!

'Things go well as a whole – but we are not moving fast enough; Tunis is anyone's who cares to walk in, but the Huns are beating us in the race... '

Admiral Sir Andrew Cunningham, naval commander for Operation Torch, to his deputy, Vice-Admiral Sir Bertram Ramsay, mid-November 1942.

Quoted in Chalmers, *Full Cycle*, p.151.

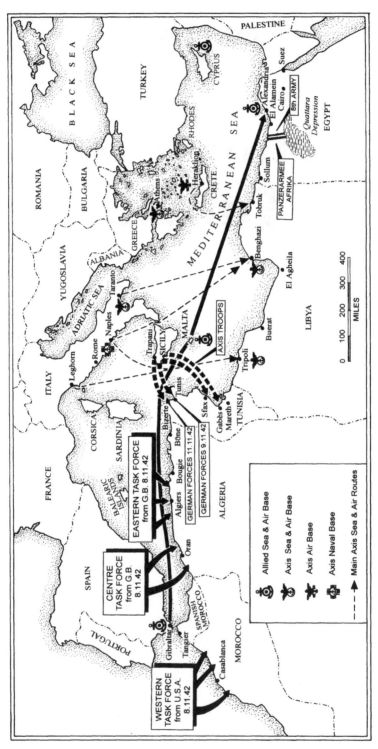

Battle Forces in North Africa and Lines of Supply and Communication
November 1942

Chapter 1
Fight Like Hell

'This is the greatest setback for German arms since 1918. The Americans will take Rommel in the rear, and we shall be expelled from Africa.'

General von Wulish, head of the German Armistice Commission, to General Auguste Nogùes, Resident-General of French Morocco at Rabat, shortly after sunrise on 8 November 1942.[1]

The American colonel's last-minute instructions had been brief and to the point: 'I want you men to hit that dock hard,' he said, 'then light out like stripy-arsed baboons up the wharf until you can get some cover. Then fight like hell.'[2]

Among the detachment of the 135th Regimental Combat Team (RCT) landing from HMS *Broke* at Algiers harbour in the early hours of 8 November 1942, was Pfc Harold Cullum. Brought all the way from Pennsylvania and among the first to get ashore, his baptism of fire was violently cut short by two bullets, the first of which blasted a hole in his stomach and the second in his arm. Sprinkling sulphanilamide powder onto the gaping wound where chunks of clothing and equipment had been driven deep into the flesh, he wrapped his shattered arm in a field dressing and, when the recall whistle blew, attempted to crawl back to his ship. Eventually taken prisoner, he ended up in a French hospital where expert attention saved his life.

Yet it was French gunfire which had wounded him in the first place. The British and Americans, in the massive gamble that they had code-named Operation Torch, had brought more than 107,000 men across the oceans to the shores of North Africa in two mighty armadas, and in three simultaneous landings placed them ashore at Algiers, Oran and Casablanca.

At Casablanca and Oran, the French resisted this invasion of their colonial territory: ill-fated attacks on Algiers and Oran harbours were bloodily repulsed; and parachute drops by Colonel William C. Bentley's 2nd Battalion, 503rd US Parachute Infantry Regiment, to secure airfields at Tafaraoui and La Senia, south of Oran, turned into near-disaster. Nevertheless, the scale and speed of the Allied invasion ensured the narrow success of their great venture, though much remained to be done to bring together warring French factions. One was led by General Henri Giraud, who had escaped from German prison camps in two world wars, and claimed imperiously that he could rally all the French in North Africa to the Allied side – the other by Amiral de la Flotte Jean François Darlan.

Operation Torch came into being principally because the two most powerful men in the Alliance, US President Franklin D. Roosevelt and Britain's Prime Minister, Winston Churchill, wanted it. Churchill had clear, long-term, objectives which he put forward with his customary vigour. An assault in North Africa would remove the Germans and Italians from the region, help to secure critical British supply lines through the Mediterranean and build a base from which Allied troops could springboard their way into southern Europe.[3] Roosevelt, who had promised Stalin that a 'Second Front' against Nazi Germany would be opened in 1942, had been caught on the point of this guarantee. Unwilling to abandon the British in their hour of need, for once during the war the President overrode the advice of his own Joint Chiefs of Staff, settling for an assault in the Mediterranean which Churchill and the British Chiefs of Staff Committee had called for time and again.[4]

In the Mediterranean, Germany was locked in a struggle not of her own making. Against the unanimous opposition of his generals, Benito Mussolini committed his forces to a desert war in September 1940, despite the unpreparedness of the army, which had few motorised vehicles, modern artillery or tanks, and a limited industrial power-base incapable of remedying these deficiencies or provisioning his troops.[5] The arrival of German forces in North Africa in the spring of 1941 was conclusive proof of the failure of Mussolini's hopes of a cheap triumph. They arrived not to pursue a particular military objective, nor as part of a broad strategic plan, but simply to support the Italians, check the British advance to Tripoli and possibly regain Cyrenaica.

The German forces in Africa were placed under control of *Comando Supremo* (Italian Supreme Command) while Hitler's headquarters, the *Oberkommando der Wehrmacht* (*OKW* or High Command of the Armed Forces), initially limited itself to advice and supplies. As German involvement increased, however, Feldmarschall der Luftwaffe Albrecht Kesselring left von Bock's Army Group Centre on the Eastern Front and flew to Rome in November 1941 where he was appointed *Oberbefehlshaber Süd* (*OB Süd* or C-in-C South).

Kesselring was ideally suited to his task. Known as 'Smiling Albert' from his habitual grin and highly optimistic temperament, he had been Chief of Staff of the Luftwaffe in 1936–37. In creating a close working relationship with the heads of the Italian armed forces he came across an old friend, General Rinso Corso Fougier, of *Superareo* (Italian Air Force High Command), who, according to Mussolini's son-in-law and foreign minister, Count Galeazzo Ciano, was 'a real pilot, not a balloon officer.' The other Italian armed forces' chiefs were Marshal Ugo Cavallero, Chief of the General Staff, and Admiral Arturo Riccardi of the *Supermarina* (Naval High Command). A man of immense organizational and administrative abilities, Cavallero was undoubtedly pro-German; indeed, he co-operated to such an extent that his own position became endangered. He was replaced by General Vittorio Ambrosio in February 1943, which 'produced joy among Italians and dissatisfaction among the Germans.'[6]

In the struggle for North Africa only the Luftwaffe was clearly and unequivocally under *OB Süd* control. Other than this, there were overlapping German-Italian commands which resulted in Kesselring taking orders from the *OKW* in some matters and from *Comando Supremo* in others. Only his strong personality held the ramshackle organization together and resolved some of the tensions arising from these confused relationships. His HQ moved from Taormina in Sicily to Frascati near Rome in October 1942, so that by his presence Kesselring could exert a stronger influence on *Comando Supremo* over German supply problems.[7]

Kesselring's ambiguous command relationships were compounded by the lack of consistent leadership from inside *OKW*, as Hitler increasingly overrode his General Staff's advice and insisted on more and more 'Führer decisions' in the face of setbacks in Russia and elsewhere. The invasion of North Africa therefore hit the German High Command at a critical moment.[8]

———◦•◦———

The first danger was averted by General Walter Warlimont, Deputy Chief of the *OKW* Operations Staff, and Kesselring, whose frantic staff work ensured that Hitler's initial response to the landings was speedily translated into the formation of a bridgehead in Tunis and occupation of Vichy France. At 0700 hours on 11 November 1942, ten divisions of the German First Army and Army Group *Felber* crossed the demarcation line between German-occupied northern France and the unoccupied territory to the south which had been governed until then by the puppet Vichy regime.[9] At the same time, two Italian divisions from Sardinia landed on Corsica and units of the Italian Fourth Army marched into the French Riviera. To the surprise of Hitler's HQ, there was virtually no resistance.

In Algiers the French were shocked by the pitiless way in which the Führer discarded the armistice of 1940. Even so, they could not reconcile their differences. Admiral Darlan ordered the French commanders in Tunisia to resist the Germans, countermanded his order and then reinstated it. At Allied Force Headquarters (AFHQ), Gibraltar, the Commander-in-Chief, Lieutenant-General Dwight D. Eisenhower, raged over the venomous squabbling and was in such a fury 'that I sometimes wish I could do a little throat-cutting myself.'[10]

———◦•◦———

Eisenhower's appointment as C-in-C had been a surprising one. He had graduated from West Point in 1915, without particular distinction, and was posted to the 19th US Infantry Regiment at Fort Sam Houston on the outskirts of San Antonio. Despite strenuous efforts, he failed to be listed for overseas duty when America entered the Great War in 1917 and remained labelled as no more than a useful trainer of troops and desk officer: 'I had missed the boat,' he later remarked.[11]

During the inter-war period he served under various powerful leaders in an effort to avoid a career dead-end, imbibing much of the politics and bureaucratic niceties characterising the higher forms of military life. Only later, under the tutelage of Roosevelt's US Army Chief of Staff, General George C. Marshall, did his career really blossom. Marshall brought Eisenhower to the War Department in December 1941, and thereafter there remained a close personal link between the two. Eisenhower was always the junior in rank, but became the best-known US military leader of the war, satisfying the public's craving for an all-American war hero. In the autumn of 1942, however, the new C-in-C was virtually unknown outside military circles. He had no combat experience and was viewed with baffled scepticism by the British who could not understand how a man could be produced from comparative obscurity to hold the highest command.[12]

Eisenhower proved to be dutiful to a marked degree, with great application to the task in hand, a keen eye for detail and a ruthless streak which implied superlative determination. He could also be impatient and brutally abrupt with those whom he discarded.[13] His public character, however, was entirely different. It was that of a friendly and relaxed small-town American, his speech peppered with homespun phrases reflecting his roots deep in his native Abilene soil. Eisenhower was adept moreover at promoting this image to the British and American publicity machines which were more than happy to play along.[14] He was in addition a peerless chairman of inter-Allied committees, arbitrating smoothly between rival plans.[15] No visionary, nevertheless he saw clearly that it was vital for American and British staffs, and the troops they ultimately commanded, to work together at all levels.

Eisenhower's deputy, Major-General Mark W. Clark, had to bear the brunt of French wrangling at Algiers. Long-limbed, beak-nosed and intensely, disagreeably ambitious, he eventually lost his temper and threatened the squabbling leaders with immediate custody and the establishment of military government. This settled matters and when Eisenhower arrived he had only to endorse the agreement which had been reached. Having now definitely joined the Allied side, Admiral Darlan was to head the civil and political government of North Africa, Giraud to be C-in-C of all French forces and General Alphonse Juin to command a reinforced French volunteer army fighting alongside the Allies; Noguès (French Morocco) and Chatel (Algeria) would retain their Resident-General posts.

Meanwhile, at *OB Süd* HQ it was not yet clear whether the German High Command planned to hold Tunisia at all costs or simply carry out a limited engagement in order to defend Generalfeldmarschall Erwin Rommel's lines of communication in the Western Desert and prevent a disastrous collapse of Italian morale.[16] The Allies for their part intended to squeeze Rommel's forces in a trap between Eighth Army, now advancing from Egypt through Tripolitania, and First Army operating from Tunisia.

From the outset, however, Allied planning had been characterised by indecision; the Americans, anxious about possible hostile reactions from the Spanish dictator, General Francisco Franco, worried about opposition from Vichy

France and fearful of a German move against Gibraltar which might close the Strait and cause havoc for the Allies, proposed to consolidate their positions in French Morocco for about three months before advancing eastwards.

British planners went for a bolder design. They had insisted on a deep strike into the Mediterranean itself, at Algiers, and, in conjunction with the Eighth Army sweeping in from the west, a swift move on Tunis before the enemy could effect a bridgehead there. Indeed, Lieutenant-General Kenneth Anderson, given the task of pushing eastwards once the Allies landed in North Africa, wanted an early attack on Tunis and even suggested that US aircraft land there on the morning of the Torch assault – though even if the bluff worked the crews would, in all probability, be taken prisoner. As the British correctly predicted, once firmly established, with their shorter lines of communication and land-based air power, the Axis forces would be difficult to prise out.

Early on the morning of 9 November 1942, two German officers, Hauptmann Schürmeyer and Hauptmann Behlau, arrived in Tunis. Under the pretext of helping the French resist the Allied invasion they discussed defence of the city with the Resident-General in Tunisia, Vice-Admiral Jean-Pierre Estèva – 'an old gentleman with a white goatee' – the *Commandant Supérieur des Troupes de Tunisie*, General Georges Barré, and the local French air force commander, General Péquin. They had been ordered by the head of the Vichy Government, Pierre Laval, to co-operate with the Germans.

While these discussions were taking place, Kesselring ordered one of Göring's intimate friends and a former fighter pilot in the First World War, Generaloberst Bruno Loezer, commanding Fliegerkorps II from Taormina in Sicily, to fly fighters and Stukas across and seize the airfield at El Aouina (Tunis). Accordingly he sent elements of the 53rd Fighter Squadron and transport aircraft, carrying supplies of fuel, oil and light flak guns. Colonel Geradot, the commander of the airfield, narrowly escaped and hastened by air to the British First Army's command post, established that day at the Hotel Albert in Algiers. He brought discomfiting news that 40 German bombers already sat on the tarmac at Tunis.[17]

The fiction that these forces were being invited to aid the French was maintained by sending Oberstleutnant Harlinghausen of Fliegerkorps II to Tunis to see Estèva.[18] Believing the French offered no opposition, he alerted *OB Süd* and, next day, a fighter group of Me-109s and Kesselring's *Wachkompanie* (personal HQ Company) carried in gliders towed behind Ju-88s, were on their way from Sicily.[19] As each aircraft taxied to a halt at Tunis, it was covered by the guns of a French armoured reconnaissance car. For a while, matters were in the balance until transport planes brought in the 5th Fallschirmjäger (Parachute) Regiment. Scrambling out, a company set up its anti-tank weapons and machine-guns and trained them on the armoured cars. The French withdrew to the outer perimeter and an uneasy peace settled over the airfield.

During this time, Loezer was again telephoned by Kesselring who told him that Barré and Estèva were communicating with the Allies via a cable linking Tunis to

Malta and by a secret radio operating on the roof of the US Consulate. Loezer was told to see that no further messages were transmitted. Arriving at Tunis, Loezer found the troops who had just flown in still organizing themselves. The resident German Armistice Commissioner warned Loezer that the situation was exceedingly delicate and it was with 'mixed feelings' that Loezer passed through French troops on his way into the city. 'The men made a good soldierly impression,' he wrote. 'I saw no officers. Machine guns and anti-tank weapons were trained on the airfield.'[20] He was met by Barré's representative, frostily polite, who could give no assurances about French co-operation. Estèva was more encouraging, assuring Loezer he had received instructions from Vichy and would do everything to help, on the understanding that the Germans were to be restricted to airfields at Tunis and Bizerte (Bizerta). French forces had orders to shoot if they strayed elsewhere.[21]

Loezer, satisfied with what he had seen and heard, made his way back to the airfield. Not a man moved to detain him though this would have been simple enough, as he observed: 'There can be little doubt that the small air forces with their planes on the ground would have been easy prey for the French troops in readiness there if they had attacked in this situation.'[22]

The same was true at Bizerte airfield, occupied on 11 November, without a shot being fired, by a single Ju-88 and two sections of the *Ahrendt* parachute engineering column. Again the French stood off and allowed the Germans to reinforce their bridgehead.

'The French behaviour is inexplicable,' complained Brigadier Haydon vice-chief of the Combined Operations staff at Gibraltar, 'The Germans, Italians and Japs appear welcome in any French possession! We who were their Allies and who are fighting for their ends as well as our own, are resisted at every turn. It is high time they were called upon to declare themselves one way or another.'[23] But the chronic indecision which beset the French leaders ensured this would not happen. 'I thought there would be some gesture of opposition, at least for the honour of the flag,' commented a surprised Ciano.[24] Its absence provided a window of opportunity for the Germans in Tunisia, which they were quick to exploit, in turn condemning the Allies to a costly and extended campaign.

Notes to Chapter 1

1 Recounted by Samuel Eliot Morison, *History of United States Naval Operations in World War II*, Volume 2, *Operations in North African Waters, October 1942 – June 1943*, p.65.

2 MacVane, *War and Diplomacy in North Africa*, p. 49. MacVane was an accredited war correspondent for the American National Broadcasting Corporation.

3 Mayer, 'The Decision to Invade North Africa (Torch) (1942)', in Greenfield ed., *Command Decisions*, p. 131. For the full background see also Matloff and Snell, *United States Army in World War II: Strategic Planning for Coalition Warfare 1941–1942*, Chaps. VIII & XII–XIII; also Matthew Jones, *Britain, the United States and the Mediterranean War; 1942–44*, Chaps. 1–3.

4 For the Torch invasion, see Breuer, *Operation Torch: The Allied Gamble to Invade North Africa*; Gelb, *Desperate Venture: The Story of Operation Torch*; Vincent Jones, *Operation Torch: Anglo-American Invasion of North Africa*; Pack, *Invasion North Africa 1942*.

5 'Never has a military operation been undertaken so much against the will of the commanders,' Muggeridge ed., *Ciano's Diary 1939–1943*, p. 289; entry for 9 September 1940. See also Deakin, *The Brutal Friendship: Mussolini, Hitler and the Fall of Italian Fascism*, p. 15.

6 Muggeridge ed., *Ciano's Diary*, pp. 552–3; entry for 31 January 1943. Ciano's views were decidedly anti-Cavallero of course: 'Cavallero who lies, consorts with the Germans, and steals all he can.'

7 General der Flieger Paul Deichmann, 'Designation of OB Süd as Supreme Commander Mediterranean Theatre (September 1942)', Foreign Military Series, MS D-008 (1947). United States Army Military History Institute (USAMHI).

8 Generalmajor Christian Eckhard, 'Study of the Situation in the High Command of the Wehrmacht shortly before, during and after the Allied landing in French North Africa, 1942', (1947) in Detwiler *et al.*, *World War II German Military Studies*, XIV, MS D-066.

9 'Greiner Diary Notes from 12 August 1942, to 17 March 1943', Detwiler *et al.*, *World War II German Military Studies*, IX, MS C065a. The situation and discussions at Hitler's HQ can be followed in more detail in Schramm, *Kriegstagebuch des Oberkommandos der Wehrmacht*, see esp. Vol. 4/II, pp. 936–7. Greiner was the custodian of the War Diary in Hitler's HQ between August 1939 and April 1943 and reconstructed much of it after the war from contemporary notes and drafts. The manuscript in the *Kriegstagebuch* is a much fuller edition of that reproduced by Detwiler.

10 Eisenhower to Bedell Smith, 11 November 1942; *The Papers of Dwight David Eisenhower, The War Years:* II, ed. Chandler *et al.*, Doc. 609.

11 Early details of Eisenhower's life have been taken from his *At Ease: Stories I tell to Friends*, and Burk, *Dwight D. Eisenhower: Hero and Politician*.

12 Notes from Sir Frederick Morgan Papers; USAMHI.

13 Major-General Albert Kenner interviewed by Dr Forrest Pogue (27 May 1948); Office of the Chief of Military History [OCMH] Collection, USAMHI. Kenner landed with Patton as Chief Surgeon of the Western Task Force in Torch and, in December 1942, became a Brigadier-General and was assigned to Eisenhower as Chief Surgeon, North African Forces.

14 See Childs, *Eisenhower: Captive Hero*, esp. p. 70.

15 Brigadier C.J.C. Molony to Lieutenant-General Sir Francis Tuker, 25 August 1959; Tuker Papers, 71/21/6, Imperial War Museum (IWM). Molony, who was one of the compilers of Volume IV in the Official History of the Second World War, United Kingdom Military Series, mentions that he has this information about Eisenhower 'on fairly good authority.'

[16] Rommel was promoted Generalfeldmarschall after taking Tobruk in the summer of 1942, the youngest Field Marshal in the German Army. 'Hitler has made me a Field-Marshal,' he wrote to his wife, 'I would much rather he had given me one more division.' Quoted by Young, *Rommel*, p. 131

[17] First Army HQ, War Diary, entry for 9 November 1942; WO/175, Public Record Office (PRO). Playfair *et al.*, *The Mediterranean and Middle East, The Destruction of the Axis Forces in Africa*, gives a total of 51 German aircraft by the end of the day at Tunis.

[18] Deichmann, 'Mission of OB Süd with the Auxiliary Battle Command in North Africa after the Allied Landing. Battles in Tunisia – Part I (November–December 1942)', Foreign Military Studies, MS D-067 (1947). USAMHI. The fiction that the Germans were aiding the French against attack was only lightly disguised: Generalfeldmarschall Albert Kesselring, 'Final Commentaries on the Campaign in North Africa, 1941–1943', Vol. 1, Foreign Military Studies, MS C-075 (1950). USAMHI.

[19] 'Das Bilden des Brückenkopfes Tunesien im Herbst 1942', *Die Oase*, No. 3 (March, 1973), p. 3.

[20] Generaloberst Bruno Loezer, 'Negotiations with the representative of General Barré and the resident of Tunis, Admiral Estèva', Foreign Military Studies, MS D-040 (1947). USAMHI.

[21] 'Report for General Nehring on the Political and Military Situation in Tunisia from 9 to 21 November 1942', (Tunis, 21 November 1942); Bundesarchiv-Militärarchiv [BA-MA], RH 19 VIII/358.

[22] Loezer, 'Negotiations with the representative of General Barré and the resident of Tunis, Admiral Estèva'.

[23] Major-General J.C. Haydon, Torch Diary, IWM 77/190/ZE, entry for 12 November 1942

[24] Muggeridge ed., *Ciano's Diary*, p. 523, entry for 12 November 1942.

Chapter 2

Death or Victory

'The dead are lucky, it's all over for them.'

Generalfeldmarschall Rommel to his wife, 3 November 1942.[1]

Hitler never attached as much importance to North Africa as the British, considering it only an annoying diversion from the war of ideology and extermination he was pursuing on the Eastern Front. For Mussolini it was much closer to home and far more than a colonial struggle. But ultimate mastery of the Mediterranean rested not only on the commanders and their toiling troops but particularly upon the complex balance of forces by which they were supplied.

On land the lengthening lines of supply and communication, which trailed behind every offensive move, granted advantages to the defender and imposed a natural balance in which the possession of Cyrenaica was crucial to both sides because everything that moved and breathed in the desert war had to be supplied by sea. 'If there must be a war the best place for it to take place is in the Desert,' observed a senior administrative officer on Alexander's staff, Major-General Miller. 'The logistics are in many respects made simpler. The further the battle from the sources of supply the weaker must the army become. Conversely the shorter the L[ine] of C[ommunication] the quicker can reorganization and reinforcement be achieved.'[2] The key to Britain's Mediterranean effort was Malta and the Axis' failure to subdue it in the spring of 1942 was, as Kesselring rightly suggested, 'a mortal blow to the whole North African undertaking.'[3]

When General Sir Harold Alexander became C-in-C Middle East in August 1942, Churchill's hand-written directive ordered him to 'take or destroy at the earliest opportunity the German-Italian Army commanded by Field-Marshal Rommel together with all its supplies & establishments in Egypt & Libya.'[4] There was little to suggest that he would be more successful in fulfilling these fine sounding phrases than any predecessor.

Alex was urbane, civilized and charming, and had impeccable credentials from his family pedigree. After serving with great personal courage in World War I, he rapidly climbed the ladder of promotion, becoming the British Army's youngest general at the age of 45 in 1937, when he was given command of the 1st Infantry Division.

During the desperate retreat to Dunkirk, General Sir Alan Brooke, Chief of the Imperial General Staff from December 1941, compared him to another outstanding commander, Bernard Montgomery, of 3rd Infantry Division. They

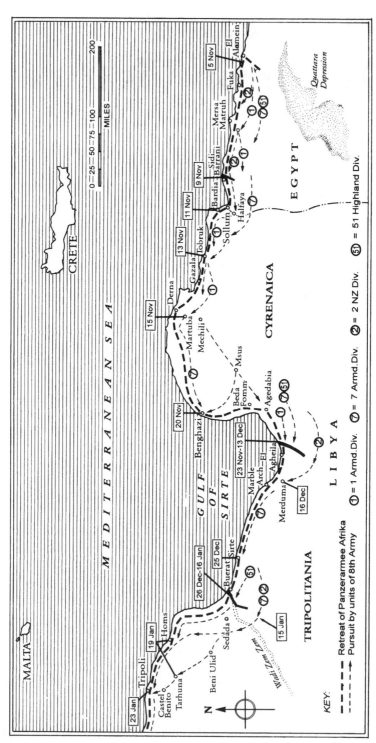

MALTA

CRETE

MEDITERRANEAN SEA

0 – 25 – 50 – 75 – 100 – 200
MILES

5 Nov
Fuka El Alamein

Mersa Matruh

Quattara Depression

9 Nov
Sidi Barrani

Bardia

11 Nov
Sollum

Halfaya

13 Nov
Tobruk

Gazala

EGYPT

15 Nov
Derna

Martuba
Mechili o

CYRENAICA

20 Nov
Benghazi

Beda Fomm o
o Msus
Agedabia o

23 Nov-13 Dec
Arch–El Agheila

Marble

Merduma o

16 Dec

GULF OF SIRTE

L I B Y A

25 Dec
Sirte

26 Dec-16 Jan
Buerat

19 Jan
Homs

23 Jan
Tripoli

Castel Benito o
Tarhuna o

Beni Ulid o

Sedada o

Wadi Zem Zem

15 Jan

TRIPOLITANIA

N

KEY:
– – – –   Retreat of Panzerarmee Afrika
– – →   Pursuit by units of 8th Army

① = 1 Armd.Div.   ⑦ = 7 Armd.Div.   ② = 2 NZ Div.
⑤① = 51 Highland Div.

Rommel's forces in retreat
November 1942 - January 1943

were, Brooke observed, totally different characters. Under the severest pressure, Alexander remained unruffled, composed, and seemed hardly to realise, 'all the very unpleasant potentialities of our predicament.'[5] Unfortunately, this merely demonstrated to some observers a failure to grasp the full tactical and strategic importance of a situation. Anthony Eden, the British Foreign Secretary, wondered aloud if Alexander, 'carried enough brains to be C-in-C,'[6] while Lieutenant-General Sir Francis Tuker, commanding 4th Indian Division in the Western Desert, thought he was, 'quite the least intelligent commander I have ever met in a high position. I cannot imagine his ever producing a plan, let alone a good plan.'[7]

Even Alexander's official biographer questioned his abilities: 'I don't think his conduct of the African campaign was more than an administrative job – it wasn't a true general's job. He was sort of a quartermaster in a way... I don't think he was a very clever man, Alex... He was an English country gentleman, almost uneducated, who never read a book or had any interest in the arts at all... But he had a particular charm and a gift for making people like him; absolutely straight.'[8]

Apart from Mark Clark, this smoothly cultivated exterior endeared him to the Americans because he fitted their expectations of the English gentleman. Senior Americans like Eisenhower, Omar Bradley, or even George Patton, who freely admitted that he was, 'not, repeat not, Pro-British,' all thought highly of him, and it is true that Alexander's personal qualities were such as to help smooth the often difficult edges of Anglo-American relationships.[9] The central problem with his style of command, however, was the lack of firm direction offered to his subordinate commanders: as Liddell Hart observed, '[Alexander] attained such early and continuous success in his career, that he never had a grindstone against which to sharpen its edges. Moreover, he had an innate reluctance to impose himself on others and in avoiding needless interference sometimes failed to provide the guidance that was needed.'[10]

Nowhere was this more sharply illustrated than in the case of Lieutenant-General Montgomery (as he was in 1942), who had his faults but was certainly, in Tuker's words, 'one of the most persistent, optimistic, determined and courageous men on the battlefield.'[11] Monty's supreme self-confidence stemmed from a lifetime of professional dedication to the Army. An iron will and military success eventually turned a shy and diffident personality into the towering example of vanity and egocentrism which he later became. On the one hand capable of deeply generous acts towards individuals, which often went unrecognised other than by his Chief of Staff, Brigadier Freddie de Guingand, Montgomery was also capable of 'breathtakingly mean behaviour.'[12] 'He has the reputation of being an able and ruthless soldier and an unspeakable cad,'[13] noted Oliver Harvey, Foreign Secretary Anthony Eden's private secretary, when Monty was appointed to command Eighth Army in August 1942.

Undoubtedly a self-publicist of real genius, Montgomery set out at once to stamp his authority on his new command. Carefully appointing his own press officer, the distinguished war correspondent, Alan Moorehead, he expertly projected an effective image by his informal mode of dress and frugal habits. And his troops responded when he revived their spirits, instilling in them the belief that they were the best in the world or, more down to earth, exhorting them: 'Kill Germans, even padres – one per week and two on Sundays.'[14] Nor did they forget Monty's influence: 'There was never a general under whom I felt it a greater honour to be serving than yourself,' wrote one much-wounded 'genuine survivor of the North African campaign,' adding, 'at least an ordinary ex-serviceman can salute from this distance and sincerely thank you for the great leadership you gave us... '[15] Said Eisenhower's invaluable chief of staff, Walter Bedell ('Beetle' or 'Beadle') Smith, 'He had transcendent ability to make his troops share his self-confidence.'[16]

'Here we will stand and fight; there will be no further withdrawal,' the new commander told his HQ staff on 13 August 1942, in the shadow of the Ruweisat Ridge. 'We will stand and fight here. If we can't stay here alive, then let us stay here dead.'[17] The effect of this address was, said de Guingand, 'electric – it was terrific! And we all went to bed that night with a new hope in our hearts, and a great confidence in the future of our Army.'[18] This assurance quickly spread throughout Eighth Army. 'It's very wonderful what an atmosphere 0 [Montgomery] has created in this short time,' wrote Lieutenant-General Oliver Leese, commanding XXX Corps, in October, 'He has great force of character and great personality.'[19] Pinned above Montgomery's desk in his campaign caravan throughout most of the desert campaign was a photograph of Rommel in classic 'Desert Fox' pose complete with sun-goggles pushed up on peaked hat, Ritterkreuz (Knight's Cross) glinting at the throat and heavy binoculars slung over the chest of his leather jacket.[20] This image was part of the battle of wits summoned up by Montgomery, with Churchill's connivance, which saw the desert war as a duel between two giant personalities.

War correspondents conspired by using romantic and sanitized terms in which the Germans were brave and the Italians, 'if not brave, then chivalrous.' British troops adopted the Afrika Korps' song, *Lili Marlene* and, in the House of Commons, Churchill complimented Rommel with the words, 'May I say across the havoc of war, a great general.'

Not all of this was entirely remote from the truth. Certainly, the conduct of the Afrika Korps was free of the bestialities which accompanied German armies elsewhere: 'Thank God, we had no SS divisions in the desert or heaven knows what would have happened,' said Generalleutnant Fritz Bayerlein, who saw active service in Africa from October 1941 to May 1943, adding, 'it would have been a very different sort of war.'[21] Rommel's own account of the desert campaign, *Krieg Ohne Hass* ('War without Hate') exemplified this approach. Troops on both sides had a respect for each other's basic humanity and fighting capabilities.

Rommel imposed his iron will on the *Deutsches Afrika Korps* (DAK), giving its 15th and 21st Panzer Divisions and 90th Light Division a powerful, cohesive identity in which men took a real and justifiable pride so that, even after the war, many former members still carried the palm-tree brassard in their pocketbooks. Unlike Montgomery, he exercised a much more immediate control on the battlefield which often involved putting himself in considerable personal danger and could cause problems for harassed staff officers in his absence.[22]

By the time Montgomery took over Eighth Army, his opponent had been in the unforgiving desert overlong. After 19 months of unremitting warfare, Rommel was suffering from desert sores, chronic stomach and intestinal catarrh, circulatory disorders and symptoms of exhaustion, as well as liver trouble. On 23 September 1942 he left to recuperate at a mountain resort near Vienna and was replaced by General Georg Stumme.[23]

Montgomery's renewed offensive at El Alamein, which began on 23 October 1942, brought Rommel hurrying back on the Führer's direct orders. He arrived at dusk 48 hours later, to learn of Stumme's death (from a heart attack) and that the enemy was smashing through the *Teufelsgarten* ('Devil's Gardens') – the mined areas on which his defences were based.

Despite the most heroic attempts, Rommel's *Panzerarmee* was unable to prevent Eighth Army breaking through. Outgunned and out-manned, Rommel signalled twice to the *OKW* his intention to withdraw along the coastal road, westwards to the Fuka line. The Führer read Rommel's second order early on 3 November – it had been intercepted, decoded and was in the hands of Brooke only hours later – and immediately ordered 'victory or death.'[24] But with only 35 tanks left and most of his ammunition shot off, Rommel had no option other than to begin a general retreat on the following day, subsequently ratified by Hitler.

In London, Churchill was impatient. Now that Rommel was on the defensive – 'Alex and Monty are hunting him hard,' he told Eisenhower on 13 November – he was anxious to push on. 'I am sure,' he added, '...that intense efforts should be made to secure the mastery in the tip of Tunis and the capture of Tripoli.'[25] Determined to prevent this scenario, Kesselring had other ideas.

In order to buy time, he ordered negotiations with Estèva to be prolonged as long as possible while reinforcements, under Oberst Lederer, were poured in to establish a bridgehead. On 12 November, 500 men were airlifted into Tunisia with 74 tons of stores and the first sea transports with ships, 17 tanks, and motor vehicles arrived. Another 600 men were flown in the next day, when Kesselring was confidently expecting the use of Gabès and Sfax airfields, 150 miles south of Tunis, and 3,000 had arrived by the 15th; they were provisioned with 170 tons of petrol and promised supplies and arms originally meant for Rommel. In fact, all air transport space had been diverted from the German-Italian Army to Tunisia for nearly a week.[26]

General Barré agreed to the occupation of the French garrisons at Tunis and Bizerte but the Germans soon realised he was playing a waiting game and had not committed his *Tunis* Division to either side. Harlinghausen became suspicious that he might go over to the Allies and ordered Leutnant Baitinger to occupy all public buildings and block the western approach roads to Tunis on the night of 13/14 November, despite Estèva's protests.

Sanitätsgefreiter (Medical Lance-Corporal) Viktor Fink, crossing Tunis alone to see that part of this order was carried out, felt distinctly uneasy: 'I must have presented a strange sight to the people,' he said, 'with my uniform and machine gun.' The tram conductor seems to have been impressed and let him travel without a ticket.[27]

Had General der Panzertruppe Walther Nehring arrived a week earlier, Barré's support might have been secured.[28] When the new field commander for Tunisia was sent by Hitler to replace Lederer and form a deep bridgehead, he discovered an alarming state of affairs at his newly-formed XC Army Corps. Nevertheless, the Allies had already forfeited the element of surprise gained by Operation Torch and were to suffer grievous disappointments as a result.

Notes to Chapter 2

[1] Liddell Hart, ed., *The Rommel Papers*, p. 320.

[2] Lieutenant-General C.H. Miller, Papers; IWM 78/20/1.

[3] Kesselring, *Memoirs*, p. 129.

[4] Churchill to Alexander, 10 August 1942; Alexander Papers, PRO WO/214/18.

[5] Bryant, *The Turn of the Tide*, p. 109.

[6] John Harvey ed., *The War Diaries of Oliver Harvey 1941–1945*, entry for 7 August 1942, p. 147.

[7] 'Some Notes by General Tuker', 6 October 1945; Tuker Papers, 71/21/6.

[8] Nigel Nicolson quoted by Hamilton, *Monty: Master of the Battlefield*, p.472. Alexander is defended more vigorously by Reid in *Churchill's Generals*, ed. Keegan, Ch. 6, *passim*.

[9] Patton Diary, entry for 11 August 1942; Patton Papers, Box 3. Library of Congress.

[10] 'The Military Balance-Sheet of World War II', Copy of notes by Liddell Hart for lecture given at the University of London, November 1960; Tuker Papers, 71/21/6. See also Liddell Hart, *The Memoirs*, II, p. 238.

[11] 'Some Notes by General Tuker'.

[12] Hamilton, *Monty: Making of a General*, p. 37. See also de Guingand, *Operation Victory*, p. 175.

[13] Harvey, ed., *War Diaries of Oliver Harvey*, entry for 10 August 1942, p. 148.

[14] Quoted by Knightly, *The First Casualty*, p. 306.

[15] 'Jock' to Montgomery, 23 October 1962; Montgomery Papers, BLM 1/119. IWM.

[16] Bedell Smith interviewed by Pogue (13 May 1947). OCMH Collection.

[17] Quoted by Hamilton, *Monty: Making of a General*, pp. 622–4.

[18] De Guingand *Operation Victory*, pp. 136–7.

[19] Leese to his wife, 22 October 1942; Leese Papers, Box 2. IWM. Leese was one of Montgomery's protégés and had replaced the luckless Ramsden shortly after the battle of Alam Halfa. 'You're not exactly on the crest of a wave, Ramsden,' said Montgomery in sacking him. See Chalfont, *Montgomery of Alamein*, p. 174.

[20] Moorehead, *Montgomery*, p. 133.

[21] Quoted by Young, *Rommel*, p. 149.

[22] Lewin, *The Life and Death of the Afrika Korps*, p. 22.

[23] Mitcham, *Hitler's Field Marshals and their Battles*, p. 184.

[24] Liddell Hart ed., *Rommel Papers*, p. 321.

[25] Churchill to Eisenhower, 13 November 1942; Eisenhower Papers, Box 23.

[26] Hinsley, *British Intelligence in the Second World War*, Vol. II, pp. 490–1; Bennett, *Ultra and Mediterranean Strategy*, pp. 190–1.

[27] Kurowski, *Endkampf in Afrika*, p. 46.

[28] Kesselring, *Memoirs*, p. 142; Kesselring, 'The War in the Mediterranean Area, Part I', Detwiler *et al.*, *World War II German Military Studies*, XIV, MS T-3 PI.

Chapter 3

Unreliable Auxiliaries

'Why don't the French start tossing the Huns out?'

Captain Harry C. Butcher, entry in his diary for 12 November 1942.[1]

Mussolini's flamboyant but empty gesture in sending his troops into Tunisia 'struck *OB Süd* like a bomb,' said the Luftflotte 2 Chief of Staff, Paul Deichmann.[2] The Germans had told the Vichy French that the Italians would not be permitted to send troops to Tunisia but on the morning of 10 November Mussolini had begun such a move by dispatching a flight of fighters. Nothing could have been better calculated to drive Frenchmen into the arms of the Allies than the arrival of Italians in fighter aircraft and torpedo boats. Kesselring was aghast and protested vigorously to *Comando Supremo*, which replied that units were on their way and could not be stopped, though it was later established that the fighter group did not take off from Sardinia until two hours after Kesselring's protest was received.

After the Italians arrived, the French broke off negotiations and Barré moved his forces westward into the mountains, establishing his HQ at Béja and maintaining contact with the Germans without actively opposing them. Although the Italians were later recalled by Cavallero, Kesselring remained convinced that the French would have rallied to the German cause had it not been for their presence.

Fifty years old, experienced in desert warfare as commander of the *DAK* from February 1942 until wounded at the Battle of Alam Halfa in August, Walther Nehring had been convalescing at Wünsdorf near Berlin. Still suffering from a festering laceration in his arm, he was anxious to return to Rommel's HQ and, while en route at Rome, was surprised to be ordered at once to Tunis.

To seal off the approaches to Tunis Nehring had only the 5th Fallschirmjäger Regiment, the 11th Fallschirmjäger Pionier Bataillon (Parachute Engineer Battalion) under the command of Major Rudolph Witzig – neither of them yet motorised – one Marschbataillon (personnel replacement transfer battalion) equipped only with small arms, an artillery battery with four 88mm guns, and a Panzerspähkompanie (armoured reconnaissance company) under Oberleutnant (Lieutenant) Kahle.

Axis Defensive Lines in Tunisia, actual and intended
1942

At Bizerte the Italians had two battalions of Marines (about 800 men) and, around Mateur, the beginnings of the Italian *Superga* Division which had disembarked on 15 November with 557 vehicles. But there was no German command system, no fully operational motorised unit combining the various arms, no signals unit – use had to be made of the highly unreliable French telephone network until late in November – no medical unit and virtually no vehicles; even Nehring had to hire a French taxi-cab for use as his staff car.[3] On an early reconnaissance he was, 'deeply impressed [by the difficulties], although hardly cheered', by what he saw.[4]

In mid-November, by sea and air, part of the battle weary *Hermann Göring* Division arrived after a difficult passage from Cognac, soon to be followed by 10th Panzer from Marseilles and Weber's newly-formed 334th Division.

Their task was formidable: they had to, 'master the almost hopeless situation,' wrote Oberstleutnant Bürker, a senior staff officer with 10th Panzer Division, 'and to use all of their determination to go into action and all of their abilities in order to prevent the enemy from quickly taking possession in Tunisia.'[5]

Nehring acted quickly to establish his close-in defences with two separate bridgeheads: one based on Tunis, guarded by the 5th Fallschirmjäger Regiment under Harlinghausen, until Oberstleutnant Walter Koch replaced him, the other on Bizerte, commanded by Oberstleutnant Stolz, who was eventually replaced by Oberst Fritz Freiherr von Broich. However, as early as 26 November, Allied wireless intercepts discovered that Nehring was bemoaning his lack of forces to defend both and wondering which he should hold, 'since neither of them can achieve much.'[6]

Stukas, reconnaissance aircraft and fighter-bombers were organized into No. 1, Air Force Command under Generalmajor Kosch. Luftwaffe ground elements were placed under the control of Generalmajor Koechy and a seasoned officer, Generalmajor Neuffer, took charge of anti-aircraft artillery units which gradually came to exceed divisional strength.[7]

Kesselring was forced to adopt a purely defensive strategy in order to keep open a line of retreat into Tunisia for the German-Italian *Panzerarmee*. Unable to defend the country for any length of time if fighting took place at the very gates of Tunis and Bizerte, his major interest lay between Tunis and old French fortifications of the Mareth Line, in the south, to which Rommel would eventually be driven. The northern third of the area was highly populated, with a well-developed road and rail system radiating from Tunis. The centre was less important, cut off from desert plains by ridges with few passes and, therefore, relatively easy to defend. Conditions in the southern third were similar, with unexplored terrain and desert making any Allied advance difficult.

Kesselring assumed, rightly, that Anglo-American troops, unaccustomed to combat and desert conditions, would not be committed in the distant southern sector of the front. With the exception of some fighter aircraft, no German forces were assigned to the southern half of Tunisia until such time as Rommel retreated there. In the central zone stood the *Superga* Division and first elements of the Italian XXX Corps.

A desirable western defence line would have extended from Bône on the coast, via Tébessa and Gafsa, to Kebili in the south, with Tozeur as a defensible outpost. Though his long-term aim was to stabilise this front, within his limited means Kesselring could only push his troops westwards as far as a line from Djebel (mountain) Abiod southwards through Béja to Sbeïtla and Gafsa and invest this as the main line of resistance. At least it had the advantage of being located far enough from the coast to absorb enemy attacks, for the hinterland was rugged and could be strongly fortified by the time the Allies were in a position to attack.

AFHQ knew that German opposition immediately after the invasion was weak, amounting to no more than small parties equipped with a few armoured cars, motorcycles, anti-tank guns and engineers sent forward to block the line of advance.[8] But they had their own problems, not least in the country through which General Anderson hoped to push his First Army.

This was extraordinarily difficult and quite unlike the desert in which Eighth Army was chasing Rommel. In the sector north of the Medjerda River, high, irregular hill ranges dominate the landscape. On their bleak shoulders, cork forests and thick scrub, at times breast high, often made the going tricky. From Souk Ahras, the Medjerda winds to its mouth between Tunis and Bizerte through a valley that sometimes narrows into a gorge and at other times is up to ten miles wide. Here, extensively cultivated ground consisted of clay soil which turned quickly into a thick, clinging, glutinous mass after rain, smearing boots and clothing and completely clogging wheeled and tracked transport. To complicate matters, valley areas were frequently intersected by deep-cut wadis (gorges) which proved to be natural tank obstacles, whether dry or turned suddenly to raging torrents after rain. Tracks turned into quagmires and the few roads inevitably converged into dangerous defiles. Bridges were usually unsafe for heavy military loads and easily mined. The winter was the local rainy season and during the Allied campaign unusually heavy rains persisted into April, later than normal, severely hampering any movement.

South and south-east of the Medjerda Valley is the Tunis Plain, lying inside a perimeter bounded roughly by the towns and villages on a line Tébourba–east of Medjez el Bab–Goubellat–Bou Arada–Pont du Fahs. On the west and east of this area was some 250 square miles of mountains and hills, irregular, flint-capped and often covered with low scrub. On their commanding, windswept escarpments a few defenders, properly dispersed and well dug-in, could observe the tank 'runs' and cover them with mines and anti-tank guns.

For about 120 miles from Pichon to Maknassy run the Eastern Dorsale mountains which then turn south-west until, some 20 miles south of El Guettar, they join the line of great Chotts or salt lakes. The Mareth Line closed the gap between these 'lakes' and the coast. Further west is the higher Western Dorsale range, running from the dominating peak of Djebel Zaghouan in the north all the way beyond Fériana, in the south. Protected by these natural obstacles, the heartland of Tunisia could not be entered lightly; any attempt to force a way through by road was likely to be very costly since passes were few and well covered.

Between the Eastern Dorsale and the sea lies the coastal plain, about 180 miles long, narrow in hilly country to the north around Enfidaville and thereafter broadening out for some 70 miles south of Kairouan and narrowing again to the Mareth position. To the south the land was largely barren and undulating desert, but further north, especially about Sousse and Sfax, a random pattern of olive groves covered much of the landscape. These features provided useful cover for tank laagers but in wet weather it was not unusual to find a unit totally immobilised by muddy ground, and gunners and tank commanders were effectively blind in such a shelter. A major road ran along the coast but vehicles moved at their peril when forced into predictable routes which picked their way beside the numerous salt lakes.

Tunisia constricted the use of tanks to an area south of Fériana–Sbeitla–Pichon, on the Kairouan and Goubellat Plains and in the Medjez Valley. Unless supported by successful offensives elsewhere, an armoured thrust could not be decisive except in the Medjez Valley because, as Map 3 (page 30) makes clear, actions north of Kairouan were bound to run up against mountainous country between Enfidaville and the Eastern Dorsale, while an offensive north-east from the region of Bou Arada and east from Djebel Rihane was barred from Tunis by the range of hills which effectively blocked the way between Bir Meherga –Ain el Asker and Ksar Tyr. 'Terrain serves to some extent as an equalizer,' observed Kesselring.[9]

On 10 November Anderson received Eisenhower's orders to initiate the eastward advance with his pitifully small forces. Anderson's willingness to do so, even before the Allies knew how Barré's French troops would react at Sétif, Constantine, and other points on the way, earned him Eisenhower's unswerving admiration: 'You were about the only senior officer of my acquaintanceship who would have accepted [this],' he said.[10]

Anderson's acerbic nature did nothing to ease troubled Anglo-American relationships. '[He] seems earnest but dumb,' was Patton's succinct and rather accurate assessment.[11] Liddell Hart heard the same criticism from Major-General Hobart who said that Anderson must have developed since his days as a student at the Quetta Staff College in the 1920s when Hobart was Commandant there, though it was, 'questionable whether he had the capacity to develop much.' Additionally, several Army Council members had serious doubts about whether he had the right qualities for a field commander, 'but they hoped that he might suffice.'[12]

Intending a series of movements by land and sea to take the ports of Bougie, Philippeville, Bône and La Calle, First Army would then start inland to take Sétif and Constantine.[13] Directed to begin First Army's advance eastwards, the commander of 78th Division, Major-General Vyvyan Evelegh, had initiated Operation Perpetual and despatched Eastern Task Force's floating reserve, 36th Infantry Brigade, commanded by Brigadier A.L. Kent-Lemon, for Bougie which lay 120 miles away along the coast. On the evening of the 10th they sailed assault stowed, accompanied by every available tank landing craft after bad weather had delayed their departure, safely escorted by the Royal Navy. Simultaneously a small mobile armoured column from 5th Northamptons, together with a squadron of 56th Reconnaissance Regiment, commanded by Major Hart and therefore known as Hart Force, set out by road from Algiers to clear a route for the brigade. They reached Djebel Abiod on the night of 15/16 November.

On the way to Djidjelli, 35 miles east of Bougie, was another transport, the *Awatea*, with commandos, RAF personnel, their stores and petrol aboard. They were to capture the nearby airfield from where air cover was to be provided but heavy surf ruined the plan and the *Awatea* returned just as the first British troops were wading ashore in high seas at Bougie. Air cover was from the carrier HMS *Argus*, which soon withdrew, and by fighters from Algiers, and this limited support left the berthed vessels sitting targets for the Luftwaffe.

During the afternoon and evening of 11 November, waves of German bombers pressed home their attacks and returned to strike Bougie at first light next day. Three ships were hit that first afternoon including the SS *Cathay*, while she was in deep water and unloading. Major Feggetter, a surgeon with the RAMC from the 69th British General Hospital, watched in horror as a bomb landed in a lighter alongside the ship, killing and wounding many troops; one man was seen to have both his legs blown off and set swimming frantically, using only his arms and supported by his life jacket, until he could be fished out.[14]

When 36th Brigade assembled ashore it was equipped on an assault scale designed for operations at a range of only ten miles or so from its maintenance area. This greatly restricted its scope as did the loss of much of its transport which was either sunk in Bougie harbour or not unloaded and returned to Algiers.[15]

The Luftwaffe attacks did not slacken off until 13 November, when No. 154 Squadron RAF became operational from Djidjelli. Flying into the airfield the previous day, the squadron was met by a party which had made its way overland from Bougie. However, lack of fuel restricted operations to one patrol of six aircraft at first, and they only became airborne after draining the rest of the squadron's tanks.[16]

Some 300 miles east of Algiers, No. 6 Commando together with some of Lieutenant-Colonel William O. Darby's 1st US Rangers and two companies of infantry, were rushed to Bône before the Germans arrived and put ashore from the destroyers HMS *Wheatland* and *Lammerton* on 12 November. They sailed into the harbour lined up on deck and singing the *Marseillaise*. The French remained polite rather than friendly.

Almost at the same time, over 300 men of 3rd Battalion, 1st Parachute Brigade, flown out from England in American C-47s of 64th Troop Carrier Command to replace the Americans squandered in the disastrous attack on Tafarouia, were dropped on the airfield at Duzerville, six miles south-east of Bône. Information of a planned German attack on the airfield had come in the previous day when Ultra code-breaking revealed orders from Kesselring.[17] They narrowly forestalled a fleet of troop-carrying Ju-52s on its way from Kairouan which turned back only when the German Fallschirmjäger spotted the billowing silks of the 3rd Battalion.

That evening, the Germans turned their attention from the naval transports and heavily bombed the airfield at Duzerville. It looked at one stage as if the troops would be forced to withdraw, despite the stiff fight they put up with Oerlikon guns taken from damaged ships in the harbour. The return of the C-47s ferrying in much needed anti-aircraft guns and supplies of fuel for the fighter aircraft, and the appearance of Spitfires over the airfield, settled matters.

A second airborne operation to broaden the basis of air operations, by seizing airfields inland, was mounted by survivors of Lieutenant-Colonel Edson Raff's 509th Parachute Infantry Battalion. From Maison Blanche, at Algiers, they flew in 20 C-47s on 15 November, accompanied by a single Spitfire, to the Tunisian border. Among them was Jack Thompson of the *Chicago Tribune*, the first American civilian to jump in combat with US troops. 'Hey Jack, it don't mean a thing if you don't pull that string,' shouted one seasoned parachutist. 'Hey Sarge, ain't Jack's chute the one you caught them silk worms in?'[18] questioned another.

Raff's men dropped near the village of Youks les Bains, ten miles from Tébessa. Welcomed by Colonel Berges, Commander of the French 3e Zouaves, they dug in at the airfield and occupied another just outside the village from where they managed to bring down a marauding Ju-88, looking for an easy kill. 'We're going right into Gafsa after the bastards,' said Raff.[19] Commandeering transport, they pushed south-east all the way to the town without support or any certainty of supplies.

From here, the paratroopers were forced to withdraw as the jaws of a pincer movement of Italian tanks closed in from Sened and Kebili. US tank destroyers, sent by Eisenhower, had not yet arrived. Before pulling back northwards to Fériana, though, the paratroops left their calling card, setting fire to a fuel dump.

Thwarted by bad weather the previous day, men of the British 1st Parachute Battalion, commanded by Lieutenant-Colonel James Hill, dropped over Souk el Arba airfield, 90 miles inland from Tunis in the Medjerda valley on 16 September. They had orders to seize the important communications centre of Béja, 30 miles away, harry the enemy and bring in the French on the Allied side.

Over 500 landed safely though one man was burned to death when he fell onto some power lines. Disguising their lack of numbers by an elaborate parade, they began the journey towards Béja, quickly enlivened when one sergeant inadvertently discharged a number of rounds from his Sten gun into the legs of the nearest soldiers. 'Not a great start,' commented Colour Sergeant Seal.[20]

Since the French might, after all, oppose Anderson's forces, it had been decided beforehand to set up an armoured regimental group, drawn from 6th Armoured Division and built around the 17th/21st Lancers. This was called Blade Force, taking its name from 78th Division's battleaxe insignia. Its task was to blaze an inland route as far as Souk Ahras and finally concentrate around the rest of 6th Armoured, coming up behind.

On 13 November Colonel R.A. Hull, Blade Force Commander, received orders to move east as soon as possible and, 'to get as near Tunis as we could – if not right into it.'[21] Hull sent on a fast column of armoured cars, anti-tank and anti-aircraft guns towards Souk Ahras while the men of a squadron of the 17th/21st Lancers were packed like sardines and despatched by rail, with their tanks to follow after. 'Next stop Waterloo,' they shouted at every halt.

Three days later the leading columns bumped into the rear of 132nd Field Regiment RA which cleared off the road to let Blade Force through amid cries of 'armour for Tunis!' Reaching Constantine just before nightfall, it got to Souk Ahras 24 hours later, to be re-joined by the 17th/21st Lancers. By any standards, this was a remarkable feat of organization and improvisation: the column had travelled from Algiers to the Tunisian border, covering 385 miles in only 47 hours with negligible vehicle breakdowns. Heavy rain that night, a foretaste of what was to come, did not dampen their spirits; 'we felt quite pleased with ourselves,' said Major (later Brigadier) Buttenshaw.

On the afternoon of the 16th, for the first time in North Africa, German infantry were fired upon by French troops, while moving on Béja. Subsequently, a strong patrol from 1st Parachute Batallion under Major Cleasby-Thompson was sent to ambush a German column near Sidi N'Sir, the last French outpost on the Mateur road before Tunis. Early on the morning of 18 November they severely mauled the Germans with Hawkins '75' grenades strung across the road on which the heavy armoured cars blew up. As their crews scrambled out they were shot down by the paratroopers who followed up with Gammon bombs.

Having knocked out six German vehicles and killed or captured a fair number of troops, the 1st Batallion paraded its spoils before the French populace at Béja. Then, with German pressure increasing on Barré's troops, it was put on immediate notice to move to the key communications centre of Medjez el Bab, accompanied by leading elements of the newly-arrived Blade Force.

Blade Force had arrived in its forward area long before it was expected and ahead of the time when 6th Armoured could catch up in the general area east of Bône. Meanwhile, as 78th Division's 36th Brigade advanced along the coastal road, Blade Force remained committed to an inland route towards Tunis, taking it over the river bridge at Medjez el Bab, 120 miles further east. The bridge was vital to any future advance since only there could tanks be sent through the mountains onto the Tunisian plain.

General Juin, commanding the French forces fighting on the Allied side, came to ask for every last man and as much equipment as possible to be sent to Medjez to help the gallant French defenders there. 'Of course,' noted Buttenshaw, 'although he did not say so it was the moral effect as much as the material effect which was really wanted.'

The news on the night of 17/18 November, that the French were under threat from Kampfgruppe *Koch* (Oberstleutnant Koch's 5th Parachute Regiment) at Medjez el Bab, brought armoured cars of B Squadron Derbyshire Yeomanry hurrying to their aid. Koch's men were a formidable bunch. Hardly any of the rank and file soldiers were over 20 years of age but their officers had been battle-hardened in the famous *Meindle* Assault Parachute Regiment, which had won its spurs at Liége and Crete.

Linking up with 1st British Parachute Battalion and then moving forward from Béja, the Yeomanry discovered the French situated on the west bank of the Medjerda river and an inconsiderable number of Germans sitting tight on the other side; neither, however, had thought to blow the bridge. Both sides were still talking to each other, the Germans trying to persuade Barré to allow their limited force to move forward, and the French for their part seeking to delay the expected onslaught.

The next morning, 19 November, Barré's men fired on four German reconnaissance aircraft and refused either to join Nehring's troops or retreat, under the excuse that the advancing Allies made it impossible for them to move.[22] Kesselring, having given Barré one last ultimatum and receiving no answer, ordered the Stukas into action: 'In war it is futile to bargain with unreliable auxiliaries,' he observed.[23]

Urgent requests to the Allied command from Giraud, Juin and General Louis-Marie Koeltz, commander of the *Algiers* and *Constantine* Divisions, for more tanks and fighter aircraft met with Anderson's thinly disguised irritation: 'It was explained to the French that, while everything would be done to assist, tanks could NOT be committed before they were concentrated in strength and fighters were at present based at Bône, which was too distant for effective fighter support.'[24]

Nevertheless, backed by a company of 1st Paras, the French fought with exemplary courage, stopping the enemy assault and driving the attackers back over the Medjerda bridge. Koch's men went berserk, several times forcing their way back into Medjez – the railway station changed hands twice in the fighting – until finally they were driven off.

Arriving a little late at the war, 175th US Field Artillery Battalion came charging to the scene and swept straight onto a forward slope in full view of the German positions. They immediately began firing at the only target visible, a church spire in the distance. 'They did not hit it,' recorded Buttenshaw rather dismissively, '... but they undoubtedly felt better and it helped them to settle down.' Extricated by Colonel Hill's paratroopers, their commanding officer explained their enthusiasm by saying that on the way into action his gun teams had realised they could be the first Americans to open fire in the war.

With the greater part of Blade Force now deployed and in action but with the arrival of 6th Armoured still awaited, a plan to attack from Medjez with a US M3 Lee battalion and march directly on Tunis was briefly considered, but this was abandoned because Blade Force had insufficient infantry. 'It was very exasperating,' recorded Buttenshaw, 'to be so near and yet so far but wise counsel prevailed.'

Notes to Chapter 3

[1] Diary of Captain Harry C. Butcher, USNR, entry for 12 November 1942. Original in Eisenhower Library; photocopy consulted in Montgomery Collection, Imperial War Museum. A truncated and sanitised version of the diary appeared as *Three Years with Eisenhower*.

[2] Deichmann, 'Mission of *OB Süd* with the Auxiliary Battle Command'.

[3] 'Das Bilden des Bruckenkopfes Tunesien', *Die Oase*; General der Panzertruppe Walther Nehring, 'The First Phase of the Battle in Tunisia', Foreign Military Studies, MS D-147 (a continuation of MS D-086). USAMHI. Also, 'Record of an interview with General Walther Nehring, Karlsruhe, Germany, 4 September 1949', by General Robinett and Colonel Potter; Brigadier-General Paul M. Robinett Papers, Box 4. Library of Congress.

[4] General der Panzertruppe Walther Nehring, 'The First Phase of the Engagements in Tunisia, up to the assumption of Command by the Newly Activated Fifth Panzer Army Headquarters on December 9, 1942 – Part I', Foreign Military Studies, MS D-086. USAMHI.

[5] Oberstleutnant Ulrich Bürker, 'Commitment of the 10th Panzer Division in Tunisia', Foreign Military Studies, MS D-174 USAMHI.

[6] Alanbrooke Diary, entry for 26 November 1942; Alanbrooke Papers, 5/1/6a.

[7] Kesselring, 'War in the Mediterranean Area', Detwiler *et al.*, *World War II German Military Studies*, XIV, MS T-3 PI.

[8] AFHQ, Cable Log, 12 November 1942; Bedell Smith, Collection of World War Two Documents, 1941–1945, Box 2. Eisenhower Library.

[9] Kesselring, 'The War in the Mediterranean Area, Part II', Detwiler *et al.*, World War II German Military Studies, XIV, MS T-3 PI.

[10] Eisenhower to Anderson, 19 September 1946; Eisenhower Papers, Box 5. See also Eisenhower, *Crusade in Europe*, p. 130.

[11] Patton Diary, entry for 10 August 1942; Patton Papers, Box 3.

[12] Liddell Hart conversation with Hobart, 28 November 1942; Liddell Hart Memoranda, 11/1942/102. Also, Liddell Hart conversation with Sir Frederick Pile, 1 November 1942; Memoranda, 11/1942/91.

[13] See Map 4: Allied Operations in Tunisia, November 1942, p. 40. The Eastern Task Force was transformed into First Army once Anderson's forces were ashore and beginning their move into Tunisia. The term 'Army' is, however, a misnomer: Anderson had little more than two infantry brigades (11th and 36th Brigades, of 78th Division), each some 4,500 strong, about 1,500 divisional troops and 1,800 men of an armoured regimental column, Blade Force.

[14] Major (later Lieutenant-Colonel) G.Y. Feggetter, TS Memoir. IWM 84/36/1.

[15] First Army HQ, War Diary, entry for 15 November 1942.

[16] Richards and Saunders, *Royal Air Force 1939–1945*, Vol. 2, p. 251.

[17] Winterbotham, *The Ultra Secret*, p. 96. For the reader interested in such matters, Lewin, *Ultra Goes to War*, Calvocoressi, *Top Secret Ultra*, and Bennet, *Ultra and Mediterranean Strategy* contain much useful information and sensible comment. The Germans used their own successful *Beobachtungs Dienst*, or naval interception unit. Unfortunately for them, their intelligence interceptions were not in the same class as those achieved by the British; see Behrendt, *Rommel's Intelligence in the Desert Campaign*.

[18] Yarborough, *Bail Out Over North Africa*, p. 90.

[19] *Ibid.*, p. 97.

[20] Arthur, *Men of the Red Beret*, p. 55.

[21] Brigadier C.G. Buttenshaw, Blade Force, War Diary. 69/11/1. Buttenshaw was a major at this time and serving as G.2 in Blade Force HQ. Blade Force comprised: 17th/21st Lancers (tanks); B Squadron 1st Derbyshire Yeomanry (armoured cars); C Battery 72nd Anti-Tank Regiment RA; G Troop, 51st Light Anti-Tank Regiment RA; a Troop of 5th Field Squadron RE; B Company 10th Rifle Brigade; two sections of 165th Light Field Ambulance; detachments of 26th Armoured Brigade Company RASC and RAOC; one section of 6th Armoured Division Provost Company; a detachment of 9th Tank Transporter Company.

[22] 'Report for General Nehring on the Political and Military Situation in Tunisia from 9 to 21 November 1942', (Tunis, 21 November 1942) pp. 3–5; Bundesarchiv-Militärarchiv [BA-MA], RH 19 VIII/358.

[23] Kesselring, *Memoirs*, p. 142.

[24] First Army HQ, War Diary, entry for 19 November 1942.

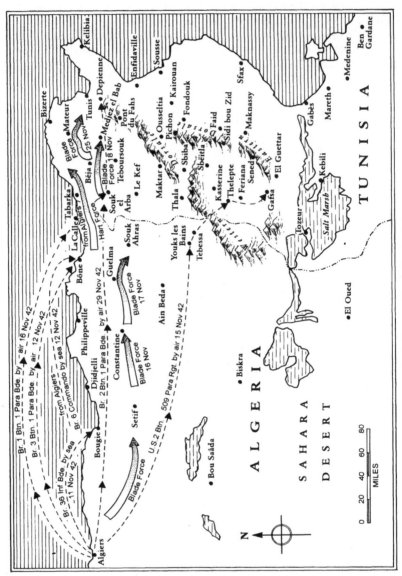

Allied operations in Tunisia
November 1942

Br. 1 Btn. 1 Para Bde. by air 16 Nov 42

Br. 3 Btn. 1 Para Bde. by air 12 Nov 42

from Algiers

Br. 6 Commando by sea 12 Nov 42

Br. 36 Inf Bde. by sea
11 Nov 42

from Algiers

Br. 2 Btn. 1 Para Bde. by air 29 Nov 42

U.S. 2 Btn. 509 Para Rgt. by air 15 Nov 42

Blade Force

Blade Force
16 Nov

Blade Force
17 Nov

Hart Force

Blade Force

Blade
Force 18 Nov

Blade
Force
25 Nov

Kelibia

Bizerte

Mateur

Tunis

Depienne

Medjez el Bab

Pont
du Fahs

Enfidaville

Sousse

Kairouan

Ousseltia

Pichon

Fondouk

Faid

Sidi bou Zid

Maknassy

Sfax

Mareth

Medenine

Ben
Gardane

Tabarka

Béja

Teboursouk

Le Kef

Maktar

Thala

Sbiba

Sbeïtla

Kasserine

Thelepte

Feriana

Sened

El Guettar

Gafsa

Gabès

Kebili

Tozeur

Salt Marsh

La Calle

Souk
el
Arba

Souk
Ahras

Youks les
Bains

Tebessa

El Oued

Bône

Guelma

Ain Beda

Philippeville

Djidjelli

Constantine

Setif

Bougie

Bou Saäda

Biskra

Algiers

TUNISIA

ALGERIA

SAHARA

DESERT

N

MILES

0   20   40   60   80

Chapter 4

Fiddling with Details

'Where is this bloody Air Force of ours? Why do we see nothing but Heinies?'

Widespread complaint among infantrymen in Tunisia, November 1942.[1]

Before arriving in North Africa General Anderson had planned, under the 'very best conditions', to get his 78th Division into a position where it could move forward from the La Calle–Souk Ahras–Divivier region and send advanced columns to Tunis and Bizerte by D+21 (29 November). This was dependent on French co-operation or passivity and on seizing coastal airfields from which fighter aircraft could operate not later than the sixth day ashore.[2] Anderson's plans were flexible but lacked imagination and a ruthless determination to concentrate his limited forces. He failed completely to impress on Evelegh the necessity of driving forward on Tunis and Bizerte before the Germans could establish a bridgehead.

Prior to the convoys sailing, Anderson had accepted that the equivalent of only four British divisions could be landed rather than the six requested. These had been spread out from Safi to Algiers but a series of quick airborne strikes, ahead of rapidly advancing Allied armour, might have won the race for Tunis. The commander of 1st Parachute Brigade thought that Anderson simply did not understand such operations; '... he was a crusty old boy who didn't know anything about parachute troops and didn't like what he had heard about them. I think he was pleased to get rid of us.'[3] The US Army was also 'incredibly naïve' in its lack of detailed planning, proper training and equipment for the exploitation east, complained Major Yarborough of the 509th Parachute Infantry. Few had looked beyond the initial gains or considered an orderly procession of air drops picking out objectives ahead of the ground troops.[4]

Early in the Tunisian campaign, Brooke was showing signs of frustration at First Army's slow progress: 'News from Tunisia rather sticky;' he wrote on 19 November, 'only hope Anderson is pushing on sufficiently fast.'[5] Faced with a journey through mountainous terrain of over 400 miles, its progress was hindered by the fact that for two weeks all available forces were split into a series of probing and only loosely-related advances.

———•◦•———

The first major clash of armour came on 17 November when a defensive force, comprised of part of the 6th Royal West Kents, two troops of Royal Artillery and part of 5th Northamptons, was guarding a bridge and road intersection at Djebel Abiod, having been sent from Tabarka the previous night. Here, at the northernmost point of Kesselring's developing main line of resistance, they met head on Gruppe *Witzig*[6] advancing from Mateur with the intention of driving them back to Bône. After a furious three-hour firefight in which the Germans used their tanks as mobile pillboxes, attempting to blast the enemy off the pass, they withdrew, leaving behind eight tanks and suffering one man killed and 20 wounded. The British lost much more; four 2-pounders, four 25-pounders and most of their carriers and other vehicles.

Everywhere in their advance the Allies were pushing against stiffening Axis resistance. The 1st Parachute Brigade and the French withdrew from Medjez el Bab to Béja on 20 November. Lack of air cover in their forward areas was daily becoming more evident in the scores of blackened and burned-out vehicles littering the roadsides. The US Twelfth Air Force was beginning a rapid build-up in Algeria but Major-General James Doolittle – hero of the famous raid over Tokyo on 18 April 1942 – had still to gather his scattered ground echelons and few forward airfields were established. Between Casablanca and the Tunisian border only four hard-surfaced runways were usable and most units were located in western Algeria, not even in the active theatre of war.[7]

From their fragile reserves and other battlefronts, the Germans hurriedly flew in bombers, fighters and transport planes to airfields on Sicily, Sardinia, and southern Italy, from where troops and weapons were to be ferried to Tunisia in an attempt to choke off the Allied advance. Aircrew in these units seldom survived unharmed for more than a few weeks. 'Our wing's operational strength,' said one bomber group commander, 'was often less than 30 aircraft, and the crews of these lasted for less than 12 missions.'[8]

Such a rate of attrition could not be sustained indefinitely despite a rapid reinforcement of Fliegerkorps II. In theory, Bruno Loezer's HQ at Taormina was allotted around 700 aircraft – bombers, fighters, reconnaissance and close-combat (Nahkampferbände) units – for the defence of the Mediterranean. But the actual number of aircraft and crews available was often far less, either through technical difficulties in transporting torpedo aircraft from northern Norway, or because of poor supply conditions which restricted activities to the use of light, single-engine formations in Africa.[9]

Numerically strong but technically inferior to its German counterpart, the Italian air force suffered catastrophic losses over Malta and was forced to discontinue daylight bombing raids after the Torch landings. The Italians were also unable to use more than one in ten of their night bombers because crews were inadequately trained. Of their two Mediterranean groups (Squadra in Italian parlance, but each composed of about 200 aircraft), one squadra was equipped with obsolete types of little operational value and was employed mainly in support of the German-Italian *Panzerarmee*. The other was used to protect the Italian mainland.

Despite these difficulties, there existed for some time a fine balance between Allied and Axis forces because the twin-engined bombers of both sides had exactly the same defects: neither could operate without fighter cover. Within their 'magic circle' of operations, Spitfires operated with some success but could not match the range of the American P-38 Lightnings at Youks les Bains and both were outnumbered by German Me-109s and Fw-190s.

Given time, the Allies could exert a decisive influence through the American B-17 four-engined heavy bomber but for the time being the Germans held the Tunisian plains where large areas were easily turned into landing grounds.[10] From there, lightweight Ju-87s operated just beyond the range of Allied artillery and were on call to give ground support within five minutes.

On the night of 20 November, a strike force of over 60 Ju-87s and Ju-88s bombed Algiers and destroyed Spitfires, Beaufighters, P-38s, Eisenhower's B-17 command plane – which he had sent forward to participate in bombing operations – and an entire RAF photographic reconnaissance unit at Maison Blanche airfield. As a parting gift, the Germans scattered thousands of razor-sharp pyramidal spikes, wrecking several Allied fighters when they blew out their tyres on trying to land, and many small booby traps resembling fountain pens, pocket wallets and watches.[11]

This was the culmination of a series of night attacks mounted from Sardinia. The raiders were free to come and go virtually as they pleased since no Allied fighters had been equipped with night interception radar equipment.[12] The tangled remains of smashed aircraft persuaded the Allies to remove their remaining B-17s out of harm's way back to Tafarouia, where the mud was reported, two days later, to be 'deep and gooey.' It was precisely at this juncture that Anderson flew back from his command post to Algiers on 22 November to see Eisenhower, who arrived after some delay the next day, about the strain on his resources and administration imposed by the advance. They agreed that there must be a 'short pause' until Combat Command B (CC B)[13] from Major-General Orlando Ward's 1st US Armored Division, further elements of 78th Division and 6th Armoured Division could arrive, after which the advance was to be resumed.[14]

The breathing space allowed 78th Division to assemble in its forward positions. A three-pronged attack, with 36th Brigade Group in the north, Blade Force in the centre, and 11th Brigade Group in the south, would press in upon the enemy, hemming him into Bizerte and Tunis and surrounding him in these pockets.

Blade Force received orders to advance west of the Medjerda River (to have gone east would have depended on taking the bridge at Medjez el Bab, still in enemy hands) and concentrated in an area east of Béja during the afternoon of 24 November. After getting strafed on the way, it waited in readiness to move onwards towards Sidi N'Sir in conjunction with Stuart tanks of 1st Armored.[15] Nearly 700 miles away was the bulk of Brigadier-General Oliver's CC B at Oran, about to be brought up with the reluctant approval of the US II Corps Commander, Major-General Lloyd R. Fredendall.

Some tanks were sent in convoy to Algiers, shipped from there to Bône, and took to the road again for the battle area, wearing out their tracks in the process. Other elements, including some tracked vehicles, were shipped to the east on railway flat cars and a number of half-tracks were driven to Souk el Arba after the personal intervention of Eisenhower and his naval aide, Captain Harry C. Butcher, greatly speeded up the process.[16]

Unfortunately, Eisenhower was out of touch with the true state of affairs at the front. 'With communications so bad,' remarked Haydon, '[the] C-in-C should call Task Force Commanders together and put them in [the] picture since [they] can have only [a] very hazy idea of what is happening.'[17] On his way to Algiers at last on the 23rd, Eisenhower's Fortress burst a tyre while landing at Tafarouia and slid off the runway into the sticky mud. Slow to grasp that Anderson's move on Tunis was badly stalled, the C-in-C immediately blamed the British for the loss of momentum. It was time, thought Butcher, for his boss to 'take [the] British by the horns,' and make them see sense.[18]

Amid mutual recriminations, Brigadier Ian Jacob, on a visit to AFHQ as one of Lieutenant-General 'Pug' Ismay's deputies, criticised the C-in-C's failure to deal with Clark's baleful influence. He 'has all along been the evil genius of the Force [AFHQ],' commented Jacob, and thought that Eisenhower should have blunted Clark's ambition to assume Anderson's command. 'General Eisenhower is far too easily swayed and diverted to be a great commander in chief.'[19]

Before the Torch landings, very little thought had been given to the question of co-operating with the French during the push into Tunisia. Only three among the American senior staff in North Africa had any grasp of their language and even when Colonel William S. Biddle arrived at AFHQ, on 6 November, in response to Clark's urgent request for a senior liaison officer, his French was decidedly rusty.[20]

The great majority of French infantry was native and varied in combat effectiveness. They were commanded by a totally French officer force and a sprinkling of French NCOs who were well trained, but everywhere poorly equipped. The French Army Detachment (DAF), commanded by Juin, was organized into Barré's Troops of Tunisia (CSTT) in the north and XIX Army Corps, under Koeltz, in the centre of the line.

Giraud, as C-in-C, was never, neither formally nor in practice, under Allied command and began to assert his independence almost immediately. Thus, there were two commanders at the front; Anderson, responsible to Eisenhower and Juin reporting to Giraud. At Algiers, Eisenhower and Giraud acted as co-equals and completed an unhappy set-up in which there was no unity of command at either level.

The fundamental reason for this uneasy compromise lay in Giraud's deep suspicions of the British and his low opinion of their military ability. He absolutely refused to place any French troops under British control and thus Anderson and

Juin had to be treated as co-equals and a boundary line determined between them, which was drawn on a line, Souk Ahras–Le Kef–Zaghouan. Anderson was most unhappy at this arrangement.

Eisenhower's intention, when he got to Algiers, was to relieve all French forces operating in 78th Division's area, thereby disentangling them from First Army formations, and concentrate them under Barré to protect Anderson's right flank. While an agreement was reached by 23 November it was tactically and logistically most unsatisfactory for there was only a single line of ammunition supply. However, due to Giraud's intransigence this compromise was as Eisenhower confessed, 'the best that could be achieved at the moment... '[21]

On the same day that the C-in-C called a temporary halt to First Army's advance, a conference took place in the shadow of the *Arco dei Fileni*, the monumental desert gate dividing Cyrenaica from Tripolitania, known to Eighth Army men as 'Marble Arch.' There, on 24 November, Bastico and Cavallero at last agreed to Rommel's repeated requests to meet and discuss Mussolini's preposterous order, agreed by Hitler, for the Mersa Brega position (known to the Allies as El Agheila) to be held at all costs.

Already, the vanguard of Rommel's defeated army had retreated along 650 miles of the *Via Balbia*, the coast road in Cyrenaica, leaving whole Italian divisions to fend for themselves. At Halfaya, long-time resentments flared into violence when both sides fired on each other as the Germans made off in all available motorised transport. So intense had been the scramble to get away that 600 'Green Devils' of the *Ramcke* Parachute Brigade were left behind. In a remarkable display of discipline and fortitude, these steel-hard troops covered over 200 miles of burning desert, seized a column of British trucks, lived off captured supplies and returned to quarrel furiously with Rommel for abandoning them.

At the *Arco dei Fileni* meeting, Kesselring tried vainly to mediate between Rommel, Cavallero and Bastico. The Italian General Staff was increasingly desperate to delay the enemy's advance and Kesselring agreed that North Africa should be held as long as humanly possible, in order to keep war away from the southern boundaries of the Reich and Italy. This view was shared both by *Comando Supremo* and the *OKW*, though not by Rommel. 'I am convinced that Rommel did not fundamentally intend to defend South and Central Italy decisively,' wrote Kesselring, 'His aim was the defence of the Alps, as a result of which... the whole war would have ended in late 1943 or early [in] 1944.'

Under enormous political and strategic pressures, Kesselring demanded a slow and measured withdrawal towards the Tunisian border. In the meantime, any delay imposed on Montgomery was to be used in building up the Axis' front through supply bases at Tunis and Bizerte. Rommel was not deceived: 'the enemy puts his pencil through all our supply calculations,' he wrote.[22] Kesselring knew, however, that while his constant requests to *Comando Supremo* for supplies of all kinds were answered only by unkept promises, once Rommel's troops entered fortress Tunisia, *OKW* and *Comando Supremo* would consider his demands fulfilled. The conclusion was inescapable: so long as Rommel struggled in the Western Desert, at least some attention would be given to provisioning Tunisia. Close to despair after the inconclusive meeting with Kesselring, Bastico and Cavallero, his army struggling along on 50 tons of supplies a day instead of 400, Rommel received an order from Mussolini to launch an attack as soon as possible against the British from the Mersa Brega position. Unable to make Rome see sense, he decided to fly unbidden to Hitler and request the evacuation of North Africa.

The meeting was a fiasco. In a paroxysm of fury, the Führer shouted that the *Panzerarmee* had needlessly retreated and thrown away its weapons. His staff, many of whom, according to Rommel, had never heard a shot fired in anger, prudently nodded their agreement. Angry and defeated, Rommel left with orders to hold the Mersa Brega position at all costs though on his return journey he managed to get Mussolini's permission for Italian infantry units to be sent to the Buerat Line further west. But a withdrawal into Tunisia as far as Gabès, where a decent defensive position was already available, was absolutely ruled out by Kesselring.

On the day that Rommel flew to see the Führer, Anderson's foremost spearheads reached the outskirts of Djedeïda, less than 16 miles from Tunis. Light forces of Montgomery's 7th Armoured Division having advanced through Egypt into Libya, covering 600 miles in 15 days, were on the approach road to El Agheila/Mersa Brega. General Marshall's optimistic forecast that the Allies might be in Tunis within three weeks seemed about to come true.

Notes to Chapter 4

1. Eisenhower, *Crusade in Europe*, p.134.
2. Anderson, 'Notes on Order of Battle,' 19 September 1942; Eisenhower Papers, Box 5.
3. Arthur, *Men of the Red Beret*, p. 28.
4. William P. Yarborough interviewed by Colonel John R. Meese and Lieutenant-Colonel H.P. Houser III, 28 March, 1975. US Army Military History Research Collection (MHRC). USAMHI.
5. Bryant, *Turn of the Tide*, p. 526.
6. A newly-formed ad hoc German battle group named after the commander of 11th Parachute Engineer Battalion, Major Witzig. He had led the famous glider-borne attack on the Belgian fortress of Eben Emael on 10 May 1940.
7. Serviceable airfields were at Port Lyautey, Tafarouia, Maison Blanche and Bône.
8. USSTAF, Historical Section, German Historians' Project, 'European Contributions to World War II – The German Air Force in the Mediterranean', (1946). 'A rough, preliminary sketch, compiled from factual and personal experiences of former officers of the G.A.F.' Spaatz Papers, Box 289.
9. General der Flieger Paul Deichmann, 'Luftwaffe Capabilities in the Mediterranean Theater after the Allied Landing in French North Africa', Foreign Military Series, MS D-017 (1947). USAMHI.
10. While it was unable to climb beyond the defensive range of the German 88mm flak, the B-17 could circumvent the limited flight radius of the German fighters.
11. Incoming message to Eisenhower, 22 November 1942; Cable Logs, Bedell Smith Papers.
12. Craven and Cate, *Torch to Pointblank*, p. 85.
13. From 1 March 1942, the US Army's creation of 'heavy' armored divisions saw the disappearance from divisional establishments of armored brigade headquarters and one of the armored regiments. In order to gain extra flexibility, two combat commands (CC A and CC B) with headquarters detachments were instituted. Each had intelligence and operations capabilities but depended on division for logistics and administration.
14. First Army Command Post – War Diary, entry for 22 November 1942. PRO WO 175/56.
15. ffrench-Blake, *A History of the 17th/21st Lancers*, p. 91.
16. Butcher Diary, entry for 26 November 1942.
17. Haydon, Torch Diary, entry for 17 November 1942.
18. Butcher Diary, entry for 26 November 1942.
19. Quoted by Ambrose, *The Supreme Commander*, p. 138; also Richardson, *From Churchill's Secret Circle to the BBC*, pp. 150–1. Ismay was Churchill's personal chief of staff and Deputy Secretary of the War Cabinet.
20. Biddle, 'The French Army of North Africa in the Tunisian Campaign', (TS, 1943), pp. 1–2. Biddle Papers, Library of Congress.
21. 'C-in-C's Dispatch, North African Campaign 1942–43', p. 20. TS Copy, Bedell Smith Papers, Box 16.
22. Rommel to his wife, 24 December 1942; Liddell Hart, Rommel Papers, p. 379.

Chapter 5

We'll Just Murder Them

'A modern battle is not at all what most people imagine it to be. There actually is *no* front line.'

Signal Corps' officer and Hollywood boss Colonel Darryl F. Zanuck in his diary, 25 November 1942.[1]

———◦◦◦———

On the long pursuit of the German-Italian Panzerarmee westwards towards El Agheila/Mersa Brega, a not uncommon sight was that of bits of vehicles and human flesh hanging from telephone wires where someone had detonated a German Tellermine, S-mine or Italian picket mine. Toiling in the rear of the *Panzerarmee*, General der Pioniere Bulowin's sappers planted many thousands of these devices. Slowed by them during the advance after El Alamein, Montgomery also blamed adverse weather conditions for his hesitant progress: 'Heavy rains interfered with my plans,' he wrote. 'The Axis forces in North Africa had sustained a crushing defeat, and indeed only the rain on 6 and 7 November saved them from complete annihilation.'[2] Monty's chief of staff offered the same limp excuse. But the rain fell impartially on friend and foe alike. 'Looking back,' wrote Brigadier (later Major-General) 'Pip' Roberts (commanding 22nd Armoured Brigade), 'it is impossible not to be critical of the pursuit.'[3] Although delayed by lack of fuel, congestion which had built up behind the front, poor tactical support from the RAF, and the absence of a fresh *corps de chasse* or pursuing force, Montgomery's cautious nature dictated that he 'over-insured' and moved forward on a broad front only after achieving overwhelming superiority.[4]

Yet Montgomery knew from an Enigma decrypt that, on 10 November, 21st Panzer Division had been reduced to 11 serviceable tanks, 15th Panzer Division had none left at all and the whole *Panzerarmee* had only one quarter of an ammunition issue (an issue was supposedly enough for a day's fighting) and fuel for only four to five days. Eighteen hours after Rommel had reported to Hitler that his army's fuel position was 'catastrophic' and his whole force virtually immobilised on 16 November, Montgomery was in possession of all these facts. Indeed, throughout the pursuit he had extensive and timely information about the state of Rommel's forces and often even advance notice of his opponent's intentions from Enigma, air reconnaissance and his Army Y service (radio interception unit).[5]

None of it hastened Montgomery's advance. There were always problems in using high grade intelligence material to the best advantage but, as Alexander said, '[He] wouldn't take risks and at times a commander should take calculated risks and not wait for 100% assurance of success before he'd undertake an operation.'[6]

Unhappy with a series of short stabbing thrusts which brought his troops round against the coast road after the enemy had slipped away, Montgomery's most senior men advised a long route through the desert to circle behind Rommel's fleeing army. Major-General Gatehouse (10th Armoured Division) wanted to drive straight for Sollum and Tobruk while the Air C-in-C, Middle East Command, Air Chief Marshal Sir Arthur Tedder, urged that the time was 'ripe for exploitation.'[7] Montgomery turned them down flat. As for the Australian commander of the Western Desert Air Force, Air Marshal Sir Arthur 'Mary' Coningham,[8] his bitter criticism of Montgomery was deeply personal. 'He never treated me properly... He won at Alamein, but he didn't follow it up. It was almost a defeat that he let Rommel get away. He could have cut across in front of Rommel, but no, despite my advice to use his air, he pushed along, pushed along... Some day the truth will be written about him and the legend dispelled.'[9] The dislike was mutual: 'The real "nigger in the woodpile" is Mary Coningham; I know him well,' Montgomery told Brooke during the campaign in Europe, 'and he is a bad man, not genuine and terribly jealous.'[10]

As if this internecine warfare were not bad enough, both Coningham and Montgomery contrived to get on the wrong side of the Americans, especially Brigadier-General Kenner, Eisenhower's medical chief, who thought Montgomery had, 'an unfavorable attitude towards us. He was a vindictive scoundrel. His own officers hated him, but the enlisted men idolized him.'[11]

Deciding to concentrate on taking the Cyrenaican airfields – a sensible precaution – Montgomery did not accept the challenge of sending units flying across the desert south of Djebel Akhdar through Msus to sever the coast road along which the *Panzerarmee* was withdrawing, at Beda Fomm or Agedabia. A force of 28 Shermans from 1st Armoured Division was rushed forward from near Sollum on 17 November, but this move, which could have been planned well in advance, came too late to isolate Rommel's forces.

By 23 November all Rommel's units had retreated inside the Mersa Brega position and Montgomery was facing the task of forcing it with a slow and calculated build-up. There was time, meanwhile, for him to visit GHQ at Cairo and for some of his soldiers to get away on leave and taste the city's dubious delights. 'There was quite a bit of stealing,' recalled A.H. McGee, 'because we'd got so many deserters about in Cairo that they were giving these wogs money to go and knock us blokes about and pinch our paybooks – we nicknamed them the free Britishers – [then they] could go up and draw our pay on our books.'[12] Soldiers whipped horse-drawn *gharis* (carriages) in frantic races through the narrow streets while the regular drivers sat quaking in the back.[13]

Montgomery thought he would be able to start his offensive about the middle of December 1942. In the lull which now descended on the desert battlefield, he questioned the wisdom of using Eighth Army to take the next major objective, Tripoli, 760 miles by road beyond Benghazi, and whether this might not be more easily accomplished by First Army.

For a time, Churchill was undecided – as was GHQ Middle East – but once Hitler had decided to create a German bridgehead in Tunisia the possibility of Anderson breaking through from the west became exceedingly remote and, in Montgomery's words, with First Army being 'seen off' by the enemy, Eighth Army would have to advance to Tripoli – and beyond. Gradually, this trickled down to the rank and file, now in confident mood: Harry Mitchell heard that First Army had landed in Tunisia: 'now it's a race to Tripoli between us and the First Army, it seemed it was about equal distance to go; [so we thought]... the Eighth Army will get up there, we'll just murder them by the time we get... there.'[14] The 'Desert Rats' would shortly discover this was greatly over-optimistic.

As Rommel's troops settled in their position at Mersa Brega, they heard enviously stories of new heavy tanks arriving in Tunisia, of the *Nebelwerfer* or multiple mortar launcher, and the *Giganten*, massive transport gliders capable of carrying a light tank or 250 men, diverted from the *Panzerarmee* to aid Nehring's forces.

Such reinforcements made First Army's task all the harder but Anderson had high expectations of his resumed attack on the night of 24/25 November: 'My intention is to start advancing tonight towards first objective, Tébourba and Mateur, thence road northward,' he signalled to AFHQ, requesting a maximum Allied bombing effort against Bizerte and Tunis.[15] At 0700 hours on the 25th, Blade Force began moving towards Sidi N'Sir in three columns with over 100 US Stuart tanks on its right, 17/21st Lancers in the centre and the Force's HQ with wheeled vehicles by road on the left, intent on patrolling the region round Tébourba and Djedeïda. Soon the carriers with the HQ group had to come onto the road as mud balled up under their sand shields, cutting their engines.

First ground contact was made at about 1300 hours when B Squadron of 1st Derbyshire Yeomanry reported it was engaging the enemy. In a copy-book attack a number of Germans were killed and 150 Italians taken prisoner who were, recounted Major Buttenshaw, 'almost more of a nuisance as POW than as active enemy as our Armoured Force has precious few infantry for guarding prisoners.'[16]

Blade Force now split, part of it moving north-eastward on Mateur while the remainder, including Lieutenant-Colonel Waters's 1st Battalion, 1st US Armored Regiment, continued eastward in its light M3 (Stuart) tanks, accompanied by scout cars. One company pushed on over the Chouïgui Pass, onto the coastal plain north of Tébourba, crossing the Tine River and punching aside Feldwebel (Company Sergeant-Major) Hämmerlein's weakened armoured reconnaissance company. By-passing the village, another column rumbled over the El Bathan bridge and breasted a ridge. Spread out before them in the late afternoon sun lay Djedeïda landing ground, guarded only by a light flak battery but shortly to be reinforced by Oberst Walter Barenthin's Fallschirmjäger Regiment – an élite unit composed mainly of fighter pilot candidates debarred from flying duties by virtue of eye or other minor physical defects.[17] German aircraft from the landing strip had been dive-bombing and strafing Blade Force all day.

There followed one of the weirdest encounters of the campaign as tanks pumped armour-piercing shells from their 37mm guns into parked aircraft. Some tried to take off and collided with each other while all around hangars and other buildings went up in flames. Before long, five Me-109s and 15 Stukas on the airfield were burning furiously. 'This cheered us up a lot,' commented Buttenshaw. American losses were relatively light: the rest withdrew to bivouac with other elements of the battalion near Chouïgui village.[18]

On the day after their success at Djedeïda airfield Waters's tanks met an enemy detachment, consisting of a Kompanie from each of the 11th Parachute Engineer Battalion, 3rd Tunis Field Battalion and 190th Panzer Battalion, rolling from Mateur towards Tébourba. This force included a number of Panzerkampfwagen IV (PzKpfw IV or Mark IV) tanks, which the Americans had never seen before, carrying the long-barrelled high-velocity 75mm gun. They were accompanied by several older and smaller PzKpfw IIIs, though these had been upgraded by being fitted with spaced armour.

The first armoured clash between Americans and Germans in World War II began on the edge of an olive grove, at a range of about 1,000 yards, when three half-track-mounted 75mm howitzers of Lieutenant Ray Wacker's assault-gun platoon scored direct hits on the enemy tanks but did little damage. The Panzers replied with flat-trajectory armour-piercing ammunition sent screaming amongst the half-tracks, which Wacker prudently withdrew to safety, while Major Siglin's 1st Platoon attacked from the flank in their Stuarts.

Six of the Stuarts were hit and burned fiercely. Siglin was killed, though grievous losses had been inflicted on the better-armed Germans. At least six Mk IVs and several Mk IIIs had been disabled, their tracks shot off or engine compartments perforated; none had 'brewed up', however. Shells had bounced off the enemy like so many ping-pong balls. This puzzled the Americans, but unknown to the tank crews, their armour-piercing shot still lay at the docks. They had been firing practice ammunition.

While the American tanks were within striking distance of Tébourba, and virtually roaming at will among the enemy's rear outposts, the southern prong of Evelegh's attack consisting of 11th Infantry Brigade Group, commanded by Brigadier E.E. Cass, reinforced by 2nd Battalion, 13th US Armored Regiment and 56th Reconnaissance Regiment, had fallen behind schedule and become pinned down on the bare and level plain near Medjez el Bab. 'As it got light,' recorded Major Knoche, 'we could make out a lot of enemy tanks... we opened fire, and gave the inexperienced Americans a painful lesson. Their return fire was very inaccurate, in fact [they were] just firing away in all directions. Even so they did cause quite a few casualties, which we could ill afford.'[19] By their determined resistance, the Germans' screening forces prevented the Allied tanks breaking through on the road south to Goubellat and Bou Arada.

During the night of 25/26 November, Kampfgruppe *Koch*, anticipating a further

American thrust towards the east which would render occupation of Medjez meaningless, withdrew from the village after inflicting heavy casualties on 2nd Lancashire Fusiliers. They had attempted to cross the River Medjerda by moonlight, faltered under heavy machine-gun fire and been cut to pieces by a deadly fusillade from Koch's men on the far bank at daybreak.

When the stone bridge was at last open, M3 Lee tanks of 2nd Battalion, 13th Armored Regiment wound their way carefully over with 1st East Surreys in support. They discovered the Germans had withdrawn their forces beyond Tébourba towards the inner defences around Tunis, though a company of Barentin's troops had, for some reason, not received the order to pull back and remained hidden in the town. An indication of other Allied problems, however, was that, as late as 23 November, many of the 2nd Battalion tanks had been immobilised through lack of grease for their bearings.[20]

Also crossing the bridge should have been Company C of 701st Tank Destroyer Battalion. In an incident which was to become hideously familiar they had been badly shot up by American P-38s which poured cannon fire into their own troops and vehicles from a height of only 50 feet. Not one round was fired back before the aircraft made off, leaving five dead, 16 wounded, towering black clouds of smoke rising from nine fiercely burning vehicles, and seven SP (self-propelled) 37mm guns out of action. It required a major effort to repair the column, at a time when every bit of Allied firepower was needed, and to get it rolling forward again within 48 hours.

By daylight on 27 November the East Surreys held El Bathan and, accompanied by Lee tanks from 13th US Armored Regiment, were also in the town of Tébourba. They successfully defended it against a German counter-attack, mounted by two columns of motorized infantry and tanks, before 5th Northamptons and Blade Force arrived. But the hold-up at Medjez el Bab made them too late to take advantage of 1st Armored Battalion's exploits.

The following day was critical in the struggle to reach Tunis and Bizerte. Climbing the heights of Djebel Maiana that morning British and American officers could see, shining and dancing in the distance, the white buildings and minarets of Tunis and the black lines of railway and roads, snaking across the meandering River Medjerda, others disappearing between ridges near Djedeïda. Hopes were high that a last push might see them in the city – perhaps even by nightfall.

In the north, while prodding laboriously past mines and booby-traps along the coastal road, one prong of Evelegh's attack was blunted by Kampfgruppe *Witzig*, reinforced by newly arrived elements of 10th Panzer Division. Oberst Barenthin, in charge of the sector around Mateur, had secured his right flank with Witzig's men taking the heights west of Djefna. This was a wise decision because he had only a thin line of defence and distrusted the fighting abilities of the two battalions of Italian infantry and one artillery battery defending Mateur itself.

As units of the 8th Battalion, Argyll and Sutherland Highlanders (part of 36th Infantry Brigade) passed between two prominent points, Bald and Green Hill – so named by the battalion's CO because, unusually, the one on the southern side of the road was free of vegetation at the top – Witzig's men were waiting, killing 30, wounding 50 more and taking 86 POW, besides destroying 10 Bren Gun carriers. To Barenthin's great surprise, the British began digging in: 'They were doing this quite openly,' he said.[21] Another attempt next day to storm the hills and force open the road was beaten back by Witzig's men after hours of bitter fighting. Renewing the advance seemed impossible after this and 36th Brigade finally withdrew to the area of Sedjenane, leaving the Germans in command of the secondary route to Bizerte.

The main Allied thrust, by 11th Infantry Brigade, came in the centre, from the direction of Tébourba with troops of the 5th Northamptons riding into battle on Lee tanks of 2nd Battalion, 13th Armored Regiment. Hauptmann Welte's 3/52 Flak Battery was well concealed and repulsed them with such effective anti-tank and machine-gun fire that the wounded had to be left in the open until nightfall when they were brought in by the light of the burning tanks. Overall, the operation had been too weak, lacked surprise and failed to co-ordinate tanks and infantry.[22]

The attack was renewed by Brigadier Cass on the following morning (29 November) using the 5th Northamptons and 12 M3 medium tanks. Again they were turned back by very heavy anti-tank and machine-gun fire. When the armour pulled out it was repeatedly dive-bombed and shelled and most of the infantry forced to withdraw nearer to Tébourba, although a defensive line on a ridge close to Djedeïda held until the Hampshire Regiment's 2nd Battalion relieved the battered Northamptons after dark.

The bulk of 11th Brigade was now stuck fast slightly north-east of Tébourba although the Germans, too, were at full stretch. When Lieutenant-Colonel Waters' tanks debauched onto the Tunisian plain from the Chouïgui Pass they were stopped by two 88mm guns of 20th Flak Division, deployed on the road to Tunis. The famous '88' was a fearsome weapon. 'We used to stand in awe of the[m],' said David Brown, '... and you only had to mention there were a few about... and there was a bit of a flap on; they were good guns, there's no doubt about that.'[23]

Nehring had only one battery of four. Contrary to all normal requirements, rules and experience, they had to be used separately on main roads as anti-tank weapons. It was, commented Nehring, 'an unparalleled situation calling for stop-gap and emergency measures,' and he personally organized the siting of each gun in order to stiffen the backbone of his defences.[24]

On 29 November there arrived strong elements of 10th Panzer under Generalleutnant Wolfgang Fischer, followed by a consignment of guns and four new Tiger tanks, shipped from Fallingbostel by Major Lüder, commanding Panzer-abteilung 501, accompanied by his brilliant company commander, Hauptmann Baron von Nolde. The Tigers, Hitler had assured Kesselring, would be 'decisive' in the campaign for Tunisia.

The PzKpfw VI or Tiger was a formidable fighting vehicle weighing nearly 60 tons. It moved on massively wide tracks and was protected by mighty armour four inches thick at the front. Carrying a lethal punch from its 88mm gun, it nevertheless suffered badly from teething troubles and lacked the reliability of other German tanks so that disaffected crews nicknamed it 'the furniture van.' These shortcomings were soon in evidence for, on arrival at Tunis, one Tiger immediately squatted immovably on the quayside and a second broke down on the road outside the city. Engines, radio apparatus and gears all caused trouble and the Tiger was a notorious guzzler of precious fuel, consuming some 50 gallons every 60 miles.[25]

Nevertheless, they gave much confidence to the infantry barring the Allied advance from the direction of Tébourba though Nehring was quite astonished at Hitler's reckless over-estimation of the Tiger's effectiveness on the outcome of the campaign, committed as they were to a front of over 300 miles. Moreover, alarming – and highly exaggerated – reports were now coming in from Arabs who swore that 1,000 enemy parachutists were dropping north of Zaghouan and 2,000 troops landing at Cap Serrat.

Despite Evelegh's decision to call a temporary halt in the trek eastwards until more air support was made available, about 500 members of the British 2nd Parachute Battalion, commanded by Colonel John Frost, clambered into American C-47s of 62nd and 64th Troop Carrier Groups at Maison Blanche. They dropped near Depienne, at 1450 hours on 29 November, with orders to destroy enemy aircraft, thought to be holding up First Army's advance, and shoot up anything at Oudna, 12 miles away – after commandeering their own transport. This last detail was symptomatic of the whole enterprise, planned with a cavalier disregard for the difficulties involved.

Depienne airstrip was found to be unoccupied; next morning the paratroopers made their way on foot to Oudna where they encountered not German aircraft on the tarmac but four enemy tanks, together with elements of 1st Company, 5th Fallschirmjäger Regiment, and Hämmerlein's armoured reconnaissance company. Supported by Me-109s they forced Frost's men to withdraw to higher ground

After a fitful night's sleep in the freezing cold, Frost's men were up early to plan an ambush. But Hämmerlein's forces, used by Nehring as the 'fire-brigade' of the Tunisian bridgehead, together with elements of the Italian *Superga* Division, arrived sooner than expected. Help appeared to be at hand for the outnumbered paratroopers when there were reports of armour coming up behind them, supposedly bearing First Army's yellow triangle recognition signal.

Alas, the reports were false for the tanks turned out to be commanded by Oberleutnant Jahn, who was shot dead in the ensuing violence which also killed or wounded many of the stubborn 'Red Devils,' including B Company's CO, Major Cleaver. In the meantime, Frost had managed to contact First Army and was told that no tanks could get beyond Tébourba. Consequently, he and his men were forced to withdraw southwards, towards the Sidi bou Hadjeba ridges, leaving behind their wounded and sent on their way by an enemy bombardment. Exploding shells ripped razor sharp slivers from the bare rocks which slashed into the hurrying men; one poor soul had his face sliced almost from his head and was desperately holding it together with his hands.

Frost's survivors were assaulted by enemy infantry and pounded by armour and artillery all day. Among them worked the medical officer, covered in blood from the injured, with nothing to staunch the wounds. Yet, just when matters appeared hopeless, the Luftwaffe mistook the yellow triangles for First Army's identification and bombed their own tanks and armour to oblivion.

After a German attack the next day, led by Leutnant Johann Ismer who was killed, a handful of paratroopers struggling towards Medjez 24 hours later were picked up by an American reconnaissance group. A few more were brought in but B Company had been surrounded and taken prisoner and C Company completely decimated on the ridges of Sidi bou Hadjeba.

Only 160 men remained of 2nd Battalion after this disaster; after one night's rest they were sent to guard the airfield at Medjez. Digging in near the railway station they became caught up in Nehring's counter-attack that was soon to follow and, not fully aware of what was happening, fought a ferocious rearguard action. Brigade HQ demonstrated little understanding or sympathy for the battalion, whose magnificent fighting qualities had been expended in a particularly ill-conceived and ultimately futile operation which outraged Frost.[26] Even Nehring was at a loss to understand its purpose: 'it was too small an action to be readily explained.'

The same could be said of the landing by ten troops, six British and four American, of 1st Commando on the coast west of Bizerte, near Sidi el Moudjad, in the early hours of 1 December, which was intended to turn Kampfgruppe *Witzig*'s right flank and harry its withdrawal. The beach selected was not easy; men had to wade ashore up to their armpits in water and five donkeys swam energetically ashore only to be found useless because of the nature of the terrain.

Dividing their forces at dawn, the commandos advanced five miles inland to two road junctions on the Bizerte–Mateur road; one group held their junction for 72 hours and the other for 24 hours. During this time, they dominated the area, stopping the enemy moving westward for it was impossible for armour to travel off-road because of the thick heather-like scrub, often over seven feet high.

Reports to Nehring of this operation were greatly delayed by the inadequate French telephone service. On hearing of it, he immediately dispatched troops – only just disembarked in Tunisia – across the wooded mountains to meet this latest challenge. Three times Arab informers gave away the commandos' positions, while for their part the 'Green Berets' confirmed reports coming in to First Army that German patrols were operating out of Mateur in Arab dress.[27]

In three days the commandos lost 134 men, including troop commanders Captain Harold Morgan and Captain John Bradford who led their men to within four miles of Bizerte. The survivors were eventually forced to retreat to Sedjenane after failing to establish radio contact with brigade HQ and running out of supplies. Beyond confirming their ability to survive and fight courageously under the most adverse situations, which was already well known, little was gained from this exploit. Since 36th Brigade Group's advance had run out of steam well short of Mateur when the operation went ahead, it is difficult to see quite what could have been achieved.

On 27 November 1942, Eisenhower and Clark at last set out for the front in a semi-armoured Cadillac, protected from aerial attack by guns mounted on two scout cars, though their elevation was 'disquietingly low.'[28]

Anderson's right flank was flung just east of Tébourba and his light reconnaissance forces stretched out to the south-east. The left of his main force was at Mateur while Blade Force was operating in support of two Brigade Groups. Soon to arrive, but not yet in line, was 1st Guards Brigade (78th Division) with Brigadier-General Lunsford Oliver's CC B from 1st Armored Division also pushing into forward areas.

In the south, 2nd Luftwaffewachkompanie (Air Force Guard Company) under Oberleutnant Kempa had occupied the airfield at Gabès on 17 November without major French opposition. Four days later they were reinforced by Italian troops arriving after a long overland march from Tripoli. Nehring's constant worry was that the Allies might break through to this important port and strategic centre, selected as the junction between the Tunis bridgehead and the *Panzerarmee*, cutting off the whole Tunisian promontory and exploiting the Mareth fortifications to which Rommel's men were retreating. He therefore stiffened the Italian forces in this region with patrols while simultaneously dispatching German demolition teams who parachuted into Gafsa and straddled the roads between Gafsa and Tébessa, in order to impede any Allied thrust to the coast.

With the object of securing the road from Tripoli, German and Italian units occupied the coastal cities of Sousse and Sfax. They were commanded by Nehring to mount an 'aggressive defence' and push out towards the west in order to keep the Allied forces at bay. In this they were only partly successful because of the low quality of some troops involved, though the Sousse battalion advanced past Kairouan and fought superior enemy forces to a standstill on the hills to the west of the city.

Dismayed by what he had seen on his tour of the front, Eisenhower was only too aware of how thinly First Army's forces were spread out. In the south, only Edson Raff's miniature blitz army was bustling about and making itself a general nuisance to the enemy. Eisenhower had instantly promoted this 'energetic, resourceful officer' to colonel and held him in high regard.[29]

On 28 November Raff was resupplied and reinforced with a battalion of the 26th US Infantry, a company of Algerian Tirailleurs, a British anti-mine engineer detachment and a company of tank destroyers. Three days later he sent a light platoon from Fériana through Kasserine to enemy country beyond Sbeïtla, with the object of attacking a German-Italian force at Faïd, the last natural barrier on the road from Tébessa to Sfax.

Faïd Pass, just to the east of the village, was full of the enemy; they were to be attacked from the rear, across their line of retreat, while Lieutenant Roworth, RE, and his squad went ahead to check for mines. 'How the hell do you know Roworth,' asked Yarborough when the road was reported as clear, 'you don't have any such thing as a mine detector with you, do you?' 'I smell 'em out Major,' was the reply. Yarborough was inclined to think this was true.[30] Four P-38 Lightnings, diving low and machine-gunning, heralded the start of Raff's attack. As they turned back to base in came the tank destroyers, followed by Algerian Tirailleurs but it took two days' hard fighting to occupy the pass and a pounding from the Luftwaffe before it was held.

Elsewhere, there was little success. Observing that the only forward formations capable of giving 'an umbrella to our foot troops' were the British Spitfires flying off Souk el Arba with about 40 P-38s and a squadron of A-20 Havocs operational from Youks les Bains, Eisenhower complained to Marshall of 'real difficulty.'[31] In a gesture to help Anderson, the C-in-C personally placed the aircraft at Souk el Arba at the complete disposal of First Army which in turn assigned them to 78th Division.

There was no lack of effort on the part of Eastern Air Command (the RAF formation supporting First Army) and the US Twelfth Air Force: in the last week of November they flew nearly 1,900 sorties and lost at least 52 aircraft against the Luftwaffe's 1,084 sorties and 63 losses.[32] But their offensive against landing grounds and transport aircraft was achieved only at the expense of neglecting the enemy's supply lines and shipping in ports. The air effort was also largely invisible to Anderson's hard-pressed infantry who were sheltering from incessant air attacks in their most vulnerable and far-flung positions.

Blade Force, stuck near Chouïgui on the afternoon of 27 November, was attacked by Ju-88s when practically devoid of any natural cover. 'What there was,' recorded Haydon, 'was allotted to the soft-skinned vehicles, otherwise we relied on good dispersion. Provided they had handy slit trenches personnel were quite safe but there was a steady drain on... vehicles at this time.' Forty-eight hours later, the Germans struck in force and blitzed Blade Force all day. In retaliation, plans were laid to attack the Axis airfields on 30 November, which was changed to an assault by US Stuart tanks and then finally cancelled because Djedeïda still had not fallen.

Despite impressing, 'every kind of scrawny vehicle that can run,' First Army was short of supplies, low on maintenance and could not stem the enemy's rate of reinforcement. Eisenhower was ready to blame everyone but himself: Anderson was, 'apparently imbued with the will to win, but blows hot and cold by turns, in his estimates and resulting demands'; Air Marshal Sir William Welsh, C-in-C Eastern Air Command, was, 'a sound statistical planner but rather devoid of imagination and... lacking in drive,' while Doolittle, 'is a curious mixture.' Only the Naval C-in-C Mediterranean, Admiral Sir Andrew Cunningham, 'a joy to have around,' and Lunsford E. Oliver had been effective.[33]

Mindful of the factors telling against him, Anderson informed Eisenhower that, unless he could mount an attack soon, he would have to withdraw his forces to an area with greater air-cover and build up his units for a major offensive. A flowing tide of men from 5th Fallschirmjäger Regiment, moving steadily along the road towards Medjez el Bab late on the afternoon of 30 November, swamped his slow deliberations. The German counter-attack had begun.

Notes to Chapter 5

1 Zanuck, *Tunis Expedition*, p. 98. Emphasis in original.
2 Montgomery, *El Alamein to the River Sangro*, p. 25.
3 Roberts, *From the Desert to the Baltic*, p. 125.
4 Carver, *Dilemmas of the Desert War*, p. 139.
5 Hinsley, *British Intelligence*, Vol. II, p. 454.
6 Answers to George Howe's questions for Alexander: Part I, North Africa and Sicily. January 1949, OCMH Collection.
7 Quoted by Hamilton, *Monty: Master of the Battlefield*, p. 59.
8 The nickname came from Coningham's proud claim to be a 'Maori', from New Zealand where he was raised, rather than an Australian where he was born. In time, 'Maori' became simplified to 'Mary.'
9 Coningham interviewed by Forrest Pogue (14 February 1947). OCMH Collection.
10 Quoted by Hamilton, *Monty: Master of the Battlefield*, p. 692.
11 Kenner interviewed by Forrest Pogue. OCMH Collection.
12 Thames Television, recorded interview for *The World at War* series. IWM 002744/01.
13 Colonel Hugh Daniel. *Ibid.* IWM 002745/02.
14 *Ibid.* IWM 002709/04.
15 Incoming message to Eisenhower, 24 November 1942; Cable Logs, Bedell Smith Papers. Anderson had 36th Brigade along the northern road from Tabarka to Mateur, where the road forks to Bizerte and Tunis. 11th Brigade was following a route 25 miles south through Souk el Arba, Medjez, Tébourba, Djedeïda and Tunis. Blade Force was operating between the two, denying high ground to the enemy.
16 Buttenshaw, Blade Force War Diary.
17 Details on the Barenthin Regiment from Colonel B.A. Dickson to Lt-Colonel Chester ('Chet') B. Hansen, 1 February, 1951; Hansen Papers, Box 28, File C. USAMHI. Hansen was a graduate of Syracuse University in journalism and Bradley used him as his PR officer. Entering the war as a second-lieutenant he ended up as a lieutenant-colonel.
18 Howe, *Battle History of 1st Armored Division*, pp. 65–6; Carell, *Foxes of the Desert*, p. 325.
19 Kurowski, *Endkampf in Afrika*, p. 69.
20 Quoted by Carrell, *Foxes of the Desert*, p. 323.
21 First Army CP – War Diary, entry for 23 November 1942. WO/214 PRO.
22 Howe, *Battle History of 1st Armored Division*, p. 73.
23 Thames Television, *The World at War* series. IWM 002705/03. The 88mm Flak 43 was the newest version of the famous dual-purpose '88' which had already seen significant use in the desert. It was specially designed for an anti-tank role, with a low silhouette and improved shield. There were about 25 of these in use in Tunisia by March 1943. Earlier types were also in evidence. See Playfair, *Destruction of Axis Forces*, pp. 499, 506; Davies, *German Army Handbook 1939-1945*, pp. 104–5.
24 Nehring, 'First Phase of the Battle in Tunisia'.
25 *Ibid.*; Battle Report from Panzer Abteilung 501, 16 December 1942, BA-MA RH19-VIII/364; Carrell, *Foxes of the Desert*; Smithers, *Rude Mechanicals: An Account of Tank Maturity during the Second World War*, pp. 125, 173–4.
26 My account is based on Frost's own story in Arthur, *Men of the Red Beret*, pp. 62–5, and on Kurowski, *Endkampf in Afrika*, pp. 83–7.
27 First Army CP – War Diary, entry for 26 November 1942.
28 Butcher Diary, entry for 29 November 1942.
29 Eisenhower to Marshall, 30 November 1942; Chandler, Eisenhower Papers, II, Doc. 673.

[30] Yarborough, *Bail Out*, p. 104.

[31] Eisenhower to Marshall, 30 November 1942. At Bône were also the RAF's No. 81 and No. 111 Squadrons but these had been badly knocked about by enemy attacks as soon as they landed there. Butcher recorded in his diary on 29th November that they were continuing to 'catch the brunt of enemy action'.

[32] Playfair, *Destruction of Axis Forces*, p. 179; First Army CP – War Diary, entry for 29 November 1942; Spaatz Diary, entry for 2 December 1942; Spaatz Papers, Box 9.

[33] Eisenhower to Marshall, 30 November 1942; Chandler, *Eisenhower Papers*, Doc. 673.

Chapter 6

A Nasty Setback

'I hope the type of piddling and disconnected action which you have evidently been subjected to will soon be stopped and I pray for an American Army.'

Major-General Ward to Major-General Oliver, 14 December 1942.[1]

———⊪●●⊪———

Oberstleutnant Koch knew exactly what was expected of him in leading the attack which Kesselring had ordered. Unhappy with the way in which Nehring had allowed his units to be pushed back towards Tunis and Bizerte, the Generalfeldmarschall visited him on 28 November, urging a much more positive view of what could be done.

Nehring's initial response was to place a soldier of great competence and vigour, Generalleutnant Fischer, in charge of the attack, scheduled to jump off on 1 December. Fischer immediately diverted substantial parts of his newly arrived 10th Panzer from support of Kampfgruppe *Witzig* and sent them instead to reinforce the front around Tébourba. Every available man and machine was flung into the assault; only 30 men remained in Tunis to keep watch on the city's 220,000 inhabitants.

Koch's 3rd Battalion advanced from Tunis towards Massicault, on the road to Medjez and pierced the Derbyshire Yeomanry's first line of defence. When the paratroops became pinned down, artillery was called up to take out the British machine-gun and mortar positions.

At the same time, the larger part of 5th Fallschirmjäger Regiment swung northwards towards El Bathan with the intention of blocking the road from Medjez to Tébourba and then turning west beyond El Bathan, thus encircling the enemy and cutting off his line of retreat. Oberfeldwebel Ahrendt led his Pionier platoon deep into hostile territory to blow up the single road bridge two miles west of El Bathan, in order to prevent the bulk of Cass's 11th Infantry Brigade Group and elements of 1st Armored Division from bringing up supplies or withdrawing. All night and throughout the next day, Ahrendt's men fought off savage attacks as the British tried to re-open the vital route.

Closing in from the south-east, a leading company of paratroopers under Leutnant Kautz found a rough path leading towards El Bathan and unexpectedly found themselves harrying the East Surreys from the rear. They were soon spotted and bombarded by American artillery and mortars but were greatly encouraged to see the flicker of machine-gun fire to the east where advance units of 86th Panzer Grenadier Regiment (10th Panzer Division) had made contact with the enemy.

Koch's men advanced in open order; storming the village, they drove the East Surreys remorselessly back until the whole Allied defence line cracked. British and American staff cars, tanks, artillery and signals units streamed south-west, towards Medjez el Bab, pursued by Oberleutnant Wöhler's 12th Company in the vanguard of 10th Panzer. The fearless Leutnant Kautz was not among them. A tank shell had exploded, killing him instantly and so severely wounding the men nearest him, Jäger Bohly and Gefreiter Vogel, that they died next day.[2] At Medjez el Bab the Panzers were stopped with unexpected ferocity by survivors of the British 2nd Parachute Battalion who delayed their advance long enough to prevent complete encirclement of the troops at Tébourba.

It was on Tébourba that the main weight of Generalleutnant Fischer's armoured drive to the west was unloaded. While Koch's regiment put pressure on the Allies' southern flank, parts of 10th Panzer Division attacked from the north and north-east and the Tiger battalion, together with two *Marsch* battalions, struck from Djedeïda.

In the Chouïgui Pass – at the northern end of the Tébourba salient – Blade Force, with Waters's 1st Battalion and the Derbyshire Yeomanry's armoured cars, felt the first impact of Battle Groups *Lüder* and *Hudel* as they attacked with 60 Mk IIIs and IVs. The defenders were driven south-eastward into olive groves near Tébourba but steady shooting by British artillery slowed up the German advance while the 17/21st Lancers were hurriedly called from the Tébourba Gap to support. However, because the Lancers were carrying out maintenance and repairs to their shockingly unreliable Crusader tanks, they were unable to re-join Blade Force in time and had five of their tanks destroyed into the bargain.

As artillery, infantry and other units streamed back through the Tébourba Gap, 2nd Hampshires were battling to hold the ridge in front of Djedeïda against another enemy advance which had developed during the afternoon of 1 December. On taking over from the Northamptons, Lieutenant-Colonel Lee had been worried that he was given permission neither to attack and hold Chouïgui village, nor to fall back on a common front with the East Surreys.

Group *Djedeïda* attacked head-on. Made up from Tunis *Marsch* battalions, their weak performance incensed Fischer who was forced personally to lead some companies, platoons and even squads: 'it is impossible to fight successfully with such troops,' he complained to Nehring. An officer, who 'lurked under cover for hours' with his men, was relieved on the spot and Fischer demanded that he be court-martialled.[3]

Despite their attackers' lack of aggression the Hampshires were up against hopeless odds, repeatedly forced into costly counter-attacks in order to hold ridge positions. With Tébourba threatened by encirclement and El Bathan falling to Koch's paratroopers, they were in imminent danger of being cut off. Indeed, their position was worse than that of Blade Force which had been driven back on Tébourba but had denied the town to the enemy by accurate artillery fire.

In bitter fighting next day (2 December) 2nd Hampshires held Group *Djedeïda* on their eastern ridge line – but only at heavy cost. As Fischer's tanks began to infiltrate their forward positions they began to pull back under cover of darkness to an area between the Medjerda River and the East Surreys' positions. Meanwhile, Tébourba was nearly surrounded by German armour and the salient pounded by Stukas, though they were forced to remain high by Blade Force's good use of light anti-aircraft guns which also deterred ground troops from pressing home attacks on its exposed positions.

Heroic efforts by part of 2nd Battalion, 13th US Armored Regiment, ordered to attack south of Tébourba, also prevented the enemy from destroying some of Blade Force's attached units, though the cost was high, as M3 Lee commander Lieutenant Philip Walker later recounted. During the engagement a nearby detonation shattered his tank's 37mm sight, blinding and wounding the gunner: 'He told Sergeant Evans to take his place, then felt for and put in a new sight himself,' noted Walker. 'We continued, firing now at Jerry tanks at 1,000 yards range... Our tank was hit and flamed up. Gave the order to abandon tank. Ran back about 70 or 80 yards to the draw, by which we had advanced. Discovered Sergeant Evans was groaning and burning. Dragged him out... Gave [him] a shot of morphine. He was conscious and uncomplaining. Put one of his eyes back into its socket and bandaged it... I was burned on my right leg and left arm but O.K.'[4] In this short firefight, lasting 15–20 minutes, eight M3s 'brewed up' and the average loss was one killed and two wounded in each.

Brigadier Cass's tanks were frittered away in such desperate engagements by pitting them against superior German armour. Ominously, Anderson reported that his army and air force units were stretched to their limits, communications were, at best, precarious and no reserve supplies had been brought forward. The arrival next day of two companies of 10th Panzer's 86th Grenadier Regiment, flown in from Italy to reinforce Group *Djedeïda*, together with first-class air support, decisively tipped the scales.

A fierce attack against the East Surreys dislodged them from Point 186, the highest part of Djebel Maiana, from where Americans and British had looked down on Tunis only five days earlier, and nearly cut off remnants of the 2nd Hampshires. Seeing German infantry taking positions on the hill they counter-attacked from an outlying peak and when this petered out, Major H.W. Le Patourel led four volunteers who bombed and shot their way deep into the enemy's positions. He was very naturally assumed to be dead and awarded a posthumous Victoria Cross; only much later was it discovered he had been taken prisoner and, happily, recovered from his wounds.[5] A counter-attack by the East Surreys in the afternoon narrowly failed to recover their abandoned guns and Lieutenant-Colonel Wilberforce was forced reluctantly to withdraw under cover of darkness along a steep and narrow track running by the edge of the Medjerda River since his retreat had been blocked by German armour. They soon came under fire; the first vehicle to blow up was a 3-ton ammunition lorry before a carrier was hit, losing a track and resisting every effort to move it. Eventually, it had to be abandoned and with it all the following vehicles.

A few guns and vehicles, some infantry and the crews of the abandoned vehicles were saved. Behind them, Tébourba lay wreathed in a pall of smoke while white Verey lights and streaks of tracer bullets revealed how the Germans were mopping up the few survivors. 'It was,' said one man, 'like Dunkirk all over again.'

This withdrawal exposed the Hampshire's left flank to attack. Completely encircled, they drew in around their battalion HQ. Lieutenant-Colonel Lee ordered 200 survivors to break out of the surrounding ring of German troops and head for Medjez el Bab. Four days later only four officers and 120 men reassembled. The battalion had virtually been annihilated.

General Evelegh's decision to vacate Tébourba and pull back 11th Brigade, stiffened with Oliver's CC B and 2nd Battalion, the Coldstream Guards (1st Guards Brigade commanded by Brigadier Copland-Griffiths), had become inevitable with the loss of Point 186, which gave the enemy an invaluable observation platform over the village and surrounding countryside.

Before the retreat could get under way a strong attack on 6 December by elements of 10th Panzer Division developed from the direction of Massicault towards Medjez el Bab. Their way was barred by CC B's tanks, but unfortunately the company commanders of Lieutenant-Colonel Hyman Bruss's 2nd Battalion, 13th Armoured Regiment, counter-attacked without decent reconnaissance and failed to co-ordinate with mutually supporting weapons or concentrate their forces. They ran onto highly accurate anti-tank fire, predictably suffering heavy losses. The subsequent retreat of Evelegh's units under constant gunfire and aerial attack, through the Tébourba Gap and up the Medjerda Valley, was arduous. Much matériel had to be abandoned.

Blade Force, put into reserve after its relief by US armour, was called upon to protect this withdrawal from an attack expected from the direction of Béja. For several days the weather was appalling; one sweep by 17/21st Lancers reported that enemy tanks had been spotted but a patrol sent out to investigate returned with the news that the 'tanks' were Arab huts. Patrol members, 'failed to report whether they were Mark III or IV,' commented Buttenshaw.

To Nehring, the outcome of the struggle for Tébourba was 'a song of praise to German valour and German endurance under the most difficult circumstances with emergency equipment.' Many wounded had to be left in agony on the battlefield because there were too few medical troops and losses were so severe. Among them was Oberfeldwebel Ahrendt, who had so skilfully led the attack at the Medjerda bridge. He was killed on 3 December by artillery fire and was posthumously awarded the Knight's Cross. Dead, too, was brilliant tank commander Hauptmann von Nolde after a shell took off both his legs as he tried to pass instructions to Hauptmann Deichmann, in turn felled by a sniper's bullet at the hatch of his Tiger during furious battles in the olive groves north of Djedeïda.

As for Cass's 11th Brigade, in four days it had exhausted its fighting value, losing 55 tanks and some 300 motor vehicles; more grievous still, over 1,000 men had been captured. The Surreys and Northamptons were each down to about 330 all ranks, the Lancashire Fusiliers, sent up with the Coldstream Guards, reduced to 450 men and the Hampshires almost wiped out. In the air losses had also been severe, especially on 4 December when nine Bisleys[6] of No. 18 Squadron, led by Wing-Commander Malcolm, were caught in the late afternoon on little less than a suicide mission. Sent without Spitfire escort on a low level attack against a landing ground ten miles north of Chouïgui, they were bounced by 60 Me-109s which shot them down, killing six complete crews. Almost the last was Malcolm, awarded a posthumous VC for his outstanding bravery.[7]

'It is obvious we have lost the race for Tunis,' noted Butcher on 6 December, though Anderson reported only that his forces had suffered, 'a nasty setback.' Cataloguing a list of Anglo-American failures and protracted enemy dive-bombing, he told Eisenhower that, above all, 'a sense of careless "dash"' had arisen after the long advance into Tunisia during which a series of successful minor skirmishes had encouraged a casual attitude. 'There were many gallant deeds in the fighting and there is no loss of spirit. But 11 Bde must have a rest before continuing: indeed all are tired.'[8] The reverse at Tébourba, had made a planned major attack on 9 December entirely out of the question although this was kept secret from the newly-activated V Corps, commanded by Lieutenant-General C.W. Allfrey with his HQ at Souk el Khemis, to whom written directions had been issued.[9]

Re-grouping his forces, Nehring planned to start a new assault on 10 December south of the Medjerda River, in a south-westerly direction on the line Medjez–Goubellat, while von Broich's forces near Mateur were reinforced and held the line without attempting to move westwards into the difficult mountainous area confronting them. In the south, the Italian *Superga* and *Imperiali* Divisions were strengthened with fresh reserves and committed step by step further south-west, improving the road link with Tripoli.

Before Nehring could execute his plan he was suddenly overtaken by a major shake-up of the German command in Tunisia. Kesselring was behind it, not through any severe disagreement with his young General der Panzertruppe over the desirability of spreading Axis positions outwards to a line Bône to Kebili, but rather from a lack of faith in his ability to see this through.[10] On 3 December 1942, Generaloberst Jürgen von Arnim was called from the Russian Front to a conference at Rastenburg where Hitler ordered him straight to North Africa. 'I have decided that our forces are too weak,' he said, 'and will create out of three tank divisions and three motorised divisions a new *Panzerarmee*, which you will command.'[11]

An old friend, Generalleutnant Heinz Ziegler had already been told he was to be von Arnim's chief of staff, carrying full powers to take decisions when his superior was away touring the front. Given new forces promised by Keitel, both von Arnim and Ziegler were confident they could advance out of the Tunis–Bizerte area, reach the mountains on the Tunisian-Algerian border, capture Bône and Philippeville harbours and move on to take the Algerian ports further west. In order to go as far as Oran, Ziegler counted on a rising of the Arab population, forcing the enemy either to re-embark or be taken prisoner. Both made the same demands for this ambitious programme: a guarantee of constant supplies and the capture of Malta.

The new commander of Fifth Panzer Army was a tall and severe 53-year-old veteran who had commanded 39th Panzer Korps at Rzhev. The call to serve in North Africa came as a complete surprise – and nearly as much to Nehring who knew he was to be sent to a command on the Eastern Front only 48 hours before von Arnim turned up at his headquarters.

Never given a clear objective, one of von Arnim's first problems was the impossibility of fulfilling a stream of contradictory orders issued by Hitler, Kesselring, Bastico, Cavallero, the OKW staff and Mussolini. Still, when he and Ziegler landed at El Aouina on 8 December 1942, it struck Nehring – generally pessimistic about the likely long-term outcome of the fighting in North Africa – that both were 'optimistic and eager for action.' They were quickly put in the military picture by Nehring's chief of staff, the capable Oberst Pomtow, and briefed by Gesandter (Ambassador) Rahn on the complicated political situation. 'Whatever happens, I need peace and order behind me and the fighting forces,' replied von Arnim, 'and somehow we have to get all these different political and national factions under one hat.'[12]

To complicate matters the French garrison of 12,000 men at Bizerte had been disarmed in a lightning action on 7 December, much against the wishes of Nehring and Kesselring since the local commander, Admiral Derrien, had remained loyal to the German cause even during the fighting round Mateur and the crisis at Tébourba. But a direct order from the Führer, delivered to Tunis by Generalleutnant Alfred Gause, could not be ignored. 'There was,' reported Nehring thankfully, 'no friction.'[13]

Safe in the knowledge that his base areas were secure, von Arnim gave orders for the advance to be resumed on Medjez el Bab, which Eisenhower had personally ordered Anderson to hold, much against the latter's wishes. The C-in-C was particularly scathing about recent events: 'I think the best way to describe our operations to date,' wrote Eisenhower, 'is that they have violated every recognized principle of war, are in conflict with all operational and logistic methods laid down in textbooks, and will be condemned in their entirety... for the next twenty-five years.'[14]

At 0830 hours on 10 December, 86th Panzer Grenadier Regiment attacked in two columns, each consisting of a company of tanks and two of infantry moving along the Medjerda. A deserter, found drunkenly weaving about on a bicycle along the Furna to Medjez el Bab road the previous day, had told some startled Americans about a much stronger force, with artillery, concentrating near Massicault. Led by Major Huedel, with up to 35 tanks including one Tiger, this force was looping through Massicault and Furna to break into Medjez from the south, where it ran into Waters's battalion, about ten miles from Medjez.

Despite prior knowledge, Waters was caught unprepared by the speed and precision of Huedel's attack. His battalion was soon split and lost five Stuart tanks, which prised open the route to Medjez. Although hindered by the accurate shooting of a French battery, Huedel's tanks outfought the Americans who were mercilessly machine-gunned as they scrambled from their burning Stuarts. The survivors sheltered in a steep-sided wadi, including one man nursing nothing worse than a damaged arm despite having been squashed into deep mud beneath the tracks of a Mk IV.

By evening, a decision had been taken to withdraw CC B's bludgeoned armour from Medjez el Bab while protecting the bridgehead against any enemy thrust which might develop from the direction of Tébourba. Directed by the senior battalion commander, Lieutenant-Colonel John R. McGinness, a long column of vehicles, guns and tanks crawled along a narrow paved road to cross the Medjerda River on the Bordj Toum bridge, slightly north-east of Medjez. A rumour spread that enemy artillery and mortars made this impossible and faced with a difficult situation, McGinness panicked. He consequently ordered the column to reverse and sent it on a dirt track alongside the river to cross the bridge at the village.

In one of the most costly and humiliating episodes in the history of 1st Armored Division, the column very quickly became mired in deep, viscous, mud. Before long the order was given to abandon vehicles and make for Medjez on foot. Left behind were 18 tanks, 41 guns, 132 half-track and wheeled vehicles and 19 trailers.[15] All had been brought thousands of miles at great cost; they remained gently rusting in their muddy graves until the Germans destroyed many of the entrapped hulks. Oliver immediately relieved McGinness of his command. 'I never felt so bad in my life,' wrote Oliver. 'The only comfort I could draw from this blunder was the fact that we still had our men, all of them having marched to safety.'[16]

On the verge of relieving all concerned of their commands, Eisenhower realised the Americans had suffered a 'crippling loss.'[17] The only positive news came from Blade Force which ran into three companies of German glider school students, decked out as assault troops. Over 100 were killed and 50 or so taken prisoner. Afterwards Blade Force withdrew without incident to Teboursouk where it was absorbed into 6th Armoured Division. 'On several occasions we had been within an ace of capturing Tunis,' commented Major Buttenshaw, 'but we never had enough infantry available to hold it.'[18] 'We just tried to do too much with too little, and too late,' agreed Waters, 'We just couldn't do it.'[19]

Despite these setbacks, Eisenhower was determined not to give up the attempt to take Tunis by Christmas and pen in the enemy around Bizerte.[20] The respite, however, enabled von Arnim to expand the bridgehead from Nehring's original defence areas into one seamless system, with the *von Broich* Division in the north, 10th Panzer Division in the centre, the Italian 1st (*Superga*) Division in the south and east and, in the extreme south, the Italian 50th Special Brigade – 'a sure indication that the Germans expect no serious attack in this area,' noted CC B HQ.[21] By 16 December, AFHQ estimated that the Axis could deploy about 25,000 combat troops and 80 tanks, supported by 10,000 service personnel. Against this, since Torch the Allies had deployed 20,000 British and 11,800 US combat troops, besides being able to call on 35,000 poorly equipped French soldiers, but were inferior in air and firepower, their preponderance in tanks and artillery being offset by superior German types and performance.

While the build-up for a new Allied attack progressed, Patton flew in from French Morocco to First Army HQ at Ain Senour – 'Jane's Ass' to the British[22] – to discover why American tank losses were so heavy. While at the front he visited Waters' battalion, which had lost two-thirds of its tanks, and found Waters himself with a bullet hole through his clothing. At Medjez el Bab he heard that the Hampshires had fought to the last against superior forces: 'when the tanks came at them,' he recorded, 'the men got in their slit trenches, and the Germans then ran up and down lengthwise and squashed them in the trenches.' Such an experience appeared to have broken the brigade commander; Patton found him 'trembling all over. He told me this was due to fatigue. From the smell of his breath I could see that it was due to something else.'[23]

Returning to Algiers on 13 December, Patton found Eisenhower and Clark trying to decide what to do next. 'Neither had been to the front,' he wrote, 'so showed great lack of decision. They are on [the] way out, I think. [They] have no knowledge of men or war. Too damned slick, especially Clark.'[24]

Within a few days Eisenhower, writing of 'tremendous' difficulties and risks, nevertheless insisted that, given 'a spell of good weather, we can do the job,' and crack open the Tunisian bridgehead despite the fact that the only glimmer of positive news came from the southern part of the front. At Fériana, north-west of Gafsa, Lieutenant-Colonel Bowen, commanding 3rd Battalion, 26th US Infantry Regiment, sent out raids under cover of darkness and scored a solid success at Maknassy on the night of 17/18 December, when his men swooped on the town and shot up a company of Italians. But Edson Raff's paratroopers were stealing the limelight: 'Serving under Raff who actually directly commanded only 80 paratroopers is a bit awkward as my command is over 900,' Bowen complained, '... it irritates every one of my men to be adding to the fame of this upstart unit which hasn't been in action against the enemy yet! It's an awkward set-up.'[25] Patton, however, was not impressed by Eisenhower's optimism; he remained convinced that the Allies possessed too little firepower to sustain offensive operations.[26]

Two days before the new attack Major-General Ward (1st Armored) visited Anderson to discuss tactics. Neither could agree on even the most fundamental issues and Ward was greatly angered by Anderson's failure to acknowledge his troops' role during the recent fighting in preventing the annihilation of 78th Division. Nor was he impressed with Anderson's personality: 'The impression was that it was a privilege to serve with him under his command. I hope that I will not have to do it.'[27]

On the night of 22/23 December, men of the 2nd Coldstream Guards lined up in pouring rain to march on Djebel el Ahmera ('the red mountain'), aptly named Longstop Hill by the Allies, nearly seven miles north-east of Medjez el Bab. Their task was to capture this important peak, which limited their view down the

Medjerda Valley, as a preliminary move before the main drive on Tunis. The Guards were to hand over to 1st Battalion, 18th RCT (Major-General Terry de la Mesa Allen's 1st US Infantry Division) who would then attempt to re-capture Bou Aoukaz, given up when Allied forces were pulled back through the Tébourba Gap.

As shells from supporting field and medium guns sought out the positions of the 754th German Infantry Regiment, the Coldstreamers battled over a series of false crests and stormed through a hail of machine-gun bullets and grenades to what they took to be the final outcrop of rock, outfighting the inexperienced German defenders, who had exhausted their ammunition and sought to defend their positions with the bayonet. Some weary hours later, the Guards were relieved by the 18th RCT which arrived late but was assured that only mopping up of a few German outposts was left.

When dawn broke, the Americans, who had not been entrusted with the original attack because of doubts about their battle worthiness, realized they occupied only part of the hill and were separated from the Germans on an adjacent peak, called Djebel el Rhar. At about noon von Arnim and Ziegler toured the front, handing out decorations and personally encouraging the troops. Oberst Rudolph Lang, who had been put in charge of the defences on 17 December, had no doubts that his men, cold, wet, and tired as they were, could be counted upon for another effort.[28]

A savage counter-attack from Djebel el Rhar by Lang's 1st Battalion, 69th Panzer Grenadier Regiment, drove the 18th RCT off its perch on Point 290. Lying up and saturated by the non-stop rain beyond Medjez and east of the Medjerda River, the Coldstreamers were ordered to re-take Longstop. Amid grumbles about incompetent Americans, they marched 12 miles back the way they had so recently come. Arriving in darkness, still buffeted by a tearing wind and the unceasing downpour, on Christmas Eve they attacked again. Having reached their former positions they tried to storm Djebel el Rahr but were driven back by overwhelming German firepower. A company of Algerian Tirailleurs, sent up to help and placed on Longstop's northern spur, was decimated by German armour.

A further attack by a Panzer group led by Oberst Hofmann eventually displaced the attackers from what the Germans called the *Weihnachtsberg* (Christmas Hill), despite determined resistance from American troops. The Coldstreamers, almost isolated by now, came back down under cover provided by two companies from 3rd Battalion, Grenadier Guards. Retiring to Medjez, they were found to have lost 178 officers and men. The 18th RCT suffered an even greater mauling; nine officers and 347 men had been killed or taken prisoner.[29]

Isolated by these setbacks were 5th Northamptons, who had set off into mist-shrouded hills to seize back the Tébourba Gap. When the attacks on Longstop were driven off Allfrey ordered a halt to further attacks for 48 hours. Increasingly desperate attempts were made by patrol and from the air to contact the Northamptons but a fall by one of their pack-mules had destroyed the crucial radio set and they had no means of knowing why the Americans were not advancing from Longstop as expected. On Christmas Eve, as sounds of gunfire grew no nearer, Lieutenant-Colonel Cook sensibly withdrew his men, who survived a wild skirmish with the enemy on the way back before staggering into a company of Surreys sent out to find them two days later.

In the meantime, while visiting Allfrey's HQ on Christmas Eve, Eisenhower saw four soldiers struggling, without success, to extricate a motor-cycle which had become bogged down off the road in sticky, cloying mud. As much as anything this incident convinced him that an attack put in under such atrocious conditions had no chance of success.[30] The push for Tunis was postponed until further notice.

Anderson confessed to being 'very disappointed' by this turn of events[31] though a young soldier, lying wounded in a German military hospital in Tunis, was cheerfully optimistic when he told von Arnim that it was futile to send him to an Italian prisoner of war camp because the British would be in the city by Christmas. 'I do not think your people will arrive that quickly,' retorted von Arnim.[32] At least one thing the bloody fighting around Longstop Hill ensured was that his confident prediction came true.

<hr>

Notes to Chapter 6

[1] Ward to Major-General Lunsford E. Oliver, 14 December 1942. Ward Papers, 1st Armored Division 1942–43. USAMHI.

[2] My account of the German actions at El Bathan is taken from Kurowski, *Endkampf in Afrika*, pp. 98–102.

[3] Quoted by Howe, *Northwest Africa: Seizing the Initiative in the West*, p. 316.

[4] Lieutenant Philip Walker to Robinett, *c*. June, 1950; Robinett Papers, Box 4. Library of Congress.

[5] Daniell, *History of the East Surrey Regiment*, Vol. IV, pp. 96–7, has the full details of Le Patourel's act of valour together with a good photograph of him.

[6] The Bisley was also known as the Blenheim Mk V.

[7] Richards and Saunders, *The Fight Avails*, p. 257. Wing-Commander Malcolm's name was commemorated in the RAF's Malcolm Clubs, the first of which opened in Algiers a few months later.

[8] Anderson to Eisenhower, 5 December 1942; Eisenhower Papers, Box 5.

[9] V Corps came into being on 6 December 1942.

[10] Generalfeldmarschall Albert Kesselring, 'Final Commentaries on the Campaign in North Africa, 1941–1943', 3 vols. (1950–51), Foreign Military Studies, MS C-075, C-075a, C-075b. USAMHI.

[11] Generaloberst Jürgen von Arnim, 'Erinnerungen an Tunesien', p. 15. Foreign Military Studies, MS C-098. USAMHI. I am indebted to Samuel W. Mitcham for sending me a copy of this MS.

[12] Dr Rudolph von Rahn, 'Aufzeichnung über die politischen Vorgänge in Tunesien vom 21. November 1942 bis zum 10. Februar 1943'; RH19-VIII/358.

[13] Nehring, 'First Phase of the Battle in Tunisia'.

[14] Quoted by Ambrose, *Supreme Commander*, p. 143.

[15] Only six light tanks, five half-tracks and one self-propelled 75mm gun were brought out by the great efforts of their crews. See Howe, *Battle History of the 1st Armored*, pp. 92–3.

[16] Major-General Lunsford E. Oliver, 'In the Mud and Blood of Tunisia', *Colliers Magazine*, 17 April 1943. Copy in Philipsborn Papers.

[17] Major-General Orlando Ward Diary, entry for 17 December 1942. Ward Papers. USAMHI.

[18] 'Blade Force' War Diary, entry for 12 December 1942.

[19] General John K. Waters interviewed by Lieutenant-Colonel William C. Parnell III, April 1980. MHRC.

[20] C-in-C's Dispatch, North African Campaign, 1942–43, p. 23. Bedell Smith Papers, Box 16.

[21] HQ CC B, Intelligence Summary, 15 December 1942. Robinett Papers, Box 12. Marshall Library.

[22] A ribald allusion to Lady Jane Seymour, wife of Henry VIII.

[23] Patton Diary, entry for 7 December 1942. Patton records that it was 3rd Battalion, 1st Guards Brigade, that had virtually been wiped out. This cannot have been the case since the Grenadiers were not engaged in the battle zone, across the Medjez bridge, until 10 December. The Hampshires were, however, part of 1st Guards Brigade.

[24] Patton Diary, entry for 13 December 1942.

[25] Lieutenant-Colonel J.W. Bowen to Colonel Stark, 22 December 1942; Box 5952; World War II Operations Reports, USNA 301-INF(26)-0.3.

[26] Patton Diary, entry for 17 December 1942.

[27] Ward Diary, entry for 22 December 1942.

[28] Oberst Rudolph Lang, 'Battles of Kampfgruppe Lang in Tunisia (10th Panzer Division)', Part I: December 1942 to March 1, 1943. Foreign Military Studies, MS D-173. USAMHI.

[29] Howe, *Northwest Africa*. Playfair, *Destruction of Axis Forces*, gives a slightly different figure of 356 US losses; see p. 188.

[30] Eisenhower, *Crusade in Europe*, p. 137.

[31] Anderson to Alanbrooke, 25 December 1942; First Army CP War Diary.

[32] Von Arnim, 'Erinnerungen an Tunesien', p. 34.

Part Two

Disaster at Kasserine

'The outstanding fact to me is that the proud and cocky Americans today stand humiliated by one of the greatest defeats in our history.'

Captain Harry C. Butcher, diary entry for 23 February 1943.

Butcher, *Diary.*

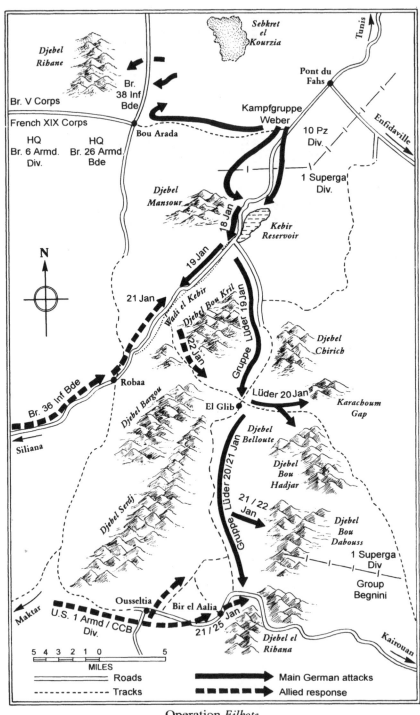

Djebel Ribane

Sebkret el Kourzia

Tunis

Br. V Corps

Br. 38 Inf Bde

Pont du Fahs

Kampfgruppe Weber

Enfidaville

French XIX Corps

10 Pz Div.

HQ Br. 6 Armd. Div.

HQ Br. 26 Armd. Bde

Bou Arada

1 Superga Div.

Djebel Mansour

18 Jan

Kebir Reservoir

N

19 Jan

21 Jan

Wadi el Kebir

Djebel Bou Kril

22 Jan

Gruppe Lüder 19 Jan

Djebel Chirich

Br. 36 Inf Bde

Robaa

Lüder 20 Jan

Karachoum Gap

Siliana

Djebel Bargou

El Glib

Djebel Belloute

Djebel Bou Hadjar

Gruppe Lüder 20/21 Jan

Djebel Serdj

21 / 22 Jan

Djebel Bou Dabouss

1 Superga Div

Group Begnini

Maktar

Ousseltia

Bir el Aalia

21 Jan

U.S. 1 Armd / CCB Div.

21/25 Jan

Djebel el Ribana

Kairouan

5 4 3 2 1 0   5
MILES

——— Roads

- - - - Tracks

⟶ Main German attacks

⟶ Allied response

Operation *Eilbote*
January 1943

Chapter 7

Battering Our Brains Out

'The critical fuel situation does not permit even minor operations at the moment.'

Extract from the War Diary of Generalleutnant Walter Warlimont, Deputy Chief of the Operations Section of the Oberkommando der Wehrmacht, *9 January 1943.*

———•◆•———

The assassination in Algiers of Admiral Darlan on Christmas Eve, 1942, faced Mark Clark with two immediate problems: who was to take Darlan's place as head of the French in North Africa and how to forestall any related mischief-making by the Axis authorities, leaving French politics as undisturbed as possible. As an immediate precaution, all Allied troops in Algiers were placed on alert.[1]

An urgent message to Eisenhower[2] brought him hurrying back to the city, which he reached after a non-stop drive late on Christmas Day. Immediately he, 'gave some discreet pushing', and with President Roosevelt's agreement, Giraud was persuaded to accept the appointment as French High Commissioner in North Africa.[3]

Darlan's death was, wrote Clark, 'like the lancing of a troublesome boil'[4] because the Americans had compelling reasons for getting rid of him and the British even better ones: 'It may raise big complications,' noted Anderson, 'but personally I think it is for the best.'[5] In return, Darlan had had few illusions about the Allies, believing the British would soon remove him and set up de Gaulle.[6]

Most of the leading Allied figures turned out in full uniform to pay their last respects to Darlan. Admiral Cunningham was standing next to Eisenhower, as Giraud knelt by the bier and 'shed a tear.' Then it was the C-in-C's turn. 'Everyone was making [the] sign of the cross,' said Cunningham, 'dipping a branch of cedar in holy water, and sprinkling a little holy water on the coffin. I punched Ike and said, "Go ahead." He said "I can't do it." Finally he doused the branch in the water, refused to make the sign of the cross, and then splashed enough water to drown the man in the coffin.'[7]

Darlan's permanent removal from the North African scene and the speedy despatch of his killer – a local 20-year-old named Fernand Bonnier – were the only morsels of good news for the Allies that bleak December.[8] A series of military setbacks, culminating in the brutal fighting on Longstop Hill, again brought out much of the latent ill feeling between the Allies. At AFHQ, American and British staffs were divided in their use of a supposedly common language: 'I had a hell of a time understanding McCreery [Alexander's Chief of Staff] for the first time,' said Lieutenant-General Bradley, after he arrived in North Africa in February 1943, complaining that his countrymen were treated as 'country cousins.'[9]

For their part, the British lost no time in venting their grievances and assuming an air of habitual superiority. 'The U.S. Army is a mutual admiration society,' recorded Brigadier Jacob, 'and any failings in this theatre can be comfortably blamed on the British.'[10] In London, Brooke noted the 'pretty shattering' report by Jacob on Eisenhower's cluttered headquarters and 'amateur' staff work. 'I do not like the Tunisian situation at all,' he added.[11]

Neither did Churchill. The delay called by Eisenhower in the north, 'makes me anxious about the condition of the First British Army,' he told the C-in-C.[12] Brigadier-General Paul M. Robinett (who took over 1st Armored's CC B from Lunsford Oliver in January 1943) wanted 'all our means and resources' to be utilised in a major push on Tunis and an end to widespread attacks which dissipated scarce resources, otherwise 'only a miracle' could bring a speedy and conclusive result.[13] Doolittle, convinced that his airmen held the key to success, suggested: 'Let's stop our wishful thinking, abandon our present 100% bitched up organization, stop trying to win the Tunisian War in a day and through forward planning, sound organization and an appreciation of what air power, when properly utilized, can do, put the God Damn thing on ice.'[14]

In the long term, the Allies could expect to win the battle of supplies but there were many immediate difficulties and disasters to be overcome. 'Rumours persist that *Strathallan* has been sunk, 400 sisters being rescued but their personal kit and some mail has gone down,' recorded Lieutenant-Colonel Shirley Smith, a British medical officer, on 24 December.[15]

The 17th Field Regiment, Royal Artillery, was on the way to Bône shortly before Christmas aboard the *Cameronia* when the ship was hit by an aerial torpedo, as Lieutenant Royle, one of the artillery officers, recorded: 'all of a sudden there was a dull explosion and the whole ship shuddered.'[16] Twenty were killed and 30 injured. Shadowed by a British destroyer, the *Cameronia* disembarked her troops at Bougie in pouring rain. 'The main road was running with muddy water and once you turned off it you slithered and squelched in inches of mud,' explained Royle. After several days in a muddy field under canvas – 'I just couldn't believe that the men were expected to sleep in such conditions but there was nowhere else,' – he reached Bône on Christmas night. 'We... sat on the deck in the warm evening listening to Xmas music over the radio and thinking of home,' noted Signalman Parker.[17] Bône was deserted after dark and, 'even the brothel did its business in daylight', because every night enemy raiders returned despite a massive defensive barrage.

Early in January 1943, as 17th Field Regiment joined 6th Armoured Division in bitter cold and heavy rain, Eisenhower's new initiative was to put in a strong mobile guard on the vast front extending from Pont du Fahs to Gafsa. Brooke was most unimpressed, complaining about, 'a ridiculous plan put up by Eisenhower for prosecution of the war in Tunisia,' adding, 'This is a dog's life!'[18]

At Eisenhower's advanced AFHQ, newly opened at Constantine under Brigadier-General Lucian K. Truscott, plans were laid for the capture of Sfax or Gabès by co-ordinating the activities of First Army and the French and US II Corps. Operation Satin was designed to cut Rommel's line of communication, choke off his supplies, and so force him either to surrender to Eighth Army or hurry back into Tunisia. Consequently, von Arnim's forces would probably be forced to shift south in his support, so freeing Anderson and Juin in the north to put pressure on Tunis and Bizerte.[19]

Much of the early drive for this operation came from Mark Clark, who sought some way of extricating American units from Anderson's control. An independent sphere of operations for US troops in central and southern Tunisia, under his own command, offered a means of getting what he wanted and also opened up the attractive prospect of encouraging Giraud's persistent refusal to allow Frenchmen to serve under First Army.

Clark got his own way but lasted only two days as commander of the southern Tunisian front. Eisenhower knew of Clark's unscrupulous manoeuvring and tipped off Marshall who cabled his confirmation, on the last day of 1942, of Clark's appointment as commander of the US Fifth Army. This had been created at the beginning of December to prepare for emergency action in rear areas and for a future invasion of the continent. Clark was to return to Oran and the field command in southern Tunisia was to be taken by a subordinate – eventually Fredendall. 'Through this action Ike rose greatly in my estimation,' noted Brooke.[20]

In planning 'to deliver a healthy kick' to Rommel's rear, Clark had wanted the US II Corps concentrated in the Tébessa–Kasserine area. On New Year's Day 1943 Fredendall received orders to move the corps from the north.[21] At its heart were strengthened elements of 1st Armored, including CC B, transferred from First Army. The intention was to strike from Sbeïtla through the Eastern Dorsale towards Sfax, while General Koeltz's French XIX Corps attacked further north, through the Fondouk Pass, which would give essential cover to any American manoeuvre on the coastal plain. The orders were imprecise and often vague.

'I am sending a letter to General Nehring [sic] this afternoon,' 'Pinky' Ward (1st Armored) exasperatedly informed Brigadier-General Oliver, 'with an air-mail return stamp, requesting from him some information as to what he thinks so few, commanded by so many, are going to do. He probably has a much better idea than some subordinates.'[22]

Beyond the lack of information given to those in the field there lay the mammoth logistical and practical problem of getting supplies forward beyond the railheads of Sbeïtla and Fériana. From there, every item would have to be trucked over 150 miles eastwards. Early in January, the difficulties had hardly been addressed – let alone solved. Anderson, unhappy at CC B passing out of his command, nevertheless informed Eisenhower that First Army would do, 'every single thing we can to help on the southern attack.' However, he was finding it necessary to 'wet-nurse' the newly-raised Corps Franc units which Giraud was 'hounding' into action in the north.[23]

There lay Evelegh's 78th Infantry Division, opposed by the *Von Broich* Division; southwards, concentrated on Medjez el Bab, was Weber's 334th Division with von Arnim's main spearhead, Fischer's 10th Panzer Division, in reserve; at Bou Arada was Keightley's 6th Armoured Division, opposed by the *Hermann Göring* Division. In effect, the British had five infantry brigades loosely strung in a 70-mile arc, opposed by two concentrated masses of German troops. Koeltz's XIX Corps lightly held the front line against the Eastern Dorsale as far as Fondouk and II Corps was in position around Tébessa. Further south still, General Joseph Welvert's *Constantine* Division had troops forward at the Faïd Pass and Gafsa.

Fifteen miles south of Tébessa, 'as high and cold as a snake,'[24] recorded Captain James Webb of the II Corps' staff, Fredendall set up his command post in a narrow, precipitous ravine, launching a major engineering operation which, said Webb, 'resembled the digging of the New York Subway.' As American units arrived they were stationed along the Western Dorsale, or on the plain below the mountain ranges. Most scattered elements of the 1st Infantry Division had been collected together and sent to join the French along a 30-mile wide sector of their front that included the flat, open Ousseltia Valley. 'Daylight movement of combat vehicles in the Valley brought almost immediate strafing. Two German planes particularly, nick-named "Ike" and "Mike" by the soldiers were very annoying in their strafing and diving tactics. Even a lone jeep was a fair target for [them]... .'[25]

Further north in the British sector, Brigadier Russell's 38th Irish Brigade – the 'Wild Geese' – had been engaged since the beginning of the year in sharp skirmishes around Bou Arada, 25 miles south of Medjez el Bab. So slender were their resources that companies had to fight in the sleet and cold as individual battle groups. An officer and two men were shot dead after wandering into their own lookouts and every man in a US signal detachment was killed after blundering into a Faughs' (Royal Irish Fusiliers) outpost. 'Think nothing of it, brother,' said the US regimental CO when told of the tragedy, 'it happens every night.'[26]

North-east of Bou Arada was a small mound, nicknamed 'Two Tree Hill' by the troops, from which a daily picket and scout car overlooked the flat landscape and, in the distance, the coast itself. The Germans eventually took the hill with the idea of pinching out the town. When the 2nd London Irish Rifles were sent in they failed to retake it and the whole brigade could do no more than stabilise the front as far as 'Grandstand Hill,' east of Bou Arada, and the Goubellat road.

On 14 January, 6th Royal Inniskilling Fusiliers were impulsively committed after a night of heavy rain and attacked while under fire from their front and both flanks in an attempt to fling the enemy back from the sector. Higher command staff work was abysmal: 'they jolly well knew the facts all right but couldn't get the message across to the old man [Anderson],' commented one of the Faughs' officers. In the evening the 'Skins' returned, minus 100 men and some of their best officers.[27]

—◦•◦—

The same day, 17th Field Regiment RA arrived in support of the Irish Fusiliers on Grandstand Hill. They were on a high state of alert with the gun crews hardly leaving their gun pits nor staff their command post. 'They say that warfare is 90% boredom and 10% terror,' noted Lieutenant Royle, one of the artillery officers, 'and so it was proving to be.'[28]

Major-General Keightley and V Corps' artillery commander, Brigadier Ambrose Platt, detested Anderson's new plan to commit the French in an assault on Fondouk, while the Irish Brigade jumped off against 10th Panzer Division on 17 January. By procrastinating, they probably saved First Army from disaster since the Allies were sent reeling by a sudden German attack the following day. It was now realised how fortunate the Inniskillings had been in failing to take Two Tree Hill. Success would have left them so far forward they would have been beyond support and nothing could have saved them.

Operation *Eilbote I* ('Express Messenger') was ordered by Kesselring to prevent a thrust by the Allies through Kairouan to the coast and intended to roll up the Allied forces in the Eastern Dorsale from north to south. Using elements of 334th Infantry and 10th Panzer Divisions, together with Panzerabteilung 501, the Germans struck at the juncture of British V Corps and French XIX Corps, where the Allied front was at its weakest.

The opening, diversionary, attack was put in on 18 January by Fischer's 10th Panzers at Bou Arada. On Grandstand Hill the Stürmregiment *Hermann Göring*, attached to 10th Panzers, ran headlong into the Inniskillings.[29] Following confused and bloody fighting, stretcher bearers from both sides met on the battlefield to find out where their men were lying. One Irish officer, shot through the temple and blinded, was discovered after wandering helplessly from the scene.

On the northern outskirts of Bou Arada, 7th Panzer Regiment collided with 17th Field Regiment. Lieutenant Brown, one of the artillery officers, seemed almost cavalier about it all soon afterwards: 'I have been up in the OP [Observation Post] and shot up the foe from there. Its the grandest sport in the world... when the thing you are aiming is a salvo of shells, and at the old Hun too, its damn good fun. How they scuttle too.' He had to admit, however, that it had been 'a hell of a battle.'[30]

Arriving just as the two sides clashed was the bulk of 2nd Lothians and Border Horse who were committed immediately to meet the German thrust. Along the road from El Aroussa their tanks approached ever nearer a low grey cloud hanging heavily ahead. 'That,' remarked a tank commander, 'is what is officially known as the smoke of battle,'[31] describing the murk created by a mixture of bursting shells, ignited haystacks, burning tanks and occasional smoke bombs. That evening, British sappers went out to blow up enemy tanks trapped in the all-enveloping mud. Some still had their engines ticking over.

While the British stood fast, the French, lacking adequate anti-tank weapons, fell back under the impact of battle groups from Weber's 334th Division, which rolled along the Eastern Dorsale and broke through with armoured and motorized columns, south of Pont du Fahs, into the Robaa and Ousseltia Valleys. Brigadier Kent-Lemon's 36th Brigade had to be rushed up to Robaa and CC B, now commanded by Robinett after Oliver was promoted, together with parts of Allen's 1st and Major-General Charles W. Ryder's 34th Infantry Divisions were sent in to bolster up the struggling French.

In five days of fighting, the Germans claimed over 4,000 prisoners and to have destroyed or captured 24 tanks, 52 guns and 228 vehicles.[32] They broke off what was only ever meant to be a limited attack and settled on a much improved defensive line, stretching from about Djebel Mansour in the north, via Djebel bou Kril and Djebel bou Dabouss to Djebel Rihane in the south.

Anderson ordered Fredendall to cover Maktar with Robinett's CC B, in case the enemy pushed through the Fondouk Pass, and sent Brigadier-General Raymond E. McQuillin's CC A to Sbeïtla to support Welvert's troops. But Fredendall also had his eye on Maknassy, at the far southern end of the Eastern Dorsale, which was in Italian hands. To capture this prize, he ordered Ward to improvise two new combat groups, CC C, under Colonel Robert Stack, and CC D, commanded by Colonel Robert Maraist.

In order to blood CC C with an easy small-scale success, Fredendall sent Stack on a hit-and-run raid on Sened Station, despite strong protests from Ward and Welvert that this would reveal the direction of the coming main effort on Maknassy. Fredendall ignored them. Stack's force set out from Gafsa on 24 January, protected by Allied air cover, and in an action which lasted barely more than three hours, took nearly 100 prisoners and left about as many dead and wounded behind. Just as Ward anticipated, however, the Germans sent a stronger force to hold Sened and were alerted to the possibility of an Allied move towards Maknassy rather than through El Guettar.

Guessing that an attack on Maknassy would take the heat off the French at the Faïd Pass, Stack's forces were then ordered to approach from the northwest via the village of Sidi bou Zid, while Maraist was to retake Sened and move rapidly east to capture the main objective.

A second German operation, *Eilbote II*, which was to have pushed onwards to Pichon, petered out because there were insufficient assault troops to carry this attack. However, on 30 January, two battle groups from a rested and re-equipped 21st Panzer Division, which Rommel had transferred from Beurat, suddenly moved on the Faïd Pass, just 24 hours before Stack's and Maraist's attack on Maknassy was to take place. Despite costly losses against a determined defence action: 'the whole day passes in fierce fighting in a hail of bombs and in a storm of bullets from American strafing 'planes,' recorded a German Gefreiter – the French garrison was surrounded and the village of Faïd taken.[33] Their increasingly urgent requests for reinforcements reached McQuillin's HQ at Sbeïtla and were relayed to Fredendall, who refused to take the sensible option of cancelling the attack on Maknassy and concentrating 1st Armored to deal with the Germans at

Faïd. Consequently, while CC C moved towards Sidi bou Zid from Gafsa, with the intention of interrupting any enemy force shifting northward from Maknassy or of helping stop the enemy's principal assault on Faïd, CC D went on to attack Sened.

Splitting 1st Armored caused confusion and near disaster. Stack's men hovered between two objectives and hardly engaged the enemy at all. Maraist got to Sened alright but ran into a powerful German and Italian defence. Troops moving up to attack positions were caught by Ju-88s: 'It was the most terrible thing I had ever seen,' commented one officer, 'not the bodies and parts of bodies near smoking vehicles, some sitting, some scattered, some blue from the powder burns – it was the expressions on the faces of those that wondered listlessly around the wreckage not knowing where to go or what to do, saying "This can't happen to us." '[34]

Artillery concentrations on the village eventually cleared the way for a final infantry-tank attack and, at nightfall on 1 February, Sened fell to CC D after fierce fighting, though a 34th Division battalion coming into support was led past the American outposts by mistake and lost most of its men as they marched straight into enemy hands.[35]

Fredendall ordered Maraist to put his infantry on the heights east of Sened Station early next morning: 'Use your tanks and shove,' he said, 'Too much time has been wasted already.'[36] It was mid-afternoon before the infantry were in position and they had hardly settled when an enemy armoured attack had to be repelled with artillery support. By now, some of the troops were showing distinct signs of nervousness at German dive-bombing and, when some field artillery was moved, it seems to have been interpreted as the signal for retreat. In the deepening gloom the road westwards was soon jammed with vehicles fleeing to the rear. Worse followed when, on the following day, 15 B-25s accidentally bombed Sened: 'our slit trenches became suddenly very populated,'[37] commented one man on the receiving end.

In the meantime, McQuillin had failed miserably to retake the village of Faïd. Lieutenant-Colonel Hamilton H. Howze (Ward's G.3) considered the divisional commander should have got rid of McQuillin because he was a 'dummy,' and, though pleasant, 'just as wooden as could be', as did Lieutenant-Colonel Simons, another 1st Armored Division officer, who thought the broad-shouldered ex-cavalryman brave but, 'in many ways a genuine blockhead.'[38] Tardy in the extreme, McQuillin took a whole day to send help to the French, and when his troops arrived on 31 January, they were badly mauled by a well-concealed enemy defensive screen. They fared no better next day when his infantry melted away in the face of determined enemy resistance. The French were left to fight their own way out and over 1,000 eventually ended up in captivity.

The result of these various actions along the Eastern Dorsale was an undoubted victory for von Arnim. Maknassy, Faïd village and the Fäid Pass itself remained in German hands: 'My nightmare is over,'[39] Arnim told one of his staff officers. 1st Armored retired to lick its wounds, thinly scattered, with only Combat Commands A and C left under Ward's direct control from his command post just west of Sbeïtla. CC A held Sidi bou Zid and the surrounding hills, to prevent the enemy debouching from the Faïd Pass, as CC C moved to Hadjeb el

Aioun, mid-way between Fondouk and Faïd. CC B was taken into First Army reserve and positioned in the Forest of Kesra near Maktar, ready to meet any enemy thrust through Fondouk, while CC D was in II Corps' reserve at Bou Chebka.

Committed once again in the north as January drew to an end, the London Irish were ordered to take Hill 286 on a low profiled ridge dominating the Allies' supply road stretching from Bou Arada south of Grandstand Hill. After the attack had gone in the Germans hit back with a spectacular night counter-attack, 7th Panzer Regiment's commanders riding into battle on top of their tanks, armed with flare pistols and guided by star shells lighting up the night sky.

Charging along the ridge from end to end, followed by *Hermann Göring* Jägers picking off any survivors, they shattered the London Irish who poured down from the heights. Anti-tank mines had been laid to stop any such performance; the Irish had forgotten to arm them. Retiring from Hill 286 on the 28th the Germans completed a classic action that effectively ruined an Irish infantry battalion.[40]

Elsewhere, the folly of attempting to take and hold inessential high ground was recognised in time. The French high command abandoned the idea of sending the 1st US Infantry to capture Djebel bou Dabouss, the commanding hill mass northeast of Ousseltia, when it became clear that reverses elsewhere in southern Tunisia would compel the Allied forces to withdraw from positions east of the Ousseltia Valley. 'Consequently it seemed futile to waste lives and material in capturing this position. In [American] football parlance taking this hill mass would have been "battering our brains out to gain a yard and a half in the middle of the field."'[41]

When Eisenhower asked about the possibility of Eighth Army action in support of Operation Satin, Alexander's reply had been non-committal. If the enemy tried to disengage at Beurat, Eighth Army would attempt to follow up as soon as possible, whereas if Rommel halted he would be attacked without delay. 'It is hoped that subsequent attacks will take Tripoli in one bound,' wrote Alexander, 'In either case it is impossible for us from this end to prevent the enemy detaching some parts of his force to meet your attacks although every effort will be made to keep up maximum pressure on the enemy.'[42]

Eisenhower's strategy relied, not unreasonably, on a respectable rate of progress by Eighth Army in its pursuit of Rommel but Montgomery was still 500 miles away in the Sirte Desert. The Desert Rats could render no assistance should US II Corps troops, having broken through to the coast, be turned upon by the enemy from two sides. This was certainly not a risk which Eisenhower's superiors at home were prepared to take. Soon he was to discover the full implications of this as he slipped towards the nadir of his command in Tunisia.

Notes to Chapter 7

1 Fredendall message to divisional and separate unit commanders, 25 December 1942; 1st US Infantry Division, Box 5776; World War II Operations Reports, USNA 301-3.2.

2 Copy in Bedell Smith Papers, Box 13. A second one was short and to the point. It read: 'Have just returned from hospital. Darlan is dead.'

3 Leahy, *I Was There*, p. 171.

4 Clark, *Calculated Risk*, p. 130.

5 Anderson to Brooke, 25 December 1942; First Army CP – War Diary; also Clark, *Calculated Risk*, p. 130.

6 See Tomkins, *The Murder of Darlan: A Study in Conspiracy*, p. 226.

7 Admiral of the Fleet Sir Andrew Cunningham interviewed by Dr Forrest Pogue (12 February 1947). OCMH Collection.

8 Early accounts conclude that Bonnier was most probably acting for a group of monarchist conspirators who hoped to replace Darlan with the pretender to the French throne, the Comte de Paris. This was the conclusion drawn at the time by an OSS agent, Kenneth Pendar, *Adventure in Diplomacy*, pp. 126–9. See also Pierre-Gosset, *Algiers 1941–1943*; Langer, *Our Vichy Gamble*; and Coon, *A North Africa Story*. A more recent account, Verrier, *Assassination in Algiers*, views the assassination in terms of a loosely-knit group of French conspirators, driven by their own, individual motives, supported by SOE and quite possibly the OSS.

9 Bradley's commentary on World War II in Hansen Papers. Bradley arrived as a major-general but was quickly promoted to lieutenant-general.

10 Jacob Diary, entry for 30 December 1942; quoted by Ambrose, *Supreme Commander*, p. 681, and by Bryant, *Turn of the Tide*, p. 554. Jacob was the Assistant Military Secretary of the British War Cabinet.

11 Alanbrooke Diary, entry for 28 December 1942, Alanbrooke Papers, 5/1/6a.

12 Churchill to Eisenhower, 28 December 1942. Eisenhower Papers, Box 23.

13 Robinett to Ward, 17 December 1942. Robinett Papers, Box 12. Marshall Library.

14 Doolittle to Spaatz, 25 December 1942; '1943 Ops File', Doolittle Papers, Box 19. Library of Congress.

15 Lieutenant-Colonel K. Shirley Smith, RAMC, Diary entry for 24 November 1942. IWM 87/31/1. The liner *Strathallan*, carrying troops and medical personnel, was sunk by a U-boat off Oran on 21 December. A young officer aboard kept a contemporary and vivid account of the event: Potter, *Tébessa?: Wherever's That?*, pp. 11–15.

16 Lieutenant P. Royle, 17th Field Regiment, RA; Memoir. IWM P370.

17 Signalman A. Parker, 17th Field Regiment RA; Memoir. 87/44/1.

18 Alanbrooke Diary, entry for 31 December 1942, Alanbrooke Papers, 5/1/6a.

19 The Satin Task Force consisted of HQ II Corps; 1st Armored Division together with 701st TD Battalion; 443rd Coast Artillery (AA) Battalion and 2nd Battalion 16th Medium Regiment attached; 26th RCT together with 5th Field Artillery Battalion and 601st TD Battalion attached; XII Air Support Command. The French *Constantine* Division was in support. See HQ II Corps, Report on Operations; II Corps, Box 3112; World War II Operations Reports, USNA 202-0.3.

20 Alanbrooke Diary, entry for 4 January 1943, Alanbrooke Papers, 5/1/6a; 'Notes on My Life', Alanbrooke Papers, 5/2/19.

21 Captain James R. Webb, 'Diary covering the activities of General Fredendall and Supporting Players, December 1942 – March 1943'; Webb Papers. Eisenhower Library.

[22] Ward to Oliver, 15 January 1943; 1st Armored Division, US Army Unit Records, 1941-50, Box 18. Eisenhower Library. The letter should, of course, have been directed to von Arnim who, by then, was in command.

[23] Anderson to Eisenhower, 1 January 1943. Eisenhower Papers, Box 5.

[24] Webb Papers, Box 1.

[25] HQ 1st Infantry Division, Summary of Operations, 8 March 1943; 1st Infantry Division, Box 5662; World War II Operations Reports, USNA 301-0.3.

[26] Recounted by Horsfall, who had the unenviable job of passing on the news to the US commander; see his *The Wild Geese Are Flighting*, p. 37.

[27] Fox, *The Royal Inniskilling Fusiliers in the Second World War*, p. 62.

[28] Royle, Memoir.

[29] The Royal Irish Fusiliers were now on 'Stuka Ridge', facing north and covering the left flank of the Inniskillings on Grandstand Hill.

[30] Lieutenant D.E. Brown (17th Field Regiment, RA) to his wife, 27 January 1943. IWM 83/16/1.

[31] Antonio, *Driver Advance!*, p. 15.

[32] General der Panzertruppe Walther Nehring, 'The Development of the Situation in North Africa', Foreign Military Studies, MS D-120. USAMHI; Playfair, *Destruction of Axis Forces*, p. 280.

[33] Extracts from Diary of a Gefreiter, 104th Panzer Grenadier Regiment, 21st Panzer Division; 8th Army Intelligence Summary No. 490 with G.2 Journal File, April 1943; II Corps, Box 3155; World War II Operations Reports, USNA 202-2.3.

[34] TS report detailing activities of 1st Armored Division, n.d. (1943); Ward Papers, 1st Armored Division 1942–43.

[35] Jackson, *The North African Campaign 1940–43*, p. 336.

[36] Howe, *Battle History of 1st Armored Division*, p. 131.

[37] Report detailing activities of 1st Armored Division, Ward Papers,

[38] Lieutenant-Colonel Hamilton H. Howze interviewed by Russell Gugeler, 12 August 1976 and Lieutenant-Colonel Robert Simons, interviewed by Russell Gugeler; Ward Papers. USAMHI.

[39] Carell, *Foxes of the Desert*, p. 340.

[40] Horsfall, *The Wild Geese are Flighting*, p. 57.

[41] HQ 1st Infantry Division, Summary of Operations, 8 March 1943.

[42] Alexander to Eisenhower, 27 December 1942; Eisenhower Papers, Box 3.

Chapter 8

Such is the Life of Generals

'If the story books tell of the African deserts, put a question mark on their inner cover. I have never worn so many clothes as at present. We have also encountered considerable rain and mud.'

Brigadier-General Paul M. Robinett to a personal correspondent, Edward Fitzgerald, 30 January 1943.[1]

<hr/>

Two weeks into 1943, President Roosevelt and Prime Minister Churchill met at Casablanca to discuss in detail Allied objectives. Debate over future grand strategy overshadowed the plans for clearing Tunisia and defeating Rommel but the pressure of fighting two wars – one political, the other military – was taking its toll on Eisenhower. Confined to bed for several days with a severe head cold and 'general grippy condition,'[2] he was summoned to Casablanca by General Marshall.

There he explained to 'Air Commodore Frankland' and 'Admiral Q,' as the Prime Minister and President were universally referred to throughout the conference, the setbacks suffered in Tunisia and the political mess involving censorship and collaboration with such undesirables as the anti-Semite, Marcel Peyrouton.[3] Many newspaper correspondents were furious at the continuation under Giraud of the late Admiral Darlan's policies, especially the absence of political freedom in French North Africa, anti-Jewish measures and the detaining of thousands of political prisoners in stinking, squalid camps where they were categorized into Jews, Communists or refugees from Franco's Spain.[4] Was this, they asked, what the Allies were fighting to uphold?

Eisenhower justified all his actions by military expediency and, while insisting that any setbacks so far had been his fault, pointed out that 1st Armored Division was being held in reserve to counter any attack against his drive on Sfax and that it was better to suffer some losses than allow his troops in the north to rot in the mud. As for the French, many were unreliable because they had families who were in the recently German-occupied south of France. The gravity of their position had been underlined when 132 men deserted from one battalion alone. Problems of leadership arose since Barré and Juin were co-operating but Giraud, who 'might be a good Divisional commander,' was giving them no scope for independent action. He was, 'dictatorial by nature and seemed to suffer from megalomania,' Eisenhower told the Combined Chiefs of Staff, and seemed 'very sensitive and always ready to take offence.'[5]

There was a coolness towards Eisenhower from the top brass, reflected in their decision on 16 January to scrap his plans for Operation Satin.[6] The 'absence of clear-cut words of thanks', convinced Butcher that the President and Prime Minister, 'had their noses to the political winds, and weren't going to be caught holding the bag for a general who had made an unpopular decision and hadn't yet got Tunisia. I told him his neck is in the noose,' added Butcher, 'and he knows it. But such is the life of generals.'[7] More than once at this time, it crossed Eisenhower's mind to ask to be relieved of his command. A pessimistic estimate prepared for him by Truscott, on 24 January, reported enfeebled French morale. 'I have the definite feeling that the French can no longer be counted on for much and that in important sectors they must be heavily supported and, to the extent possible, immediately rearmed.'[8]

In an effort to gain some kind of understanding, Colonel William Biddle was sent from II Corps as liaison officer to Juin's HQ. He was expected to form a judgement at any time on the combat value of French troops: 'job no sinecure,' he wrote, 'Will demand all my ingenuity, and will require my capitalizing on good will which I've built up with [the] French.'[9]

Determined to tackle the parlous state of American preparedness for the battles ahead, Eisenhower was alarmed at the inability of Americans to apply their training to battle conditions and 'innumerable instances' of poor discipline. Insisting that matters must be put right, he wanted men who were hard, 'capable of marching distances of up to twenty-five miles a day without a halt, going without sleep, subsisting on short rations.' Their officers, especially the younger ones who were reluctant to admonish or reprimand subordinates, had to impose discipline and obey orders.[10]

General Marshall noticed the same slackness and disregard for authority when visiting North Africa at the end of January. Coming across a tank destroyer battalion encamped on a hillside he was deeply shocked by a, 'lack of disciplinary leadership and training that was glaring and meant that it was not useable [sic] for battle against the Germans... The men were all right,' he added, but 'the training was seriously wrong.' Infuriated by this 'bad business,' Marshall fired off several angry letters but experienced officers were spread very thinly indeed, often due, in Marshall's opinion, to the gross overstaffing of US headquarters all over the world.[11] The quality of manpower had declined visibly towards the end of 1942 as the air forces had made tremendous inroads on the number of college graduates, resulting in only 15–20 per cent of each intake entering army officer candidate schools.[12]

At Casablanca, Churchill and Roosevelt insisted that de Gaulle, who could not command the allegiance of French Army officers in North Africa, attend the Anfa

Hotel in the hope that he might be brought to work with Giraud, who had little administrative ability. On the final day they agreed to a joint communiqué which, at least, was what Harold Macmillan called, 'the beginning, though only just the beginning, of the loosening out of a complicated situation between the various French peoples.'[13]

As Eighth Army approached Tunisia, a new structure agreed at the conference co-ordinated its actions with those of First Army, and with US II Corps and French XIX Corps. Logic dictated that overall control should be handed to the Americans but the British Chiefs of Staff, unhappy with Eisenhower's performance to date, produced a scheme in which Alexander was to be brought from the Middle East and appointed as Deputy C-in-C to Eisenhower.

Alexander's command was the group of armies on the Tunisian front (eventually 18th Army Group – that is First and Eighth Armies, together with all American and French land forces) while Eisenhower, in Brooke's words, was pushed, 'up into the stratosphere and rarified atmosphere of a Supreme Commander, where he would be free to devote his time to the political and inter-Allied problems, whilst we inserted under him one of our own commanders to deal with the military situation and to restore the necessary drive and co-ordination which had been so seriously lacking.'[14] The Americans were flattered and pleased by this plan for they had expected the British to demand Eisenhower's demotion to serve under Alexander. Now they were being offered the very opposite. Marshall and his colleagues fell for this apparent act of generosity and, as Brooke happily admitted, 'did not at the time fully appreciate the underlying intentions.'[15] They were beguiled by the fact that, once Eighth Army crossed the Tunisian frontier, Eisenhower would exercise supreme command *on paper* over the group of armies fighting there, together with French forces under Juin and US Fifth Army in Morocco, which seemed a big enough job for anyone.[16]

In addition, a new and cohesive air umbrella over the whole of the Mediterranean was set up, on 17 February, in which the Air C-in-C, Tedder, was placed directly under Eisenhower's command, although Admiral Cunningham for one was not sure about his abilities: '[He is] nice enough but never knows what his staff is doing.'[17] Reporting directly to Tedder were Major-General Carl A. ('Tooey') Spaatz commanding a new formation known as Northwest African Air Forces, Air Chief Marshal Sir Sholto Douglas, AOC Middle East and the AOC Malta, Air Vice-Marshal Sir Keith Park.[18]

Yet the C-in-C was not even equal in rank to some of his subordinates; but as Marshall explained to Roosevelt at Casablanca, it was simply not practicable to give Eisenhower a fourth star while his army was still mired in the mud. If anything, the President was even more astringent, replying that, 'he would not promote Eisenhower until there was some damn good reason for doing it, that he was going to make it a rule that promotions should go to people who had done some fighting, that while Eisenhower had done a good job, he hasn't knocked the Germans out of Tunisia.'[19]

At this low point in his fortunes, even Berlin radio forecast that Eisenhower would be transferred back to London and Alexander take over in North Africa. It came at a time when critics both in Washington and London were snarling at his heels and calling for his replacement; he was, noted the faithful Butcher, 'the centre of controversy.'[20] Marshall, however, never wavered in his support and backed him to the hilt, as did the highly respected Cunningham with whom Eisenhower developed a close friendship. Always dressed in freshly laundered full 'whites', Sir Andrew was a marvellous, if somewhat eccentric host. It was his influence with Churchill and Roosevelt which helped secure for Eisenhower the coveted fourth star and rank of full general as early as 15 February. Lord Ampthill, a Royal Navy staff officer, observing Cunningham (known as ABC from his initials) at close quarters, thought that, 'ABC did as much or more than anyone else to give Ike confidence, and also to blend the Br. and U.S. staffs into a reasonably smoothly working Allied Force Head Quarters... His name worked magic with Americans, British and the French... '[21]

The date fixed at Casablanca for Operation Husky (the invasion of Sicily) during the favourable moon period in July, put Eisenhower under pressure because it was absolutely necessary to get Tunisia wrapped up well before then. Just before the assembled dignitaries left Casablanca came welcome news. Early on the morning of 23 January a squadron of the 11th Hussars had entered Tripoli, hard on the heels of the retreating Germans. 'TRIPOLI is OURS!!,' exulted Signalman Beaumont of 7th Medium Regiment, RA, 'after 2 yrs desert and dust – and at last a little green and some trees.'[22] It was a triumph, of sorts, for Montgomery's troops, though they would have little time to savour it.

There were no victories now for the German troops, falling back fast towards the Tunisian border. On the last day of 1942, Rommel had received permission from Mussolini to retreat from the Beurat position. 'We carried on to a place some km beyond Tripoli,' noted a German Gefreiter in his diary, 'Bombing attacks day and night.' Amidst unceasing air attacks on 24 January he observed: 'All our forces from Libya are flooding back towards Tunisia. The road is blocked with traffic.'[23]

At the beginning of 1943, there were in excess of 100,000 Axis troops in Tunisia and about 50,000 in Rommel's *Panzerarmee*.[24] To keep only the German part of the *Panzerarmee* in being required somewhere between 17,000 and 23,000 tons of essential supplies each month instead of the 5,871 tons it was actually receiving. Everywhere the situation was the same, whether it was fuel, ammunition or food. From the start of 1943 the bread ration for every man had to be reduced, from 500 to 375 grams per day. The situation was, explained a report with much understatement, 'not particularly rosy.'[25]

Apart from a small US naval contingent, Motor Torpedo Boat Squadron 15, all offensive seaborne operations throughout the whole of the Mediterranean after the Torch landings until Operation Husky fell to the Royal Navy which caused havoc along the enemy's main supply route. This ran from Sicilian ports to Tunis and Bizerte by way of an open sea passage of about 100 miles which involved some ten hours' sailing. So great was the Axis' need for supplies that they risked attacks by day and night until, late on 1 December 1942, Allied air reconnaissance alerted a British submarine patrol and Force Q, commanded by Rear-Admiral C.H.J. Harcourt, to an enemy convoy hurrying toward the North African coast.[26]

Three British cruisers and two destroyers pounced at point-blank range just after midnight. All five transports and three destroyers in the convoy were sunk or set on fire amidst scenes of dreadful carnage. When morning crept above the horizon, the sea was seen to be littered with debris. Tossed amongst the thick oil staining the surface of the water were dozens of corpses, still afloat in their lifebelts.

In contrast, by clearing ports as fast as possible and pushing through convoys with air cover and naval escorts against savage attacks, the Allies put over eight million tons of supplies ashore in North Africa between the Torch landings and March 1943, losing only 2.4 per cent to enemy action in the process.[27] 'Keep hammering away at the damned submarine!,' Eisenhower instructed Spaatz.[28]

Despite Admiral Dönitz's warnings that the coastal waters of the Mediterranean were too shallow for ideal operations and that the surface and air defences ranged against his U-boats were too powerful, the German Naval High Command ordered him to attack follow-up landings after Torch and subsequent Allied supply convoys.

After some initial successes in November and December 1942, 14 German and Italian submarines were soon lost in the central and western Mediterranean. Appalled that this extravagant sideshow was seriously impeding operations in the Atlantic and, sensing a major defeat, Dönitz requested permission to call it off but it was not until 23 December that this was agreed.[29] Despite German U-boats sinking nearly half a million tons of merchant shipping in the Mediterranean all were eventually destroyed. The Italians could offer little assistance because, lacking maritime aircraft, they were forced to use their submarines as reconnaissance vessels. They were never able to destroy the British convoy system, despite the most severe losses.[30]

The British 8th Submarine Flotilla (Captain Fawkes) at Algiers and 10th Flotilla (Captain Phillips) from Malta, raided constantly against Axis supply vessels in the dangerous Sicilian Channel. Yet, despite the Mediterranean's many minefields and their primitive fire control systems, reliable torpedoes and a high standard of marksmanship among the 32 British submarines helped account for an impressive tonnage of shipping in the last two months of 1942.

During January 1943, the Axis lost about a quarter of their transhipped supplies and in the next month, for every submarine on patrol, three ships went to the bottom. Seventy-two, totalling 221,000 tons, were sunk in five months while seven British submarines were lost, including the redoubtable *Turbulent* whose captain, Commander J.W. Linton, was awarded a posthumous Victoria Cross to go with his DSO and DSC.[31]

After the mauling by Force Q most Axis personnel sent to Africa were brought in by a massive, hastily arranged airlift; this began in November and reached its peak during the early months of 1943. Directing the operation from Rome was

Generalleutnant Ulrich Buchholz, appointed *Lufttransportführer Mittelmeer* (Air Transport Commander, Mediterranean) in December 1942, with three *Geschwaderen* (Groups) under his command, one in Sicily and two in mainland Italy.[32]

Transport flights of 100 aircraft commonly set out at dawn, landing at Tunisian airfields before 0700 hours to avoid attack. A second flight would approach Farina or Cap Bon shortly after noon in staggered formation, separating to land, either at field runways southeast of Tunis or at Bizerte. In the evening Geschwader S would send in another wing (*Gruppe*) which often remained overnight.

Retaining any sort of defensive formation demanded an exceptionally high flight performance, especially since fighter protection was available only from Sicily to the Tunisian coast. Between Naples and Trapani, transports of Geschwader N had to avoid RAF and USAAF interception by flying at a height of 50 metres (150ft), out of touch with each other apart from messages from the leading aircraft of the wing's wedge formation. Even when they eventually met their fighter cover there were further problems; the fighters' speed had to be adjusted to that of the slowest Ju-52, about 180–190km/h (110–120mph).

To incorporate Ju-52s and giant six-motored Me-323s in the same flight was very difficult because the latter became spectacularly unstable if throttled back, under full load, below their cruising speed of 220–230km/h (135–145mph). Consequently, as the formations approached Tunisia, they were often strung out over miles of sky and, more often than not, their fighter cover had failed to arrive, though Buchholz could recall no occasion on which a transport turned back on account of this. Even when fighters were present, this protection usually consisted of fewer than a dozen medium and long-range aircraft which simply could not cover the vast arc through which a transport formation became dispersed.

The inevitable result was that the courage, nerve, determination and sacrifice of the transport pilots was not enough. They suffered terrible casualties between November 1942, and April 1943, in ferrying an average 585 tonnes (575 Imperial tons) of supplies daily into Tunisia together with thousands upon thousands of troops. 'Untiring in their flights... often under severest enemy interference,' wrote Buchholz, 'and with only negligible support from our own pursuit planes, they have completed their mission... carrying it out to the bitter end.'[33]

This perilous supply situation inflamed the already tortuous relationships between the Axis partners and in conference at Rastenburg on 19 December 1942, Hitler agreed with Cavallero and Ciano that the Tunisian supreme command should come into line with that in Libya and pass to *Comando Supremo*. By this arrangement Hitler placed von Arnim's Fifth Panzer Army under Italian control though, angry at the supply situation, he had no intention of giving them any real influence in its command.[34] This move was calculated in part to remove difficulties between Rommel and von Arnim. Neither seemed to know much about the other's plans and dispositions. During protracted meetings with Göring and Hitler on 11/12 January, Kesselring proposed that Rommel be put in command of an army group headquarters when he reached Tunisia, hoping that, 'this promotion would arouse his ambitions and improve his performance.'[35] To make this politically acceptable this had to be under Italian command – *Comando Supremo* – though Kesselring hoped secretly that the day would be far off when this happened. At a second Italo-German conference this was agreed.

The upshot was that, late in January, Mussolini named General Giovanni Messe to command the Italian First Army when it came into being. Determined and ruthless in his priorities, Kesselring did his best to hinder this by installing the whole of his German operations staff during the same month into *Comando Supremo* headquarters which led to much friction between the two sides.

Unlike the Allied integrated air command, Germans and Italians remained rigidly independent of each other, apart from a few special operations. After US fighter-bombers drove the enemy from his last air bases at Zuara, in Tripolitania, on 24 January, nearly 400 German and Italian aircraft had to be based in Tunisia. They were controlled from *Fliegerkorps Tunis* or from *Comando Aeronautica Tunisia*.[36]

On the last day of 1942, Alanbrooke cabled Montgomery telling him that, due to the slow progress of the Allies in Tunisia, his troops might well have to operate west of Tripoli.[37] This meant moving everything over 800 miles of road from the port of Benghazi, which Rommel had abandoned on 19 November, until Tripoli could be properly opened up. In order to remain active, an infantry division needed 300 tons of supplies a day, and an armoured division 400 tons; in each case half the total was accounted for by fuel. If Eighth Army had also to feed a starving populace at Tripoli matters would be very difficult: '50,000 thousand screaming women would be a proper party,' wrote Montgomery, 'however, we would handle it somehow.'[38]

If Tripoli was not reached within ten days of the opening assault at Beurat, his troops would have to retreat again. Operation Fire-Eater was programmed to take the Beurat position and rush forward with such impetus that Rommel would have no time to settle in the Tarhuna–Homs position, 200 miles further west, and be pushed out of Tripoli itself.

Montgomery wanted Benghazi working at full pressure until the end of January but a severe gale on the 3rd lashed the harbour and caused extensive damage. More delay in unloading was caused by further storms; Lieutenant-General Brian Horrocks' X Corps had to be 'grounded' and its vehicles driven day and night, bringing up supplies for other units from Tobruk to Benghazi and roadheads further westward.[39]

Before Operation Fire-Eater began on 15 January, Montgomery knew beyond doubt from Enigma intercepts the true nature of Rommel's difficulties. With only 36 German and 57 Italian tanks, and supply trucks sometimes stranded without fuel for days at a time, he could not put up a protracted defence in Tripolitania. Meanwhile, Mussolini raged at, 'that madman Rommel, who thinks of nothing but retreating in[to] Tunisia' and Kesselring was puzzled as to why Rommel had not slashed at Montgomery while the Eighth Army was assembling its forces before the Beurat Line. Opportunities must surely have been missed: 'the Rommel I knew in the old days would not have passed [them] up... '[40]

But these were not 'the old days' and Rommel had to organize an orderly withdrawal, which might be dangerously – perhaps fatally – hampered by the presence of his Italian troops, who had no real stomach for the battles ahead. They included so called 'shock troops' of the Tunisian Battalion, all of them volunteers in fact with only a fortnight's training, whom General Bagnini thought were a greater danger to their own side than the enemy. As for the Italian artillery, it had been a 'total disaster' until put into action under German direction, when it had proved 'surprisingly' successful. Italian infantry units had to be stiffened by German support; they then fought with far greater steel in their souls.[41]

Early in January Rommel heard that Mussolini had agreed that his non-motorised Italian divisions should be sent back to the Tarhuna–Homs Line because once the British attacked at Beurat, it would be too late to remove them.[42] The Eighth Army was to be delayed before Tripoli for somewhere between three and six weeks on the Tarhuna–Homs position. Here, *Comando Supremo* assured him, was a line ideally protected by mountains over 700 metres (2,300ft) high which the enemy could not outflank.

Realising that Mussolini had no grasp of the situation, Rommel issued orders that his Afrika Korps was only to hold the Beurat position until the enemy was in such strength that they could attack or outflank the defenders, and that under no circumstances were his troops to allow themselves to be encircled. As soon as the code 'Movement Red,' was transmitted, they were to fall back in the direction of Sedada.[43]

In order to forestall an Allied attack at the Gabès defile – lying half way between Tripoli and Tunis – which could divide the Axis armies, he suggested that one or two divisions be sent back to guard it. With Kesselring's agreement 21st Panzer Division, leaving its tanks and weapons behind for other units to use, began withdrawing towards the Tunisian border (where it would re-equip) on 13 January. The choice of this division was, thought Kesselring, probably dictated by strained relations between Rommel and the divisional commander, Generalmajor Hans-Georg Hildebrandt.

In the meantime, Montgomery methodically built up his forces in front of Beurat, bringing up 450 tanks to set against Rommel's puny reserves, but refused to use French troops other than for guarding airfields. Apart from coping with this mundane task they were 'quite useless,' while French infantry brigades, 'merely let you down. A very essential part of my doctrine is that there shall be no failures; if I tackle anything it must succeed; I train the troops in the technique I am going to use in the next battle, and I do not crack off until I am ready.'[44]

By the time he was ready to 'crack off' against the Beurat line, 23rd Armoured Brigade was in the centre flanking the 51st Highland Division – nicknamed the 'Highland Decorators' from their habit of painting their 'HD' sign on anything and everything, whether it moved or not. The armoured brigade was to face up to Rommel's troops and force a withdrawal before the Highlanders were fully committed in their approach up the axis of the coast road. On the far left, 7th

Armoured Division and 2nd New Zealand Division, under XXX Corps' commander, Oliver Leese, were to sweep forward and threaten to outflank the enemy.

Eighth Army's assault was preceded by substantial bombing raids from fighter-escorted Bostons, Baltimores and American Mitchells of the Desert Air Force which hit the enemy's forward landing grounds and motor transport. By night, Bostons did further damage to landing grounds and Wellingtons of 205 Group, aided by flare-dropping Albacores, attacked roads and traffic.

Steadily and unspectacularly, Montgomery's troops pushed forward to the Beurat line. As they did so, Rommel's forces began to slip away, frustrating plans to bottle them up and destroy them. British units then began advancing strongly against 90th Light and 15th Panzer Divisions which, losing touch with each other, provoked a sudden crisis in the German command, although 90th Light Division drove out the 51st Highlanders from their own rearguard positions which had been penetrated. Low on fuel, Rommel's units found themselves unable to sustain their rearguard action in open countryside, despite knocking out 20 enemy tanks, and were forced to retreat on 17 January to the Homs–Tarhuna line.

Montgomery now sent his tanks in a wide flanking movement from the southeast by road towards Tarhuna and on to Castel Benito from the direction of Beni Ulid. On 19 January, Major-General John Harding's 7th Armoured and Lieutenant-General Sir Bernard Freyberg's New Zealand 2nd Division began their move against Rommel's southern group just as the Desert Fox arrived at the advanced headquarters of General de Stefanis, commanding XX Army Corps, north-west of Tarhuna. While there he spotted enemy tanks only six miles away moving on the Djebel Garian mountain range to the south. If the column carried on he foresaw there would be little to prevent it coming in behind the *Panzerarmee* and wreaking havoc by nightfall.

Part of 164th Light Division and elements of the *Ramcke* Parachute Brigade, together with a reconnaissance group were hurriedly dispatched to stiffen 15th Panzer Division. The whole of Rommel's artillery laid down a heavy carpet of fire on the approaching tank column which was hit by every available aircraft that the Luftwaffe could get off the ground.

Arriving back at his own HQ, Rommel told his relieved staff that Montgomery had been unable to resist a flanking movement without engaging the German artillery at the same time. But Rommel had grossly miscalculated the strength of the attack on Garian. What was apparently an armoured division was no more than 4th Light Armoured Brigade (which had no heavy tanks at all by 20 January) and Rommel's defences were thrown off balance as he committed most of his heavy forces to meet it. This left Freyberg's New Zealand Division, running with only 14 tanks, to bypass Tarhuna to the west and reach Azizia on 22 January, while 7th Armoured Division, with only 30 tanks, smashed its way into Tarhuna, after a massive artillery bombardment ordered on the 19th by the young and highly energetic Harding, who, in Montgomery's words, was 'a fine natural leader.'[45]

Unfortunately, Harding was badly injured on 19 January when a German shell almost blew off one of his hands. Leese's attack slowed almost to a walk but Montgomery immediately sent another young soldier, Brigadier 'Pip' Roberts from 22nd Armoured Brigade, to take temporary command whereupon 7th Armoured resumed its rapid advance.

While the mass of German defenders was drawn from the coastal road towards events further west, 51st Highland Division was driven furiously by Montgomery towards Homs. Personally directing operations, he led 22nd Armoured Brigade on a route from the west which cut across that of the advancing Highlanders.

Anxious to capture Tripoli without delay, Montgomery was particularly hard on the Highlanders who were short of shells, transport and petrol, much to their commander, Major-General Wimberley's, disgust. Nevertheless, having whipped on his leading formations, Wimberley attacked the main Homs defence position at dawn on 20 January and, when that advance was held up, ordered an outflanking march by the seashore to come in behind 90th Light. When the defenders withdrew some miles to the west, he sent in his leading battalion of Seaforth Highlanders by moonlight.

Montgomery now had Tripoli threatened along the coastal axis as well as by Leese's outflanking movement. Rommel had already abandoned the Tarhuna position on the night of 19 January, upon learning that an enemy column was within 30 miles of Garian, having cut the main Tarhuna–Garian highway. Mussolini immediately accused him of shifting his forces westwards too impulsively, thereby disobeying instructions to hold the Tarhuna–Homs line for at least three weeks.

During a tempestuous meeting on the afternoon of 20 January, Rommel told Cavallero, Kesselring and Bastico he had never accepted the time limits imposed on him for holding the Tarhuna–Homs position, which he now thought wholly untenable. 'You can either hold on to Tripoli for a few more days and lose the army, or lose Tripoli a few days earlier and save the army for Tunis. Make up your mind,' Rommel stormed at his furious superiors.[46]

The crucial decision had already been made. That morning, gigantic explosions had been heard from the direction of city. At the harbour, German demolition experts were destroying dock installations; further inland the airport was systematically demolished. Still convinced that the New Zealanders' thrust in the west threatened to encircle his troops, Rommel ordered a fighting rearguard from the 90th Light to abandon Tripoli shortly after midnight on 23 January. Precious ammunition was destroyed and such food stocks as could not be evacuated were distributed to the civilian population.[47] So serious was Rommel's supply situation that his retreating troops could fall back only 60 miles towards the Tunisian border, when all mobility would have to cease as they ran out of fuel.

'A very wonderful day,' Leese wrote to his wife on 23 January. After three hundred miles of 'the most frightful going', Montgomery, driving along the coast axis, and Leese, swinging around from the west, met at the city which had been captured after so many miles of desert slogging. 'The town still has many Wops and Wogs,' Leese noted, 'We've been through it with Armoured Cars and Tanks.'[48]

The entry of B Squadron, 11th Hussars, into the city, followed closely by companies of 1st Battalion, Gordon Highlanders, who rode in the twilight of pre-dawn on a squadron of tanks from 50th Battalion, Royal Tank Regiment, was the signal for a day of celebration and reflection but Montgomery was determined that his troops would not be seduced by the fleshpots on offer. 'Much fighting lies ahead and I cannot have my Army getting "soft" and deteriorating in any way. I have forbidden the use of houses, buildings, etc., for HQ and troops. The Army will live in the fields,' he ordered, 'and in the desert, and will retain its hardness and its efficiency.'[49] He immediately set an example by locating his HQ about four miles outside the city.

Leese, however, knew when to be realistic. After only a few days, numerous brothels – separate for officers and men – were doing a roaring trade, averaging three minutes per visit. 'We have got a partial check on drink and I am having all the tarts inspected and policing the brothels – the latter in the teeth of the doctors and Church,' he observed, and was quite unrepentant about this policy: 'as there are no more Boches in Tripoli one might as well fight them!!!'[50] For most of Eighth Army, however, Tripoli was only barely glimpsed as they sped beyond its walls. 'We have passed Tripoli now,' wrote Signalman Beaumont on 24 January, 'thought we might have had a rest, but if we have him [Rommel] beat I suppose it's best to follow up.'[51]

The Desert Fox's downward spiral of depression and frustration, compounded by nervous strain, is clearly recorded in a letter to his wife on 25 January: 'I simply can't tell you how hard it is for me to undergo this retreat and all that goes with it. Day and night I'm tormented by the thought that things might go really wrong here in Africa. I'm so depressed that I can hardly do my work... K[esselring]... is full of optimism. Maybe he sees in me the reason why the army has not made a longer stand.'[52]

Private Crimp, an Eighth Army infantryman, was more concerned by events in the north: 'There, however, things don't look so good. The British 1st Army and the Americans (green troops, I suppose) after struggling desperately all through the winter, are now tied down in the mountains. Jerry, on the other hand, having saved Tunis and pushed out a tough defence of the city, is said to be actually bringing large reinforcements over from Italy. (Doesn't the bastard know when he's bloody well whacked?) So we shall be up there soon, dead cert.'[53]

Certainly, the Eighth Army was going to Tunisia. Equally without doubt, some of them would be dead before its vanguard ever reached the border.

Notes to Chapter 8

[1] Robinett Papers, Box 12.

[2] Butcher Diary, entry for 12 January 1943.

[3] Years later, Eisenhower told Hopkins that he had been wrong over the question of censorship in North Africa; see *The White House Papers of Harry L. Hopkins*, p. 674. Peyrouton was formerly a Minister of the Interior in the Vichy Government and closely connected with its anti-Semitic laws.

[4] See Hurstfield, *America and the French Nation 1939–1945*, Ch. 9, *passim*.

[5] 'Situation in North Africa', Combined Chiefs of Staff, 57th Meeting, ANFA Conference. Bedell Smith Papers, Box 1; Eisenhower to CCS, 23 January 1943; Alexander Papers, PRO, W0214/2.

[6] Proceedings of the ANFA Conference, 16 January 1943, 'The North Africa Situation', Bedell Smith Papers, Box 1.

[7] Butcher Diary, entry for 20 January 1943 (not 17th as in published version). Harry Hopkins told Eisenhower not to blame himself for the setbacks.

[8] Truscott Memorandum to Eisenhower, 24 January 1943; Truscott Papers, Box 9. Marshall Library.

[9] 'Notes on Liaison Mission'; Biddle Papers. Library of Congress.

[10] Eisenhower to Hartle, Clark, Allen, Fredendall, Anderson, etc., 15 January 1943; Chandler, Eisenhower Papers, II, Doc. 770. See also 'Notes on Recent fighting in Tunisia', (No.2), AFHQ, 7 January 1943, in Biddle Papers.

[11] Marshall to Major-General A.D. Bruce, 30 January 1943; Marshall to Lieutenant-General L.J. McNair, 1 February 1943; Marshall Papers. Marshall Library.

[12] McNair to Marshall, 2 February 1943; *ibid*.

[13] Harold Macmillan, *War Diaries*, p. 10. Macmillan was sent out by Churchill at the start of 1943, ostensibly to help Eisenhower on local politics but actually to make sure British views were kept before the C-in-C.

[14] Bryant, *Turn of the Tide*, p. 556.

[15] Quoted by Bryant, *Turn of the Tide*, p. 556 and Alanbrooke, 'Notes on My Life', addition to diary entry for 20 January 1943. In order to confirm Eisenhower as commander of the US military forces in Tunisia, the North African Theatre of Operations (NATOUSA) was created. Eisenhower was appointed to command this new body on 4 February 1943. *Cf.* Tedder, *With Prejudice*, p. 396.

[16] ANFA Conference Proceedings, 20 January 1943; Bedell Smith Papers, Box 1.

[17] Cunningham to Admiral Sir Algernon Willis, 17 January 1942; Cunningham Papers, CUNN 5/9.

[18] US Secretary's Office at Casablanca meeting to Eisenhower, SHAEF Cable, 21 January 1943; Eisenhower Papers, Box 130. See also Richards and Saunders, *The Fight Avails*, pp. 259–61. The subordinate commands under Northwest African Air Forces (Spaatz/NAAF) were Northwest African Strategic Air Force (Doolittle/NASAF); Northwest African Air Service Command (NAASC); Northwest African Tactical Air Force (formerly Air Support Command under Kuter – then NATAF under Coningham which took the Desert Air Force under its operational control); Northwest African Coastal Air Force (Barrett replaced by Lloyd/NACAF); Northwest African Training Command (NATC); Northwest African Troop Carrier Command – formed 18 March 1943 (NATCC); Northwest African Photographic Reconnaissance Wing (Roosevelt/NAPRW).

[19] Sherwood, *Hopkins' White House Papers*, pp. 686–7.

[20] Butcher Diary, entry for 28 January 1943.

21 Lord Ampthill to Oliver Warner, Cunningham Papers, CUNN2/1.

22 Signalman J.W. Beaumont, diary entry for 23 January 1943; Beaumont Papers and Diary, IWM 83/36/1.

23 Extracts from Diary of a Gefreiter, 104th Panzer Grenadier Regiment.

24 The exact figure for troops in Tunisia was given in a German strength return as 49,412. This was comprised of 20,000 army, 12,000 Luftwaffe, 2,000 marines and 15,412 Italian troops; 'War in Tunisia', Report for 3 January 1943; RH19-VIII/355. These figures are obviously rough estimates and, even for combat troops, seem far too low. Howe in the official American history, *Northwest Africa*, puts the figure nearer 100,000, with about 74,000 Germans and 26,000 Italians in Tunisia. The fact that Kesselring estimated that 60,000 tons of supplies were needed per month to sustain both von Arnim's and Rommel's troops suggests that Howe's is the accurate figure. British intelligence estimated that there were 55,000 troops facing Montgomery at this time, of whom 30,000 were Germans. This estimate was remarkably accurate; a German report on 1 February gives the German strength as 1,054 officers and 29,649 NCOs and men – a total of 30,703. This figure was far below the theoretical establishment of 1,841 officers and 60,685 NCOs and men who should have made up the various German parts of Rommel's *Panzerarmee*. Figures taken from 'German Army Strengths, listed and actual, 1 February 1943' (includes armament strengths); RH19-VIII/40. BA-MA. Desmond Young, in his *Rommel*, is surely wrong in writing of Rommel's 25,000 Italians, 10,000 Germans and 60 tanks on the retreat through Tripolitania; p. 178.

25 TS Battle Reports covering *Deutsch-Italienische Panzerarmee* for period 23 October 1942 to 23 February 1943, Text, Volume 1; Battle Report for 3 January 1943. RH19 – VIII/31; BA-MA.

26 Force Q consisted of the cruisers *Aurora*, (Captain W.G. Agnew); *Argonaut* (Captain E.W.L. Longley-Cook); *Sirius* (Captain p. W.B. Brooking) and the destroyers *Quentin* and HMAS *Quiberon*. Harcourt was aboard his flagship, *Aurora*.

27 This figure reduces to 1.5 per cent if the assault period of Operation Torch is excluded.

28 Eisenhower to Spaatz, 12 November 1942. Eisenhower Papers, Box 9.

29 Terraine, *Business in Great Waters*, pp. 497–9.

30 A total of 62 German U-boats entered the Mediterranean of which all were destroyed; see Hezlet, *The Submarine and Sea Power*, pp. 157–8. The Italians lost 34 submarines and a combined total of 243 warships (totalling 33,500 tons) and merchant ships (totalling 325,000 gross tons); see de Belot, *The Struggle for the Mediterranean 1939–1945*, p. 203.

31 Hezlet, *The Submarine and Sea Power*, p. 153. In six months from 8 November 1942, the British 8th Flotilla sank well over 200,000 tons of shipping and damaged another 30,000 tons. The 10th Flotilla claimed 130,000 tons sunk and 40,000 tons damaged. See Bartimeus, *The Turn of the Road*, pp. 117–18.

32 Buchholz had an advanced command post at Trapani. In the German set-up, a wing (*Gruppe*) consisted of four squadrons (*Staffel*), thus totalling 48 aircraft. The usable strength on average, however, between December 1942, and May 1943, was 315 Ju-52s and 15 Me-323s. Generalleutnant Ulrich Buchholz, 'Supply by Air of the Enlarged Bridgehead of Tunis (December 1, 1942 – May 11, 1943),' (1947), Foreign Military Studies, MS D-071. USAMHI.

33 Buchholz, 'Supply by Air of the Enlarged Bridgehead of Tunis'.

34 Fifth Panzer Army actually came under *Comando Supremo* operational control as from 26 January 1943.

35 Kesselring, 'The War in the Mediterranean Area, Part 1', p. 30.

[36] *Fliegerkorps Tunis* was set up under General Seidemann with his tactical HQ at La Fanconnerie on 15 February 1943, and was directly responsible to *Luftflotte 2*. Two groups were established which were controlled by *Fliegerkorps Tunis*; *Fliegerführer 2* (which replaced *Fliegerführer Tunisien*) with a tactical HQ at Tunis under Colonel Benno Kosch; *Fliegerkorps 3* (which replaced *Fliegerführer Afrika*) commanded by Colonel Walter Hagen from his tactical HQ at Gabès. General of Air Brigade Gaeta commanded *Comando Aeronautica Tunisia*, from his HQ at Tunis. Set up on 6 January 1943, it controlled three groups; *Settore Aeronautico Est*, commanded by Colonel Carlo Draga; *Settore Aeronautico Ouest*, commanded by General of Air Brigade Ruggero Bonomi; and *Settore Aeronautico Centrale*, commanded by Colonel Augusto Bacchiani. On 15th February, *Comando Aeronautica Tunisia* was absorbed by General of Air Army Mario Bernasconi's 5th *Squadra*, with an HQ at El Hamma. Two subordinate commands were newly-created; *Settore Aeronautico Nord* commanded by Colonel Augusto Bacchiani and *Settore Aeronautico Sud*, commanded by Colonel Carlo Drago.

[37] Brooke to Montgomery, 31 December 1942; Montgomery Papers, BLM 49/11.

[38] Montgomery to Brooke, 2 January 1943; Montgomery Papers, BLM 49/12.

[39] Notably at El Agheila, Nofilia and Misurata.

[40] Muggeridge, *Ciano's Diary*, p. 543, entry for 5 January 1943; Kesselring, 'War in the Mediterranean Area'.

[41] Report on relationships in the field between German and Italian troops from 21 January to 5 February 1943; RH19VIII/357. BA-MA.

[42] At the same time, the 164th Light Division was to be withdrawn to the Tarhuna–Homs position but was re-routed to the south to secure Rommel's flank; Outgoing message from *DAK*, Corps' Order 3 January 1943, RH24-200/82; Incoming message to DAK, 4 January 1943, RH24-200/78. BA-MA.

[43] Outgoing message from *DAK*, Corps' Order, 6 January 1943. *Ibid*.

[44] Montgomery to Brooke, 2 January 1943; Montgomery Papers, BLM49/12.

[45] Montgomery's Situation Report, 26 January 1943, 'The Advance on Tripoli,' Montgomery Papers, BLM 30/1-3. Details of tank numbers from Hamilton, *Monty, Master of the Battlefield*, p. 118.

[46] Liddell Hart, *The Rommel Papers*, p. 389.

[47] *Ibid*., p. 390; TS Battle Reports covering *Deutsch-Italienische Panzeramee* for period 23 October 1942 – 23 February 1943, Text, Volume 2; Battle Report, 23 January 1943. RH19-VIII/32; BA-MA.

[48] Leese to his wife, 23 January 1943; Leese Papers, Box 2.

[49] Montgomery's Situation Report, 26 January 1943. The entry of the 11th Hussars into the city of Tripoli was stage-managed but only fair. They were the original 'Desert Rats,' who had exchanged the first shots of the desert war with Italian posts at Sidi Omar on the night of 11/12 June 1940. A patrol of 1/5th Queen's Royals had actually entered very early on the morning of the 23rd. Just outside the city a patrol of 1/6th Queens Royals had come across a notice bearing the wildly optimistic claim: 'Tommy, we shall return.' Foster, *History of the Queen's Royal Regiment*, p. 186.

[50] Leese to his wife, 27 January 1943; Leese Papers, Box 2

[51] Beaumont Diary, entry for 24 January 1943; Beaumont Papers and Diary.

[52] Liddell Hart, *Rommel Papers*, pp. 390–1.

[53] Crimp, *The Diary of a Desert Rat*, entry for 23 January 1943, pp. 158–9.

Above: US Army Chief of Staff General George C. Marshall (right) with Lieutenant-General Dwight D. Eisenhower. Marshall was instrumental in securing Eisenhower's appointment as Commander-in-Chief of the Torch Operation in 1942.

Left: Generalfeldmarschall Erwin Rommel. Montgomery pinned a photograph of the 'Desert Fox' above his desk during the North African campaign, an act suggestive of his view of the desert war as a battle of wits between two military giants.

Far left: Alexander (left) and Montgomery. Alex's easy-going charm stood in contrast to Monty's self-confidence, and alleged ruthless streak.

Left: 'Freddie' de Guingand, Monty's invaluable chief of staff.

Right: Paratroops in a transport plane en route to Tunisia from Algiers.

Below: American troops land at Surcouf, 20 miles east of Algiers, on 9 November 1942.

Left: General Kenneth Anderson, commander of First Army (centre), flanked by (left) Generals Allfrey and (right) Evelegh, two of his principal subordinates.

Right: (Left to right) General Giraud, President Roosevelt, General de Gaulle and Prime Minister Churchill, photographed during the Casablanca Conference.

Below right: The shattered gun turret of a German Mark III tank on the Bou Arada battlefield, 19 January 1943.

Below: General Fredendall inspecting a Royal Marine Guard of Honour on board a British aircraft carrier.

Left: An SAS patrol photographed on 18 January 1943 after returning from a three-day sortie behind the enemy's lines.

Right: RAF Boston medium bombers on a mission over North Africa in early 1943.

Below left: General Leclerc (right), pictured with Montgomery. Leclerc's Free French force was incorporated into Eighth Army as Force L after an epic 1,600-mile march from Chad to Tripoli.

Below right: A German Tiger tank, knocked out in Tunisia by Allied anti-tank fire.

Above left: GIs of the 2nd Battalion, 16th Infantry marching through the Kasserine Pass on 26 February 1943.

Above: A Valentine tank, bogged down in the Wadi Zigzaou, March 1943. Monty was criticised for choosing to head his attack with this obsolescent type of tank.

Left: A cameraman filming Sherman tanks as they move up in the advance on Kasserine.

Right: General Patton's reputation as a 'hard-hitting, fast-thinking American hero' soared after the successful occupation of Gafsa by his troops in March 1943.

Above: A young German prisoner receives water through a barbed wire fence at Gafsa POW camp, March 1943.

Above right: Lieutenant-General Freyberg, the vastly-experienced commander of the New Zealand Division.

Above, far right: Lieutenant-General Oliver Leese, commander of XXX Corps, was often critical of First Army's performance.

Right: Allied tanks and infantry advance through Gafsa, 5 April 1943.

Left: RAF commanders Coningham (right) and Broadhurst. The two clashed over the role the air force should play in the battle of the Mareth Line.

Left: Gurkhas emerging from a smokescreen at the summit of a hill, near Medenine, on 16 March 1943.

Right: A Black Watch soldier watches British tanks crossing the anti-tank ditch at the entrance to the Gabès Gap, on 6 April 1943.

Below right: Lancashire Fusiliers resting below a typical craggy Tunisian cliff, 14 April 1943.

Below: A captured German 88mm gun being used in action by New Zealand Division artillery, near Enfidaville on 15 April 1943.

Above: Stretcher bearers of the East Surrey Regiment move up Longstop Hill under fire, 23 April 1943.

Above right: Crouching beside bomb ruins, an American patrol awaits the order to move forward into Bizerte, 8 May 1943.

Left: Lieutenant-General Horrocks was buoyant on hearing that he was to command the main attacking front at Tunis, deeming it a test of 'the real art of generalship'.

Right: The liberated population of Tunis cheers a Churchill tank and its crew on 8 May 1943.

Above: General von Arnim steps down from an Allied transport plane at Algiers on 14 May 1943, now a prisoner of war.

Above: (Left to right) General von Sponeck is received by Generals Freyberg and Keightley at Bou Ficha on 13 May 1943.

Below: General Montgomery with captured commanders General von Liebenstein (seated right) and Marshal Messe (seated left). They are deciding assembly points for surrendering Axis units.

Chapter 9

Promises of More Hard Fighting

' I'm sick and tired of this bloody desert and the sooner I get out of it the better I shall like it. I think I've done more than my share in this war, and it's about time somebody took my place.'

Bombardier J.E. Brooks, 64 Medium Regiment, RA, in a letter home, 12 February 1943.[1]

The entry into Tripoli had been a tremendous achievement but was imbued with a sense of anti-climax. Suddenly, far from the dream of a ship to take them home, Eighth Army veterans realized there was much more fighting to be done.[2] Before a triumphal parade on 4 February there was endless spit and polish, heartily resented by most of those involved. 'Inspected today by Corps Commander – C-in-C coming tomorrow – all guns lined up together,' noted Signalman Beaumont, 'glad to get it over.' Lieutenant McCallum, a Scottish infantry officer, hated the enforced preparations: 'It would be ludicrous to pretend that the honour of a visit from the Premier had any appeal to the soldiers of the [51st] division. The idea of a ceremonial parade was galling in the hours of meticulous preparation and rehearsal that it required.'[3]

Sublimely indifferent, Churchill was in his element on the reviewing stand on 4 February, with Montgomery beside him, as he watched the greater part of 51st Highland Division swing past to the tunes of 80 massed pipers and drummers. On foot came famous Scottish regiments: Seaforths, Black Watch, Argylls, Camerons and Gordons. Atop Mussolini's triumphal arch, silhouetted against the sky, a lone kilted soldier stood motionless as the troops marched past. It was pure theatre and the Prime Minister, tears in his eyes, loved every minute of it.[4]

After lunch, Churchill went on to visit 8,000 men of the New Zealand 2nd Division. Before the assembled troops he was characteristically upbeat but warned them of the impending struggle: 'The enemy has been driven out of Egypt; out of Cyrenaica; out of Tripolitania. He is now coming towards the end of his means of running, and in the corner of Tunisia a decisive battle has presently to be fought.'[5] Lieutenant-General Freyberg thought the event, 'the most impressive and moving parade of my career,' but others, such as Second Lieutenant Boord, were not impressed. 'We were all keyed up to hear what the PM had to say, hoping we would hear something of our future once the Tunisian campaign is completed,' he wrote home, 'but we were disappointed. Beyond congratulations and promises of more hard fighting we heard nothing.'[6]

Preparations for that eventuality were already under way. 'Today we have settled in earnest to plan our next battle,' wrote Leese. 'It is a big task. We must and will achieve. We have some 500 miles to Tunis while the 1st Army at one time only had 20 miles. It's a good bet we will get there first.'[7]

Between Benghazi and Tripoli, the Germans had killed or wounded over 1,000 of their pursuers on mines. At one crossroads Major Rainier, an Eighth Army engineer staff officer, came across a New Zealander who had just stepped on an S-mine. A crimson stream gushed from a hole the size of a man's hand in his chest, while beside him knelt a colleague, trying desperately to staunch the flow with a wad of cotton. Further on a truck passed him: 'Blood was running through the cracks in the floorboards and splashing on the shiny surface of the road like red paint. In that lorry were the remains of eleven South African sappers who had just been caught by an S-mine.'[8]

But there was no let up on Rommel's men hurrying westward from Tripoli, despite the delaying tactics of German sappers of Panzer Pionier Bataillon 200 and a Luftwaffe Feldbrigade who sowed nearly 200 Hungarian and German Teller mines in a random pattern along the 58 kilometres (36 miles) of road between Zuara and the Tunisian border. For good measure they also blew 19 bridges and constructed various anti-tank obstacles.[9]

In the vanguard of the advance, men of the Queen's Royal Regiment (7th Armoured) moved forward on foot and 12th Lancers (1st Armoured) were often forced to clamber down from their armoured cars and accompany them; they were slowed on 25 January by sand dunes, which made it impossible for the tanks to outflank the German positions, while delayed-action mines in the Tarhuna Pass interrupted the supply columns on which they depended.[10]

On 13 February elements of 15th Panzer Division – the last of Rommel's forces engaged in continuous rearguard action – crossed the Tunisian border. Two days later they reached the old French defensive fortifications lying between the Matmata Hills and the sea, some 80 miles inside Tunisia itself, known as the Mareth Line and selected by *Comando Supremo*.

The position was formidable. From the Matmata Hills in the west, many wadis ran across the low-lying sandy plain towards the sea, about 22 miles away. The most important of these were the Wadi Zeuss and, over three miles behind it, the Wadi Zigzaou. Between these natural obstacles there were pre-war French fortifications and the Germans had turned these into even stronger field-works, mainly nests of pill boxes, some of them capable of holding half a battalion, with the main defences resting on the Wadi Zigzaou, which had been deepened and widened particularly where it neared the sea. About 19 miles of the front were covered with wire obstacles and approximately 100,000 anti-tank and 70,000 anti-personnel mines had been laid.

Rommel knew that the position could be outflanked by a determined onslaught and Montgomery was aware of this from a French officer formerly of a Tunisian rifle battalion, Captain Paul Mezan, who had helped plan and build the Mareth Line. In the name of de Gaulle, he had requisitioned an ancient black taxi which he used as his caravan, office and fighting vehicle and put himself at the disposal of 50th Division. He knew the location intimately and the best crossing places over the Wadi Zigzaou.[11] More news of the enemy's defensive preparations came from other sympathetic French officers, photographic reconnaissance carried out day after day by RAF aircraft, and from the activities of the Long Range Desert Group (LRDG).

During Eighth Army's advance towards Tripoli, LRDG patrols had been busy keeping watch on the coast road, sending back information about Rommel's retreating forces and harrying his rearguards.[12] At the same time, a Rhodesian half-patrol of the LRDG, led by Lieutenant Jim Henry, provided a radio link with Eighth Army while accompanying General Leclerc's Free French Forces on the first part of their historic 1,600-mile march across the desolate wastes from Chad in French Equatorial Africa to Tripoli.[13] On reaching Montgomery's HQ, they were incorporated into Eighth Army as Force L, which Leclerc subsequently commanded with distinction.

Patrols of the LRDG carried out the 'careful and detailed reconnaissance' ordered by Montgomery, for the production of 'going maps' in case Eighth Army had to by-pass the Mareth Lane to the south and swing inwards towards Gabès. This was risky work; one patrol north of Scimered lost four trucks with their passengers, and another officer was killed when his vehicle hit a land mine in Hon on 15 January. Their task was further complicated by the activities of 1st Special Air Service Regiment (SAS) which 'beat up' roads and, noted the LRDG's Intelligence and Topographical Officer, stirred enemy patrols to furious activity.[14]

When Eighth Army was making its push for Tripoli, a group of David Stirling's SAS had put on a demonstration of strength on the west side of the city in order to alarm the enemy and persuade them to withdraw before demolishing port installations. This was mostly unsuccessful; the harbour entrance had been completely blocked and there had been much destruction, some due to the earlier intensive Allied bombing. Great efforts were made to clear the port and German reconnaissance reports on 1 February recorded that the Allies were unloading supplies with small vessels.[15] Churchill was there to see the first large merchant ships enter the harbour three days later.

An SAS officer, Captain Jordan, with a group of three French patrols, was also ordered to disrupt Rommel's supply lines stretching from Sfax and Gabès while another group closed up to the Mareth Line and observed the enemy's defensive preparations. Stirling himself was to lead a further group through southern Tunisia, reconnoitre a path for Freyberg's New Zealanders around the Mareth Line and link up with First Army. Much later, he admitted that this particularly hazardous venture was part of his plan to claim brigade status for the SAS by becoming the first fighting force to establish contact between First and Eighth Armies.[16]

With Eighth Army HQ urging the necessity of speed, Stirling consolidated all patrols into two larger groups. However, both groups were subsequently captured in the Gabès Gap, stretching 18 miles between the sea and the Chott lakes north of El Hamma. This passage, dominated by the Wadi Akarit at its northern end, offered the only direct route through to the Tunisian coastal sector but was crawling with enemy troops. The loss to the SAS of its dynamic head was certainly a calamity, such was his leadership and popularity.

'The capture of Lieutenant [sic] David Stirling, Commander 1st SAS Regiment at Oudref 17 kilometres north-west of Gabès,' noted a German tactical report on 10 February, 'gives us an important insight into the organization of the disruption and sabotage ability of the Eighth Army.' Before being sent to a POW camp in Italy, Stirling supposedly disclosed details of his last raid and the coded signals by which his men recognised one another. Furthermore, the Germans believed they had discovered how the SAS was set up within Eighth Army and the organization of its raiding forces.[17] They realized that, while SAS operations would continue, without Stirling's leadership the raids would not carry the same punch, though a few survivors, one set led by a brilliant Rhodesian from the LRDG who had transferred to the SAS, Mike Sadler, and the other by Lieutenant Martin, of the Free French Forces attached to the SAS, did get through to Allied lines and were the first Eighth Army men to link up with First Army.

Sadler's group looked so villainous after their trek that they were put under armed guard by the Americans and only cleared by intelligence after they had been taken to Gafsa. Later, they accompanied Freyberg's New Zealanders on their sweep around the Mareth Line, covering the same ground they had reconnoitred previously under such difficult conditions. 'It was good to know,' said Sadler, 'that the original journey had not been in vain.'[18]

On 12 January 1943, a LRDG patrol led by a New Zealander, Captain Nick Wilder, beat Stirling's men by a short head to be the first Eighth Army troops to cross the border into Tunisia. In conjunction with the Indian Long Range Squadron, each of the LRDG's ten patrols was responsible for reconnoitring an area approaching the Mareth Line, and in the Matmata Hills to the west. It was there that Wilder discovered a route (naturally known later as 'Wilder's Gap') northwest into the Dahar plain by which a force could outflank the Mareth Line.

A following patrol, under Lieutenant Tinker, accompanied by Lieutenant-Colonel Vladimir Peniakoff's No 1 Demolition Squadron, the smallest independent unit in the British Army – known as 'Popski's Private Army' (PPA) – set out on 18 January and managed to penetrate right through the Tebaga Gap and beyond, ending up within 25 miles of Gabès, confirming that a strong force of all arms could indeed be put through Wilder's Gap into the Dahar and then through the Tebaga Gap.[19]

By 3 March 1943 all the topographical reconnaissance patrols, which relied on brilliant feats of navigation by the LRDG, SAS and PPA, were complete, and, as the LRDG's commanding officer somewhat wistfully remarked, 'The country north of Tripoli, over which the 8th Army proposed to advance, was of a much too inclosed nature for the operation of L.R.D.G. patrols.'[20] Eight days later, the LRDG ceased to be under Eighth Army command.

——————

During the first week in February, light elements of Montgomery's forces approached the Tunisian border. Behind them came the whole might of Eighth Army, including the 11th Hussars who spotted a signboard reading, 'Goodbye and Keep Smiling signed Ramcke.'[21] If the *Ramcke* paratroopers were still in good heart there was also certainly no weakness of morale among their pursuers. In one place where a tank had halted, Godfrey Talbot of the BBC saw where a soldier artist had traced a huge advertisement for his favourite Lancashire beer in the sand. Later, he was approached in a particularly isolated spot by an elderly Bedouin begging tea; around his shoulders hung a once-white towel with the bold inscription, 'Nottingham Baths, 1938.'[22]

Far ahead on the inland route, in pouring rain and high winds, the armoured cars of 12th Royal Lancers advanced past frequent minefields and badly cratered ground towards Pisidia on the Tunisian frontier. Here, the coastal road was so destroyed they were forced to detour southwards and entered the salt pans of Sebkret et Tadet. By 7 February they had reached a narrow mud causeway, south-west of Zeltene at Oglat el Haj Sayid, the only frontier crossing between the salt marshes and the sea, dominated by at least 30 German tanks.[23]

The bad weather, revealed in a letter home by Oliver Leese as 'blowing like hell and showery,' continued relentlessly. Godfrey Talbot described it in one of his broadcasts as 'breezy,' which exasperated the general beyond measure: 'He's a very silly man though I've never seen him,' wrote Leese. 'I keep well away from all the Press. They twist everything anyone does or says to suit their own desire for sensation though they tell me *The Times*, [Daily] *Telegraph* and *New York Times* people are better.'[24]

Talbot's 'breezy' weather filled bomb craters on both sides of the causeway with rainwater and reduced it to an impassable morass. Lieutenant-Colonel Hunter (Commander, Royal Engineers, 7th Armoured Division) had the task of throwing a causeway across the mud to take the whole of the division's wheeled transport.

The first 'regular' Eighth Army men to cross into Tunisia consisted of a small detachment from 1st Battalion, The Buffs (Royal East Kent Regiment) on foot, followed closely by men of the 5th Royal Horse Artillery and Staffordshire Yeomanry, whose tanks towed across vehicles of the 12th Lancers and other units. While they established and held a bridgehead, in 48 hours of unremitting toil interrupted regularly by German dive-bombing, Hunter's sappers built a wooden structure strong enough to support the rest of the advancing forces.[25]

Across it drove part of 8th Armoured Brigade (a combination of 1st The Buffs and Sherwood Rangers) together with 69th Medium Regiment, RA, and 131st Queen's (Lorried Infantry) Brigade from 7th Armoured Division, now commanded by Major General 'Bobby' Erskine. They advanced rapidly side by side on the village of Ben Gardane while 153rd Brigade of 51st Highland Division moved quickly along the coast road to counter stiffening enemy resistance.

As the Highlanders marched past the solitary border stone on 14 February to the triumphant skirl of the pipes, army photographers recorded the occasion but the event was marred when a truck blew up on a mine. Only a few days later an RAF staff officer, Flight Lieutenant Chadwick, nearly had his name added to the casualty list when his vehicle exploded almost at the same place: '[I had] several very stiff drinks and went to bed, glad to be able to do so.' The ever-present dangers meant the loss of good friends: 'since leaving Tripoli we had an indifferent few days, but things just went on the same and you didn't... mention them again.'[26]

On 15 February Ben Gardane fell to the British and within 48 hours 8th Armoured, down to only 12 active tanks, was replaced by 22nd Armoured Brigade, led by scout cars from 4th County of London Yeomanry ('the Sharpshooters').[27] At the same time, the Highlanders bivouacked outside the village to the sound of distant gunfire but were delighted to find a well which for once did not contain a putrefying corpse – a common tactic used to deny the enemy fresh water.

———※•※———

Back in Tripoli, Montgomery held a 'study week', on 14–17 February, to which he invited senior officers from England, Tunisia (including the Americans), Syria and Iraq. Besides lectures and discussions there was a demonstration by troops from 51st Highland of mine-clearing techniques, one of a night attack by 7th Armoured and another by the New Zealanders of movement and deployment in the desert.

Privately, Patton thought Montgomery's talk was 'very well done,' as was the use of Scorpions (Valentine flail tanks) and mine-detectors by the Highlanders.[28] 'The four days of lectures and demonstrations were most instructive... I learned a great deal,' he told Marshall.[29] That he had attended at all was a measure of his genuine interest in the art of soldiering. Others might have benefited but failed to turn up. Montgomery was very disappointed at the turnout, especially in the absence of anyone of substance from Tunisia; no British or American divisional commanders made an appearance, sending instead their staff officers.

———※•※———

During ten days in the first half of February 1943, Generalleutnant Warlimont, Deputy Chief of Staff at *OKW*, visited Tunisia to review the chaotic command situation. His visit took him by way of Kesselring's HQ and *Comando Supremo* in Rome to talks with von Arnim and Heinz Ziegler, at Tunis. After visiting various units and discussions with Rommel he returned to East Prussia on 15 February and the next day was summoned to the Führer's HQ to attend the usual midday conference.

Unlike Kesselring's evaluation, presented to the Führer at a conference held in Berlin and East Prussia on 11/12 January, Warlimont's was deeply pessimistic about the long-term situation in North Africa. To any rational strategist his revelations gave real cause for concern. Within the operational reserve of 10th and 21st Panzer Divisions, Warlimont discovered only the latter had been refitted and equipped while 90th Light was down to 2,400 men. Rommel had likened the German situation to a house of cards; adequate forces to resist a serious attack were nowhere available and artillery, ammunition, supplies of every kind and transportation space all suffered from critical shortages. Under such conditions, said Warlimont, 'the conduct of any offensive action by the German forces must be regarded as extremely hazardous and utterly audacious.'[30]

It was on such offensive action, however, that von Arnim and Rommel had already embarked. Kesselring calculated that, with Eighth Army's forces deployed and scattered in depth on the limited road net, which prevented Montgomery's units advancing parallel to one another, the southern sector would remain quiet for several weeks before a major assault was made on the Mareth Line. In the west, extension of the Allied lines to Faïd completed their strategic concentration and along its entire length their front line was occupied.

Assuming, correctly, that this activity had not gone entirely smoothly, Kesselring planned to attack the two fronts in succession with the idea of delaying enemy attacks by weeks or months. In the south, a series of good defensive lines could be secured, anchored on both flanks and rearguards left behind. But in the west, the Allied line still pinned von Arnim's troops uncomfortably near the coast. A series of frontal attacks was to be staged along its length to keep the enemy off balance and push parts of the line further west from where future assaults could be mounted.

Kesselring's plan was approved by *Comando Supremo* and the *OKW*. Four days after von Arnim had revealed his intention, on 24 January, to mount an attack on Faïd in order to deter any American movement on Sfax or Gabès (Eisenhower's ill fated Operation Satin), *Comando Supremo* ordered him to send two armoured formations to capture the Faïd area, destroy the Americans at Tébessa and occupy the Gafsa basin. At the best of times the commander of Fifth Panzer Army cut a stiffly patrician figure; his reply was glacial. The operation against Faïd was already in hand, he loftily informed the Italians, while two armoured divisions were insufficient to mount an attack on Tébessa and, in any event, were unavailable because 10th Panzer was needed in his northern sector and 21st Panzer was not yet at battle readiness.

As for the commander of 10th Panzer, Generalleutnant Wolfgang Fischer, he would never again lead his men in battle; on 5 February he drove into an inadequately marked Italian minefield west of Kairouan. His driver and aide were killed outright and his chief of staff, Oberstleutnant Bürker, badly wounded. The blast also tore off Fischer's legs and his left arm. In his death throes he called for pen and paper and wrote to his wife. His last words were, 'It will soon be over.'[31] He was immediately replaced by von Broich, promoted Generalmajor accompanied by a new operations staff officer Oberstleutnant Graf von Stauffenberg, an outstanding organizer and later involved in the 'July Plot' against Hitler.

Discord within the Axis command worsened when Rommel, convinced that the Allies would strike from Gafsa towards the coast, proposed a spoiling attack to be carried out by a battlegroup from Fifth Panzer Army and another from the German-Italian *Panzerarmee* under a single commander. His plan also involved the transfer of mobile troops from von Arnim's 10th and 21st Panzer to the south since he could not release his own 15th Panzer Division.

Von Arnim viewed Rommel as a lucky and self-advertising upstart while Rommel had slight regard for the Prussian soldier-aristocrat who, 'had little or no battle experience with our western enemies and hence had no means of knowing anything of their weaknesses of command.'[32] Matters were not helped by a series of directives from Ambrosio, who had taken over from Cavallero at *Comando Supremo* and displayed, thought Kesselring, 'an unfriendly, even hostile attitude.'[33] These called for attacks involving mobile troops drawn from both armies, though neither commander was willing to provide them.[34]

In an attempt to resolve these difficulties, Kesselring met von Arnim, Rommel and Messe on 9 February. Unknown to them, Anderson had ordered that Gafsa was not to be held at all costs but they knew of the consequences of his decision for some American units had already been reported as pulling out. Consequently, von Arnim was to mount an attack within a few days in the Sidi bou Zid area; afterwards 21st Panzer was to help Rommel attack Gafsa and turn north, hitting the Americans before they could recover their balance. In private, Kesselring told Rommel, who was pessimistic about the chances of a successful assault, that if the way was opened to Tébessa he could expect overall command of the final thrust and for any greater operations which might follow.[35]

Rommel's directive, issued the next day for Operation *Morgenluft* ('Morning Air'), planned to destroy enemy units in their assembly areas, form a special *Deutsche Afrika Korps* Kampfgruppe (Battlegroup) commanded by Generalmajor Freiherr Kurt von Liebenstein, take the heights north of Gafsa and obliterate enemy positions in Tozeur and Metlaoui. But his mind was already looking to wider possibilities: with the help of 21st Panzer, still expected from von Arnim, a continuation of the campaign 'according to the developing situation' was mentioned.[36]

At the same time he was sensibly cautious, insisting that he would take no risks since a reverse would have 'a catastrophic effect' at the Mareth Line, 'there being no more reserves at the army's disposal,' and intent on using von Arnim's 10th Panzer Division since his own 15th Panzer was needed to hold Montgomery in check.[37] Again von Arnim refused, claiming that he needed all his forces for a more limited attack code-named *Frühlingswind* ('Spring Breeze').

This operation was to be mounted by Ziegler with Oberst Pomtow leading the assault, spearheaded by the Tigers of 1 Company, Panzerabteilung 501 (attached to 10th Panzer). They were to break out of the Faïd Pass and enter Sidi bou Zid from several directions; meanwhile, other elements were to encircle most of the 1st US Armored Division and annihilate it.

In the south, Rommel received news of strong Allied reconnaissance forces moving out from Gafsa and, worried by the possibility of losing his Italian line of defence south-west of El Guettar, postponed his attack from 13 to 18 February. He proposed to spring from heavily camouflaged assembly areas and drive swiftly along the road from Gabès towards Gafsa. In the meantime, confident in his own plans, von Arnim omitted to tell either Kesselring or *Comando Supremo* that Ziegler's attack was due to open in the early hours of 14 February.

——◆◆◆——

In charge of intelligence analysis at AFHQ was a British officer, Brigadier Eric Mockler Ferryman. One US intelligence officer who knew him well thought him 'a splendid person; Galahad type; not ruthless enough to please some people [he] took full responsibility for mistakes of his subordinates.'[38] Others, like Montgomery were not so impressed, assessing him as, 'a pure theorist', without practical experience.[39]

Anderson thought the Germans would strike in the north, against Pont du Fahs. From past experience, Mockler-Ferryman was aware that the Germans' precarious supply situation, rate of reinforcement and absence of information about a more serious offensive, did not necessarily rule out such a possibility. But his usual avenues of information were blocked off in the early part of February 1943 when command changes at *Comando Supremo* seriously upset readings of the enemy's routine signals. The difficulty of deciphering Enigma intercepts at this time was further compounded by changes in the Allied command structure which impeded field intelligence staffs in their work of collecting and co-ordinating material from air reconnaissance, POW interrogation, agents' reports and Y service radio eavesdropping.[40]

In effect, Mockler-Ferryman was working almost in the dark when he informed Anderson that a limited German offensive would be launched in the Ousseltia Valley region, at Fondouk Pass through the Eastern Dorsale. Such Enigma evidence as did become available, and on which he relied to a considerable extent about Operations *Morgenluft* and *Frühlingswind*, was almost wholly misleading and became entangled with information about another proposed operation, appropriately codenamed *Kuckucksei* ('Cuckoo's egg'), which they superseded.

Since Anderson was not to know that warnings of an attack from the direction of Fondouk were based on an excessive reliance on Ultra and misplaced confidence in other unreliable evidence, he was somewhat surprised but unshaken when visiting Tébessa on 13 February to be confronted with evidence of a different kind from Colonel 'Monk' Dickson, Fredendall's Intelligence officer at II Corps HQ. Basing his estimate on battlefield intelligence – interrogation of POWs, observation of the enemy's artillery command surveying for targets, and air reconnaissance – the German attack, he reported, would come further south at Faïd or, more probably, Gafsa. After questioning him closely Anderson remarked, 'Well young man, I can't shake you,' but told Fredendall later that his staff officer was a 'pessimist' and 'alarmist.'[41]

——◆◆◆——

After less than four weeks the attempt to make national commands directly responsible to Eisenhower had failed. Given command of all armies on the Tunisian front, Anderson tried to organize the British, French and Americans into three sectors, with a corps commander in executive charge of all troops in each of them. Matters did not run smoothly and he had, by 7 February, to address the problem of commanders meddling in each other's sectors while expressing deep concern about, 'the lack of close co-operation in some instances between British and French, or American and French… [which] must be overcome.'[42]

The beating administered to French units at the Faïd Pass during the last days of January forced Eisenhower to issue Anderson with modified instructions. In an effort to squeeze the French out of the front line, elements of the 1st US Infantry Division were scattered thinly in the Ousseltia Valley. The southern flank of the French XIX Corps was covered by the 34th Infantry Division and 1st Armored, but they fared little better. Near Pichon was 135th RCT, while Anderson kept Robinett's CC B east of Maktar. Stack's CC C was at Hadjeb el Aïoun, roughly midway between Pichon and Sidi bou Zid, and McQuillin's CC A somewhat dispersed near Sidi bou Zid, reinforced by 168th RCT (less 1st Battalion); these units were controlled by II Corps through Headquarters, 1st Armored Division.

Major-General Ward, at his HQ in a large cactus patch slightly west of Sbeïtla, controlled very little of 1st Armored, and what he did was subject to the most detailed dispositions from Fredendall, acting on recommendations made by one of his assistant operations staff officers, Lieutenant-Colonel 'Red' Akers, who had visited McQuillin's HQ. Fredendall's directive, issued on 11 February, ordered Ward to contain the enemy at the Faïd Pass but, against all US military doctrine which normally gave the local commander much freedom of action, was unusually detailed in its exact placing of Ward's units and ended with a postscript written in Fredendall's own hand: 'I want a very strong active defense and not just a passive one… The enemy must be harassed at every opportunity. Reconnaissance must never be relaxed – especially at night. Positions must be wired and mined now.'[43]

Relations between Ward and Fredendall were rapidly worsening: 'F[redendall] and his staff continue to command this div[ision] in detail,' complained Ward privately. 'Even arranging platoons. Get no missions. Fed up.' A few days later, Fredendall told him to mind his own business after a request for photo-reconnaissance. Ward was enraged: 'He is a spherical SOB [son-of-a-bitch]. Two-faced at that.' Fredendall's tendency to hit the bottle also deeply offended Ward; on one visit to II Corps HQ he came across a paralytic Fredendall, surrounded by his cowering corps staff, unable to give orders: 'a drunk, a coward, and incompetent,' was how Ward summed him up. Others severely criticised included Anderson, merely 'a juggler of red arrows' (on situation maps) without any real fighting experience.[44] Some of Ward's own senior officers, hearing him sound off openly about the British, found it surprising and ill-advised, especially as word had filtered down from Eisenhower that such sentiments would not be tolerated.

Ward also had difficulty handling the activities of Brigadier-General Robinett who was 'not only smart but… a pretty dominant sort of guy.'[45] Determined to act as a semi-autonomous commander, Robinett was often criticised over his style of operations. Lieutenant-Colonel Simons thought he was a martinet, '[he] has a small man complex… a mean and difficult man,'[46] while Truscott later wrote of him as 'conceited' and one author termed him 'cocky.' Robinett was swift to reply:

'Self confidence can be confused with conceit or cockiness. The point of view of the observer determines that.'[47]

Troubled by the bewildering jumble of his command, Eisenhower decided to visit the front on 12 February. His main concern was how to meet von Arnim's attack which Mockler-Ferryman had told him would come through Fondouk and the thinness of the American line guarding the Allies' prime airfield at Thélepte, south of the village of Kasserine and just east of the Western Dorsale.

Guarded by a specially trained mechanized cavalry platoon, Eisenhower arrived at II Corps HQ where he discovered Fredendall's tunnelling efforts. Having warned against, 'our generals staying too close to their command posts', he was greatly annoyed and after Anderson had outlined his troop dispositions even more so: 'I had no idea at all that you had scattered the Americans in this fashion,' he snapped. 'The American people will take a good deal from me. But they won't take this even from me when they learn how you've scattered these troops of ours under British and French command.'[48] With this, Eisenhower started out on an all-night inspection of the front, accompanied by 'Red' Akers.

He saw men of 1st Armored, 1st Infantry and 34th Infantry Divisions, not yet battle-hardened, and spoke to their officers who had failed to grasp elementary tactical lessons of preparing defensive positions and mine-laying. Even more worrying was the dispersed nature of 1st Armored. Fredendall had ordered Ward to place defensive forces on two hills, just west of Faïd, which dominated the road to Sbeïtla. To the north, around and on Djebel Lessouda, sat Lieutenant-Colonel Waters's tanks, infantry and artillery, and in the south, on Djebel Ksaïra and on a smaller hill, Djebel Garet Hadid, Colonel Drake's 168th RCT, including untrained infantry, many of whom had arrived only days earlier and allegedly had never handled a bayonet or entrenching tool or even fired a rifle. Below them and to the west was a mobile armoured reserve force of 40 Sherman tanks commanded by Lieutenant-Colonel Hightower, who was to launch a counter-attack from Sidi bou Zid while Waters blocked any German attack through the Faïd Pass and Drake cut off enemy units moving up from Maknassy through the Maizila Pass in the south. Quite what Hightower should do if both passes came under attack had not been considered.

At 1st Armored's HQ Eisenhower talked at length with Ward, Robinett – who had come down from the north on his own initiative – and Schwartz, commander of French troops in the Sbeïtla area. Robinett brought further disturbing news. His reconnaissance troops had been right along the Eastern Dorsale in the French sector and witnessed no signs of an impending enemy attack through the Fondouk Pass.

Determined to bring to the C-in-C's attention other discrepancies, Robinett questioned the positioning of American troops on Djebels Lessouda and Ksaïra who might disastrously be cut off from CC A, straddling the wide gap between the two hills on the plain below. The same point was made when Eisenhower got to McQuillin's command post at Sbeïtla.

After pinning a Silver Star on Colonel Drake for his bravery in the recent operations around Sened Station, Eisenhower stepped out of his sedan; leaving behind his driver, Kay Summersby, he walked a short distance across the sands. Ahead, he could make out a black mountain mass, cut cleanly by the Faïd Pass. After a few moments for reflection Eisenhower turned away, as unaware as Anderson and Fredendall where the main thrust would come. At that very moment, only a few miles away on the other side, Ziegler's forces were moving to their assault positions.

<hr />

Notes to Chapter 9

[1] Bombardier J.E. Brooks, Letters. IWM 84/13/1.

[2] Moorehead, *African Trilogy*, p. 485.

[3] McCallum, *Journey with a Pistol*, p. 79.

[4] Pawle, *The War and Colonel Warden*, p. 229; Brigadier Jacob's notes for 4 February 1943, quoted by Gilbert, *Road to Victory*, p. 331.

[5] Eade, ed., *Onwards to Victory: War Speeches by the Right Hon. Winston S. Churchill*, p. 12.

[6] Quoted by Burdon, *24 Battalion*, p. 154.

[7] Leese to his wife, 5 February 1943. Leese Papers.

[8] Rainier, *Pipeline to Battle*, pp. 194–5. *Cf.* Bentwich and Kisch, *Brigadier Kisch: Soldier and Zionist*, pp. 178–9.

[9] Report 1 February 1943; Supplement to Kriegstagebuch Nr. 9, Dept. 1a, *DAK*; Outgoing messages, orders, etc. RH24-200/83 BAMA.

[10] Verney, *The Desert Rats*, pp. 149–51.

[11] Clay, *The Path of the 50th*, p. 113.

[12] See Lloyd Owen, *The Desert My Dwelling Place*, p. 261. He became commander of the LRDG in November 1943. Also of interest is his *Providence Their Guide: A Personal Account of the Long Range Desert Group 1940–45*.

[13] Leclerc was a pseudonym adopted by Vicomte Philippe de Hauteclocque to protect his family who were incarcerated in Picardy during the German occupation. With the rank of capitaine he fought with immense bravery in the Battle of France and escaped to London from where he was sent by de Gaulle to rally French Equatorial Africa. Later, he commanded with great distinction the crack French 2e Division Blindée.

[14] Lloyd Owen, 'Notes from Theatres of War LRDG'. IWM P219. The intelligence and topographical officer was W.B. Kennedy Shaw who later wrote *Long Range Desert Group 1940–43*, partly based on the 'Phase Reports' which he prepared at the time and which are reproduced by Lloyd Owen (later commander of the LRDG) in his 'Notes.' There was never any doubt about Lloyd Owen's admiration for Stirling: 'I have no doubt that David Stirling was a genius in the field of guerilla warfare.' *The Desert My Dwelling Place*, p. 112.

[15] Battle Report, 1 February 1943. RH19 – VIII/32.

[16] Cowles, *Who Dares, Wins: the Story of the Phantom Major*, p. 233.

[17] 'Tactical Report on Enemy Positions and Units', 10 February 1943; RH19-VIII/364.

[18] Cowles, *Who Dares, Wins*, p. 251.

[19] Stevens, in his *Bardia to Enfidaville*, gives the date as 27 January when Tinker set out. He fails to mention that Peniakoff accompanied the patrol and, as 'Popski' appears meticulous about dates in his account (though not always reliable in other details) I have preferred his version; see Peniakoff, *Popski's Private Army*, p. 298.

[20] Lloyd Owen, 'Notes from Theatres of War LRDG.'

[21] Messenger, *The Tunisian Campaign*, p. 44.

[22] Talbot, *Speaking from the Desert*, p. 129.

23 Ministry of Information, *The Army at War: Tunisia*, p. 18; Verney, *The Desert Rats*, p. 150.

24 Leese to his wife, 14 February 1943. Leese Papers.

25 Knight, *Historical Records of the Buffs*, p. 159; Verney, *loc.cit.*

26 Flight-Lieutenant E. Chadwick, letter home on 24 May 1943. IWM 85/30/1.

27 Onslow, *Men and Sand*, p. 108.

28 Patton Diary, entries for 14/15/17 February 1943.

29 Patton to Marshall, 22 February 1943. Marshall Papers, Box 79.

30 Greiner Diary notes, 16 February 1943; Detwiler *et al.*, *World War II German Military Studies*.

31 Recounted by Carell, *Foxes of the Desert*, p. 339. Horsfall correctly gives the name of Fischer's chief of staff as Bürker and says he was killed at the same time as his commander, see *The Wild Geese are Flighting*, p. 48. Carell is mistaken in naming him Bürklin.

32 Liddell Hart, *Rommel Papers*, p. 401.

33 Kesselring, 'Final Commentaries'; C-075.

34 Ambrosio replaced Cavallero as Chief of Staff of the Italian Armed Forces at *Comando Supremo* on 4 February 1943. Exchange of messages, Cavallero to Rommel, 2 February 1943; Rommel to Cavallero, same date; Ambrosio to Rommel, same date; Rommel to Ambrosio, 3 February 1943; RH19-VIII/40.

35 Noted by Rutherford, *Kasserine: Baptism of Fire*, p. 66.

36 Rommel's Orders for attack on Gafsa, 10 February 1943; RH24200/80. BA-MA.

37 Generalmajor Freiherr Kurt von Liebenstein, 'The Drive via Gafsa against Kasserine Pass', (1947), Detwiler *et al.*, *World War II German Military Studies*, IX, MS D-125.

38 Colonel J.O. Curtis interviewed by Dr Forrest Pogue, (n.d., *c.* 1947–8). OCMH Collection.

39 Hamilton, *Monty: Master of the Battlefield*, p. 144.

40 Hinsley, *British Intelligence*, II, pp. 582–3.

41 Anderson's remark to Dickson is from an interview with Colonel B.A. Dickson (13 December 1950), OCMH Collection, and his comments afterwards to Fredendall from a letter from Dickson to Hansen, 9 May 1949; Hansen Papers, Box 28 (a).

42 HQ 1st Infantry Division, Intelligence Notes, Memorandum from First Army, 7 February 1943; 1st US Infantry Division, Box 5679; World War II Operations Reports, USNA 301-2.1.

43 Copy in files of 1st Armored Division, 1942–1943; Ward Papers, Box 2. Emphasis shown is in original. Also quoted in full with slight variations from this copy by Howe, *Battle History of 1st Armored Division*, pp. 136–38.

44 Entries in Ward's diary, 29 January, 2 and 8 February 1943; also interview by Russell Gugeler with Lieutenant-General Gordon Sumner, April 1976, in which he mentions Ward told him of Fredendall's drunken behaviour at II Corps HQ. Ward Papers.

45 Hamilton H. Howze interviewed by Gugeler. Howze was Ward's G.3 Divisional Operations Officer and lost his post when Ward was relieved of his command. He went to 13th Armored Regiment where he talked his way into the 81st Armored Reconnaissance Battalion and fought with conspicuous bravery in tank engagements during May 1943.

46 Lieutenant-Colonel Robert Simons interviewed by Russell Gugeler; Ward Papers.

47 Brigadier-General P.M. Robinett, comments on Blumenson, *Kasserine Pass*; Robinett Papers, Box 6. Library of Congress.

48 Recounted by Bradley in conversation with Chester Hansen; Hansen Papers, Box 23. See also Eisenhower to Fredendall, 4 February 1943; Eisenhower Papers, Box 42.

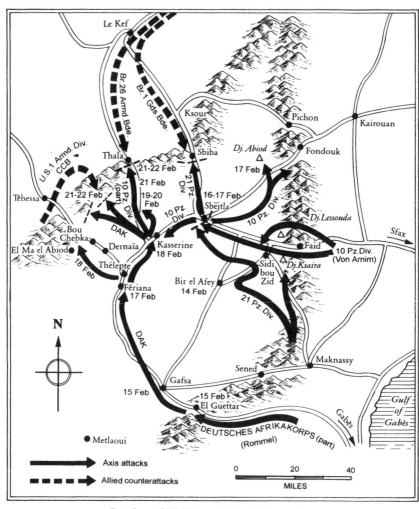

Le Kef

Br. 26 Armd. Bde.

Br. 1 Gds. Bde.

Ksour

Pichon

Kairouan

U.S. 1 Armd. Div. CCB

Thala

Sbiba

Dj. Abiod △

Fondouk

21-22 Feb

21 Feb

17 Feb

Tébessa

21-22 Feb

10 Pz. Div. (part)

19-20 Feb

16-17 Feb

Sbeïtla

10 Pz. Div.

Dj. Lessouda

Sfax

10 Pz. Div.

DAK

Bou Chebka

Dernaïa

Kasserine

18 Feb

Faid

Dj. Ksaira △

10 Pz. Div. (Von Arnim)

El Ma el Abiod

Thélepte

18 Feb

Sidi bou Zid

Bir el Afey

14 Feb

21 Pz. Div.

Fériana

17 Feb

N

DAK

Maknassy

Sened

Gafsa

15 Feb

15 Feb

El Guettar

Gabès

Gulf of Gabès

Metlaoui

DEUTSCHES AFRIKAKORPS (part)
(Rommel)

→ Axis attacks

⇢ Allied counterattacks

0   20   40

MILES

Battles of Sidi bou Zid and Kasserine
February 1943

Chapter 10

I Know Panic When I See It

'Dabney, open up the bottle. Let's have a drink.'

Major-General Fredendall to his chief of staff at the height of the Kasserine Pass crisis, February 1943.[1]

Before dawn broke on St Valentine's Day, 14 February 1943, the defenders on Lessouda and Ksaïra heard the unmistakable sounds of approaching armour. All along the Allied front a message had been flashed from First Army HQ warning of an immediate German attack. This was based on Enigma decrypts showing that Fifth Panzer Army was about to open its offensive, but Anderson still firmly believed this would come at Fondouk with a diversionary move virtually anywhere. However, as the sun rose in a great ball of fire above the Faïd Pass, gigantic Tigers, supported by lorried infantry and anti-tank guns came nosing through a violent sandstorm, firing and then deploying. Operation *Frühlingswind* was under way.

Troops of 7th Panzer Regiment and 86th Panzer Grenadier Regiment (10th Panzer Division), comprising Group *Gerhardt*, moved to encircle Djebel Lessouda from the north while others, with Tigers, headed south-west. Waters's small tank force sent to block the northern advance was brushed aside while German aircraft, in what was to be the first of day-long raids, devastated Sidi bou Zid. Hardly any American air defence had got off the ground.

Before 1000 hours, Waters was completely surrounded and Louis V. Hightower's tanks were sent in to 'clear up the situation.' They met Group *Gerhardt* as another German tank force, Group *Reimann*, was cutting past Lessouda on its southern side in a drive from Faïd straight for Sidi bou Zid. Greatly outnumbered and outranged by the Germans, Hightower radioed McQuillin that he could put in no more than a delaying attack. In the meantime, Group *Gerhardt* had paused after encircling Djebel Lessouda and waited near the Faïd–Sbeïtla road hoping for sight of mobile elements of 21st Panzer, with 91 tanks, which had travelled northwards along the Eastern Dorsale. After disgorging from the Maizila Pass, Group *Schütte* drove northwards from Maknassy to outflank Sidi bou Zid and Group *Stenckhoff* moved west and then north-east to attack the village from the rear. McQuillin telephoned Ward for help but Ward thought only a local attack might be in progress. Nevertheless, Lieutenant-Colonel Kern was sent with 1st Battalion, 6th Armoured Infantry, and a company of Stuart tanks, to take up a blocking position along a defensive line running through an intersection on the Faïd–Sbeïtla highway, known thereafter as 'Kern's Crossroads'.

By mid-morning, Hightower's tanks were heavily engaged in stubborn resistance in the north as Schütte and Stenckhoff began their moves from the south. Drake reported that he had counted 83 German tanks around Djebel Lessouda and that men were abandoning their artillery positions and deserting the battlefield in panic. 'You don't know what you're saying,' McQuillin told him curtly. 'They're only shifting positions.' 'Shifting positions, hell,' Drake radioed. 'I know panic when I see it.'[2]

At noon the enemy was right on top of CC A Command Post, forcing McQuillin to shift several times south-westwards, harassed by German dive-bombing and slowed by much sediment and water which had mysteriously appeared in the fuel tanks of his thin-skinned armoured vehicles.

Schütte's tank force had been delayed by soft sand on its drive from the Maizila Pass. Ziegler therefore,ordered Groups *Reimann* and *Gerhardt* to carry out the attack on Sidi bou Zid from the north-east while Group *Stenckhoff* moved up during the afternoon, troubled by enemy mobile patrols but able to make contact eventually with 10th Panzer Division. On Djebels Lessouda, Ksaïra and Garet Hadid, the defenders were totally marooned in a sea of German troops, but under orders from higher authority Ward refused to order their retreat – though promising a counter-attack next day to relieve them.

By late afternoon much of McQuillin's CC A had been badly mauled. Had it not been for Hightower's stubborn resistance even more of 1st Armored might have been overrun for, abandoned on the plain between Faïd and Kern's Crossroads, were wrecked and burning field and anti-tank guns, 59 half-tracks, over 20 trucks and 44 tanks.

One of these tanks was Sergeant Basker Bennet's Sherman. He had been in the thick of the fighting with 1st Armored Regiment in front of the Faïd Pass until two 75mm shells winged their way through the turret and set his tank on fire. 'I called down to the driver and radio man but they must have been hit because they didn't answer,' said Bennet. 'The tank was burning badly now so I jumped out with the remainder of the crew.' Crouching in a ditch the survivors watched the stricken vehicle trundle on with its dead for hundreds of yards before burning out completely. After hiding for several hours as the battle raged about them, Bennet and his men were forced to surrender when a German tank threatened to crush them in their trench. 'Where is your carrier?' asked the tank commander, in excellent English. Pointing to the burned-out wreck, they explained what had happened. To their immense surprise they were directed back to their own lines; 'We took off quickly', added Bennet.[3]

Through the heat and smoke as he retreated from Sidi bou Zid in a general exodus across the desert, Sergeant Clarence W. Coley, another of Hightower's men, could see half-tracks, Jeeps, motorcycles and trucks, all moving in the same general direction. By the time they reached safety Hightower was left with just seven serviceable tanks.

———•◦◦•———

On his way back to Algiers, Eisenhower learned of the Faïd Pass attack at Fredendall's HQ. There he was assured that it was limited in extent, involved only 21st Panzer and could comfortably be handled by CC A. With no apparent cause for alarm, he only heard of the disaster at Sidi bou Zid late in the afternoon of St Valentine's Day when he arrived at Constantine.

Anderson, still not ready to disregard Mockler-Ferryman's firm prediction of a more northerly attack and having no Enigma information that 10th Panzer – with its 111 medium tanks and a dozen Tigers – had been committed, refused to release Robinett's CC B for it to move south and bolster Ward's severely damaged forces. Ward himself remained, 'calm and level-headed and optimistic,' according to his aide, Captain Ernest C. Hatfield on 15 February: 'Germans really got us bad yesterday but we hope to retaliate today. Three more days like yesterday and they can scratch the 1st A D off the books.'[4]

During the evening of 14/15 February, Ward began preparations for a counter-attack to relieve Waters and Drake and asked Fredendall for assistance. He ordered Colonel Stack's CC C southwards after dark to Kern's Crossroads where it was joined by Lieutenant-Colonel Alger's 2nd Battalion, 1st Armored Regiment, which had been with CC B under First Army command.

Alger had 54 brand new Shermans, supported by tank destroyers, armoured infantry and field artillery but his mission was far beyond the means available. His battalion had no battle experience and only a very hazy idea of what lay ahead of it; even the maps available were of the wrong scale. Lying in wait were over 100 German tanks, carefully deployed by Ziegler, led by capable and experienced commanders who knew exactly how to ambush the inexperienced Americans.[5] Anti-tank guns had been set up in cactus patches beyond Sidi bou Zid, among houses in the town and behind hedges. As Robinett remarked, the attackers were, 'like lambs... entering an unknown and difficult terrain infested with wolves familiar with the area.'[6]

In the early hours of 15 February, Alger's battalion set off across the plain towards Djebels Ksaïra and Lessouda. One tank destroyer platoon was dive-bombed and brought to a halt but the rest carried on until they reached the second of several steep-sided and damp wadis. Bunching together on a single crossing the leading tanks hesitated under accurate gunfire and air attacks and ran straight into the German ambush. Having observed the axis of Alger's advance, the Germans had sent part of their armour to the north-east of Sidi bou Zid and another to the south-west: as the pincers closed intensive fire poured into the Shermans from the flanks, penetrating their thinner side armour. Caught in the trap the battalion was scattered and reduced to a series of wrecked and fiercely burning hulks. Realizing that Alger was never going to reach Djebel Ksaïra by nightfall, Stack informed Ward and soon after radioed Alger to ask how he was doing. 'Still pretty busy,' was the unflustered reply.[7]

By 1540 hours the armoured infantry had been forced to make a run for safety in order to avoid German tanks coming up rapidly from the south. The 68th Field Artillery Battalion, after being surrounded, managed to march westward and reached safety after dark. Pounded by artillery and dive-bombers the remains of Alger's battalion, without Alger himself who had been taken prisoner, struggled back towards their rallying area at Kern's Crossroads. Only four of the new Shermans returned with a few dismounted crews. Fifty tanks were lost. Two months later when the area was re-captured, it was seen that all but one, which had broken down, had been badly holed.[8] The battalion had virtually been annihilated, with 15 officers and 298 men listed as missing in action.

Late that evening Ward still had little idea what had happened: 'We might have walloped them or they might have walloped us,' he radioed Fredendall.[9] By the light of burning vehicles, Germans were out on the battlefield, salvaging what they could. 'Plenty of booty,' reported one soldier, 'No sleep all night. I was on guard over prisoners of war and helped to load wounded Americans onto ambulances.'[10] German casualties had been relatively light – 100 men, up to 20 Mk IV tanks and five 88mm guns, together with various other artillery pieces and trucks. To Ziegler's men went the honours and a set of captured documents giving in full the US order of battle. For 1st Armored the action had been a catastrophe; in 48 hours the best part of two tank battalions and much divisional artillery had been destroyed; and those troops stuck on the hills around Sidi bou Zid still awaited their grim fate.

When Hightower's tanks had been mostly destroyed on the open plain the previous day, Lieutenant-Colonel Waters sent his driver to inform Major Robert R. Moore, commander of 2nd Battalion, 168th Infantry (34th Infantry Division), of his intention to withdraw. Before long, the driver was back, ashen faced, in great pain, with a gaping hole in his chest. He had been shot by a jittery American patrol. Waters was later captured by a German patrol, probably brought in by Arabs; they were methodically stripping the body of his driver as he was marched to a mobile HQ. He was sent eventually to Oflag VIIB at Eichstätt in Germany where the guards kept a close eye on Patton's son-in-law.[11]

Orders to bring out the entrapped Americans were dropped by aircraft on Djebel Lessouda where command had devolved upon Major Moore. He was faced with the difficult task of getting nearly 650 men (the rest of the battalion were with Drake on Djebel Ksaïra) and a number of prisoners across the enemy-infested plain to Kern's Crossroads. Early on the morning of 16 February, he reached there hugging his sleeping bag having carried it all the way: 'The Germans could have my tin hat,' he said, 'but I wasn't going to give them my English fleabag.'[12] Gradually, nearly 300 men arrived, some still guarding their prisoners.

The troops isolated on Djebel Ksaïra and Garet Hadid had a longer line of retreat which took them close to Sidi bou Zid. Orders to withdraw were sent by radio and airdropped on the night of 16/17 February. They had been relentlessly pounded by German attacks and were completely out of food and short of water.

When daybreak came the enemy spotted them on the open plain, well short of the protecting slopes of Djebel el Hamra. Encircling the exhausted men with armoured and motorized troops, the Germans cut them to pieces with heavy machine-gun fire. The 1,400 or so who survived were driven into large cactus patches and the great majority captured. Amongst the prisoners was Colonel Drake, who ended up at Eichstätt with Waters and Lieutenant-Colonel Alger.

As the scale of the German attack in the south gradually became clear, Anderson was fearful that the whole of his forces might be outflanked. Unable to concentrate an adequate blocking force forward of Sbiba and Sbeïtla he decided, on the evening of 15 February, with Eisenhower's approval, to pull back in 24 hours time and establish a new line for II Corps to hold on the Western Dorsale, running from Sbiba south to Sbeïtla and then south-west through Kasserine to Fériana.

Orders were also issued for the evacuation of Gafsa, in order to shorten the most southerly part of the Allied front. The Americans pulled out hurriedly on the night of 15/16 February in drenching rain amidst crowds of bedraggled and frightened civilians who clogged the narrow road to Fériana, 40 miles to the northwest. Several prostitutes, known as the 'Gafsa girls,' were among the evacuees. One officer, 'credited with the rescue, received high praise from all sides for this supreme devotion to duty,' noted Captain Webb, who added, 'The girls themselves made no comment.'[13]

Hard on the heels of 1st US Ranger Battalion as it fled, elements of Grenadier Regiment *Afrika* and the Italian *Centauro* Division occupied the town without a shot being fired. Meanwhile, infected by the mood of defeatism and despair, American troops had begun demolitions at Fériana where a mixed force under Colonel Alexander N. Stark prepared to regain Gafsa when the enemy had been dealt a decisive blow elsewhere.

A key objective of Operation *Morgenluft* had been achieved before *DAK*'s Group *Liebenstein* had even been able to mount its attack. This persuaded Rommel to send reconnaissance troops to strike at Fériana and Thélepte airfields, which Eisenhower admitted were 'impressive in extent' and of great value to the Allies. At the same time Rommel sent his *Kampfstaffel* south-west, to Metlaoui, with instructions to blow up a railway tunnel and take the village. There they discovered hidden American stores of precious fuel and railway trucks.

Rommel had urged von Arnim to follow up the success at Sidi bou Zid by capturing Sbeïtla, where engineers had blown up a huge ammunition dump before leaving, but Ziegler's troops paused on the morning of 16 February while Kesselring's permission was sought for their advance. This allowed time for Robinett's CC B (which First Army had released) to reach the remote wind-swept, arid plain on which Sbeïtla stood.

In the north, 21st Panzer still lay under von Arnim's command; since Gafsa had fallen he assumed Rommel had no need of its support. Furthermore, he had dissipated his forces by despatching 10th Panzer on a wild goose chase after Koeltz's XIX Corps, which had been given permission by Anderson to withdraw from the Eastern Dorsale and retire to Sbiba. Unable to cut them off, the Panzers found themselves pursuing shadows in the scrubland around Fondouk and Pichon.

Not until the night of 16/17 February did von Arnim resume his attack when, under a pale moon rimmed with frost, three parallel columns of Group *Gerhardt* and Group *Pfeiffer* (21st Panzer) advanced on CC A which had just taken up positions at the edge of extensive olive groves, three miles east of Sbeïtla, after falling back from near Kern's Crossroads. As the Germans manoeuvred to attack, they set off a barrage of rocket flares and rifle fire at extreme range, worrying the inexperienced Americans and igniting supply dumps near McQuillin's CP. Some troops stampeded and scattered a group of minelayers from CC B holding positions to the south and south-east of the town.

There followed a wild flight to the rear as soldiers and vehicles stampeded in an irresistible panicking mass, hastened by the sounds of gunfire and explosions as engineers burned all fuel, oil, rations and ammunition. At around 2030 hours, a colossal explosion announced that the pump house on the aqueduct to Sfax had been demolished; this was mistaken for evidence of increased enemy activity which strained to breaking point the nerves of the exhausted, confused soldiers.

A few units did stand and fight, including tanks commanded by Hightower and Lieutenant-Colonel Crosby (CO of 3rd Battalion, 13th Armored Regiment). Together with elements of CC A artillery they fought off the German attack but, thinking his defence line had been pierced, Ward contacted II Corps. Anderson became thoroughly alarmed and authorized the evacuation of both Sbeïtla and Fériana on the morning of the 17th. Ironically enough, just as Ward was radioing the bad news to II Corps HQ, Ziegler – who displayed a fumbling, tentative handling of armour throughout the operation – was informing von Arnim that Sbeïtla was heavily defended and was consequently told to wait until morning before attacking the town.

When dawn broke the retreat westwards had not subsided and there were numerous violations of radio security as many troop dispositions and intentions were radioed in clear.[14] CC B's tanks, camouflaged with wet clay smeared on their plates, had orders to hold their position as long as possible to cover this retreat while, further north, a reorganized CC C shielded the town which was shaken periodically by inexpert demolitions, unplanned and uncoordinated.

On the morning of the same day, Hauptmann Meyer's 2nd Battalion of Special Group 288 led the advance of von Liebenstein's Kampfgruppe along the tarred road leading from Gafsa to Fériana which was to be evacuated by the Americans as the Allied line swung westwards on its southern hinge. In the lead was Oberleutnant Schmidt's company accompanied by heavy Panzerjäger ('tank hunters' – self-propelled anti-tank guns) and engineers with mine detectors. Although shelled by artillery and, despite the miserable weather, dive-bombed by units of the US XII Air Support Command, they reached Fériana just as the last Americans were withdrawing.

From out of the houses poured men, women and children; they were, wrote Schmidt, 'waving and shouting in the false jubilation which these people always accorded any apparently victorious troops.'[15] At the Thélepte airfields they discovered the smashed remains of 34 unserviceable aircraft which the Americans had been unable to fly out and a towering cloud of smoke billowing from 60,000 gallons of fuel and burning airport facilities. Tacked on a dugout door was a newspaper map of the latest Russian offensive.[16] The effect was lost on von Liebenstein who had been wounded by a mine at Fériana; command of the *DAK* Kampfgruppe had that morning been turned over to Generalmajor Karl Bülowius.[17]

Further north at Sbeïtla, CC B under Robinett began a methodical and skilful withdrawal at 1530 hours, using three routes south of the town. There was sharp fighting for 2nd Battalion, 13th Armoured Regiment, which lost ten tanks including that of its commander, Colonel Gardiner, who was wounded and his driver killed. Eventually, what remained of 1st Armored reached the village of Kasserine, passed north-westward through the Kasserine Pass and stopped south-east of Tébessa, blocking the road from Fériana. There, concealed in a wooded area, the division began to recuperate from its staggering losses of the past four days: 2,500 casualties, 112 medium tanks, ten tank destroyers, 16 self-propelled 105s and five 75mm howitzers as well as 280 other vehicles. 1st Armored had been reduced, on its own estimation, to not more than 50 per cent combat efficiency.[18]

Rommel now half-embraced the distinct possibility of a huge strategic surprise – though always with one eye on Montgomery's advance to the Mareth Line – which involved a concerted attack by forces formerly engaged in *Frühlingswind* and *Morgenluft* through the Western Dorsale and on to the great Allied centre of Tébessa. From there the way would be clear for a drive northwards, deep into the rear of First Army as far as Bône, forcing the Allies on to the defensive, delaying their preparations for offensive operations and forcing them to think of abandoning Tunisia altogether.

Some steadying influence in the Allied ranks was badly needed. On 16 February a 'Most Secret' message was flashed from Brooke to Alexander: 'Eisenhower making urgent enquiries whether you arrive Algiers as expected 17 Feb. Consider your presence to give confidence most important.'[19]

On taking up his command two days later Alexander thought the general situation, 'far from satisfactory. British, American and French units,' he explained to Brooke, 'are all mixed up on the front, especially in the south. Formations have been split up. There is no policy and no plan of campaign. The air is much the same. This is the result of no firm direction or centralized control from above... We have quite definitely lost the initiative.'[20]

To exploit his temporary advantage Rommel requested support for the thrust on Tébessa but von Arnim replied firmly that 21st and 10th Panzer Divisions were occupied in the Sbeïtla and Fondouk areas.[21] Due to a desperate lack of ammunition and fuel, no troops could go forward of the Eastern Dorsale unless they depended on captured supplies because deliveries promised from Italy were so uncertain.[22] Nevertheless, on learning of the Allied withdrawal Rommel signalled to *Comando Supremo* and Kesselring his intention to make for Tébessa with 10th and 21st Panzer under his own command. That message was not decrypted by Allied intelligence until the afternoon of the 19th.[23]

In the very early hours of that day, however, Rommel was ordered to undertake a softer tactical option. While von Arnim was to carry out holding attacks in the north, *Comando Supremo* rather ambivalently ordered Rommel to strike at Thala and thence to Le Kef, though it did not specifically limit him to this move. This 'appalling and unbelievable piece of shortsightedness,' caused by a want of boldness and 'lack of guts,' raged Rommel,[24] threatened to undo the greater strategic enveloping movement and run his thrust line too close to the Allied front, exposing it to their reserves. Knowing that only by retaining an element of surprise could he break up the Americans' assembly areas, he decided to move at once on Thala.

Sending a message to von Arnim requesting armoured units be placed formally under his control – von Arnim refused claiming, untruthfully, that many tanks were under repair and kept the Tigers for himself – Rommel ordered 21st Panzer to advance through the Western Dorsale at Sbiba on to Ksour while 10th Panzer concentrated at Sbeïtla, ready to support the success of either 21st Panzer or *DAK Kampfgruppe*, which was to take the Kasserine Pass, 25 miles south-east of Sbiba. Meanwhile, during this time of Axis indecision, Anderson had ordered his troops to hold Tébessa, the plain between Le Kef and Thala, the Sbiba Pass and all the main exits westwards into Algeria from Tunisia. Alexander, newly arrived, agreed.

In the Sbiba area – nominally under command of Koeltz's XIX Corps but actually under control of First Army – was much of Keightley's 6th Armoured Division together with 1st Guards Brigade from 78th Division, 18th RCT from Allen's 1st Infantry Division, three battalions of 34th US Infantry Division, three American field artillery battalions, parts of the 72nd and 93rd Anti-Tank Regiments (RA) and, in the north, the French Light Armoured Brigade under Saint-Didier and a small unit, Detachment *Guinet*.

Fifty-five miles away, 1st Armored around Tébessa was re-organizing and bracing itself for further action. 'Pinky' Ward was co-ordinating his plans with General Welvert to defend the passes at Dernaïa, Bou Chebka and El Ma el Abiod. Artillery support was to be given to the defenders of the Kasserine Pass, where Lieutenant-Colonel Moore commanded 26th RCT, elements of the 19th Combat Engineer Regiment, 33rd Field Artillery Battalion, 805th Tank Destroyer Battalion and a battery of 75mm guns from the French 67th African Artillery.

At Thala, where a threat might develop towards Le Kef from the Kasserine Pass, Brigadier Charles Dunphie's 26th Armoured Brigade (less 16th/5th Lancers held in support of the Guards at Sbiba) awaited the hurried arrival of 2/5th Leicestershire Regiment (139th Brigade) which had only just landed in North Africa. The 2nd Lothians were ordered to Thala which involved an unremitting 35 hours of continuous driving shared between the crew members.

By infilling, patching and intermingling of units Anderson strove to meet the coming onslaught. The cost was a blurred command structure, confused responsibilities, and a deluge of adjustments virtually overwhelming Fredendall's CP, which had been moved from its rock-hewn safety in 'Speedy Valley' to La

Konif. On the other hand, when Rommel put in a probing reconnaissance at the Kasserine Pass on the evening of 18 February, which alerted Fredendall to an imminent attack, he had little idea of the opposing forces. Some locations, like that of 6th Armoured Division at Sbiba, had been established by radio intercepts; the whereabouts of much of 1st Armored together with parts of 1st and 34th US Infantry Divisions were roughly known but the exact position of their various elements could not be ascertained.[25]

Perturbed by these reconnaissance activities, Fredendall telephoned Colonel Stark: 'I want you to go to Kasserine Pass right away and pull a Stonewall Jackson. Take over up there.' Stark was amazed: 'You mean tonight General?' 'Yes immediately.'[26] In fog and swamping rain, Stark relieved Moore at the pass, 2,000 feet above the Sbeïtla plain, dominated on the right by Djebel Semmama (4,447ft) and on the left by the highest peak in Tunisia, Djebel Chambi (5,064ft). A metalled road from Kasserine, some five miles away, bisected the pass, emerging on the western side to cross the huge basin of scrub, cactus and low outcrops of rock whose clay soils became gluey in wet weather, known as the Bled Foussana, and so northwards to Thala. A southern unmetalled branch ran off from a fork just east of the narrows to Djebel el Hamra where a trail led towards Tébessa. Both main road and railway crossed the Hatab River, no more than a stream in the bed of the pass, on a bridge which Moore's engineers had already destroyed.

A triple belt of mines was laid across both roads, shortly after they forked and more demolitions in the narrows of the pass were intended to stop enemy armour at the eastern end, which Moore planned to discourage still further by using his own artillery. Much of his infantry was astride the road to Thala and his engineers, desperately short on combat experience, blocked the minor road; 2,000 more troops held a thin line astride the two roads extending three miles across the Bled Foussana, covering the exit from the pass whose heights on both sides were defended only by patrols.

When leading troops of the famed Aufklärungsabteilung 3 (Reconnaissance Battalion 3) from the *DAK* Kampfgruppe first appeared, not all defensive measures had been completed and the general plan, to compress the attackers into a narrow channel and destroy them there, was not understood by many of Moore's troops.[27] So green were the engineers that their first sight of the enemy, on the afternoon of 18 February, set some off in panic to the rear from where they had to be rounded up and returned to their posts.

It was on Sbiba as well as Kasserine that Rommel's double-handed attack fell during the morning of the 19th. Generalmajor Hildebrandt's 21st Panzer was committed towards Sbiba but was badly delayed by waterlogged roads and mines. Indeed, so bad was the weather that neither side could fly air support, which was marginally to Rommel's advantage for his men had to advance with little cover. Running into rather more determined opposition than expected, Hildebrandt's tanks were shelled unmercifully by defenders who occupied the high ground, despite having their dispositions given away by Arabs. An outflanking move eastwards was rebuffed by infantry of 34th Division, though 16th/5th Lancers in support lost four tanks.

Around the Kasserine Pass, Stark's undermanned defences held out as well. The Germans' 3rd Reconnaissance Battalion suddenly attempted a breakthrough at daybreak but the defenders had been alerted by British intelligence officers attached to II Corps. They flung back the attack and so Bülowius committed Gruppe *Menton*, made up from two battalions of the Panzer Grenadier Regiment *Afrika*, to work its way along both sides of the road through the pass.

Above them, two companies from Special Group 288 were detailed to gain the dominating heights. Led by Oberleutnants Schmidt and Bucholz, these veterans scaled soaring cliff faces and ridges, skilfully avoiding American artillery and small arms fire. Far below, however, Oberst Menton had underestimated both the Americans and the particular demands of mountain warfare by confining the main body of his troops to the bed of the pass. His attack collapsed.

On his way to Sbiba, Rommel arrived at *DAK* Kampfgruppe HQ at 1300 hours and ordered Bülowius to put in an outflanking attack. In mid-afternoon, a powerful force of infantry and tanks ran into American minefields on their northern approach and were then hit by shells, anti-tank rounds and machine-gun fire. Another effort from the west failed when American engineers fought back and knocked out five tanks. Meanwhile Hildebrandt was urged to punch a narrow corridor through the Allied defences, but accurate shooting by British 6-pounder anti-tank guns left 12 German tanks smouldering, while 25-pounders shot up the self-propelled guns behind, hurling them from their mountings and killing their crews.[28] It was not until darkness fell that 21st Panzer got to the outskirts of Sbiba at last, only then to be pulled back to a defensive line about seven miles south of the town.

Kesselring arrived at von Arnim's HQ to find out exactly what had happened in Operation *Frühlingswind*, suspecting that 10th Panzer had not been released, in turn limiting Rommel's scope for movement. Rejecting von Arnim's alternative proposals for an attack on Le Kef he radioed urgently to Rommel, ordering him to disregard *Comando Supremo* and make for the important nerve centre of Tébessa which could be by-passed in an enveloping attack. The next day he flew to the forward HQ of Kampfgruppe *DAK* north-west of Kasserine amidst a blanket of fog and swirling sandstorms.[29]

Hearing the sounds of the Kasserine battle from 35 miles away at Thala, the commander of 26th Armoured Brigade, Brigadier Dunphie, hurried to see Stark who seemed confident that the German attack could be held. Dunphie was alarmed at what he took to be the imminent breakdown of Stark's defences and told Anderson that a counter-attack should be mounted but, with few reserves other than two poorly armed regiments of tanks, Anderson instead sent his Brigadier General Staff, Colin McNabb – killed two months later in the struggle for Longstop Hill – to review the situation.

Everything seemed quiet enough but, concealed by the night of 19/20 February, Bülowius' troops had encircled and captured one pocket of American defenders and scared off a company of engineers who, not for the first time, broke in panic. Knowing nothing of these developments, there seemed to McNabb no cause for immediate alarm. Fredendall sent Stark the 3rd Battalion, 6th Armored

Infantry and, while retaining Dunphie's 26th Armoured as insurance against any attack at Thala, allowed him to send forward a small detachment commanded by Lieutenant-Colonel Gore of 10th Rifle Brigade and known naturally as 'Gore Force,' which took up a position towards the pass that same night.[30]

No one knew who exactly commanded which forces. Increasingly angry with the hapless Ward, Fredendall telephoned Truscott to insist on something drastic being done; 1st Armored was, 'in a state of utter confusion', and he doubted if the 'present incumbent can cut the mustard.'[31] He also reported to Eisenhower that Ward, 'appears tired and worried and has informed me that to bring new tanks in would be the same as turning them over to the Germans.' Under these circumstances he needed someone 'with two fists immediately,' and suggested Truscott.[32]

Events were now moving even further beyond Ward's control. Robinett received orders directly from II Corps – thereby gratuitously by-passing Ward – on 20 February to move his CC B from El Ma el Abiod Pass through Thala towards Kasserine in order to relieve Stark. This added to Ward's worries for, as well as Fredendall's hostility towards him, he now believed that Robinett, too, was trying to stab him in the back and have him removed from his command. Here was a sure recipe for disaster.

With both points of his attack stalled, Rommel had decided to focus the weight of his assault on the Kasserine Pass and, through the mist and dampness of 20 February, 20th Panzer Grenadiers and crack Italian mountain troops of the 5th Bersaglieri Battalion (*Centauro* Division) attacked fiercely at 0830 hours under cover of a huge artillery barrage. For the first time, the troops of Gore Force heard the terrifying howl of the German *Nebelwerfers*, multi-barrelled rocket launchers capable of firing six heavy high explosive shells in 90 seconds. Nevertheless, even as Stark's control disintegrated, Gore Force was successful in slowing the German attack along the Thala side of the pass.

Again in touch with von Broich, Rommel was furious at the delay in committing 10th Panzer which had been brought up. But 19th US Engineers on the Tébessa side of the pass were in serious trouble: 'Enemy overrunning our CP,' radioed Moore at noon. Increasing pressure from two battalions of 10th Panzer, now committed behind 21st Panzer and the Bersaglieri, eventually unhinged the American defence which fell to pieces. At the head of 1st Battalion, 8th Panzer Regiment, Hauptmann Hans-Günter Stotten broke through the pass towards Djebel el Hamra, where CC B was arriving from its position in reserve at El Ma el Abiod.[33]

Near Haidra, 20 miles north-east of Tébessa, Robinett met Fredendall, who had driven back from the Kasserine Pass, unsure and gloomily pessimistic: 'There is no use Robbie,' he said, 'they have broken through and you can't stop them.' Robinett's reply was typically pugnacious: 'Well, God damn it, general, we'll go down and try.' Fredendall seemed relieved that someone was going to make a stand: 'If you stop them this time, Robbie, I'll make you a Field Marshal.' Robinett said, 'I took this remark more as a gesture of confidence in me and my command than anything else,' adding, 'It was just as well I did.' Robinett now commanded all forces south of the Hatab River, while Dunphie controlled those to the north.[34]

To its eternal credit a stand was being made by Gore Force which withdrew slowly towards Thala, fighting all the way. Superbly marshalled by Major A.N. Beilby, who was killed later in the day, the seven Valentine and four Crusader tanks of C Squadron, 2nd Lothians, heavily outranged but hull down in wadis, withstood the German self-propelled guns all afternoon. After all the tanks had been destroyed, the surviving crew members withdrew through the 17th/21st Lancers, covered by six American Lee tanks. Four of these were set alight and in the fiery glare from their blazing hulks all the British 6-pounder guns were wrecked, though the 25-pounders managed to escape.

The shattered remnants of Stark Force had already broken off hostilities and got away in small groups towards Djebel el Hamra. Completely unblooded previously in combat, they had managed to hold Rommel's veterans for 72 hours but, unable to account for nearly 400 men and with another 100 wounded, they had had enough. At Stark's CP, Major Conway witnessed their collapse: 'That night, rain, cold and all, they just streamed back along the road there in the dark and I talked to several and asked them, "What's going on?" And they didn't know where they were going, they knew... [only] – to the rear. They lightened their loads is what they called it – they got rid of them.'[35]

Eventually they were stopped and turned round by Stark's own efforts or by Robinett's CC B making its way to the front but with the pass now in German hands the situation was critical – would Rommel now make for Tébessa or Thala? About to pay the price of the original blunder was the unfortunate Mockler-Ferryman. That same day, General Paget (C-in-C Home Forces) set out from London for Eisenhower's HQ to handle, 'the replacement of Mock in such a manner that he will not be discredited... However, Ike insists we need a G-2 who is never satisfied with his information,' noted Butcher, 'who procures it with spies, reconnaissance, and any means available.'[36] In March, Brigadier Kenneth Strong arrived to take over.

Allied intelligence officers were tolerably certain that Rommel would strike for Thala and confirmation of this was received at midnight on 20/21 February from a decrypt of an intercepted *Comando Supremo* order.[37] Poised to advance from the Kasserine Pass, Rommel was nervous of a counter-attack and uncharacteristically hesitant which gave the Allies a few welcome hours of breathing space during which the untrained 2/5th Leicesters were trucked in to hold a final defensive line four miles south of Thala. Seeing them digging in after being on the move for 48 hours one of Eisenhower's staff, Major Conway, who had no idea just how raw they were, was impressed: 'I talked to some of the Britishers... just digging there, the shells are flying and all that, and all they are doing is spitting on their hands and using the pick and shovel. The whole damn battalion just digging in. The Americans hadn't thought of that... or at least they didn't demonstrate they had.'[38]

Hurrying from Morocco was the 9th US Division's artillery, driving over 800 miles in four days; further reinforcements were struggling over appalling roads from Sbiba – where Hildebrandt's Panzers had failed again to break through determined American defences – but as a result of the deepening crisis at Kasserine, the whole Allied command organization was becoming ever more cumbersome. 1st Armored HQ believed that Robinett had been given control of all forces at the pass. However, Fredendall had also ordered Terry Allen to assume control of the entire area south of Foussana, from Djebel Chambi to El Ma el Abiod. In the meantime, Dunphie had also been ordered to combine the action of his own 26th Armoured Brigade, CC B and the remains of Stark force, although he had neither the staff nor signals organisation to do so.

Anderson, thoroughly alarmed by the evening of the 20th, decided to by-pass Fredendall, who seemed increasingly out of touch, and appointed Brigadier Cameron Nicholson to command the entire Allied effort north-west of the pass, under the name 'Nick Force.' This was a curious decision. Nicholson, unhurried and courteous, was older and second-in-command to Keightley (6th Armoured) who would have been the natural choice. Nicholson's own 2i/c was Colonel Dick Hull, former commander of Blade Force. There were now so many overlapping responsibilities that the Allied command structure was in severe danger of overload.

———————

Knowing the strength of the enemy's forces from papers captured the previous day and reasoning that a double thrust from the Kasserine Pass would divide and weaken the opposition, Rommel took a crucial decision on the 21st to split his attack; von Broich's 10th Panzer was to advance on Thala and Bülowius' Kampfgruppe on Djebel el Hamra – leading to Tébessa – while Hildebrandt's Panzers remained on the defensive to prevent Allied troops reinforcing from the north.[39]

At a commanders' conference held by McNabb late the previous day it was decided that Robinett would cover the passes to Tébessa and Haidra (though the boundary between his area of command and that of Terry Allen to the south was vague) while the road across the ridges to Thala was to be held by Dunphie; the Hatab River defined their adjacent areas. A single push on either axis by Rommel's forces could thereby be attacked from either flank.

The advance on Thala and Djebel el Hamra dissipated Rommel's strength though far away to the north, around Béja, British troops were thoroughly shaken by the sight of Jeeps hastening through from Kasserine, their windscreens smeared and clotted with blood.[40] As one officer remarked, on that 'Panic Sunday,' while German reconnaissance units probed the American and British defences, 'Oflag [POW] bags [were] being packed.'[41]

Through the rising mist of early morning, Kampfgruppe *DAK* led again by two battalions of Special Group 288, pushed along a track leading to the summit pass of Djebel Hamra. This time they met their match in Robinett's CC B. Tanks and self-propelled 105s slowed the advance: 'the day grew wilder,' remarked Oberleutnant Schmidt, 'shells seemed to rain on us from all directions.'[42] Under cover of darkness they were forced to withdraw. Robinett, confident, experienced and never short of ideas, had given 1st Armored its first real taste of success.

On the other prong of the attack, 10th Panzer drove 26th Armoured Brigade back in grim fighting, ridge by ridge. To the east of the Thala road, the heavily outgunned Lothians and opposite them 17th/21st Lancers in their Valentines and a few Crusaders, fought to stem the German tide. Several times, when the attack seemed to be stalled, Rommel was in the thick of things, directing von Broich to send in his lorry-borne troops behind the tanks. Badly mauled, what remained of the two armoured regiments was ordered to withdraw through a gap in the Leicesters' defensive line. They were followed on foot by surviving crews from blazing tanks while the wounded and dying were brought out on Bren Gun carriers and scout cars.

In front of Thala the remaining tanks were just settling into a laager, though there had been no time to close a defensive minefield laid across the road, when the Leicesters spotted a British tank approaching. Suddenly, it slewed across their trenches and began firing. Behind were others; the Germans had infiltrated the defences, using a captured Valentine.[43]

Many of the Leicesters stood no chance at all as the Panzers swept on until a fuel dump at the side of the road went up in flames, revealing them to the 17th/21st Lancers. For several hours the armoured duel swayed back and forth across the final ridge before Thala. By about 2000 hours, the Germans had lost 15 tanks – including the rogue Valentine – and withdrew to re-group and resume the attack next morning. They had inflicted grievous damage, taking 571 prisoners and destroying 38 tanks as well as 28 artillery pieces.

The exhausted defenders were reinforced just in time by Brigadier-General S. LeRoy Irwin who arrived in the early evening with 9th Division's artillery. Drunk with fatigue, Irwin met Brigadier Jack Parham, the Brigadier RA from First Army, and in rain, fog and darkness they carefully sited 48 American howitzers. In front of them was a thin screen of Leicesters, numbering about 100 men, together with early infantry arrivals from 2nd Hampshires and 16th/5th Lancers with Sherman tanks, some still hurrying from Sbiba. Less than a mile away assembled 2,500 men with 50 tanks, 30 guns and other weapons, determined to annihilate them.

'I'm sorry,' said Lieutenant-Colonel ffrench-Blake of the Lothians to his assembled tank crews in the small hours of 22nd February, 'but we've got to go out on a forlorn hope.'[44] With his remaining ten tanks, he had been ordered by Dunphie to take a hill overlooking the British position. At 0500 hours they started out in chilling rain but seven immediately ran full tilt over a ridge directly into the waiting Germans and were destroyed in vicious fighting. Their unintended sacrifice bluffed the Germans into thinking that a much bigger counter-attack was about to begin. This was reinforced by the roar of Irwin's guns, firing at daybreak. Instead of ordering his 10th Panzers to issue the *coup de grâce*, von Broich paused while his own 88s laid down a terrific barrage, pinning the remnants of Nick Force in their trenches for six hours.

While von Broich hesitated undecided in front of Thala, Bülowius had ordered his men westward towards Djebel el Hamra Pass, ready for a dawn infantry attack.

In heavy rainstorms they lost their way while trying to get around Robinett's extreme southern flank and ended up advancing on a camel track into the Bou Chebka Pass, seven miles from their destination which landed them in the Foussana Valley.

In the confused fighting that followed elements of Kampfgruppe *DAK*, some in captured French and American uniforms, attempted to close on Djebel el Hamra with 25 tanks and assault guns.[45] They were stopped by determined opposition from a heavily reinforced 16th Infantry Regiment (1st US Infantry) and just as they prepared to withdraw in the late afternoon through Bou Chebka Pass, were hit by a counter-attack. Pounded by 1st Infantry's guns and, from the north-east, the combined firepower of Robinett's CC B, Axis discipline disintegrated. Hundreds of men fled pell mell into the gathering darkness, leaving behind many vehicles intact. Rommel ordered the Kampfgruppe *DAK* to be recalled though success had been nearly within Bülowius' grasp: 'It was "touch and go" for a short time', admitted 1st Infantry HQ.[46]

Rommel had been visibly depressed by the failure of von Broich's attempt to break through to Thala as well as the setback at Bou Chebka. Burdened by intelligence reports that Allied resistance north-west of Kasserine was stiffening, he calculated that the odds stacked against him were far too high.

During the afternoon of the 22nd, as low cloud cover dispersed, Spitfires escorted fighter-bombers in attacks on German armoured vehicles and motor transport approaching Thala while American bombers, operating from the over-crowded single steel plank runway at Youks les Bains, and P-40 Airacobras strafed enemy traffic in the Kasserine Pass. Orders were issued to Kampfgruppe *DAK* that the position in front of Thala must be held to the last bullet and there was to be no retreat without specific orders.[47] But as he set off back to Frascati, Kesselring ordered von Arnim to meet him at Bizerte airport where he demanded furiously why Rommel's requests for reinforcements had not been met and elements of Ziegler's Kampfgruppe moved north instead of reinforcing the *DAK*'s right wing. Evidence of continuing antagonism between his commanders confirmed Kesselring's decision to call off the Kasserine Pass offensive.[48]

On the same evening, Bülowius received orders to pull out, followed by von Broich, while Hildebrandt remained near Sbiba and got ready to retreat. Early next morning came an official directive from *Comando Supremo*: the bulk of Kamfgruppe *DAK* was to go to First Italian Army (*AOK 1*), formerly the German-Italian *Panzerarmee*, re-named on 20 February, when General Messe had reluctantly taken command at Rommel's insistence. 10th Panzer was to guard the Kasserine Pass during the withdrawal and then itself retire to join 21st Panzer at Sbeïtla, after it had pulled out from Sbiba. Both armoured divisions were then to make their way back through the Faïd Pass, whereupon the 10th would turn north to Pichon and the 21st south to Sfax.[49]

As his forces retreated, Rommel received a directive on the evening of the 23rd appointing him *Oberbefehlshaber* (C-in-C) of *Heeresgruppe Afrika* (Army Group

Africa), combining Fifth Panzer Army (von Arnim) and First Italian Army (Messe). Very late in the day *Comando Supremo* was insisting on a unified command. 'I've moved up a step in command and have given up my army as a result,' he wrote to his wife, 'Bayerlein remains my Chief of Staff. Whether it's a permanent solution is doubtful.'[50]

Meanwhile, the Allies had also been trying to disentangle their command structure. Back in Morocco at Mamora – 'Boring Acres' to the troops – with 2nd US Armored Division in reserve, Major-General Ernest N. Harmon, known to his men as 'the poor man's George Patton' because of his crude language, had heard 'sketchy reports' of the deteriorating situation at Kasserine. On 20 February, he was called by AFHQ for 'limited field duty' and was surprised when Eisenhower revealed news of dissension between Fredendall and Ward, that Robinett was disloyal to Ward, and that 1st Armored Division was rated non-combat-worthy by the British.[51]

Eisenhower then ordered him to take over command of either II Corps or 1st Armored. 'Well, make up your mind, Ike, I can't do both,' exclaimed Harmon.[52] Eisenhower thereupon told him to act as deputy corps commander, help Fredendall restore the situation and then report directly back as to whether he should relieve Ward or Fredendall. Driven next day (22 February) to Constantine and on to Tébessa he met a panic-stricken mass of Jeeps, trucks and vehicles of all kinds streaming away from the front. Reaching Fredendall's HQ he was shocked by his first words. 'We have been waiting for you to arrive... Shall we move the command post?' Harmon took an instant decision: 'Hell no!,' he said. 'All right,' retorted Fredendall turning to the others, 'that settles that. We stay.'[53]

Handed typewritten orders by Fredendall, Harmon discovered he had been given battlefield command of 1st Armored and 6th Armoured Divisions. His first task was to visit his divisional commanders. Ward took his demotion well, after Harmon had told him: 'I'm about a thousand files behind you [junior in terms of service] but these are my orders and that's how it is.' Captain Hatfield, one of Ward's aides, was bitter, however: 'Fredendall just won't give my general a command,' adding, 'We licked [the] Germans yesterday and they withdrew through [the] pass. No one can take credit for that except Gen[eral] Ward.'[54]

Sympathetic and tactful, Harmon was entirely proper in his conduct of a tricky situation.[55] Ward issued a special message to his troops: 'All units will be alerted at dawn for movement in any direction except to the rear.' In the meantime, Harmon went on to see Brigadier 'Cam' Nicholson, dirty and unshaven after several days and nights without sleep. 'We gave them a ······ bloody nose yesterday and we are damned ready to given them another one this morning,' he said. Harmon liked this; 'he and I were going to get along together just fine.' Harmon had arrived too late to influence the Kasserine Pass operations but was responsible for following up the retreating enemy. He adopted what was essentially the 'Howze Plan,' established on the night of 19/20 February, for Dunphie's and Robinett's forces to counter-attack together.[56]

Only gradually on the morning of 23 February did it dawn upon the beleaguered defenders that the Germans had pulled out. At Djebel el Hamra, CC

B could find no targets, and near Bou Chebka Terry Allen's men reported they were out of touch with the enemy. Conscious of 34th Infantry Division's losses – 50 killed, 200 wounded, 250 missing in action – Major-General Ryder ordered patrols forward at Sbiba before cautiously ordering a pursuit the next day.

On the road to Thala Nicholson ordered all guns to cease firing that afternoon. Reconnaissance patrols advanced three miles without opposition, passing the spot where Nick Force had made its final stand. Two wrecked Bren Gun carriers lay nose on to a German tank with its turret blown off, shattered and burnt-out enemy tanks were surrounded by shell-cases, tins of food, scattered papers, bits of equipment, mess tins, knives and forks. A dead Arab in his snow-white burnous lay where he had been caught in the crossfire. Beside one tank was a tall, blond German, blue eyes wide in the surprise of sudden death. In his pocket was a letter from the Ruhr, posted only five days earlier. A grave was being dug and an Army chaplain was pulling a surplice over his uniform, ready to read the burial service.

As soon as he realized the battle was over, Harmon went to see Fredendall and discovered him lying drunk in bed, having partied too well on whisky, but for others there was no time for celebration.[57] They were picking their way through hundreds of mines and booby traps towards the Kasserine Pass in a vain pursuit. One haunting image was burned ineradicably into Nigel Nicolson's mind – a British soldier blown apart by a mine, his body lying divided on either side of the road.[58]

The Germans suffered 201 men killed, 536 wounded and 252 missing and had lost numerous guns, half-tracks, tanks and vehicles. They claimed over 4,000 prisoners, many vehicles, much ammunition and equipment. The Americans, particularly, had suffered a body blow from which it would take time to recover. Over 20 per cent of II Corps was wasted; of 30,000 Americans involved about 300 were killed in action, some 3,000 wounded and nearly 3,000 posted as missing.[59]

More than this, the enemy had thrown the Allies off balance and, as Alexander admitted, prolonged the war in Tunisia by several months.[60] Time, lives and equipment had been lost. Some 3,400 men, mostly volunteers and all but 400 of them infantrymen, had to be sent from the 3rd US Infantry and 2nd Armored Divisions to replace troops lost at Kasserine.[61] By the time the Germans pulled back through the pass, a major Allied inquest had begun.

Notes to Chapter 10

[1] Webb Diary, entry for 3 February – 16 March 1943. Webb Papers, Box 1.

[2] Blumenson, *Rommel's Last Victory*, p. 144.

[3] Conversation with Sergeant Basker Bennet, Coy. H, 1st Armored Regiment, Omar M. Bradley, Report of North Africa Operations, 2 April 1943; US Army Ground Forces, Observer Board Papers. USAMHI.

[4] Diary of Captain E.C. Hatfield, entry for 15 February 1943, transcribed by Russell Gugeler; Ward Papers. USAMHI.

[5] Comment on Battle of Sidi bou Zid by Major Hudel of 10th Panzer Division; Ward Papers, 1st Armored Division 1942–43.

[6] Robinett's comments on Blumenson, *Rommel's Last Victory*.

[7] Blumenson, *Rommel's Last Victory*, p. 162.

[8] Colonel Hamilton H. Howze interviewed by Lieutenant-Colonel Robert Reed, 5 February 1973; Howze Papers. USAMHI.

[9] Howe, *Northwest Africa*, p. 422.

[10] Extracts from Diary of a Gefreiter, 104 Panzer Grenadier Regiment.

[11] Blumenson, *Rommel's Last Victory*, pp. 164–5; Waters interviewed by Parnell.

[12] Austin, *Birth Of An Army*, p. 87.

[13] Diary, résumé entry for 3 February – 16 March 1943; Webb Papers, Box 1.

[14] Major Martin Philipsborn, 'The Sbeïtla Operation', Intelligence Report, 28 February 1943; Philipsborn Papers. USAMHI. Philipsborn was an Intelligence officer with HQ CC B.

[15] Schmidt, *With Rommel in the Desert*, p. 158.

[16] Pyle, *Here is Your War*, p. 176. Pyle was one of the best-regarded American war correspondents. He was killed by a Japanese sniper on 18 April 1945.

[17] Message timed at 1415 hours from *AOK* to *DAK*, 17 February 1943; RH 24-200/81. BA-MA.

[18] Truscott to Eisenhower, 19 February 1943; Eisenhower Papers, Box 116; Blumenson, *Rommel's Last Victory*, p. 207; Butcher Diary, entry for 20 February 1943.

[19] CIGS to Alexander, 16 February 1943; Alexander Papers, WO/214/18. In the same file is a copy of Eisenhower's directive to Alexander appointing him Deputy C-in-C.

[20] Quoted by Playfair, *Destruction of Axis Forces*, p. 304.

[21] Personal message from Rommel to von Arnim, 18 February 1943; RH19-VIII/41. BA-MA. The enemy would not be able to see the possibilities of a manoeuvre on Tébessa, claimed Rommel.

[22] Major Richard Feige, 'Relationships between Operations and Supply in Africa (as of January 1943)', 25 April 1947; Detwiler *et al.*, *World War II German Military Studies*, XIV, MS D-125; von Arnim, 'Erinnerungen an Tunesien'.

[23] Report, *Deutsch-Italienische Panzerarmee*, 18 February 1943; RH19-VIII/32; Hinsley, *British Intelligence*, II, pp. 589–90.

[24] Liddell Hart, *Rommel Papers*, p. 402.

[25] Evening Report, *Deutsch-Italienische Panzerarmee*, 19 February 1943; RH19-VIII/41.

[26] Quoted by Howe, *Northwest Africa*, p. 447.

[27] Howe in *Northwest Africa*, mentions the 33rd Reconnaissance Battalion but Rommel the 3rd Battalion in Liddell Hart, *Rommel Papers*, p. 402. Aufklärungsabteilung 3 is still famous amongst *Afrika Korps*' veterans for its daring exploits.

[28] D'Arcy Dawson, *Tunisian Battle*, p. 146. D'Arcy Dawson was a war correspondent for the London *Daily Sketch*, *Sunday Graphic* and *Sunday Times*.

[29] Battle Reports, 19 and 20 February 1943; RH 19-VIII/32.

[30] 'Gore Force' consisted of a company of the 10th Rifle Brigade, a squadron of 2nd Lothians and Border Horse with seven Valentine and four Crusader tanks, a battery of RHA and a troop from 93rd Anti-Tank Regiment, RA.

[31] Two messages Truscott to Eisenhower, 19 February 1943; Eisenhower Papers, Box 116.

[32] Fredendall to Truscott, 19 February 1943; *ibid.*, Box 42.

[33] Kurowski, *Endkampf in Afrika*, p. 191. For this attack Stotten later received the *Eichenlaub zum Ritterkreutz des Eisernen Kreutzes* (Oak Leaves to the Knight's Cross of the Iron Cross).

[34] Philipsborn to Howe, 18 February 1952; Robinett to Howe, (Memorandum 1) 4 March 1952; Robinett Papers, Box 4. Library of Congress.

[35] General T.J. Conway interviewed by Colonel Robert F. Ensslin, 29 September 1977. MHRC.

[36] This entry for 20 February appears in the fuller, unpublished text of Butcher's diary and is also quoted by Lewin, *Ultra Goes to War*, pp. 273–4.

[37] Neither Anderson nor Alexander's intelligence chief, Lieutenant-Colonel David Hunt, thought that predicting Rommel's intention to attack through the Kasserine or Dernaïa Passes (the latter between Fériana and Tébessa) and then striking northwards towards Le Kef was difficult. See Hunt, *A Don at War*, pp. 161–2. Given a free hand, Rommel's objective almost certainly would have been Tébessa.

[38] Conway interviewed by Ensslin. MHRC.

[39] Supplement to Battle Report, *Deutsch-Italienische Panzerarmee*, 20 January 1943; RH19-VIII/41.

[40] Observed by Gunner Greenwood, 70th Field Regiment, RA, Sound Archives recording, IWM 4767/7.

[41] Shirley Smith Diary, entry for 21 February 1943.

[42] Schmidt, *With Rommel in the Desert*, p. 215.

[43] ffrench-Blake, *17/21st Lancers*, pp. 120–1.

[44] Austin, *Birth of an Army*, p. 91.

[45] Some Germans were using American uniforms, 'and our helmets coloured nearly white,' noted the S.2 Journal, CC B, 1st Armored Division, on 22 February 1943; Robinett Papers, Box 13; Marshall Library.

[46] HQ 1st Infantry Division, Summary of Operations, 8 March 1943.

[47] Battle Order from *Deutsch-Italienische Panzerarmee*, 22 February 1943; RH19-VIII/32.

[48] Kesselring, 'War in the Mediterranean Area;' *Memoirs*, pp. 151–2.

[49] Blumenson, *Rommel's Last Victory*, pp. 286–7; Playfair, *Destruction of Axis Forces*, p. 305.

[50] Liddell Hart, *Rommel Papers*, p. 409.

[51] Harmon to Robinett, 23 June 1971; Robinett Papers, Box 5. Marshall Library. Robinett hotly disputed this charge of disloyalty, though Ward believed it at the time. Harmon thought Ward was a great personal friend of Marshall who must have passed the word along to Eisenhower.

[52] Harmon, *et al.*, *Combat Commander*, p. 112.

[53] Harmon interview by Dr George F. Howe (15 September 1952). OCMH Collection.

[54] Hatfield Diary, entry for 23 February 1943.

[55] Howze interviewed by Reed.

[56] Harmon to Howze, 24 February 1948; 'Correspondence 1908–1945;' Howze Papers.

[57] Harmon, *Combat Commander*, p. 119; confirmed by Ward Diary, 26 February 1943.

[58] Nicolson, *Alex*, p. 176. Alexander's biographer Nigel Nicolson was serving as an officer in the Grenadier Guards at this time.

[59] Blumenson, *Rommel's Last Victory*, p. 303. Eisenhower gives slightly different figures in his *Crusade in Europe*, p. 164.

[60] Had Rommel acted more decisively and not split his forces, he might have got to Tébessa though this would not have changed the outcome of the campaign but only extended its duration; see 'The Story Behind the Story: The logistical reasons the Nazis lost in North Africa in World War II', HQ US Army Command Information Topics, No. 20-65, 1 September 1965; RH24200/117. BA-MA.

[61] HQ 3rd Infantry Division, Report of Operations 1942–44; 3rd US Infantry Division, Box 6097; World War II Operations Reports, USNA 303-0.3.

Chapter 11

A Complete Dog's Breakfast

Thud,
In the Mud.
Thank Gud,
Another dud.

The poet Richard Spender's last piece, written while retreating with the 2nd Parachute Battalion from the Tamera Valley on St Patrick's Day 1943, just 11 days before he was killed.[1]

———◆◆◆———

The battle of Kasserine Pass confirmed that the M3 Light (Stuart) tank was useful only for reconnaissance and the M3 Gun Motor Carriage – an old 75mm mounted on a half-track as a makeshift 'tank-destroyer' – was nothing less than a death trap. Asked if machine-gun fire was stopped by these vulnerable 'Purple Heart Boxes,' one soldier replied: 'Oh yes, Sir, the bullets usually penetrate one side and rattle about a bit.'[2]

Fredendall's strategy and Stark's original dispositions had been faulty. Open space might have been traded for defensible terrain but Fredendall dispersed his units where they could be cut off and defeated in detail. Either the Faïd Pass should have been sealed or a swift retreat to Sbeïtla and Kasserine ordered, thereby extending the enemy's supply lines and making him vulnerable to swift counter-attacks. Stark deployed his troops as if stopping a cattle stampede across the flat plain of the Foussana Valley, where there was no cover, and allowed the enemy to climb the shoulders of the pass and gain a decisive advantage. Stark was later sent home on rotation to become a Brigadier-General – a deplorable policy, thought Bradley.[3]

In November 1944 Fredendall showed his fiercest critic all the orders issued by First Army for defence in the American sector. 'It interested me,' wrote Ward, 'as I had blamed him for the very meticulous and detailed way in which he handled each of my battalions. I now find that General Anderson of the British Army was responsible. The placing of our troops so off-centre and so exposed like a sore thumb at Sidi bou Zid and Bizzerti [sic] was Anderson's decision. Fredendall recommended otherwise.'[4]

Nine years later, Ward was still of this opinion: 'I now even have sympathy for the Corps Commander [Fredendall],' he told Robinett but added, 'He had a most difficult task and I might add was not too well suited to accomplish it.'[5] In return, Robinett believed that Fredendall was not entirely to blame for Kasserine. 'He was merely a compliant subordinate caught in the web of faulty Allied command arrangements. I was well aware of the situation some time before he came into the picture. I agree, however, that he was not the man for the job.'[6] The row rumbled on as Fredendall bitterly attacked Anderson: '[he] scattered my command from hell to breakfast over my 150 mile wide front. By direct orders he placed every one of my units, even down to battalions and companies. He never permitted me to collect my armor into a powerful mobile striking force.' Furthermore, nothing was ever done about Anderson, 'who had powerful supporters in Eisenhower's H.Q., where British influence was paramount.'[7]

Eisenhower wisely refused to comment on allegations in the American press but 'Monk' Dickson, in 1948 a Philadelphia warehouseman but formerly Fredendall's G.2, had no hesitation: 'Anderson has General Fredendall tied up in knots,' he commented. 'In my opinion the disaster at Kasserine is 100 per cent Anderson's job.'[8] Colonel Dickson had every reason to be bitter; correctly anticipating where the Germans would strike he had been snubbed by Anderson. Only a few people emerged from the unhappy episode with reputations enhanced. 1st Armored's CC B was competently and aggressively handled; Robinett claimed to the end of his life that only he blunted the German attack on the road to Tébessa, thereby forcing von Broich's men to bide their time before Thala. Rommel himself confirmed that failure to clear the Americans off the Hamra plateau by *DAK* Kampfgruppe prevented 10th Panzer from freeing his western flank and Fredendall admitted that, 'General Robinett certainly saved our bacon with his tanks.'[9]

Ward remained unconvinced by Robinett's self-promotion.[10] In fact the arrival of Irwin's artillery at Thala, the desperate defence by the Lothians' and Lancers' tanks and quiet but steadfast leadership by Dunphie and Nicholson were equally important. Not least, too, was Rommel's own inclination to break off the operation at the earliest possible moment. If Eisenhower intended Harmon to sort out problems between Fredendall and Ward he should either have been sent earlier, before the storm broke, or later when the Germans were back beyond the Western Dorsale. Coming late on the scene, he had little influence on the Kasserine Pass battle but was unduly blamed for the slow follow-up as the enemy retreated.

<hr>

Although Eisenhower had assured Fredendall on the evening of 22 February that he was perfectly safe in taking any reasonable risk in launching properly supported local counter-attacks, II Corps failed to realise for 24 hours that Rommel had begun a total withdrawal. Not until the 25th was any action taken and by then it was too late; the quarry had escaped.

Following instructions issued by *Comando Supremo*, 10th Panzer moved to an area around Sidi bou Zid and 21st Panzer to Sbeïtla and the northwest.

Kampfgruppe *DAK* retreated to Gafsa and was dissolved, its components reverting to their normal units on the Mareth front.[11]

The Allied advance towards the Kasserine Pass by 16th Infantry Regiment, supported by a battalion of medium tanks, 804th Tank Destroyer Battalion and two companies of 601st Tank Destroyer Battalion, was slow and cumbersome when speed was vital; German intercepts revealed their pursuers were badly hampered by mines.[12] The man on the spot, Harmon, had not had time to get to know all that was going on. Only XII US Air Support Command's Fortresses harassed the retreating enemy; in the space of 15 minutes on the 23rd, 104 hostile aircraft were counted by the Panzers who had never witnessed such intense concentrations before.[13]

Fredendall was unaware that RAF Bisleys had carried out night attacks on 23/24 February and failed to tell Robinett of the continuing aerial bombardment. 'This emphasizes [the] necessity for the Corps Commander passing on to his lower echelons the air attacks that are going on,' remarked Spaatz, 'since Robinett may have pushed forward more vigorously had he known of the attacks going on on the other side of the [Kasserine] Pass.'[14] Following his refusal to relieve Ward of his command and falling foul of Fredendall because of it, Harmon arrived back at AFHQ on 28 February amid scenes of jubilation. 'Well, what do you think of Fredendall?,' asked Eisenhower. 'He's no damned good,' replied Harmon, 'You ought to get rid of him.'[15]

After the enemy withdrew from Kasserine Churchill demanded a searching inquiry into what had gone wrong. Under Anderson's command the Americans had been, 'spread about by him or someone over a large, loosely held line in bits and pieces... there was no proper spirit or knowledge of what was going on in the First Army.' Since 'Boniface' (Churchill's code for Enigma intelligence) had given ample warning of Rommel's attack, why had a sensible withdrawal not been effected? Now the situation had been restored, 'incompetence or inadequacy' was not to be overlooked. Until he had Alexander's report, added the Prime Minister, his confidence in Anderson was suspended.[16]

Alexander replied that his best officers had been sent to give urgent instruction to the Americans, 'in battle techniques and training for war.' He went on: 'I am frankly shocked at whole situation as I found it. Although Anderson should have been quicker to realize true state of affairs... he was only put in command of the whole front on January 24th [sic]. Real fault has been lack of direction from above from very beginning resulting in no policy and no plan. Am doubtful if Anderson is big enough for the job although he has some good qualities.'[17]

On the same day, writing to Brooke that the French were, 'good chaps and willing to fight,' he complained about the Americans, 'so badly trained – this is the case from top to bottom, and of course entirely inexperienced.'[18] While Alexander's arrival produced a calming influence on the more hysterical elements during the Kasserine Pass crisis, his patronising view of American capabilities caused much offence – not least to Marshall – which was hardly surprising given his comments on the state of II Corps in April. The troops were, 'very nice... fine looking men if on the soft and fat side. They have excellent equipment and weapons too,' he observed, but this was futile because, 'they simply do not know their job as soldiers, and this is the case from the highest to the lowest, from the general to the private soldier.' Telling Brooke that the problem was, 'very serious indeed', he warned that, 'unless we can do something about it, the American Army... will be quite useless and play no useful part whatsoever.'[19]

Even when Americans were bearing the brunt of the fighting later in Sicily and Italy, Alexander refused to change his opinions. Before long, he had Ward relieved of his command of 1st Armored Division and yet did nothing about Anderson who had dispersed its units into 'penny packets' and had clearly forfeited its respect. Despite telling Brooke that command of an army was beyond the man's capabilities: 'He is a good plain cook and not of the calibre we must now look for in our army commanders', Alexander avoided a final decision. Instead, he tried to shift it onto the CIGS who was quite unsure as to whether Alexander was recommending the replacement of Anderson or not.[20] Unwilling to grasp the nettle, Alexander temporised and allowed Anderson to stay by default while others lost their commands.

'The Pass is ours,' Ward informed Fredendall on 25 February. A preliminary artillery bombardment by American 155mm guns fell on nothing but undefended rock and the Kasserine Pass was retaken by elements of 26th Armoured Brigade, CC B and troops from 16th Infantry Regiment. By nightfall American forces were in the villages of Kasserine and Fériana.[21] 'In my opinion, wrote Major Gardiner, CO of 2nd Battalion 13th Armored Regiment, 'what really caused the Germans to pull back through the Pass, once they found the way blocked, was not the pressure we put on them but the realization that the Eighth Army was about to resume its drive and the holding of Kasserine was of no particular value with them.'[22]

Before the crisis broke Montgomery had confidently, 'fixed up a plan of campaign to finish off the N. African War.' It was 'quite simple,' he told Brooke, 'and everything is really based on getting Eighth Army north of the GABES gap and out into the open; I will then roll the whole show up from the south, moving north with my right on the sea.' With First Army withdrawing from Gafsa, however, Alexander was unfortunately saddled with, 'a complete dog's breakfast in Tunisia and... an absence of good chaps over there.'[23]

At the height of the Kasserine emergency, Alexander urgently ordered Montgomery to exert force on the Mareth Line in order to divert Rommel's attention.[24] Monty subsequently made much of this: 'I speeded up events and by the 26th February it was clear that our pressure had caused Rommel to break off his attack against the Americans.'[25] Such a claim was patently untrue and dismissed by his chief of staff, de Guingand – not that Montgomery took much notice.[26] Alexander's directive was sent shortly before midnight on the 21st; discouraged by the severe check to his offensive before Thala and Djebel el Hamra Pass on the 22nd, Rommel called off his assault. However, not until the 24th was Leese writing about, 'driving against the Mareth Line so as to help the Americans and our 1st Army. We are very nearly in close contact with it and are now starting to try and drive in his covering troops.'[27] This was at least 48 hours too late to have created significant pressure.

———•·•———

Having been warned explicitly by Alexander not to over-extend elements of Eighth Army, Montgomery proceeded to do exactly that, for the whole of X Corps was at Benghazi, 1,000 miles away, and the nearest division which could be brought up as reinforcement to the lead units was the New Zealand, back at Tripoli. These were anxious times: 'There is no doubt that between 28 Feb[ruary] and 3 March I was definitely "unbalanced",' recalled Montgomery.[28] Leese had little confidence in approaching the Mareth Line: '… our left flank was completely exposed to the German threat from the mountains.' But after much feverish activity he was convinced on 2 March that Rommel had, 'missed his great chance and now we are calm, confident and ready.'[29]

During the time when his forces were most exposed to attack, Montgomery rushed up 2nd Armoured Brigade's tanks from Tripoli to Ben Gardane. Also hurrying forward was 23rd Armoured Brigade with units of 50th Division, 201st Guards Brigade and 2nd New Zealand Division which drove up from Tripoli non-stop in 36 hours.

By morning on 4 March, Montgomery had established a powerful force at Medenine, an undistinguished collection of white houses and mud huts, about 20 miles south of the Mareth Line. Under command he had 51st, 7th Armoured and 2nd New Zealand Divisions, all XXX Corps artillery, nearly 400 tanks, 350 field guns and 470 6-pounder anti-tank guns.

'It's a very big thing and please God we have made the right decision to stand and fight here,' noted Leese on 5 March.[30] But there was no other place to stand and fight unless Montgomery had withdrawn again beyond Tripoli. He had no intention of doing so and was supremely confident: 'I am in fact sitting "very pretty", and Rommel can go to hell', wrote Montgomery. 'If he attacks me tomorrow (as he looks like doing) he will get an extremely bloody nose; in fact it is exactly what I would like him to do.'[31] Rommel was about to oblige.

———•·•———

While the withdrawal from Kasserine was taking place von Arnim flew to Rome, without Rommel's approval. There, he obtained Kesselring's permission to mount a new major offensive by Fifth Panzer Army in the northern third of Tunisia, from the coast to the Bou Arada valley. Operation *Ochsenkopf* ('Oxhead'), scheduled to begin on 26 February, was planned in the belief that the Allies had been badly unbalanced through having to move their forces from the north during the recent crisis. When told of this Rommel was dumbfounded at the 'nincompoops' of *Comando Supremo*.[32] Ambrosio, however, was equally astonished wh n he heard about it because von Arnim had already called off a spoiling attack in the Medjez el Bab area for want of sufficient forces.

Ochsenkopf's principal aim was to advance towards Béja from Mateur through

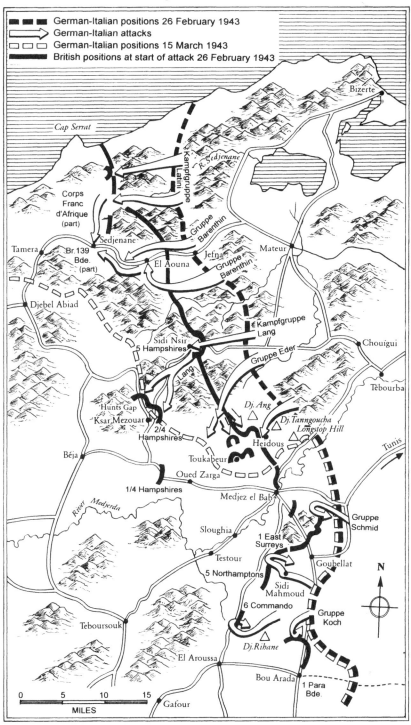

Legend:
- ■■ ■■ German-Italian positions 26 February 1943
- ⇒ German-Italian attacks
- ▭▭ ⇨ German-Italian positions 15 March 1943
- ▬▬▬ British positions at start of attack 26 February 1943

Bizerte

Cap Serrat

R. Sedjenane

Kampfgruppe Latini

Corps
Franc
d'Afrique
(part)

Gruppe Barenthin

Sedjenane

Tamera

Br.139
Bde.
(part)

Jefna

Mateur

El Aouna

Gruppe
Barenthin

Djebel Abiad

Kampfgruppe
Lang

Sidi Nsir
5 Hampshires

Chouïgui

Gruppe Eder

Lang

Tébourba

Hunts Gap
Ksar Mezouar

Dj. Ang

2/4
Hampshires

Dj. Tanngoucha
Longstop Hill

Béja

Heidous

Tunis

Toukabeur

Oued Zarga

1/4 Hampshires

Medjez el Bab

River Medjerda

Gruppe
Schmid

Sloughia

1 East
Surreys

Testour

5 Northamptons

Goubellat

N

Sidi
Mahmoud

Teboursouk

6 Commando

Gruppe
Koch

Dj. Rihane

El Aroussa

Bou Arada

1 Para
Bde.

0   5   10   15
MILES

Gafour

Operation *Ochsenkopf*
February 1943

Sidi Nsir with an armoured battlegroup of 77 tanks (including 14 Tigers) commanded by Oberst Rudolph Lang, part of Generalmajor Weber's Korpsgruppe. The rest of Weber's forces including Oberst Audorf's 754th Grenadier Regiment, composed of older men and some wounded from the Eastern Front, together with units of *Hermann Göring* Division and others from 10th Panzer Division which had not taken part in Operation *Frühlingswind*, were to support in the centre and south. Two battlegroups would encircle and destroy the British at Medjez el Bab and a third entrap the enemy in the Bou Arada Valley by means of a pincer movement before advancing to Gafour. In the north Oberst Hasso von Manteuffel, commanding the former *von Broich* Division, was to mount a secondary attack, codenamed Operation *Ausladung* ('Unloading'), in the Sedjenane Valley and cover Weber's northern flank.

The first in what was to be a complicated series of nine offensives by von Arnim's troops along a 60-mile front opened on the morning of 26 February when Lang's infantry, supported by 74 tanks, including 14 Tigers, advanced along the road between towering heights to Sidi Nsir.[33] Defending this patrol base – hardly more than a small white building and wooden platform where the road curved close to the railway track – were 5th Hampshires supported by 155th Battery, 172nd Field Regiment, which had placed its eight 25-pounders well forward of the infantry.

Soon after dawn a vicious slogging match developed as Lang was forced to commit more and more of his armour in trying to dislodge the Hampshire's anti-tank gunners and infantry who stuck doggedly to their posts despite low-level attacks from German fighters causing havoc among their supply lorries. As Oberst Barenthin's paratroopers picked their way over steep hills to envelop the Hampshires, tanks crossed the Sidi Nsir–Béja road during the afternoon cutting the defenders' supply line. After his telephone lines had been sliced, radio put out of action and observation post smashed, the artillery commander, Major John Raworth, still reported, 'German tanks attacking. Everyone in good heart.' Gun after gun was overrun but even when ammunition in the gunpits was blazing others went on firing. There came a final message, 'Tanks are on us,' followed by the 'V' sign before the last surviving gun of the dying 155th Battery was silenced. A lone gunner was seen to charge the German tanks, brandishing a sticky bomb.[34]

After 12 hours' continuous fighting German tanks broke through 5th Hampshire's defences and their CO, Lieutenant-Colonel Newnham – later awarded a DSO – at last ordered a phased withdrawal.[35] By then, he was in touch with only one of his four rifle companies. As darkness fell he put a time bomb into the station at Sidi Nsir, burned all his bedding and, 'the pictures of my lovelies on the walls. "Can't let the Germans look at you, my darlings,"' he said, and led what remained of his battalion back over the hills.[36] Only 120 struggled to Hunt's Gap, a railway station on a rise of ground nine miles from Béja, to be strengthened and reinforced there by 128th Infantry Brigade. Of 130 officers and other ranks from 155th Battery, nine returned – two of them wounded.

Oberst Lang had lost 40 tanks, though his engineers were soon out at work repairing where possible and cannibalising those beyond saving. Already, his ability to reach Béja had been significantly reduced but this was by no means evident next day as the Panzers pushed on towards Hunt's Gap after heavy overnight rain had delayed the offensive and made off-road going impossible. About midday Lang's leading tanks were in contact with 2/4th Hampshires and the remnants of 2/5th Leicesters, newly arrived from Thala, who held a thin line across three miles of open countryside. Stopped once more, Lang tried again on the 28th after another night of heavy rainstorms which confined his tanks to the narrow ribbon of road. During the hours of darkness, the defenders had been reinforced by 2nd Hampshires, extra anti-tank guns and the North Irish Horse with 12 Churchill tanks. These had been introduced in First Army – 58 to a Regiment – only recently when a mixed squadron of 142nd (Suffolk) Regiment, RAC, rode into battle at Sbiba on 21 February, losing four in the process.[37]

By the fourth day, (1 March), the strain of holding the German attack was beginning to tell on brigade HQ, situated about three miles from Béja. Brigadier Pratt, normally the corps artillery commander, was a worried man, unsure as to whether he could prevent the Tigers from advancing on Béja and Medjez el Bab. However, late in the afternoon the guns stopped firing at Ksar Mezouar. A tank commander cautiously approached six German tanks which had tried to entice the Churchills out to fight and discovered their turrets thrown open and crews gone. They had abandoned haversacks of letters, towels, pipes and tobacco, pudding powder, tinned food and, in one tank, even postcard sets of 'Arab Beauties,' purchased in Tunis.

The Churchills, now in pursuit, trundled towards Sidi Nsir. Lang had only five 'runners' amongst his tanks and Weber ordered him to withdraw, go on the defensive, and hand over his command to Oberst Buse of the 47th Grenadier Regiment, from Korpsgruppe reserve. Disgruntled, Lang's troops nicknamed him 'Tank-Killer'.

Onto bare hillsides barring an advance up the Béja–Mateur valley clambered the 8th Argyll and Sutherland Highlanders to relieve most of 2/4th Hampshires. Then, for 18 days, they lay out on the open ridges, unable to move while it was light. The officer in charge of organizing supplies of food, water and ammunition on trackless slopes by farm-horse and mules, Euan Grant, admitted that bringing everything up under cover of darkness was a massive strain; he was, he said, 'awful shagged.'[38]

While the battle at Hunt's Gap was the most hard-fought of von Arnim's offensive, further south troops of the Jäger Regiment *Hermann Göring*[39] climbed hill paths leading out of the Goubellat Plain. At midnight on 25 February under the garish light of flares and a furious mortar bombardment, they fell upon a company of 1st East Surreys at 'Fort McGregor,' no more than a sharp rocky knoll, 1,000 yards ahead of the main defensive line. 'The hill was being torn apart with mortar and machine gun fire,' wrote Lieutenant Kinden of the Surreys, 'at times it was as light as day and then suddenly very dark. The noise of bombardment and men shouting, the groaning of the wounded and dying and the smell of exploding ammunition and death was everywhere. This entire situation was all about war and what it really means to be in close combat.'[40]

By daybreak the East Surreys were cut off while the Algerian Tirailleurs, holding Djebel Djaffa on their right, were driven back exposing Brigadier Cass's 11th Brigade HQ and his gun lines. There followed a tremendous assault but a reserve company of East Surreys, with support from 2nd Lancashire Fusiliers, a field company of Royal Engineers, 56th Reconnaissance Regiment and a few Valentines of 17/21st Lancers, mounted a strong counterattack on Djebel Djaffa and re-took it. All available firepower was concentrated on Fort McGregor and at dusk on 26 February a patrol found only six Germans still on their feet. The bodies of 15 East Surreys were extricated from the debris; some had been killed after their capture by British artillery fire including Major Brooke Fox, the East Surreys' company commander. Around them about 60 Germans lay dead.[41]

Some way south, German tanks and infantry forced their way between 11th Brigade and 38th Irish Brigade at first light on 26 February. In the Irish sector, slightly north of the village of Bou Arada, the line on Stuka Ridge and its adjoining features was held by 2nd London Irish Rifles, young men who reportedly scarcely knew each other. Hit by the 2nd Battalion of Jäger *Hermann Göring* and Koch's paratroopers, they were scattered as the enemy attacked Steamroller Farm (there was a steamroller in the farmyard), on the rear slopes of Djebel Rihane where Lieutenant-Colonel Scott, Irish Brigade commander, had his HQ. Here they ran into a small unit of Lieutenant-Colonel Derek Mills-Roberts' No. 6 Commando, whose 250 strong force had been established on the western slopes and was patrolling eastwards at irregular intervals.

Only after engaging the enemy with his HQ troop and setting his other three troops to drive them eastwards did Mills-Roberts realize he was up against a much stronger force than expected. From the north there appeared more troops shouting, 'Jäger, Jäger', to which the defenders retorted with equal vigour, 'Commando, Commando'. After the Germans brought up four tanks the commandos were forced to withdraw, hunted by the enemy who introduced patrol dogs into the dense scrub, though many in this area of steep hills and gullies managed to link up with 56th Reconnaissance Regiment. Re-forming, they wreaked havoc by pumping 60 mortar shells into the Germans' tank harbour. During the entire action, No. 6 Commando suffered exactly 100 killed, wounded or missing (40 per cent of its strength).

Next in line on 26 February, 2nd Parachute Battalion of 1st Parachute Brigade was involved in, 'a bewildering course of action.'[42] Acting as shock troops, they spent much of their time in carriers being ferried hastily from one place to another, in action by night and travelling by day.

It was the misfortune of a large force of Italian infantry, attempting to advance from Djebel Mansour through trackless, wild country south of Bou Arada, to be waylaid by them. As the Italians disappeared into the many ravines, the paratroopers' support company fired into them all their normal stock of ammunition, their reserve, and further replenishment brought up by mule train. When night came, a sweep of the whole battle area brought in 90 very dispirited prisoners and, 'a collection of rifles, machine-guns and other ironmongery of typical Italian design.'[43]

Meanwhile, 1st and 3rd Parachute Battalions held a determined attack on their position – which centred on a feature known as Argoub, south of Djebel Bou Arada – by Austrians and Italian Alpini reinforced by men of 756th Mountain Regiment from Audorf's 334th Infantry Division. Under cover of a short bombardment, 1st Parachute Squadron, RE, was sent in to bolster up the hard-pushed 3rd Battalion. Charging uphill, with bayonets fixed and firing Bren Guns from the hip, they forced the enemy from the Argoub until they reached a horseshoe-shaped wadi at the foot of Djebel Mansour. There the Axis troops became trapped in an area which had been ranged by 3rd Battalion the previous day and in 90 minutes were pulverized by 3,000 mortar shells. In all, 3rd Battalion took 150 prisoners and killed over 250. When searched, some prisoners had pamphlets in their pockets detailing the best way to fight *Die Roten Teufel* – the 'Red Devils.' The paratroopers were delighted; no higher honour could have been bestowed on them.

Around Steamroller Farm, the enemy's progress towards El Aroussa, from where Brigadier 'Nelson' Russell was commanding his scratch 'Y' Division (made up from the Parachute Brigade and 38th Irish Brigade), had been slowed by stubborn resistance from armoured cars of 1st Derbyshire Yeomanry.

On 27 February the Irish attacked and stabilised their front; at the same time, 1st Guards Brigade arrived on the road to El Aroussa. Next day, a company of 2nd Battalion, Coldstream Guards, supported by seven Churchills from 51st Battalion, RTR, charged Steamroller Farm but intense shelling and dive-bombing burned up five Churchills and stopped the Coldstreamers in their tracks. Undeterred, Captain Hollands carried on in his Churchill under repeated fire from two 88s. Both missed at point-blank range, whereupon Hollands wrecked them, broke through into the enemy's rear, caught the German transport echelon and set it ablaze. Shortly afterwards he was joined by Lieutenant Kenton and, when two Mk IIIs attempted to intervene, they destroyed them as well.

The Churchills then opened fire on the massed Germans who fled screaming through the bushes, trying to get to the hills behind. In hot pursuit the tanks crushed many beneath their tracks and shot up 25 wheeled vehicles, eight anti-tank guns, two anti-aircraft guns, mortars, ammunition, radio sets and much else. They killed 200 men and were described in a German transmission, which the British intercepted, as a 'mad tank battalion,' which had scaled 'impossible heights.'[44]

On the following day 3rd Grenadier Guards walked into Steamroller Farm. The whole area, observed Sergeant-Major Bryen, RSM of 6 Commando, was littered with, 'distorted bodies which had lain there for two days or more, shell holes, burning lorries, guns and motor cycles, arms, ammunition, kit, uniform strewn everywhere, both our own and the enemy; shell, cartridges, grenades, heaped in confusion, with plenty of very obvious booby traps.'[45] In recognition of their parts in the action, Mills-Roberts of 6 Commando and Hollands were awarded the DSO.

Before the start of von Arnim's offensive, the British CIGS hoped that Brigadier Flavell's parachute brigade might be withdrawn, refitted and retrained because it consisted of, 'expensive personnel hard to get and hard to train, and which we are having great difficulty in replacing.'[46] The Germans had also used their seasoned parachute troops as line infantry, blocking holes here and there, dissipating their efforts in roles for which they had never been intended.

When the US 26th RCT accordingly arrived in the Bou Arada sector, 1st Battalion reported their hand-over was so noisy it sounded like, 'Blackpool beach on a summer Sunday afternoon in Wakes Week [a traditional holiday period].'[47] Flavell's brigade was then sent to Tamera Valley in the north where the German offensive had been most successful and was pitchforked straight into a critical situation. On 2 March, the towns of Medjez el Bab and Sedjenane had come under serious attack. Two weak battalions of Algerian Tirailleurs had been driven off Djebel Ang, overlooking the Plain of Medjez. They in turn dragged off a detachment of 138th Infantry Brigade which had been holding Toukabeur at the southern extremity of the mountain range.

By then the Germans had cut the Medjez–Béja road and controlled all routes to Medjez except from the south. While the British still held Oued Zarga, a settlement on the road roughly mid-way between Béja and Medjez, everything going to Medjez now had to be sent over the mountains via Tebersouk along 25 difficult miles of road. Meanwhile, the Germans shot up anything which moved and the threat to Medjez increased when strong enemy forces were reported in the prehistoric caves of the tiny village of Heidous, at the base of Tanngoucha, as well as on the mountain ridge between Oued Zarga and Medjez.

The engineers had rapidly constructed a road over desolate, broken country from a point near Testour, in the Tebersouk Valley, to link up with Oued Zarga from the rear. Ammunition, artillery and Brigadier 'Swifty' Howlett's 36th Infantry Brigade accompanied by other assorted units were moved up to open a front east and west of Oued Zarga.[48] They extended the line from 6th York and Lancasters defending the northern edge of Medjez. Further forward, east of the River Medjerda, 2/4th King's Own Yorkshire Light Infantry hung on to Grenadier Hill.

Howlett was transferred to take command of 139th Brigade on 3 March, temporarily replacing the unfortunate Brigadier Chichester-Constable who had suffered severe losses in defending the far north of the Allied line against attacks by elements of Division *von Manteuffel*. These began with Rudolf Witzig's rugged troops from 11th Fallschirmjäger Pionier Bataillon scrambling over the hills on their way to the iron-ore mining village of Sedjenane. His objective was to push on as far as Djebel Abiod, cut the road to Béja from the north and hold up any offensive against Bizerte. In dire peril of being surrounded on 27 February, 6th

Lincolns withdrew hastily from their position facing Green and Bald Hills, leaving behind in the clinging mud all their guns.

An attack on Witzig's forces by 16th Durham Light Infantry, not yet battle-hardened, was easily repulsed and another broken up with heavy losses. This left only 2/5th Sherwood Foresters defending Sedjenane. The battalion, one of those badly mauled at Dunkirk, was occupying poor defensive positions, about three miles east of the village. It was decimated by a German attack on 2 March and only a remnant got away in darkness to safety.

For these setbacks Chichester-Constable was sacked. The holder of two DSOs, 'he knew the Germans were going to attempt a big break-through and had quite rightly asked if he could move his defensive position,' commented Colonel Frost. 'Not only did they say no but took one of his battalions away [2/5th Sherwood Foresters – later returned]. The Germans attacked and completely overwhelmed him. He lost his guns, his men and his career. They had made him a scapegoat. I took careful note.'[49]

When it arrived at Sedjenane 1st Parachute Brigade joined the 2nd Coldstream Guards, which had hastened from El Aroussa to block the western approaches. The brigade was placed astride the main road; on its left was the Corps Franc d'Afrique under Colonel Durand, which had held up well against attacks by the Italian Bersaglieri in what the paratroopers referred to, without disrespect, as the 'Second Eleven Match.'

After the Germans had fought their way house by house along Sedjenane's long, muddy street, the Coldstreamers withdrew leaving the Red Devils to block the advance. At dawn on 8 March Barenthin's Fallschirmjäger Regiment attacked through dense woods and head-high scrub covering the hills. They caught the 2nd Parachute Battalion, having only just taken over from 6th Lincolns in the dark, somewhat off balance. A Company immediately began to suffer casualties. The A Company commander rang battalion HQ and said calmly, 'We appear to be completely surrounded now, but I am sure it will be all right.'[50] Only by suffering considerable losses was 3rd Battalion able to prevent Barenthin's troops slicing between 1st and 2nd Battalions. On the 10th, in pouring rain and bitter cold, the Germans attacked again and were badly cut up by the paratroopers who took over 200 prisoners in hand-to-hand fighting.

For the next seven days the parachute brigade stuck it out, though 1st Battalion was completely overlooked by German positions on Djebel Bel, a wooded hill on the right of the brigade's position. An attack by the luckless Sherwood Foresters, ordered by Lieutenant-General Allfrey, was bloodily repulsed whereupon a determined attempt to force 2nd Battalion out of the woods nearly succeeded until a squadron of Stukas arrived and mistakenly bombed their own forward troops, from 10th Panzer, to extinction. However, the weight of attacks on the Corps Franc d'Afrique finally stove in their front and Brigadier Flavell had to allow Colonel Durand to withdraw. This unhinged his defence and made the parachute brigade's positions untenable. Even then, 2nd Battalion, which had taken over 150 casualties, was reluctant to retreat.

This involved swimming and wading down the Oued el Madene, carrying all their weapons and under continuous shellfire. Soaking wet and exhausted, the battalion took up positions on three bare rocky hills, known as the Pimples and then handed over to the Leicesters. The key to the whole position was the highest hill, named 'Bowler Hat,' south-west of Sedjenane and unfortunately on the enemy's side of the river. A strong attack by Panzer Grenadiers now fell upon the Leicesters. Major Vic Coxen of 1st Paras, probing forward with a couple of platoons to find out what was happening sent Platt, his signaller, to their HQ. Back came his response: 'That you, sir?' 'Yes.' 'They've fucked off.' 'Who have?' 'Those fuckers; they've all fucked off.'[51] From this Coxen gathered that the Leicesters had apparently retreated and a counter-attack, mounted hastily by 3rd Parachute Battalion, failed miserably.

Another attempt on the 20th was much better organized. Following a heavy and well-directed bombardment, Lieutenant-Colonel Pearson's 1st Battalion charged the hill, supported by a flanking attack across the river using a bridge laid down by the Parachute Field Squadron. Ferocious war cries of 'Waho Mohammed' were heard as the paratroopers stormed forward, driving before them startled German infantry who had just relieved the Panzer Grenadiers. At small cost, the battalion took the hill and secured it. The fighting in the north, for the time being, was over.

——◆◆◆——

Elsewhere, too, von Arnim's offensive had ground to a halt. These short but savage battles, ranging over 60 miles of the front, had caused him losses, which he could ill-afford. Weber's Korpsgruppe alone reported 900 wounded, 24 tanks destroyed (including the total loss of two Tigers) and nearly 50 disabled, as well as the destruction of many anti-tank guns and mortars.[52]

About 2,500 British soldiers were on their way to Italian POW camps. Among them was Gunner Greenwood of 70th Field Regiment, RA. While in transit a German remarked to him: 'You've got the bloody Americans and we've got the Italians. Between us we could rule the world.'[53] Despite their differences, however, in the long run the Allies could make good their loss of weapons, ammunition and stores. Proportionately, von Arnim had managed to inflict greater damage on himself than on Eisenhower who, as Kesselring remarked, was not fighting 'a poor man's war.'[54]

——◆◆◆——

Notes to Chapter 11

[1] Quoted by Arthur, *Men of the Red Beret*, p. 71.

[2] Bradley, 'Memoir 1893–1945', Unpub. TS; Bradley Papers, Box 1. USAMHI.

[3] Recounted by Bradley in conversation with Hansen; Hansen Papers, Box 23.

[4] Ward to Henry Hannington (his father-in-law), 3 November 1944; Ward Papers.

[5] Ward to Robinett, 15 December 1953; Robinett Papers, Box 4. Library of Congress.

[6] Robinett to Ward, 22 December 1953; *ibid.*

[7] Article in *Chicago Daily Tribune*, 15 February 1948.

[8] Quoted in *Chicago Tribune*, 15 February 1948; cuttings in Webb Collection, Box 1.

[9] *Ibid.*

[10] Ward Diary, entry for 26 February 1943. Robinett got a DSM but not the promotion he thought he deserved.

[11] Nehring, 'Development of the Situation in North Africa'.

[12] Behrendt, *Rommel's Intelligence*, p. 217.

[13] Report from *Deutsch-Italienische Panzerarmee*, 23 February 1943; RH19-VIII/32.

[14] Spaatz Diary, entry for 3 March 1943; Spaatz Papers, Box 11.

[15] Harmon, *Combat Commander*, pp. 119–20.

[16] Churchill to Alexander, 24 February 1943; Alanbrooke Papers, 6/2/17; and in Alexander Papers, WO 214/11.

[17] Alexander to Churchill, 27 February 1943; *ibid.*

[18] Alexander to Brooke, 27 February 1943; Alanbrooke Papers, 6/2/17.

[19] Alexander to Brooke, 3 April 1943; *ibid.*

[20] Brooke to Alexander, 8 March and reply, 12 March 1943; *ibid.* Quite where the description of Anderson as 'a good plain cook' originated is unclear. Montgomery apparently used exactly the same term to Anderson's chief intelligence officer, Kit Dawnay, during the Tripoli study week (February 1943).

[21] Eisenhower's 'Despatch on the North African Campaign, 1942–43', p. 36; Blumenson, *Rommel's Last Victory*, p. 295.

[22] Colonel Henry E. Gardiner, 'We Fought at Kasserine', *Armored Cavalry Journal* (March–April 1948), pp. 9–17.

[23] Montgomery to Brooke, 16 February 1943. Montgomery Papers; BLM49/17.

[24] Alexander, *Memoirs*, p. 65.

[25] Montgomery, *Memoirs*, p. 158; *El Alamein to the River Sangro*, p. 44. He claimed that Alexander's 'very real cry for help' was sent on 20 February, but was mistaken.

[26] De Guingand, *Operation Victory*, p. 242.

[27] Leese to his wife, 24 February 1943; Leese Papers, Box 2.

[28] Montgomery's Situation Report, 'Preparations for moving Westwards from Tripoli against the Mareth Position', 20 March 1943. Montgomery Papers, BLM 31/1-4.

[29] Leese to his wife, 2 March (mis-dated 2 February) 1943. Leese Papers, Box 2.

[30] Leese to his wife, 5 March 1943, *ibid.*

[31] Montgomery to Brigadier Simpson, 5 March 1943; quoted by Hamilton, *Monty: Master of the Battlefield*, p. 161.

[32] Rommel, *Krieg Ohne Hass*, pp. 363–4.

[33] Lang's Group had been provided with 12 Mk IV Specials, eight Mk IVs and 40 Mk IIIs as well as the 14 Mk VI Tigers; Macksey, *Crucible of Power*, p. 182.

[34] Clifford, *The Conquest of North Africa*, p. 68; Austin, *Birth of an Army*, pp. 94–5; D'Arcy Dawson, *Tunisian Battle*, p. 164; Marshall, *Over to Tunis*, p. 74. Marshall was one of the bevy of war correspondents in Tunisia.

[35] Daniell, *Regimental History: The Royal Hampshire Regiment*, Vol. 3, p. 104.

36 Austin, *Birth of an Army*, p. 96.

37 Perrett, *Allied Tanks North Africa*, p. 44.

38 Austin, *Birth Of An Army*, p.98.

39 Oberstleutnant Koch's 5th Fallschirmjäger Regiment was renamed the Jäger Regiment *Hermann Göring* in February 1943. This involved merely a tactical regrouping and did not represent any increase in the total German paratroop strength in Tunisia. The regiment was correctly estimated by the Americans to be, 'a first-class fighting outfit.' Koch retained an attenuated independent battlegroup of his own.

40 Lieutenant R.F. Kinden, TS Memoir. IWM84/50/1.

41 Blaxland, *The Plain Cook and the Great Showman*, pp. 172–3.

42 R. Priestley, Memoir. IWM 83/24/1.

43 Stainforth, *Wings of the Wind*, p. 100.

44 Perrett, *Allied Tanks North Africa*, p. 51; also Austin, *Birth of an Army*, pp. 101–02; D'Arcy Dawson, *Tunisian Battle*, pp. 165–6.

45 Saunders, *The Green Beret*, p. 145.

46 Brooke to Alexander, 20 February 1943.

47 Saunders, *The Red Beret*, p. 111.

48 D'Arcy Dawson, *Tunisian Battle*, p. 168.

49 Quoted by Arthur, *Men of the Red Beret*, p. 68.

50 Saunders, *The Red Beret*, p. 112.

51 Arthur, *ibid.*, p. 52.

52 Battle Report of Operation *Ochsenkopf*, 3 March 1943; 'War in Tunisia, 1 March 1943 – 27 March 1943'; RH19-VIII/352. BM-MA.

53 Gunner Greenwood. Sound Archives recording, IWM.

54 Kesselring, *Memoirs*, p. 147.

Chapter 12

Every Objective Must Be Held

'My son's birthday, he is four years old. I hope I shall soon be home with him, I have missed so much of his life.'

Sergeant J.R. Harris, 4th County of London Yeomanry, in his diary, 10 March 1943.[1]

'I must confess that instead of becoming hardened by war and battles I find the reverse to be the case and I am if anything more nervy than I was 3 years ago. It's a pity and not what you'd expect.'

The Rev. J.E.G. Quinn while with the Coldstream Guards at Medenine, 11 March 1943. Quinn had already won the MC and twice been wounded: six months later he was killed at Salerno.[2]

———

'We will stand and fight the enemy in our present positions,' ordered Montgomery at Medenine. 'There must be NO WITHDRAWAL anywhere, and of course NO SURRENDER.'[3] Ultra had given clear evidence of Rommel's intention to mount Operation Capri with an encircling attack using what was left, after Thala, of 10th Panzer together with half 15th Panzer and 21st Panzer Divisions, though his precise thrust line was not known until the actual day of the assault. Every angle of approach was covered. Anti-tank guns were sighted to kill German tanks and not simply to protect the infantry. There was no wire and few mines in front of the troops, but they were well dug-in and covered by concentrated artillery whose fire could quickly be shifted in any direction.

Interception of radio signals by British Army Y detected the southwards movement of Rommel's troops supported by 160 tanks and 200 guns, and air sightings of 10th Panzer and other armour suggested he would attempt a decisive thrust from the west.[4] By mischance, the BBC revealed on the eve of the attack that the New Zealand Division was moving into the front line. For some reason the Germans apparently missed this useful nugget of information.[5]

Rommel stood in a open car on the morning of 6 March, appearing pale and jaundiced, a dirty neck bandage covering the festering desert sores which plagued him, to observe the start of his attack. Precisely at 0600 hours his artillery opened up as Panzers rumbled out of early morning mist from the hills to the north and west of Medenine. Their only hope of success lay in a feint along the coast road by 90th Light Division, joined by battlegroups from the Italian *Spezia* and *Trieste* Divisions.

Coming up against the British flank between Tadjera Khir and Medenine, 15th and 21st Panzer soon discovered that this ruse had failed. In the very centre of the advance, Hermann Frömbgen of 5th Panzer Regiment (21st Panzer) got to within 1,000 metres of the foot of low hills before Metameur, slightly north-west of Medenine, when, as he recalled, 'all hell broke loose.' From real gun pits, located 40 yards behind hastily abandoned dummies, the Panzers were suddenly engulfed by extraordinarily heavy artillery fire. Low-flying RAF aircraft rocketed the tanks, while deadly machine-gunning forced them to close up their armoured panels; the shooting then swept the lorried infantry in their rear, causing much disorganization and heavy casualties.[6]

On every side, 15th and 21st Panzer and 90th Light were taking heavy losses and by late evening it was all over. Out on the battlefield, in torrential rain, British sappers were demolishing abandoned tanks. 'Under heavy fire and in profound darkness we had to return to our start point,' noted one Gefreiter, 'The sacrifice was in vain.'[7] Behind them they left 52 smashed tanks and had suffered 645 casualties, over two-thirds of them German. By comparison, Eighth Army losses were moderate indeed; 130 men of all ranks killed or wounded and not a single tank lost. The battle had been, as de Guingand rightly remarked, 'a little classic all of its own,' and on its success Montgomery's vanity began to inflate alarmingly.[8]

For Rommel, Medenine had been a catastrophe: 'A great gloom settled over us all,' he wrote. 'The Eighth Army's attack was now imminent and we had to face it. For the Army Group to remain longer in Africa was now plain suicide.'[9] On 8 March he handed over *Heeresgruppe Afrika* to von Arnim who remarked grimly, 'One of us was enough here to be liquidated.'[10] Next day Rommel flew to Rome to see Ambrosio at *Comando Supremo* in an attempt to save his troops from certain disaster by persuading the high command to shorten the front in Tunisia from 400 to 100 miles, adequately supply defenders of well-fortified positions and use small motorized forces to squeeze out enemy penetrations of the line. The Führer thought him over-pessimistic and after decorating Rommel with the Oakleaves with Swords and Diamonds, sent him off to Semmering on sick-leave.[11]

Few on the Allied side knew Rommel had gone until an Enigma intercept on 18 March revealed the fact; the first signal, signed by von Arnim as *Oberbefehlshaber* of *Heeresgruppe Afrika*, was decrypted 24 hours later. This information was withheld from all commands by the War Office for fear that the Germans might get to know that their machine ciphers had been broken and it was not until 24 April that an Eighth Army intelligence summary revealed Rommel's departure from Africa.[12] Other changes in the German command structure at this time put General der Panzertruppe von Vaerst, who arrived in

Rome on 3 March, in command of Fifth Panzer Army while Generalleutnant Hans Cramer replaced Generalleutnant Ziegler, who had temporarily commanded the *Afrika Korps*.[13]

No final decision was taken about Rommel's return but Hitler and Kesselring had lost faith in him. Although his troops still fought and died there, Rommel's African days were over. In the year or so left to him the Desert Fox never again saw the arena in which he had forged such a mighty reputation.

<hr>

Just as Rommel's star waned, Montgomery's ascended. In England he had become a celebrity, much to his surprise and delight: 'In defeat unthinkable, in victory insufferable,' Churchill was supposed to have said.[14] Apart from Monty's own troops, no one else could fight: '... the Americans were complete amateurs at fighting' and since First Army was led by Anderson, whom he thought, 'quite unfit to command an Army in the field', Eighth Army would do the job by itself.[15] Alexander was also concerned about Anderson's shortcomings and wrote off most Americans apart from Fredendall, whom he liked and supported.

Eisenhower, however, now had grave misgivings about II Corps and his commanders in the field. 'The problem plagues me all the time,' he wrote to Marshall. Robinett was a puzzle: 'He has the best fighting record of any Combat Commander on the front', but had a loose tongue and appeared, 'intelligent but entirely without judgment, except in a tactical sense.' Terry Allen was doing, 'a satisfactory job', as was his assistant divisional commander, Brigadier-General Theodore (Teddy) Roosevelt,[16] one of the genuine maverick characters of 1st Infantry and, like Allen, liable to ignore army regulations: 'Aw cheer up,' he once told his men after a particularly hard battle, 'when this is over, you can go back to Algiers, beat up a few MPs [Military Police] and feel better.'[17] He shared with Allen a well-earned reputation as an exceptionally courageous and superlative leader in the field.

Major-General 'Doc' Ryder also passed scrutiny but Fredendall's staff was weak and the C-in-C had spent much time travelling, 'just to assure myself that he was doing the job successfully.' Worried at Fredendall's inability to select good men and get the best out of them, Eisenhower was already looking for a substitute to replace him.[18]

<hr>

On 14 March, Eighth Army was ordered by Alexander to take the Mareth position and II Corps to capture Gafsa, advance on Maknassy and capture El Guettar, thereby threatening the enemy's line of communication north of Gabès. Hitler had ordered 'limited but concentrated attacks' and a 'reserve line' in the Gabès area which was to be fortified 'most strongly and at once' with a doubling (and later tripling) of sea transport and increased offensive activity by the Luftwaffe.[19]

That such grandiose plans bore virtually no relationship to reality did nothing to dent Kesselring's habitual sunny confidence, even after he had inspected the defences in Tunisia. Yet the defence line was only lightly held in places and in others not at all. Since Allied strength was calculated at some 210,000 fighting troops, 1,600 tanks, 1,100 anti-tank guns and 850 field guns, they might well defeat each of the Axis armies in turn. In face of this overwhelming preponderance of men and matériel, there seemed little chance of building up adequate defences, which in any case demanded an increase in monthly shipments of supplies to 140,000 tons.

The most impossible job in Tunisia belonged to Oberstleutnant i.G. Brand, *Oberquartiermeister Heeresgruppe Afrika*, responsible for supplies to the Axis armies. As an absolute minimum on which to subsist, they required approximately 75,000 tons of supplies every month.[20] In April, not more than 23,017 tons arrived and about 3,000 tons during the early part of May. By then, a catastrophic 77 per cent of supplies was being lost in transit.

On 13 March Fifth Panzer Army reported that it had absolutely no reserve stocks whatsoever left. Daily meals in the line often amounted to no more than half a mess-tin of cold rice, one and a half slices of bread and two potatoes.[21] Symptomatic of a rapidly worsening situation was Hitler's decision to cancel the consignment of important documents by air from Italy to Africa.[22] Troops sent as reinforcements to Tunisia no longer went through the Africa acclimatisation course and the best that could be done was to make some arrangements after they arrived.[23]

About the only positive development was the arrival on 17 March of one infantry regiment (two battalions) of 999th Light *Afrika* Division to reinforce Fifth Panzer Army. Apart from specially selected officers and NCOs, it consisted of troops punished for offences against army discipline, men who had been reduced to the ranks and *Schwarzschlaechter*.[24] They were given the chance to work out their punishments by demonstrating bravery on the battlefield. Roughly ten per cent of the division's personnel deserted at the first opportunity but units which later fought around Fondouk did so with exemplary courage. Even so, since transport space was so limited, only one other rifle regiment arrived in April. The divisional commander, Generalleutnant Kurt Thomas, was killed when his aircraft was intercepted on its way to Tunisia.[25]

Oberstleutnant Brand's opposite number on the Allied side was Major-General C.H. Miller, who took over a supply line growing in strength and vigour. The situation at Eighth Army was 'pretty strong' but at Fériana, at II Corps HQ, there was talk of being stretched to the limit. '[I] rather doubt this statement actually,' he noted, 'as they have had little fighting, but no doubt the adm[inistration] is suffering from excessive demands from the fwd troops.'[26] In reality, front-line troops got only a residue of supplies due to persistent pilfering while in transit, though Anderson remarked that there was never any real shortage of ammunition.

———◆◆———

Eisenhower finally lost patience with Fredendall, especially after listening to Alexander, who had changed his mind and was now 'quite worried' about his lack of ability to plan the next operation.[27] Commanding US I Armored Corps in French Morocco, Patton was chafing for active command when the C-in-C ordered him to be ready for extended field service. Realising that he was, 'taking over rather a mess', from Fredendall, Patton was, nevertheless, full of confidence: 'I think I will have more trouble with the British than the Boches.'[28] Fredendall's staff was outraged, believing Anderson (rather than Alexander) had done the dirty on him. 'Pinky' Ward was mightily relieved: only a day or so before the news came through, he had written: 'The situation re Fredendall is still dangerous. He will get me if he can.' Afterwards, 'Glory be,' everything had changed.[29]

Fredendall was greatly surprised by his removal on 5 March although Eisenhower cabled Marshall that same day explaining that, 'no stigma should attach to him in connection with this relief because in many respects he did a very soldierly job in the recent fighting.'[30] Six days later Fredendall left North Africa for good. Physically timid to the last, he refused to fly to Constantine and left by road at what he thought was the safest time, in the small hours of 7 March. 'I think Fredendall is either a little nuts or badly scared,' remarked Patton.[31] Above all, Fredendall and his staff assumed that the deceitful British were behind his replacement.

'He may have been used to some extent as a goat to protect Gen[eral] Anderson – I can't be sure about that,' wrote Captain Webb, and, 'though he showed amazing self-control considering the provocation, he occasionally popped off about the British.' Observing that, 'It's strictly a British show over there and the only reason an American [Eisenhower] happens to be in titular command was that the French would not accept an Englishman,' Webb was bitterly critical. 'To them will go the glory and all the news will be slanted to play up the British and play down the Americans... all the time we were getting trimmed the BBC was broadcasting about "green American troops," but the moment we held and broke the Germans it suddenly became "Allied troops under Gen. Anderson." You don't like that.'[32]

One of the first things Eisenhower told Patton at Algiers on 5 March was that criticism of the British must stop. 'I fear he has sold his soul to the devil on "Cooperation" which I think means we are pulling the chestnuts for our noble allies,' noted Patton. Travelling on to meet Alexander, 'a snob in the best sense of the word', with whom he was much impressed because of his fighting record – he knew that, 'It is clear that I too must "cooperate" or get out.'[33]

Patton blew in like a whirlwind. Within hours of arriving at Fredendall's HQ in a smothering cloud of dust thrown up by a procession of scout cars and half-tracks, sirens blaring, bristling with machine guns, he issued orders to smarten up the corps HQ staff. This had a stunning, not to say devastating, effect. Incredulous officers and men were fined $25 for wearing improper uniform and speed limits and other traffic regulations were strictly enforced. "I guess I am a S.O.B. but Discipline will win the war,' he told Eisenhower.[34] All this, thought Bradley, appointed deputy corps commander to gain battle experience, was designed to emphasize a new and very different leadership though some, like Martin Philipsborn of 1st Armored's CC B, considered it counter-productive.[35]

'A grand chap and a born leader,' thought Major-General Penny, head of Signals for the Middle East Command, 'Smart, blasphemous, fit and "Glamorous"! Very rich and a fighter. Possibly a better soldier than one thinks but born in the wrong century.'[36]

Wherever he went the tall, straight-framed Patton acted up to his brash image. At 1st Infantry Division's HQ, a small oasis near El Quettar, Patton was irate at seeing slit trenches dug all around. 'What are all these things for?' he inquired in his high-pitched voice. 'Well, you know,' said one officer, 'there is a lot of enemy air here.' Patton went over to Terry Allen. 'Terry, which one is yours?' 'That one right over there General,' said Allen. Whereupon Patton walked over, unbuttoned his flies and urinated. 'Now use it,' he retorted.[37]

Behind such outward exhibitions, however, lay years of professional training and a retentive memory in which was stored anything of military application. Eisenhower appreciated this but was anxious to curb Patton's more unbridled behaviour – a further reason for Bradley's appointment as an understudy.[38] 'I want you as Corps Commander – not as a casualty,' Eisenhower told Patton, adding that he was to rehabilitate the Americans under his command and prepare with all speed for the attack ordered by 18th Army Group for 14 March.[39]

II Corps had too little strength to mount other than a limited offensive. Scattered along 120 miles of front were only about 90,000 men in four divisions and supporting units.[40] To their left on the Western Dorsale were 50,000 Frenchmen and, further north again, about 120,000 British. A major worry was that the enemy might punch through the passes between 1st Armored and 34th Infantry Divisions, cutting the Americans' line of communication.

Much to Patton's frustration, restraint was the order of the day but his officers were more circumspect: 'I agreed completely with this idea that we ought to go down [onto the desert before Gafsa] buttoned up, ready for anything with our flanks secure,' commented Lieutenant-Colonel Porter of the 1st Infantry Division staff, 'We didn't need another Kasserine right then.'[41]

Alexander's initial plan was for II Corps to reopen the Thélepte airfields, move through Fériana and take Gafsa by 15 March, though this was later put back two days. Patton ordered 1st Infantry to take Gafsa and 1st Armored to drive on Maknassy, which entailed furious preparations. His other two divisions remained in reserve to cover any surprise Rommel (who was assumed to be still in Tunisia) might pull.

Montgomery, in the meantime, was positioning his forces on the Mareth front, ready to attack on the night of 20/21 March. Operation Pugilist-Gallop was designed to smash through the Mareth Line, push onwards without pause through the Gabès Gap, drive northwards on Sfax, Sousse and finally capture Tunis. Strong support was to be provided by Air Vice-Marshal Harry Broadhurst, new commander of the Desert Air Force. An ex-Battle of Britain fighter pilot sporting a brilliant war record, Broadhurst had acted as Air Marshal Coningham's chief of staff until his boss assumed command of the Northwest African Tactical Air Force, formed the day after Coningham took over what was the Allied Air Support Command, from Brigadier-General Kuter, on 17 February.[42]

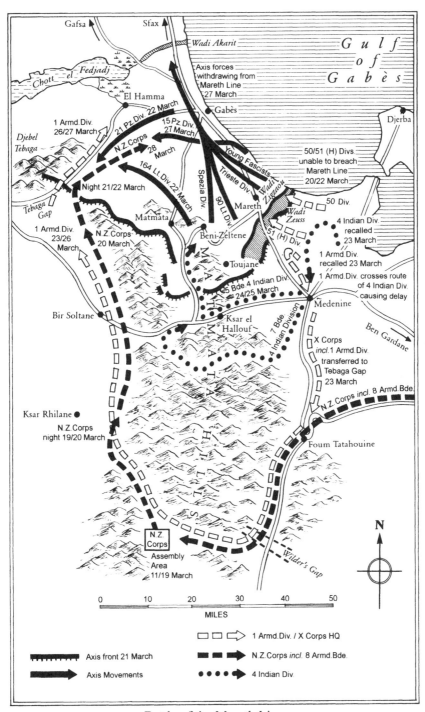

Gafsa

Sfax

Wadi Akarit

G u l f
o f
G a b è s

Axis forces
withdrawing from
Mareth Line
27 March

Chott el Fedjadj

El Hamma

Gabès

Djerba

1 Armd. Div.
26/27 March

Djebel Tebaga

21.Pz.Div. 22 March

15.Pz.Div.
27 March

N.Z. Corps

28 March

164 Lt. Div. 22 March

Young Fascists

50/51 (H) Divs.
unable to breach
Mareth Line
20/22 March

Night 21/22 March

Spezia Div.

Trieste Div.

Wadi Zigzaou

50 Div.

Tebaga Gap

Matmata

90 Lt. Div.

Mareth

Wadi Zeuss

4 Indian Div.
recalled
23 March

1 Armd. Div.
23/26 March

N.Z. Corps
20 March

Beni-Zeltene

51 (H) Div.

1 Armd. Div. recalled 23 March

1 Armd. Div. crosses route
of 4 Indian Div.
causing delay

Toujane

25 Bde. 4 Indian Div.
24/25 March

Bir Soltane

Ksar el
Hallouf

7 Bde.

4 Indian Division

Medenine

Ben Gardane

X Corps
incl. 1 Armd. Div.
transferred to
Tebaga Gap
23 March

Ksar Rhilane

N.Z. Corps
night 19/20 March

N.Z. Corps incl. 8 Armd. Bde.

Foum Tatahouine

N

N.Z.
Corps

Assembly
Area
11/19 March

Wilder's Gap

| 0 | 10 | 20 | 30 | 40 | 50 |

MILES

☐ ☐ ⇨ 1 Armd. Div. / X Corps HQ

▰▰▰➤ N.Z. Corps *incl.* 8 Armd. Bde.

⬟⬟⬟⬟⬟➤ Axis front 21 March

➤ Axis Movements

●●●●➤ 4 Indian Div.

Battle of the Mareth Line
March 1943

Montgomery and Coningham had little time for each other and their prickly relationship had deteriorated steadily throughout the desert campaign.[43] Known by the soldiers for his bloody-minded temperament, Coningham was a strong proponent of equality in air-ground co-operation which, so far, was notable by its absence during operations in Tunisia, not least because the US War Department insisted that the USAAF remain subservient to the land forces.

Coningham's subordinate commands were 242 Group RAF (Air Commodore Kenneth Cross) operating with First Army; the Desert Air Force (Broadhurst) with Eighth Army; and 12th US Air Support Command (Brigadier-General Paul L. Williams) with II Corps. His insistence on an independent tactical air doctrine inevitably caused some ruffled feathers but for the first time in Tunisia Allied air power was no longer to be a mere adjunct to land operations – providing an air umbrella over the troops – but a striking, flexible, offensive force, what Coningham termed, 'a combination of shield and punch.' However, this was not what Broadhurst had in mind. On taking over the Desert Air Force he ordered aircrews to concentrate on ground-air co-operation, using stationary captured vehicles laid out in the desert to show how difficult it was to score direct hits.

Montgomery favoured Broadhurst's line and knew such teamwork would be essential in helping to crack open the Mareth Line's formidable defences. Nearest the coast were elements of General Sozzani's *Young Fascist* Division and, holding a position as far as the main Gabès–Mareth road, General La Ferla's *Trieste* Division. Blocking the main road in front of Mareth itself and covering the Wadi Zeuss were von Sponeck's 90th Light Division's Panzer Grenadier Regiments with an attached battalion of 47th Panzer Grenadier Regiment. Further inland was the *Spezia* Division and General Falugi's *Pistoia* Division out on the far flank at Toujane. Directly southwards the Hallouf Pass in the Matmata Hills was protected by von Liebenstein's 164th Light Division.

Behind the Mareth position stood Borowietz's depleted 15th Panzer Division with Hildebrandt's 21st and von Broich's 10th Panzer. While the 15th was kept in reserve, 21st Panzer was forward of the Gabès Gap, a passable stretch of desert 25 miles to the rear of the Mareth Line. It lay between the village of El Hamma, 20 miles inland, and Gabès and could be reached by road from the Tebaga Gap, at the northern extremity of the Matmata Hills. North and west of El Hamma lies a great salt lake, the Chott el Fedjadj, and it was at its northern exit, 15 miles from the Gabès Gap and pinched between the salt lake and the sea, that the Wadi Akarit provided another substantial natural defence.[44] Immediately behind it was deployed 10th Panzer.

Broadhurst could put up 535 fighters, fighter-bombers and tank-busters, 140 day-bombers, 80 Halifax and Wellington night-bombers of No. 205 Group and all the Mitchell and Marauder day-bombers of the NASAF. Against this massive force the Germans had only 83 serviceable aircraft in southern Tunisia and about 40 Italian. Montgomery could also deploy many more tanks yet, despite such numerical odds, he was extremely cautious.[45] Using information about the enemy's dispositions from the Army's Y service, POW interrogations, captured documents and Enigma, he planned to put in a heavy frontal attack with 51st

Highland Division pushing forward along the main coastal road axis. On its right, 50th Northumbrian Division, commanded by Major-General 'Crasher' Nichols, was to breach the Wadi Zigzaou anywhere between Hamra Rass and the sea.

In reserve, Horrocks' X Corps, with a strong, mobile armoured force consisting of 1st and 7th Armoured Divisions under command, waited to meet any enemy threat that might develop between the main thrusts and, once the initial breakthrough had been made, would pass through Leese's XXX Corps and exploit towards Gabès.

When Tuker's 4th Indian Infantry Division was brought up on the left rear of 50th Division, he was told that his command was to be split between X and XXX Corps and Eighth Army HQ. A short, sharp conversation with Horrocks quickly established that, with his presence no longer required, he could clear off back to India. Montgomery informed the irate Tuker that the idea had come from Horrocks. 'I knew that Horrocks was trying to grab troops in order to get in on the Mareth battle and so compete with Leese,' noted Tuker, 'I do not yet know which of the two, Horrocks or Monty, was most to be believed (then, or at any other time).'[46]

To complicate matters, at XXX Corps Leese had the knife out for one of his subordinates, Major-General G.W.E.J. Erskine, who had taken command of 7th Armoured Division on 24 January after John Harding had been wounded. 'Bobby Erskine... has risen to great fame here of late but I am sure that he is ultimately a complete shit... He is at present frightened of me...'[47]

⎯⎯⎯❖⎯⎯⎯

Prior to the main attack, scheduled for 20 March, Freyberg's New Zealand Division (designated a corps at midnight on 11/12 March because of its special tasks and extra attached units) began to gather its 25,600 men, 151 tanks, 112 field guns and 172 anti-tank guns in a staging area south-east of Foum Tatahouine. Under command were 5th and 6th New Zealand Infantry Brigades, 8th Armoured Brigade (from XXX Corps), Leclerc's L Force (Free French), the armoured cars of 1st King's Dragoon Guards, and additional artillery regiments. Freyberg was to force the corps through Wilder's Gap around the western slopes of the Matmata Hills, reach the entrance to the Tebaga Gap (objective 'Plum'), advance to El Hamma ('Peach'), and capture the hills northwest of Gabès ('Grape') bringing his troops well into the rear of the Mareth Line.

Monty's latest version of his 'left hook' involved an approach march of 250 miles over open country and was not without risks for, if Leese's attack faltered in the main sector, Freyberg would be way out in the wilderness, threatened by 15th and 21st Panzer Divisions.[48]

Screening Wilder's Gap from enemy reconnaissance probes was Leclerc's force, lying up by day between the sand sea called Le Grand Erg Oriental (the 'Great Oriental Urge' to soldiers) and the Matmata Hills. They were attacked on 10th March by a strong reconnaissance force from 21st Panzer consisting of armoured cars, artillery, and infantry in tracked carriers and trucks, supported by Me-109s and Stukas. The French had been forewarned and with RAF assistance, summoned by a radio 'air tentacle' unit, repulsed the attackers. 'The British... also did great execution, particularly of armoured cars,' noted Captain Peers Carter, a liaison officer with Leclerc's force, 'The battlefield was simply littered with German dead when they pulled out.'[49]

Freyberg's troops were able to start off unmolested through Wilder's Gap on 11 March, led by Lieutenant Tinker's LRDG T2 patrol and accompanied by Mactroop, a highly individualistic team of volunteers from 9th and 51st HAA Regiment, RA, commanded by Brigadier H.M.J. McIntyre, who deployed to maximum effect, a number of captured German 88mm guns.

From their staging area the New Zealanders turned northwards towards Bir Soltane and the Tebaga Gap. Travelling at eight miles an hour on a nine-vehicle front through broken country, with 'L' Force covering his line of communication, Freyberg's corps on the move was a formidable undertaking. On 20 March, just east of Ksar Rhilane, a squadron of RAF Kittihawks inadvertently strafed the column, causing numerous casualties and setting some vehicles on fire. 'The RAF is supposed to be on our side,' complained Sergeant Caffell of Mactroop.[50]

Freyberg's attack on objective Plum (the Tebaga Gap) was to coincide with an assault by Leese's XXX Corps, forcing the Axis command to meet simultaneous threats from two directions. Preliminary moves on the night of 16/17 March included attempts to drive in the enemy's outer bastions on the Mareth Line during Operations Canter and Walk.

In Canter, elements of two divisions, the 50th (69th Infantry Brigade – 5th East Yorkshires and 6th Green Howards) and 51st (153rd Infantry Brigade – 5/7th Gordon Highlanders) cleared out isolated pockets of Italians from the flat coastal area without much trouble and went beyond the Wadi Zeuss, forward of Wadi Zigzaou. But on their left, 201st Guards Brigade ran into awful difficulties in carrying out Walk on the bare, whalebacked hills at the south-west end of the Mareth defences dominating the main road to Mareth and known from their configuration as 'The Horseshoe.'

Very little opposition had been expected and an over-confident Montgomery told the Guards: 'It is going to be a party, and when I give a party it is always a good one!'[51] So men of the 3rd Coldstream, advancing with 6th Grenadiers on their right, were relaxed, even exchanging jokes, as they crossed the start line at 1040 hours supported by three medium and five field regiments of artillery.

After fording a large wadi about 400 yards from the start line, they stumbled into a large and dense minefield whose location had not been established by British intelligence. To make matters worse, the Germans had captured a gunnery officer and knew from his map the supporting fire plan and its exact timings. The unwounded who managed to extricate themselves fought their way up bare hillsides with matchless courage. Verey lights on the Grenadier's side announced they had secured their objectives but despite superhuman efforts the Coldstreamers took only one of theirs. 'Well I am still alive and that was more than I dared to hope twelve hours ago, when we were caught... by mortar and machine gun fire of terrific intensity,' recorded the Rev. Gough Quinn, a Coldstream padre. 'Our attack was a complete failure... Every attempt to get through was wrecked by

[a] devilish minefield on which scores of men were killed and [those] going to help them were in turn blown up... Most of our casualties we could not get at. The shelling was terrific.'[52]

The Grenadiers lost 363 killed, wounded and missing and the more experienced Coldstream battalion, 159. Even recovering their bodies proved difficult: 69 Grenadiers were later brought in – an effort which necessitated lifting 700 mines. 'The most damnable thing has happened,' wrote Leese, blaming himself. 'I had thought it would be an easy blooding for them.'[53] It was certainly a blooding though hardly as Leese had expected. Yet despite this setback, Montgomery's confidence in Leese and his own abilities remained undiminished. Writing to Brooke on 17 March he boasted: 'I had no difficulty at all in the area where my real thrust is to go in [with 50th Division across the Wadi Zigzaou], and I am pretending that I am not really interested in that area at all.'[54]

On the other side, von Arnim's intelligence sources revealed Montgomery supplying his main front while heavy traffic and reinforcements at Ksar Rhilane suggested a possible thrust west of the Matmata hills. Captured documents and POW interrogations gave a reasonably accurate picture of the opposing battle array and signals intelligence reported an unusual silence on all Eighth Army's wireless nets on the Mareth front – and after 16 March on the communications of the flanking New Zealand group – suggesting preparations were virtually complete. 'Similar signs had been observed before all large scale attacks by Eighth Army,' noted a senior German intelligence officer.[55]

Oliver Leese was unshaken after the mauling suffered by 201st Guards Brigade but critical of what American help was on offer. Alexander had virtually written them off, relegating II Corps to a subordinate and supporting role, limited to reaching Gafsa and then merely demonstrating down the Gabès road. 'Don't let them be too ambitious,' cautioned Monty, telling Alexander that once he was through the Mareth Line and breaking through the Gabès Gap, 'I do not want the Americans in my way.' Alexander agreed, confining American and French troops west of a clear-cut boundary extending along the hills from Maknassy to Faïd and thence along the Eastern Dorsale to Fondouk.[56]

Newly-promoted Lieutenant-General on 12 March, Patton began Operation Wop five days later when US aircraft laid on fragmentation bombing at 0930 hours, half an hour before 15,000 men of the 'Big Red One' (1st Infantry Division) moved through pre-dawn darkness along desert trails branching off the Fériana–Gafsa road. They were directed by military police, 'with the same calm ill nature exhibited by New York traffic cops.'[57] Against very little opposition and in pelting hail and rain they occupied Gafsa by mid-morning, the enemy pulling out along the Gabès road and sowing mines to cover his retreat.

Back home, this easy victory was the subject of much enthusiastic publicity. Patton, 'a hard-hitting, fast-thinking American hero', received the lion's share. American confidence soared still higher when El Guettar, ten miles east of Gafsa, was taken by 1st Ranger Battalion (attached to 26th RCT, 1st Infantry) on 18

March. Most of the Germans had pulled out 48 hours earlier, taking with them all the Italians' trucks and even the wheels from their field guns, leaving the *Centauro* Division no option but to stand and fight. Demoralized, they offered little resistance to the Rangers' fired-up aggression though marauding Ju-88s caused some nasty casualties.

In his wartime book Captain Ralph Ingersoll describes how he came across one of the injured doughboys sitting on a rock, his rifle across his knees. Looking up, face contorted and tears running down his cheeks, the soldier held out his left hand: 'Please, sir, get them quickly and have them take it off.' Ingersoll saw what remained of a hand. 'There was,' he wrote, 'no back to it. There were some bones and some red and white patterns, like the patterns in medical textbooks.' Again the soldier asked plaintively, 'Please, have them take it off so I don't have to look at it.' Near the road to El Guettar, Ingersoll met a lieutenant, his face white with anger, picking up ugly, jagged pieces of blue-grey steel. 'You see this,' he panted, 'You see this? I got a place for this. I got a place in a God-damn booby trap for those God-damned bastards.'[58]

While his troops consolidated their positions, Patton heard that 1st Armored was, 'largely stuck in the mud' but was determined that Ward should advance on Maknassy whilst infantry and artillery took Sened Sation. On 19 March he went to see Ward, travelling over 42 miles of new road carved out by army engineers in filthy weather. 'Wet, dirty, and isolated, they keep right at it. I stopped and talked to each group and complimented them on what they had done and they seemed pleased.' Further on he observed a squadron of Derbyshire Yeomanry on reconnaissance duties as usual: 'They were drying their blankets on cactus bushes, which either indicates great hardihood or great stupidity.'[59]

On arriving, he found Ward's tanks mired in a sea of glutinous sludge. Robinett was defensive and, curiously, lacking in confidence. Nevertheless, his, 'violent passion for war', aroused, Patton was raring to go and ordered Ward to advance on Maknassy and take the heights beyond, even if it meant using only infantry, ferried forward in half-tracks.[60] Returning to his HQ at Fériana, Patton found Lieutenant-General Dick McCreery, Alexander's chief of staff, waiting with new orders. While holding Gafsa, Patton was to halt at the limit set for 1st Armored's advance. 'These instructions definitely prohibit an American advance to the sea,' he fumed, '... this is to pinch us out so as to insure a British triumph. I kept my temper and agreed. There is nothing else to do, but I can't see how Ike can let them [the British] pull his leg so. It is awful.'[61]

The day after the Americans took Gafsa there appeared, at the eastern entrance to the town, large signs emblazoned with the insignia of First Army (a Red Cross of the Crusaders) and a message in a scroll above the shield: 'The First Army welcomes the Eighth Army.'[62] But such a meeting was to be delayed longer than anyone could reasonably have expected.

Committed to a narrow break-in front at Mareth, Montgomery warned 4th Indian Division that the battle would be, 'a slogging match'. Brigadier Bateman (commander, 5th Indian Infantry Brigade) thought, 'no worse approach to any battle objective could have been selected.' It was, he observed, 'a flat and featureless plain, across which it was quite bad enough to follow behind an attack let alone carry it out.'[63] That unenviable task fell to 50th Division's 151st Infantry Brigade (commanded by Brigadier Beak, VC) whose 9th Durham Light Infantry had orders to cross the Wadi Zigzaou and capture an outlying enemy position, Ksiba Ouest at the same time as 8th Battalion, 1,200 yards away on its left, took Ouerzi Est. In the meantime, 7th Green Howards were to protect 151st Infantry Brigade's left flank by securing a prominent fortification named the Bastion.

The RTR's 50th Battalion would then cross the Wadi Zigzaou and keep going while 6th Durham Light Infantry mopped up behind. Close up, in reserve, waited 4th Indian Division ready to carry out various possibilities of which the most ambitious was to exploit towards Gabès. On standby was 51st Division, prepared to advance up the main road towards Gabès and Sfax if a breakthrough was effected while X Corps awaited a rapid advance on Gabès should a route become available. By aerial reconnaissance, patrols and flash-spotting, the enemy's gun positions on the Wadi Zigzaou had been located. All XXX Corps artillery was involved and divided its barrage into three phases with suitably martial names – 'Hawk', 'Falcon', and 'Eagle' – whose success was to be identified by signal rockets, though some bright character had chosen the same signal for both first and third phases.

Great sheets of flame lit up the dark night of 20th March as the preparatory barrage opened up. The heavy 5.5-inch guns were each sending over shells weighing 100 pounds, fused to explode just above the ground, spreading a lethal hail of metal. In the gunpits, sweating gunners reeled from the deafening concussions, the barrels of their guns too hot to touch. 'You can close your eyes and plug your ears with cotton,' said an officer, 'but you can't get away from that terrific concussion. It's no fun to fire for four hours at a stretch like that.'[64]

In order to maximise the effect of the creeping barrage that followed the troops had to advance, over favourable terrain, within 100 to 150 yards of the line of bursting shells, taking losses from them if necessary. 'Until and only until the infantry suffer casualties from our own guns are the infantry getting within fighting distance of the enemy and doing the job,' observed Brigadier Dimoline, commanding the artillery of 4th Indian Division.[65]

The first British assault troops into action were Green Howards' special fighting patrols who proudly labelled themselves 'The Thugs.' Moving about 500 yards ahead of 7th Battalion in small parties with the sappers they quickly came under murderous fire. Struggling through a minefield they cleared a path and raised scaling ladders to clear the enemy's anti-tank ditch. Wiping out the first machine-gun post they got through another minefield, attacked a machine-gun post and took about 30 Germans and Italians prisoner. Meanwhile, the main body of the battalion had started out but was caught by severe shell and mortar fire in the anti-tank ditch. Lieutenant-Colonel Seagrim rallied the shaken troops and won a VC – though he was killed at Wadi Akarit two weeks later. Fighting on in the maze of trenches and defence works making up the Bastion, 7th Green Howards took it by daybreak, 6th Battalion being brought up to secure their left flank.

The Durham Light Infantry's assault troops who started out for the Wadi Zigzaou moved as if they were on their way to a picnic. Their confidence quickly dissipated however, once they ran into enemy shelling and mortaring which crowded them behind the leading Scorpion tanks.[66] Reaching the edge of their first major obstacle, they found all the features already known from reconnaissance – a steep and well-defined bank, up to 20 feet high, and a ditch often filled with stagnant water which had turned to a sticky morass. Parallel to the wadi on either side was a deep and wide anti-tank ditch. Pill boxes, the size of an ordinary bedroom but with concrete walls two feet thick and equipped with ¾-inch thick steel doors, were connected by an elaborate network of deep trenches.

Scrambling down precipitous banks, the 8th and 9th Durham Light Infantry squelched through a black sponge of knee-deep mud and set their scaling ladders and cat-walks (hooked poles with metal struts) against the opposite bank of the wadi. Up they went, carrying 18-foot ditching planks and, where ladders and poles would not reach, men formed human ladders.[67]

In the meantime, huge stores of brushwood, duck boards, steel mesh and timber had been piled up to bridge the Wadi Zigzaou but the sappers ran into trouble as soon as they attempted to construct a firm crossing for 50th RTR's Valentines. Working under intense enemy enfilading fire and a stream of bombs and shells pouring down from the Matmata Hills, they slaved away only to see the brushwood and timber sinking into the mud as the leading tank slipped into the morass. Other fascines were set on fire by the Valentines' exhausts.

Four tanks managed to manoeuvre round their stricken leader before another tank churned to a helpless standstill. 'As dawn was very near,' recalled one RTR commander, 'there was nothing for it but to turn back to avoid being caught in the open in daylight.'[68] Throughout the next day (21 March) the tiny bridgehead was held while day-bombers of the Desert Air Force and American Mitchells blasted the enemy's positions; others struck at landing grounds far and wide. Unable to counter-attack, the Germans reinforced the *Young Fascist* Division with a battalion of 200th Panzer Grenadier Regiment, anti-tank guns, and 15th Panzer's artillery as well as moving up a battalion of Luftwaffe Jäger.

Orders were issued by Eighth Army HQ that, come what may, XXX Corps was to construct at least one crossing on the night of 21/22 March. As tired sappers of 50th Division tried again to build a causeway around the mired Valentines, 6th Durham Light Infantry moved forward, to extend the bridgehead. They took Ouerzi Ouest and another position, Zarat Sudest, quite easily with Italians surrendering in droves, but 9th Durhams suffered heavy casualties in capturing several other strongpoints, including Ouerzi Est. On the far right flank 5th East Yorkshires also secured part of Ksiba Est but were unable to extend their advance toward the coast through complex defensive works.

Across the causeway advanced 42 Valentines of 50th RTR. After a 'very rough ride', they came across, 'quite a few bodies of our infantry boys lying still in the sand obviously having been caught in the shelling of the previous night.'[69] No support was available because the tanks' tracks had so torn up the sappers' handiwork that 6-pounder anti-tank guns were unable to follow. This was potentially disastrous for, somewhere ahead, 15th Panzer was manoeuvring to attack, protected by the miserable weather which had grounded Allied air cover.

Montgomery chose this moment to inform Alexander that 50th Division had secured a bridgehead which was being extended and suggested that, 'you now announce that my operations are proceeding satisfactorily and according to plan.'[70] In fact, Leese had no more than four battalions of infantry – the Durhams much depleted – and some outgunned Valentines across the Wadi Zigzaou, no anti-tank screen and a single crossing, fast becoming impassable in heavy rain, which was shelled and machine-gunned unmercifully.

At corps and divisional HQs there was much confusion and great pandemonium at the crossing itself. In mid-afternoon murderous bursts of machine-gun fire heralded 15th Panzer's attack. They were supported by a brigade of infantry from 90th Light, Panzer Grenadiers, and *Ramcke* paratroopers. Receiving news that the Durhams were withdrawing, 'Crasher' Nichols' forward brigade commander charged onwards in a jeep, 'shouting out to the divisional commander that he was going to stop "the b——s"!'[71]

Driven back to the anti-tank ditch, the exhausted Durhams cut themselves a fire-step and settled grimly to their task. Before them lay the hulks of 27 Valentines. Eleven surviving tanks perched on the edge of the wadi to give support while away to their right the 5th East Yorks were still in position, though vulnerable to being pushed back which would expose the Durhams' flank.

A few days later, Montgomery boasted that, 'we never lost the initiative, and we made the enemy dance to our tune the whole time.'[72] Such a claim is totally at odds with what happened. He was out-of-touch, still planning to put through Shermans of the 22nd Armoured Brigade, 7th Armoured Division, as soon as the bridgehead had been established and ordering a renewed assault for the evening of 22 March.

Sappers and miners of 4th Indian Division had the arduous task of constructing another crossing; until they did so the whole of Eighth Army's coastal advance was held up. Lieutenant-Colonel Blundell, the division's fearless and highly popular chief engineer, decided to rush up two temporary bridges of steel mesh stretched over fascines. Between dusk and moonrise the necessary materials were carried forward and sappers began to break down the eastern bank for the approach ramps as others dropped into the bed of the wadi to work on the crossings.[73] Labouring under a canopy of screaming artillery shells, mortar and machine-gun fire, surrounded by dust, fumes and towering flames, Madrassi and Sikh sappers and miners worked away with the imperturbable Blundell everywhere, cheerily pointing out that, since he was so tall and had not been hit, others must be safe. This laughing assertion was somewhat offset by the fact that the peak of his cap had been shot away.

At 0145 hours, amidst another torrent of shells, the men withdrew so that the infantry could attack. In order not to panic them, Blundell ordered his troops to walk back casually, chatting and joking, stopping to explain the situation. XXX Corps' artillery support had been delayed and various infantry units jumped off too soon, adding to the confusion amid the dreadful congestion on the approach to the crossings where 6th and 7th Green Howards were painfully making their way forward under fire as streams of wounded struggled the other way.

The mistimed attack forced the cancellation of the artillery fire plan and convinced Leese that nothing but certain slaughter awaited his men. At 0200 hours, he saw a newly-awakened Montgomery in his map lorry where he confessed that Eighth Army had, 'lost its bridgehead.'

'What am I to do, Freddie?'[74] Montgomery, badly shaken by this news, asked his chief of staff. For once, he seemed insecure and indecisive. On how soon he recovered depended Eighth Army's fortunes, those of the Allies in Tunisia and, more immediately, the fate of the living soldiers still crouching in their shallow graves at the Wadi Zigzaou.

Notes to Chapter 12

[1] Sergeant J.R. Harris, Diaries 1942–43. IWM 86/5/1.
[2] Rev. J.E.G. Quinn, Diaries, 1940 – September 1943. IWM P247.
[3] Quoted by Hamilton, *Monty: Master of the Battlefield*, p. 167.
[4] Hinsley, *British Intelligence*, II, p. 595.
[5] Hunt, *A Don at War*, p. 166.
[6] Alexander Clifford, *Three Against Rommel*, p. 369; Barclay, *The History of the Royal Northumberland Fusiliers in the Second World War*, p. 100. Frömbgen's account is from *Die Oase*, No.4, April 1973.
[7] Extracts from Diary of a Gefreiter, 104th Panzer Grenadier Regiment.
[8] De Guingand, *Operation Victory*, p. 243. Sergeant Crangle on No. 7 gun of an anti-tank platoon of 1/7th Queen's, managed to knock out 14 tanks – more than any other in a single action in Tunisia. Eventually disabled, its gun-shield pierced in 20 places, it was recovered and went back to an honoured place in the regimental depot. Foster, *History of the Queen's Royal Regiment*, p. 194.
[9] Liddell Hart, *Rommel Papers*, p. 416.
[10] Von Arnim, 'Erinnerungen an Tunesien', p. 73.
[11] Report of 11 March 1943; War in Tunisia,' RH19-VIII/352.
[12] Eighth Army Intelligence Summary, 24 April 1943; II Corps, Box 3155; World War II, Operations Reports, USNA 202-2.3.
[13] 'Note on new posts permitted by the Führer in Africa', n.d.; Rommel's Personal Files December 1940 – April 1943 [Copies]; RH19-VIII/322. BA-MA. As his chief of staff, von Arnim was sent Generalmajor Gause while Oberst Bayerlein became chief of staff at First Italian Army, where he vigorously safeguarded German interests. Messe's chief of staff was Brigadier-General Guiseppe Mancinelli.
[14] Moorehead, *Montgomery*, p. 158.
[15] Montgomery's Situation Report, 'Preparations for moving Westwards from Tripoli against the Mareth Position', 20 March 1943; Montgomery to Brooke, 17 March 1943. Montgomery Papers, BLM 49/23.

[16] Eisenhower to Marshall, 3 March 1943; copy in Eisenhower Papers, Box 80. The original is in Marshall Papers, Box 66, Folder 49; also in Chandler, *Eisenhower Papers*, II, Doc. 860.

[17] Recounted by Bradley in conversation with Hansen; Hansen Papers, Box 23. Teddy Roosevelt was the eldest son of President Theodore Roosevelt (1859–1919).

[18] Eisenhower to Marshall, 3 March 1943.

[19] Warlimont, *Inside Hitler's Headquarters 1939–45*, p. 312.

[20] Feige, 'Relationship between Operations and Supply in Africa'.

[21] Playfair, *Destruction of Axis Forces*, p. 384.

[22] 'War in Tunisia', 13 March 1943; RH19-VIII/352.

[23] Message from *OKH* to *OB Süd*, 16 March 1943; *ibid*.

[24] 'Black butchers' – that is soldiers discovered illegally slaughtering livestock for food.

[25] General der Panzertruppen Gustav von Vaerst, 'Operations of the Fifth Panzer Army in Tunisia', Foreign Military Studies, MS D-001 (1947). USAMHI.

[26] Major-General C.H. Miller Diary, entry for 21 March 1943. Miller Papers. IWM 78/20/1.

[27] Alexander interviewed by Howe.

[28] Patton Diary, entry for 4 March 1943.

[29] Ward to his wife, 4 and 5 March 1943. Ward Papers.

[30] Eisenhower to Marshall, 5 March 1943. Bedell Smith Papers.

[31] Patton Diary, entry for 6 March 1943.

[32] Webb to his mother and Cox, 20 April 1943. Webb Papers, Box 1.

[33] Patton Diary, entry for 5 March 1943.

[34] Patton to Eisenhower, 13 March 1943. Eisenhower Papers, Box 91.

[35] Philipsborn to Robinett, 1 April 1957. 'I felt they [the troops] resented all of the nonsense Patton imposed on us right after Kasserine.' Robinett Papers, Box 4. Library of Congress.

[36] Major-General Sir (William) Rowell Campbell Penny (Signal Officer-in-Chief Middle East, 1941–3; Commander, British 1st Infantry Division, October 1943–4), Diary entry for 9 March 1943. TS account, written up from diary at later date. Penny Papers 3/2, Liddell Hart Centre. By far the best biography of Patton is D'Este, *Patton: A Genius for War*.

[37] Hansen interviewed with Bradley by Kitty Buhler (1966). Bradley Papers, Box 1.

[38] 'Ike sent Bradley up to II Corps as Deputy Commander to restrain Patton whom Ike and I thought might need restraint.' General Marshall interviewed by Roy Lamson, *et al* (25 July 1949). OCMH Collection.

[39] Eisenhower Memorandum to Patton, 6 March 1943; Chandler, *Eisenhower Papers*, Doc. 865.

[40] 1st Armored/Orlando Ward; 1st Infantry/Terry Allen; 9th Infantry/Manton Eddy; 34th Infantry/Charles Ryder, together with 13th Field Artillery Brigade and 1st Tank Destroyer Group.

[41] General Robert W. Porter interviewed by Lieutenant-Colonel John N. Sloan (1981). OCMH Collection.

[42] Brigadier-General Kuter had commanded the Allied Air Support Command, hastily formed on 22 January 1943, to co-ordinate the activities of the US 12th Air Support Command and No. 242 Group, RAF. On 18 February it became NATAF and the Desert Air Force came under its operational control five days later.

[43] See Orange, *Coningham*, pp. 120–1.

[44] The Wadi Akarit was known sometimes as the Gabès Gap or by the Germans as the Chott position.

[45] Playfair, *Destruction of Axis Forces*, p. 334. Axis tank strengths were: Fifth Panzer Army (on the Mareth front) 44 German medium tanks, 8 Tigers, 19 Italian; First Italian Army 29 German, 27 Italian; *DAK* 94 German tanks. The resulting total of 221 tanks differs from Playfair (142), *ibid.*, and from that revealed by Enigma (195). Exact figures are hard to ascertain but my figures are based on a return to *Heeresgruppe Afrika* on 16 March by First Italian Army; RH19-VIII/352. Montgomery could deploy 743 tanks, a huge advantage.

46 'Some Notes by General Tuker.'

47 Leese to his wife, 13 March 1943. Leese Papers.

48 The many problems associated with such an outflanking move as that assigned to the New Zealand Corps, and Freyberg's briefing to his commanders, are fully dealt with by Barber and Tonkin-Covell, *Freyberg: Churchill's Salamander*, pp. 134–45.

49 Quoted by Maule, *Out of the Sand*, p. 152.

50 Sergeant (later Lt.) E.W. Caffell, Memoirs (1982); IWM P469. These typescript memoirs are based on the author's diaries. See also Stevens, *Bardia to Enfidaville*, pp. 176–7.

51 Quoted by Jackson, *North African Campaign*, p. 361; Blaxland, *The Plain Cook*, gives a slightly different version on p. 194. They both add up to the same cocksure boast.

52 Quinn Diaries, entry for 17 March 1943. IWM P247.

53 Leese to his wife, 19 March 1943. Leese Papers.

54 Montgomery to Brooke, 17 March 1943. Montgomery Papers, BLM 49/23.

55 Behrendt, *Rommel's Intelligence*, p. 220–1.

56 Montgomery to Alexander, 8 and 11 March 1943; Alexander to Montgomery, 14 March 1943; quoted by Nicolson, *Alex*, pp. 180–1.

57 Draft of memoirs and article on Allen and 1st Division in North Africa and Sicily (based on articles by A.J. Liebling in the *New Yorker* in 1943). Major-General Terry de la Mesa Allen Papers, Box 1. USAMHI.

58 Ingersoll, *The Battle is the Pay-Off*, pp. 184–5.

59 Patton Diary, entry for 19 March 1943.

60 Wellard, *The Man in the Helmet: The Life of General Patton*, p. 8. Wellard was a war correspondent with Patton in North Africa from November 1942 onwards.

61 Blumenson ed., *The Patton Papers 1940–1945*, p. 195.

62 D'Arcy Dawson, *Tunisian Battle*, p. 179.

63 Major-General D.R.E.R. Bateman, 'Some Notes on War in the Western Desert and North Africa', 11 February 1959. 72/117/1.

64 Quoted by Hill, *Desert Conquest*, p. 235.

65 'Instructional History of 4th Indian Division Artillery for the Period of the North African Campaign: El Alamein to Tunis, September 1942 to May 1943'. Brigadier H.K. Dimoline Papers. IWM 73/40/1.

66 Lewin, *Life and Death of the Africa Korps*, p. 241.

67 Ward, *Faithful: The Story of the Durham Light Infantry*, p. 497.

68 Quoted by Messenger, *Tunisian Campaign*, pp. 78–9.

69 *Ibid.*, p. 80.

70 Quoted by Playfair, *Destruction of the Axis Forces*, p. 340.

71 Bateman, 'Some Notes on War'.

72 Montgomery, Situation Report 31 March 1943, 'The Battle of Mareth.'

73 Anon., *The Tiger Kills*, p. 255. The account given here of Blundell's work at the Wadi Zigzaou is interesting but inaccurate in some respects, especially in its timing of events.

74 Quoted by Hamilton, *Monty, Master of the Battlefield*, p. 193.

Chapter 13

We Stopped the Best They Had

'It is a miracle I am still alive. If it goes on like this, Tommy will soon finish us off in Africa.'

German Gefreiter in his diary, 24 March 1943.[1]

Far removed from the carnage at Wadi Zigzaou, Freyberg's New Zealanders moved forward over difficult, soft ground and waited under nearly a full moon only a few miles short of their first objective – the Tebaga Gap (Plum). Early on 21 March, Eighth Army Intelligence reported 21st Panzer as likely to bar the way at Peach (El Hamma) with 70 tanks while 15th Panzer waited in readiness with 50 tanks, unless required at the Mareth Line.[2] Messe had also ordered 164th Light Division from Mareth to the Tebaga Gap; it arrived on the 22nd. This was not revealed to Freyberg by Enigma or Y sources until the next day.

Concerned at the mounting delay, Montgomery twice urged Freyberg to smash through towards El Hamma and hasten on to Gabès while II Corps moved east from Gafsa, 'which should give enemy further bellyache.'[3] But Freyberg was worried about lack of manpower in his division which was 2,400 short of its 16,000 establishment. Aware that serious losses might lead to the complete withdrawal of New Zealand troops from the Middle East, he kept such worries to himself.

Many fires were started in the Tebaga Gap after it was bombed at 0800 hours on the 21st but Freyberg's armour, lacking infantry support, was held up. Despite the pre-arranged orange smoke signal, some returning aircraft strafed the New Zealanders, fortunately with minimal casualties. An attack on Point 201, isolated, flat-topped, in the centre of the gap by 25th and 26th Battalions of Brigadier Gentry's 6th Infantry Brigade and a squadron of tanks from 3rd RTR, was delayed while a minefield was cleared and all the corps' artillery positioned in support. Mactroop moved to within 300 yards of the enemy: 'We are hit by a salvo of shells,' recorded Sergeant Caffell, 'which kills Bdr. Bert C—— and wounds [other] Gnrs... All possible praise to the NZ [New Zealand] army MO... who was on the gun position within minutes tending the wounded under fire. We are forced to move guns back about 1,000 yards then continue in action barraging to cover our infantry. During the night we are attacked by enemy a/c [aircraft] with cannon fire and anti-personnel bombs by moonlight.'[4]

Despite intense small-arms fire the infantry cleared the first trenches with bayonet, grenade and rifle, taking the forward defence line and Point 201 (though it changed hands several times in intense fighting), losing 11 killed and 68 wounded or missing.[5] In cold and windy weather next day, over 800 Italian POWs began filtering back through the New Zealanders' lines complaining about the way they had been shelled.

Having captured Point 201, Brigadier Gentry urged Freyberg to put 8th Armoured Brigade through the Tebaga Gap rather than wait until daylight. Instead, Freyberg merely gave its commander, Brigadier Harvey, permission to do so – instead of issuing a direct order – and throughout the 22nd carefully widened the corps' salient. His natural caution was reinforced by Lieutenant-Colonel Kellet (2i/c 8th Armoured) having his head blown off while Freyberg was actually talking to him. Miraculously, Freyberg escaped injury but five others nearby were wounded.[6]

After his indecision on the night of 22/23 March, Montgomery was up early, extraordinarily rejuvenated, his self-confidence restored. With XXX Corps stuck on the Wadi Zigzaou and Freyberg's men making sound but unspectacular progress on the left flank, he decided to close down the too narrow attack and concentrate everything on a 'left-hook' by backing up Freyberg with the British 1st Armoured Division. Lieutenant-General Horrocks was to go along with his X Corps' HQ and take charge. Freyberg was senior to Horrocks, disliked the arrangement and was, 'grim, firm, and not at all forthcoming', when Horrocks arrived.[7] Major-General Tuker thought Horrocks was, 'unlearnt militarily', afraid of Montgomery and 'lacked moral courage'.[8] But at least Leese was pleased when 50th Division was withdrawn: 'Off you go, Jorrocks [sic],' he said condescendingly, 'and win the battle.'[9]

It took all de Guingand's diplomatic skills and some sensibly tactful behaviour by the comparatively unknown Horrocks to placate Freyberg who was, in any case, too experienced to let his annoyance get the better of his tactical good sense. Some disagreements did, naturally, arise which de Guingand did his best to smooth over by ensuring that every communication sent from Eighth Army HQ went to both commanders.

'Gertie' Tuker was not pleased by what had happened so far: 'This battle's a mess,' he wrote on 23 March, 'It has been fought badly by 30 Corps and 50 Division.'[10] Much to his surprise, however, 4th Indian Division was about to take an active part. Ahead lay the mountains, where men of the Punjab, Nepal and Baluchistan could call on their specialised knowledge, already learnt on the Indian Frontier, Abyssinia and Eritrea.

From earlier reconnaissance by 5th Brigade and from local French sources Tuker knew that what was shown on Allied maps as a poor cart-track, climbing into the Matmata Hills from Medenine and then traversing to the Hallouf Pass, 35 miles to the west, was in fact a decent, if narrow, tarmac road. Just inside the hills the road forked, the northern branch giving access to the crests at Toujane and Téchine to the north-east, when it became a cart-road dropping precipitously down through Matmata village and Beni-Zeltene onto the Gabès Plain. If the division could gain control of these mountain tracks just as the New Zealanders arrived at Peach (El Hamma), 150 miles would be cut off their supply lines. Granted power of manoeuvre for 40 miles from the sea to El Hamma Pass, magnificent opportunities opened up for a thrust into the enemy's rear areas behind the Mareth Line.

On the 23rd, Montgomery ordered Tuker to assemble 4th Indian Division and open the Hallouf Pass. Speed was essential to Tuker's ambitious strategy of turning the enemy's flank but bringing his division through Medenine proved difficult because 1st Armoured, *en route* to reinforce the New Zealanders with an armoured brigade of 7th Armoured Division on its tail, claimed absolute precedence. Tuker could only wait impatiently before getting his troops started into the hills on the night of 24/25 March.

At 18th Army Group HQ, Alexander was pleased with Patton who was, 'doing well and cooperating in every way.' US 1st Infantry Division had also proved itself in the recent fighting – unlike 1st Armored which, he informed Churchill, had been 'very sticky.'[11] Patton intended to do something about Ward's slowness in taking the hills beyond Maknassy but the second phase of II Corps' operations was delayed by mud engulfing Ward's armour. His divisional HQ bivouac area was covered in a rippling surface of water; not far away McQuillin's CC A was parked in waist-deep floods.

Ward fulfilled Patton's orders to take Sened Station – by way of careful manoeuvre rather than a storming attack along the Gafsa–Maknassy railway route. Threatening a frontal attack by McQuillin's CC A, which had managed to extricate itself from its watery pit on 20 March, Stack's CC C and Colonel DeRohan's 60th RCT (from 9th US Infantry Division) outflanked Sened Station from the north. DeRohan's men climbed and contoured 600 feet above the valley floor to command the heights while Stack's tanks crossed a series of awkward ridges, blocking off the northern road route out of Sened Station. McQuillin, too, had to cope with mud and mines but was rewarded with minimal casualties and over 500 prisoners.

As soon as Sened Station had been secured on the 21st, 1st Infantry Division's 18th and 26th Infantry Regiments, with 1st Ranger Battalion, were scheduled to move east of El Guettar. By mid-morning of the next day they had captured a major position, formerly occupied by 6,000 men of the Italian *Centauro* Division, and dug in along Gum Tree road.

Patton was furious at Ward who was diffident in advancing 1st Armored on Maknassy and 'dawdled all day' before entering the town – which proved easy since the enemy had already departed. There was another delay while Ward sized up the task of putting tanks onto ridges to the east. On the evening of 22 March, Ward sent his tanks forward in an effort to take the pass, five miles away, leading to Mezzouna and seize the heights of the Eastern Dorsale commanding it. Despite having only a short time in which to set mines, erect barbed-wire and position their machine-guns, a few Germans and Italians of Special Brigade 50, organised by Generale di Brigata Imperiali de Francavilla, stopped the attack, virtually without artillery. It was resumed next morning with extra support. Imperiali had to come into the front line to stiffen his troops who were giving themselves up at an alarming rate, but what saved the day was fanatical resistance by about 80 men of Rommel's former *Begleitkompanie* (bodyguard) under Major Medicus, accompanied by troops from Reconnaissance Unit 580, and the appearance of Oberst Rudolph Lang, summoned hastily to take charge of leading elements of a Kampfgruppe from 10th Panzer.[12] Getting hold of a few energetic young officers from an 88mm Flak-Abteilung, he ordered them to use every means, including their personal weapons, to prevent one additional man or vehicle retreating. A straggler line was set up and later several battalions were sent up to reinforce the hard-pressed defenders.[13]

At El Guettar, Kesselring had wanted to move 10th Panzer closer to the southern sector of the front but leading elements only arrived on the 22nd and 23rd when a determined attempt was made to pinch out the American advance. British Army Y intelligence gave precise advance warning of a serious attempt on the second morning; the Germans thought they had been betrayed, increased their security and re-timed their attack on 1st Division, dug in behind a series of low ridges which guarded the entrance to the long El Guettar plain, four to five miles wide and confined by two mountain ranges.[14] Advancing rapidly over a carpet of yellow daisies and poppies, the attacking German tanks were followed by lorried infantry and supported by dive-bombers, strafing the American gun positions.

A roaring storm of shells fell on the leading Panzers as the US field artillery opened up and tank-destroyers appeared out of the wadis to blast them at short range. After struggling through three miles of defences and getting to within two miles of Allen's HQ, they were forced to withdraw back to 'Hot Corner' – a road junction between the eastern end of the valley and the road running south to Kebili.

Displaying great fortitude, they regrouped and advanced, finishing off the tank-destroyers which, contrary to Patton's instructions, pursued the Panzers without having sufficient advantage in speed or armour to fight them. But the attack was again eventually repulsed leaving the hulks of 30 tanks, some of them burning, on the battlefield.[15] When the area was being cleared in the second half of April, amidst piles of spent shell casings, gutted tanks and the occasional unburied corpse, the body of a 1st Division infantryman was located in one of the forward positions. By his side was a half-finished note to his family which began: 'Well folks, we stopped the best they had.'[16]

When 1st Armored had still failed to take the heights beyond Maknassy on 24 March, Patton ran out of patience and ordered Ward to lead the attack himself. Thus, at 0030 hours next morning a battalion assault against Djebel Naemia was, to universal astonishment, led by the division's commanding general over ridges swept by enemy fire. 'Damn it, men. You're not going to let a fifty-one year old man run your tongues out?' shouted Ward, 'Let's get up that mountain.' Nevertheless, little headway could be made and he received a nasty gash in the corner of his left eye from a flying splinter of rock. At 0600 hours, Ward and his aide decided to retreat in order to allow 1st Armored's artillery to flush out Germans drilled into the bare rock.[17]

Patton thought he had, 'made a man of Ward' and decorated him with the Silver Star; Ward had thought he might refuse it.[18] Nowhere, however, had 1st Armored's troops been able to advance far and Patton was exasperated by the certain knowledge that, had Alexander allowed him to push beyond Gafsa on 17 March, he would in three days have reached the second phase of operations since the Italians were on the run and 10th Panzer had not had time to block his path.[19]

Oberst Lang came precisely to the same conclusion. After the fall of Gafsa he considered there was no serious resistance to the American advance. The Italians were strong only in numbers and those who did not run away as soon as the enemy attacked, surrendered. One 'reliable' battalion, which Imperiali requested Lang put into the front line, broke and scattered as soon as the enemy appeared; re-formed and re-committed after measures had been taken against its commanders, the battalion then deserted en masse.

Facing no real opposition other than the remnants of one Italian battalion which did stand and fight – each of its soldiers was awarded the Iron Cross, Second Class – the Americans ought to have stormed ahead and would have reached the Maknassy Pass at the latest by 20 March. From there, they could have cut into the rear of First Italian Army and severed its supply route. Instead a series of set-pieces, in which the highly accurate US artillery became separated from the infantry, slowed the advance against Tigers and 88mm guns. As Lang observed, 'the enemy was well aware of his material superiority and therefore was no longer willing to accept the necessity of severe infantry casualties.'[20] There is no doubt that for his part Patton was affected by the sight of German losses, telling Bradley that when they attacked at Gafsa on 23 March, he saw the German infantry slogging on and on through the combined fire of 16 battalions of artillery. Under the rain of shell fragments, 'you could just see these fine infantrymen melting away. He just hated to see good infantrymen murdered in that way.'[21]

Alexander insisted that II Corps should exert increasing pressure at all possible points along the Eastern Dorsale and send an armoured task force down the Gafsa–Gabès road to the Wadi Akarit, the next natural defensive position to which First Italian Army could retreat after Mareth. He released 9th US Infantry Division (less 60th RCT), which was to fill the line south-east of El Guettar, and 34th Infantry Division moved to Sbeïtla to demonstrate through the Fondouk Gap towards Kairouan. In the northern part of its sector, 1st Armored was to leave CC B and position a greatly reduced force east of Maknassy with 60th RCT. The rest of the division was to pass as a mobile armoured formation towards Gabès through a hole punched by elements of 1st and 9th Infantry Divisions. Unfortunately, these orders were too late and poorly conceived. They involved an attack through a desolate land mass composed of tumbling ridges, riven by deep wadis, in which resolute defenders would have many advantages. Nevertheless, the threat held 10th Panzer Division in check and Enigma revealed that it was in serious difficulties.

On Eighth Army's front, 21st Panzer and 164th Light, now lying near the Tebaga Gap, had orders to respond only if attacked, and there were serious doubts as to whether they could hold, 'the new thinly-occupied main defence line'.[22] Leclerc's Force L had come under Freyberg's command and its fierce Senegalese infantrymen had taken with the bayonet a series of dominating mountain ranges. Brigadier Kippenberger of 5th New Zealand Infantry Brigade was, therefore, able to obtain a perfect view of the enemy's lines. 'It was,' he remarked, 'the only reconnaissance I ever made in which I could see everything that I wanted to see.'[23]

Overlooked by the New Zealanders and French, 164th Light reported that 21st Panzer might not be strong enough to re-capture this high ground and feared that a mass tank attack could not be stopped. They were given permission on 25 March to retreat to El Hamma if in danger of being overrun.

In the wake of 1st Armoured, 4th Indian Division had set off from Medenine, sending 7th Brigade southwards through the Khordache Pass to encircle the main Matmata buttresses. 5th Brigade was to push straight through the mountains westwards to Hallouf, turn north to roll up the enemy, to be followed by 7th Brigade in support. Having taken the summits, both brigades would become mobile battlegroups and descend onto the Gabès Plain. This was no mean task for Brigadier Donald Bateman's 5th Brigade, with 1st Battalion, 9th Gurkha Rifles in the lead, which was in difficulties as soon as it approached the Hallouf Pass on the night of 24/25 March. Here was encountered every type of mine – Teller mines, Italian N-mines like lengths of rail, paratroop anti-tank mines, square French mines, S-mines, and limpet mines shaped like Chianti bottles – many armed for delayed action.

A road demolition caused further severe delay until the afternoon of the 26th when the junction of the Téchine trail and Hallouf road was reached; 1/4th Essex then turned northward and upward, covering ten miles against light opposition with 1/9th Gurkhas close behind. Reaching Hardy Crossroads, on the very crest of the Matmata Hills, accurate German gunfire prevented further movement along a knife-edged ridge.[24]

South of the Khordache Pass, 7th Brigade was, 'wading through a sea of mines', noted Tuker. 'They're buried so deep that the detector and bayonet can't reach them but the vehicle puts them off.'[25] After losing all their available mine sweepers Brigadier Lovett's leading elements reached the western entrance of the Hallouf road before dark, following the trail blazed by 5th Brigade towards Téchine, a troglodyte village, where the inhabitants lived underground and only their tombs were on the surface.[26]

As 4th Indian Division crossed the Matmata Mountains, plans had been finalised by Montgomery, Freyberg and Horrocks to lay on a blitz attack at El Hamma. Plainly worried at the prospect, Monty requested 1,500 immediate reinforcements by air to replace Eighth Army's casualties together with 56th British Infantry Division and troops from 10th Indian Infantry Division. Attempting to force Alexander's hand he warned: 'If we do not finish this business there will be NO repeat NO HUSKY... '[27] Since Husky was the planned invasion of Sicily and the next big Allied move, this was not far short of blackmail and Alexander bought him off by sending 11,500 men while asserting that only 56th Division would be available in addition and would be transported, as originally planned, by road.

Montgomery had decided to call the attack on El Hamma, Supercharge II, a reference to the successful breakout at El Alamein. With the sun immediately behind them, 300 tanks were to advance right through the Tebaga Gap and along the axis of the main Kebili–El Hamma road. Opposing them, 164th Light and 21st Panzer had about 70 tanks, though these were scattered all along the front. In fact, they were unable even to match Brigadier Roscoe Harvey's 8th Armoured Brigade total of 150-plus, let alone the 67 Shermans, 13 Grants and 60 Crusaders of Brigadier Fisher's 2nd Armoured Brigade (1st Armoured Division). 15th Panzer's 50 tanks were still held back in order to be able to support either at the Mareth Line or Tebaga Gap and it was important for the Allied attack to go in before this division could be moved.

In Harry Broadhurst's crucial air support system, strafing of low-level targets was to be controlled by an experienced pilot flying a Spitfire above the Kittyhawk squadrons and a ground controller operating what later came to be known as the 'cab-rank' system. Sitting next to the commander, 8th Armoured Brigade, he was to call-up fighter-bombers, directing them onto the army's targets, warning them if they looked like shooting up friendly troops and giving them confidence that he would not fly them into masses of flak.[28] Coningham thought the Desert Air Force was being misused and sent his chief of staff, Air Commodore Beamish, to remind Broadhurst that his permanent rank was only squadron leader: 'One kick up the arse and you've had it,' Beamish told him. Even his own pilots shouted 'Murderer!' when he briefed them.[29]

Before the main attack, bombers from 205 Group RAF and the Desert Air Force, including American squadrons, plastered targets in the battle area by day and night. An artillery 'stonk' on Point 184, which overlooked the start line, was followed by a bayonet attack by 21st Battalion (New Zealand Corps). In a quick and 'clean' operation they cleared the hill of troops from 104th Panzer Grenadier Regiment (21st Panzer), killing 18.

A crucial part of Supercharge II involved putting 1st Armoured Division through after 8th Armoured Brigade had punched a hole in the Tebaga Gap bottleneck. With recent memories of abortive actions at the Ruweisat and Miteiriya Ridges, Freyberg had to be assured by Horrocks that he would rapidly follow up, but remained doubtful about charging a gun line. Freyberg told Kippenberger, 'I thought it was going to be tough. Reply: "It will be tougher for him" [the enemy].'[30]

185

As three formations of light and heavy bombers blitzed enemy positions on 26 March, at precisely 1600 hours Shermans from 8th Armoured Brigade began moving steadily forward through an enveloping sandstorm. On the right were the Nottinghamshire Yeomanry, abreast of them the Staffordshire Yeomanry and on the left 3rd RTR. Next came lighter Crusader tanks and carriers with the New Zealanders' 28th (Maori), 23rd and 24th Battalions, ranged from right to left. Over their heads roared shells from 200 guns of the combined divisional artillery hitting the enemy's own artillery lines and infantry, 3,000 yards ahead.[31]

After making good progress on the eastern or right flank, a well-sited 88mm gun on Point 209, occupied by 2nd Battalion, 433rd Panzer Grenadier Regiment (164th Light *Afrika*), knocked out three Shermans. 28th Battalion halted and deployed to attack the lower features, later named Hikurangi by the Maoris, and its higher western extremity.

In the centre, the Staffordshires drove right through their second objective, losing six Shermans, but to their rear 23rd Battalion was delayed on its right flank by some determined but ultimately short-lived opposition from men of 1st Battalion, 382nd Panzer Grenadier Regiment (164th Light). By 1800 hours the New Zealanders had also penetrated almost 2,500 yards beyond their first objective.

On the left, 3rd RTR's tanks lost their earlier precision after striking an unsuspected minefield covered by the anti-tank guns of 1st Battalion, 125th Panzer Grenadier Regiment (164th Light). Further to the west, the other side of the gap and the lower slopes of Djebel Tebaga were defended by a formation of Italians, 5th Panzer Regiment (21st Panzer) and 1st Battalion, 433rd Panzer Grenadier Regiment.

Losing contact with the tanks, 24th Battalion was badly cut up by German machine-gun posts which the Shermans had by-passed, losing 50 dead and 62 wounded though it took over 500 prisoners. In a straightforward fire-fight at ranges up to 200 yards, Major Andrews reported: 'On my immediate front, our accurate fire bowled most of them and some Italians began yelling and throwing up their hands, but were rallied by two Germans, a sergt. and a Red Cross chap, both of whom we killed. (The sergt. had on him the Iron Cross and Italian Croce di Guerra so must have been a hot number.)'[32]

Only a single company reached its final objective at 1800 hours but by then 2nd Armoured Brigade's three regiments (Queen's Bays, 9th Queen's Royal Lancers and 10th Royal Hussars) obeying Brigadier Fisher's orders – 'Speed up, straight through, no halting' – had led hundreds of Eighth Army tanks in nine columns irresistibly through the Tebaga Gap to a forward staging area, where 1st Armoured laagered until the moon rose to light the rest of the way to El Hamma. In an extraordinary drive the division had smashed right through two German divisions, pinning them between its own rear anti-tank screen and the New Zealanders.

In order to protect his front after the combined assault, von Liebenstein requested 15th Panzer to act as his reserve for a counter-attack but Bayerlein, at First Italian Army, did not issue orders until three hours later due to severe delays in communications. By then 5th Panzer Regiment had been bulldozed aside and 1st Battalion, 125th Panzer Grenadier Regiment, scattered. Around 1900 hours, just as the first elements of 2nd Armoured Brigade arrived on their first objective, 5th Panzer Regiment began to pull back and Hildebrandt sent two elements of 21st Panzer Division, 3rd and 33rd Reconnaissance Units, to construct a defence four miles south of El Hamma.

At midnight on 26/27 March, 1st Armoured again set off with 2nd Armoured Brigade leading a fantastic race against von Liebenstein's troops retreating in a parallel direction south-west of El Hamma, all units intermixed in a headlong dash. Von Liebenstein had placed his anti-tank screen across the road but, confused by the sight of tanks approaching them at night, the gunners presumed they were retreating Panzers. A big mistake: 2nd Armoured Brigade thrust past them and was stopped only by a few 88s, and some other anti-tank and field guns which von Liebenstein hastily scraped together and sited about three miles from El Hamma.

Coming up late in support, 15th Panzer tried to break in with its surviving ten tanks but was beaten off by the combined firepower of powerful new 17-pounder anti-tank guns of 76th Anti-Tank Regiment, RA, 1st Royal Northumberland Fusiliers and 8th Armoured Brigade. In the confusion the New Zealand Divisional Cavalry was repeatedly fired on by 1st Armoured Division's rearguard. 'On my asking them later if they knew what the recognition signal was,' noted Lieutenant-Colonel Bonifant of the New Zealanders, 'I was informed that they had never heard of it.'[33]

By-passed by the main force, the Maoris of 28th Battalion were engaged in a private war of their own. Neither they nor 443rd Panzer Grenadier Regiment, holding the saddle connecting the steep underfeatures of Hikurangi to Point 209's real summit, realized that 1st Armoured had nearly reached El Hamma. During desperately bitter fighting on the night of 26/27 March, when only about 20 yards separated the two sides, parts of the hill mass changed hands several times. At one stage, the Germans broke into a sector where Second Lieutenant Ngarimu drove off the attackers with his Tommy-gun and then with a hail of stones after his ammunition ran out. In the morning, he was seen on the crest of the hill, gun in hand, summoning his men on until a burst of fire cut him down. His outstanding courage was recognized by a posthumous VC.

At around 1700 hours Captain Matehaere's company, braving severe automatic and rifle fire, charged from the saddle to the summit cheered on by others standing on Hikurangi dancing and chanting their *hakas*. Unable to retreat – they had no transport – the German resistance suddenly collapsed; just 231 came off the hill, among them their CO, Major Meissner.

Visiting the scene, Kippenberger came across what he described as 'a most horrible scene of slaughter. There were,' he continued, 'dead and mangled Germans everywhere, more than I had seen in a small area since the Somme in 1916.'[34] At the New Zealanders' regimental aid post lay 30 or 40 bodies, mute witnesses to the murderous effects of artillery fire on the stony ground. Ninety-two Maoris had paid with their lives for the occupation of Point 209, isolated and soon forgotten.

———————

In equally remote country, 4th Indian Division had struggled to gain a position where it could threaten the rear of the Mareth position in the shorter of Montgomery's two 'left hooks.' Early on the morning of 27 March, Major Gregory's company of 1/4th Essex advanced against the Italians along a narrow, bare ridge from Hardy Crossroads. After they put in a bayonet charge and broke into the *Pistoia* Division's positions the defenders fled, leaving behind 116 prisoners and numerous dead and wounded. For some time the Italians had been increasingly jittery about holding fixed positions. Messe was convinced his Italian troops were no longer useful fighting material and on 22 March *OB Süd* ordered German staff of First Italian Army to examine reports that they had given up without a struggle and put out white flags in abject surrender.[35]

Against weakened opposition, 5th Brigade (4th Indian Division) made good progress despite the rugged nature of the Matmata Hills. While the 1/4th Essex reached Téchine and explored forward towards Matmata itself, 4th Battalion, 16th Punjab Regiment (normally under 7th Brigade but temporarily with the 5th) pushed on to Toujane in order to protect 5th Brigade's right flank. On the same day (27 March) patrols from 7th Brigade passed beyond Téchine and, travelling fast north-eastwards, reached the top of the defile, 1,500 feet above Beni-Zeltene. Working like beavers, Blundell's 4th Bengal Field Company of engineers gingerly hauled down two huge compressors and a bulldozer and began shoring up the road which had fallen away in several places. By next morning, 4th Indian had opened a supply route for the New Zealanders and was making ready for 7th Brigade to debouch onto the Gabès Plain below.

But the Mareth position had already been abandoned by their enemies. In great haste, Italian non-motorised units began to withdraw in accordance with von Arnim's instructions on the night of 25/26 March and by the 28th all remaining troops of 90th Light were hurrying back towards Gabès or further north to the Wadi Akarit. There, they were shielded by a rearguard of 164th Light assisted by von Liebenstein's skilful delaying action at El Hamma and Lang's continuing denial of American forces at Maknassy.

At Gabès and Sfax, demolitions of electricity works, harbour installations, unloading facilities and all useful factories and workshops were set. Meanwhile, reports received by *Heeresgruppe Afrika* from Italian intelligence sources at Gibraltar suggested that the next attacks would be mounted in the Tunis–Bizerte area, supported by amphibious landings and a heavy naval presence.[36]

Held up before El Hamma, Horrocks asked Freyberg to stage another Supercharge. Slow to respond, Freyberg was more intent on destroying any remaining opposition at the Tebaga Gap and bringing up his artillery. This was a dangerous business: 'Troop leader made elementary mistake of leaving defined track to cross open ground,' noted Sergeant Caffell, 'with result our convoy runs into minefield... we return to track.' One man was killed and another badly wounded.[37]

Unsure of his line of communication, Freyberg argued instead for a move which would by-pass El Hamma and strike north-east towards Gabès. By the time this had been agreed by Montgomery any major advantage gained by the speed of the break-through at Tebaga had been lost. The Axis forces were already streaming from the Gabès Plain: 'Under a hail of English bombs we broke through the enemy and headed for Gabès,' recorded the Gefreiter from 104th Panzer Grenadier Regiment. 'It was a miracle... that we got out again.'[38] Inching 7th Brigade's guns down the Beni-Zeltene gorge on the 28th, 4th Indian Division watched in frustrated impotence as the enemy slipped away. Despite a magnificent effort – 'everyone is very pleased with them,'[39] recorded Major-General Miller – they were marginally too late due to the bottleneck which had cost the division precious time at Medenine.

———◆◆◆———

By 0900 hours that same day, Eighth Army had at last taken possession of the Mareth Line. Crossing the Wadi Zigzaou, Major Rainier thought it a thoroughly evil spot: 'Our dead guardsmen lay strewn before the wire like autumn leaves. I estimated sixty in one small area... [the place] reeked of death. I mean potential death, not the death of past days which was evidenced by bodies lying bloated in the sun.[40]

With little room for its artillery positions, supported only by undergunned 2-pounder Valentines, lacking space to form up its infantry properly, none whatsoever for its own HQ and an exit on the far side of the enemy which was itself a bottleneck, 50th Division had suffered directly as a result of Montgomery's inept plan. Had the Hallouf Pass been seized early on his flanking movement would not have been, as Tuker observed, 'a lengthy, clumsy and obvious operation, visible from any position on the Matmata heights... But 8 Army,' he added, 'was a ponderous machine.'[41]

In sending Freyberg to attack the Tebaga Gap by an obvious route, Montgomery claimed this was intended to divert attention from Leese's assault on the Wadi Zigzaou. Before he knew from Ultra, however, that the New Zealanders had been discovered as early as 19 March at Wilder's Gap, he intended them to move in great secrecy. Only after their route became known did he try to turn this to advantage: 'having... received a setback on my right, I recovered quickly, and knocked the enemy out with a "left-hook".' Despite the fact that Mareth was what he termed 'the toughest fight we have had since Alamein,' Montgomery was in no doubt it had been, 'the most enjoyable battle I have fought. Alamein was a slogging match. Mareth gave considerable scope for subtlety, and for outwitting the opponent.'[42] But the cost was high. Leese's XXX Corps suffered nearly 2,000 casualties and the Mareth Line was still claiming victims in its minefields long after the battle had moved on.

———◆◆◆———

189

As 51st Highland Division continued to advance along the main coastal road towards Gabès and 4th Indian Division concentrated at Beni-Zeltene, the New Zealanders moved north and east on 28 March on rough tracks, traversing wadis where bulldozers had improved the crossings. On their western flank, 1st Armoured put in a holding force at El Hamma (which the enemy vacated the next day) and prepared to move in the small hours of the following morning into the 20-mile gap to Gabès.

The New Zealanders' 6th Brigade cleaned up the opposition while 5th Brigade, together with Leclerc's Free French, came abreast on a different axis towards Gabès. In the vanguard was Kippenberger, with a squadron of King's Dragoon Guards and artillery. They met little opposition and on the morning of 29 March, after smashing a line of pill-boxes with well-directed fire, he sent an advanced party of Dragoon Guards and Bren Gun carriers of 23rd Battalion flying into Gabès; they arrived just as the last elements of 15th Panzer left the town, destroying a bridge on its northern limits.

Although only a small place, it was the first town with a sizeable European population to be liberated and was afforded much publicity by newspaper reporters who flocked there. Despite pattern-bombing by the Americans which had left hardly a building standing in the centre, the Allied troops were given a huge welcome by the local populace, including French police and, noted Kippenberger, 'some astonishingly nicely dressed girls whom we looked on with some relish.'[43] Not that there was much time for fraternization; the New Zealanders had already begun to move northwards on the main road before Freyberg's tactical HQ arrived.

In the meantime, forward patrols of 4th Indian Division's 7th Brigade raced across the Gabès plain, over-running an Italian rearguard of 100 men and taking them prisoner. When they reached the town they had to wait while the 51st Highlanders put on their kilts and marched through. This sealed 4th Division's intense dislike of the Scots; Major Jephson, one of their officers who won a MC in the Matmata Hills, thought they were made to pause because Montgomery undervalued the Indians as fighting soldiers.[44] Such resentment was widespread and shared by Tuker who believed that Monty had, 'no use for Indian troops', so that they were the last to be called into action once XXX Corps ran up against the Mareth Line.[45] 'All these people seem to think 4 Div ought not to be put up against Germans,' he remarked. 'I only want to have one really good Boche slaughter to convince the rest of this Army that they play at fighting – we don't – it's our profession.'[46]

It was the Americans, above all, whom Eighth Army thought were merely playing at fighting. Leese despised them together with First Army, the BBC and press, whom, he wrote, 'I quite frankly loath.'[47] In return, there were many who believed that Eighth Army was, quite unfairly, grabbing all the headlines for itself.

Notes to Chapter 13

[1] Extracts from Diary of a Gefreiter, 104th Panzer Grenadier Regiment.

[2] Overall tank strengths on 16 March were as follows: Fifth Panzer Army (on Mareth front) 44 German + 8 Tigers + 19 Italian; First Italian Army 29 German + 27 Italian; *DAK* 94 German. Figures compiled by *Heeresgruppe Afrika*, 16 March 1943. RH19VIII/352.

[3] Montgomery to Freyberg, 21 March 1943; quoted by Barber and Tonkin-Covell, *Freyberg*, p. 151.

[4] Caffell Memoirs, Diary entry for 21 March 1943.

[5] Norton, *26 Battalion*, p. 242; Stevens, *Bardia to Enfidaville*, p. 183.

[6] Corps Commander's diary, entry for 22 March; quoted by Barber and Tonkin-Covell, *Freyberg*, p. 154.

[7] Stevens, *Bardia to Enfidaville*, p. 199.

[8] 'Some Notes by General Tuker'.

[9] Horrocks, *A Full Life*, p. 150.

[10] Tuker's War Diary as GOC 4th Indian Division, entry for 23 March 1943. Tuker Papers, IWM 71/21/2.

[11] Alexander to Churchill, 24 March 1943; Alexander Papers WO 214/11.

[12] Von Arnim, 'Erinnerungen an Tunesien', p. 85.

[13] Oberst Rudolph Lang, 'Report on the Fighting of Kampfgruppe Lang (10th Panzer Division) in Tunisia: Defensive Fighting at Mezzouna-Maknassy, March-April 1943', Foreign Military Studies, MS D-166. USAMHI.

[14] Enigma also gave notice of the 10th Panzer attack but Patton was not a recipient of Ultra information at this stage and may not have received this to reinforce the warning he received from Army Y; see Hinsley, *British Intelligence*, II, p. 601. The Germans had no inkling that Enigma was responsible as is clear from a report dated 23 March 1943; RH19-VIII/352.

[15] Patton Diary, entry for 24 March 1943; Patton to Marshall, 29 March 1943, Marshall Papers, Box 79, Folder 12.

[16] Terry Allen, 'A Factual Situation and Operations Report on the Combat Operations of the 1st Infantry Division during its Campaigns in North Africa and Sicily during the period 8 November '42 to 7 August '43'; Allen Papers, Box 4.

[17] Hatfield Diary, entry for 24 March 1943.

[18] Ward to his wife, 25 March 1943; Ward Papers. Patton thought Ward's action would have merited the DSC 'except for the fact that it was necessary for me to order him to do it.' Patton Diary, entry for 27 March 1943.

[19] *Ibid.*, entry for 25 March 1943.

[20] Oberst Lang, 'Report on the Fighting of Kampfgruppe Lang (10th Panzer Division) in Tunisia'.

[21] Bradley interviewed by Buhler, 1966.

[22] Quoted by Hinsley, *British Intelligence*, II, p.601.

[23] Quoted by Henry Maule, *Out of the Sand*, p. 154.

[24] Tuker, *Approach to Battle*, p. 299; also Martin, *The Essex Regiment 1929–1950*, p. 286.

[25] Tuker, War Diary, entry for 26 March 1943.

[26] Anon., *The Tiger Kills*, p. 261.

[27] Montgomery to Alexander, 25 March 1943. Alexander Papers, WO/214/18.

[28] De Guingand, *Operation Victory*, pp. 257–60; Copy of letter from Major-General Miller, 28 March 1943 (with Miller Diary). The RAF controller in the air was Wing Commander Darwen, a superb fighter pilot, later killed in Italy.

[29] Hamilton, *Monty: Master of the Battlefield*, p. 200.

[30] Freyberg's GOC diary entry for 26 March 1943; Barber and Tonkin-Covell, *Freyberg*, pp. 170, 173.

[31] See Paul Freyberg, *Bernard Freyberg V.C.*, pp. 428–9.

[32] Burdon, *24 Battalion*, p. 176.

[33] Quoted by Stevens, *Bardia to Enfidaville*, p. 235.

[34] Kippenberger, *Infantry Brigadier*, p. 289.

[35] Orders from *OB Süd* to German staff, *1. Italienische Armee*, 22 March 1943. RH19-VIII/352.

[36] 'War in Tunisia, 28 March 1943 – 28 April 1943'; RH19VIII/351. BM-MA.

[37] Caffell Diary, entry for 27 March 1943.

[38] Extracts from Diary of a Gefreiter, 104th Panzer Grenadier Regiment; entry for 29 March 1943.

[39] Miller in letter from Eighth Army HQ, 28 March 1943; Miller Papers.

[40] Rainier, *Pipeline to Battle*, p. 220.

[41] Tuker, 'History of 4th Indian Division: Some Notes for its Wartime Commanders'. Tuker Papers, 71/21/6.

[42] Montgomery Diary, entry for 31 March 1943; 'The Battle of Mareth – Reflections on the Battle'. IWM BLM 32.

[43] Kippenberger, *Infantry Brigadier*, p. 292.

[44] Major Francis Jephson. Sound Archives recording. IWM 8941/16.

[45] 'Some Notes by General Tuker'.

[46] Tuker War Diary, 31 March 1943.

[47] Leese to his wife, 28 and 29 March 1943. Leese Papers.

Part Three

Masters of the North African Shores

'As you know, there has all through this campaign been an incessant accompaniment of belittlement, sneering, rumour and at times almost slander: all to the effect that 1 Army is no good & that had 8 Army had the job etc. etc... it has hurt & riled me intensely and has been so un-British in every way. It is quite damnable.'

Lieutenant-General Kenneth Anderson to Captain G.C. Wynne, who had visited Eighth Army as a member of the Cabinet Office's Historical Section, 18 May 1943.

Wynne Papers 8/1, Liddell Hart Centre for Military Archives.

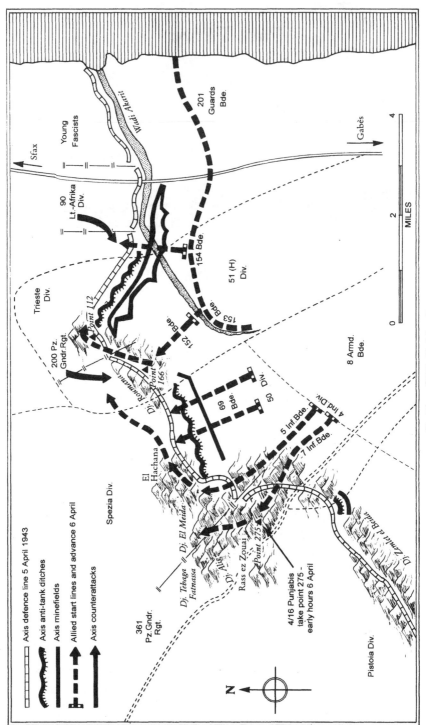

Battle of Wadi Akarit
April 1943

Axis defence line 5 April 1943
Axis anti-tank ditches
Axis minefields
Allied start lines and advance 6 April
Axis counterattacks

Sfax

Young
Fascists

Wadi Akarit

201
Guards
Bde.

Gabès

90
Lt.-Afrika
Div.

154 Bde.

51 (H)
Div.

153 Bde.

Trieste
Div.

200 Pz.
Gndr.Rgt.

Point 112

152 Bde.

Dj: Roumana

Point 166

69
Bde.

50
Div.

8 Armd.
Bde.

5 Inf Bde.

4 Ind.Div.

7 Inf Bde.

El
Hachana

Spezia Div.

Dj: El Meïda

Dj: Tebaga
Fatnassa

Dj: Alig

Rass ez Zouai

Point 275

4/16 Punjabis
take point 275 -
early hours 6 April

361
Pz. Gndr.
Rgt.

Dj: Zemlet el Beïda

Pistoia Div.

MILES
0   2   4

N

Chapter 14

Into the Furnace

'We now hold the initiative and I intend to keep it – pounding here and there and making the enemy dance to my tune... '

General Sir Harold Alexander to General Sir Alan Brooke, 30 March 1943.[1]

On hearing that four American divisions were to drive towards Gabès, Tuker was certain that this, 'ought to fix the Boche if Yanks just walk forward in big squares.'[2] But fighting in such forbidding terrain was not quite so simple as, to his immense and growing frustration, Patton was discovering. His troops were spread over a front of more than 100 miles: 'However, this is not as bad as it sounds,' he told Marshall, 'because three divisions are well-grouped and the fourth – the 34th – is on a sort of raiding mission to the northeast [Fondouk].' Anticipating some 'very hard' fighting and losses in battalion and company commanders 'higher than average,' he added that should anything go drastically wrong the general scope of operations was laid down by Alexander and he was merely carrying out orders: 'We are trying to be simple, not change our plans when once made, and keep on fighting.'[3]

Attempting a breakthrough in the wild and mysterious country east of El Guettar, however, was a formidably difficult undertaking. Forced to navigate by re-photographed French maps last surveyed in 1903 which were hopeless in scale (1:100,000), the infantry could not obtain accurate co-ordinates nor pinpoint their own positions. Compass-bearings had to be taken from high points which exposed those doing this to murderously accurate fire from German snipers supported by 88s.[4]

When the attack opened on 28 March, 1st Infantry were badly cut up by terrific mortar and machine-gun fire from the broken yellow and red stone mass of Djebel Chemsi. Colonel Fechet reported, 'mines, booby traps... and trip wire... Wops in forward positions, Germans in rear... Wops faked surrender and then threw hand grenades. Mountains... strongly held by automatic weapons.'[5] Fighting through these powerful defences, Terry Allen's men struggled as far as the western end of the hill on the first day. Across the valley, however, 9th Infantry could make no progress through the shimmering heat to take Djebel Kreroua nor clean out the enemy artillery observation posts on the high, bare wall of Djebel Berda.

By clever use of interlocking fire zones, the Germans pinned down both prongs of the attack and pounded supply trucks which raced between the palms and blossoming fig and plum trees in the El Guettar oasis.

With the 1st and 9th Infantry lost in a confusing mass of jumbled rock and deeply-cut wadis, the 34th failing in its feint at Fondouk, where Ryder had been told to, 'Go out in the area and make a lot of noise but don't try to capture anything', and the attack from Maknassy abandoned, Patton's troops had come to a grinding halt everywhere.[6] Prior to this setback he had planned that units of 1st Armored would undertake a meteoric 80-mile drive from El Guettar to Gabès. Now Patton pinned his hopes on Ward's former chief of staff, Colonel 'Chauncey' Benson. Before Ward lost his command he had sent Benson to 13th Armored Regiment. Despite a reputation for heavy drinking, Patton admired his aggressiveness.[7]

Blocking the route were newly-arrived mobile elements of 21st Panzer, sent to reinforce 10th Panzer near El Guettar. In support, the Luftwaffe stepped up its attacks on US artillery which laid down a heavy barrage on 30 March to clear enemy positions in front of 1st Infantry. At noon, Benson's Sherman and Lee tanks rolled through the narrow gap in the ridge at El Guettar. Self-propelled guns followed, then half-tracks carrying infantry, tank-destroyers and Jeeps. Well dug in and superbly sited, the Germans slowed this force with an extensive minefield and then plastered it with accurate anti-tank gunfire. When 13th Armored was forced to retreat from this ill-coordinated and costly assault, the burning remnants of 13 tanks and two tank-destroyers were left behind.

In the meantime, Manton Eddy's 9th Infantry had crawled along the foothills of Kreroua but could do little more than hang on by their fingernails. Suddenly in their midst appeared a British military policeman, dressed incongruously in razor-smart uniform, who was to direct the first elements of Eighth Army to their supply dump in Gafsa. He was hurriedly sent back, having arrived 'a trifle early.'[8]

Next day, Patton told Benson to try again and expend a whole company if necessary. Simultaneously, to take the heat off Benson, and off Ryder's 34th Infantry stuck at Fondouk, he ordered Ward to attack at Maknassy, disregarding any number of casualties. 'I feel quite brutal in issuing orders to take such losses, especially when I personally am safe,' he noted, 'but it must be done. Wars can only be won by killing, and the sooner we start the better.'[9]

US intelligence was very pessimistic and worried about the effect of this holdup on the whole Tunisian campaign, 18th Army Group nervous and uncertain, and Patton himself in no doubt that reports of enemy withdrawals, in front of 1st and 9th Infantry Divisions, were the product of 'wishful thinking.' Benson's second effort went ahead at 1230 hours on the 31st in advance of co-ordinated artillery and air support which Patton had planned. Sure enough, while 2nd Battalion, 1st Armored Regiment managed to pass through a lane cut through the enemy's minefield, its tanks then became marooned and could penetrate no further against determined resistance.

A tremendous effort by the Luftwaffe over II Corps' area of operations and the new longer-range offensive strikes ordered by Coningham, rather than Broadhurst's more effective air umbrella, temporarily offset the Germans' loss of numerical superiority. During a sudden attack by a dozen Ju-88s on 1 April, the death of Captain Richard N. Jenson, his aide, seems temporarily to have driven Patton over the brink of frustration at the inability of his troops to make any progress.[10] On the same day a Sitrep (situation report) from II Corps HQ complained that: 'Forward troops have been continuously bombed all the morning... enemy aircraft have bombed all division C.Ps. Total lack of air cover for our Units has allowed German Air Forces to operate almost at will.'[11] This intemperate claim might not have called for much response but as Spaatz explained, '[it] caused great concern as to its inaccuracy and the unjustness of its accusation plus the widespread distribution given it by Patton.'[12]

At Ain Beida, 50 miles south-east of Constantine where 18th Army Group had its HQ, Spaatz's deputy, Brigadier-General Larry Kuter, read the report and was inclined to think it, 'obviously exaggerated and emotional', but the short-fused Coningham exploded with rage. Next morning he fired off a bellicose response which carried worldwide, including even to the official historian at the Pentagon. After accusing Patton of deliberately exaggerating his previous day's casualties and recalling that 362 Allied fighters had been in the air, including 260 over II Corps' front, Coningham retorted: 'It is... assumed that there was no intention... of using air force as an alibi for lack of success on ground. If sitrep is in earnest and balanced against... facts it can only be assumed that II Corps personnel concerned are not battleworthy in terms of present operations.'[13]

Tedder realized at once this was, 'dynamite with a short, fast-burning fuse', for it struck at the very heart of inter-Allied relations. Americans were stunned and infuriated by this attack on the fighting ability of their soldiers, none more so than Eisenhower who, deeply wounded and angered, drafted a signal to Washington asking to be relieved since he could not control his subordinate commanders. Only Bedell Smith's timely intervention stopped him sending it.[14]

At once, Tedder ordered Coningham to withdraw and cancel his signal and made it absolutely clear that he took 'the gravest exception' to comments which, he said, 'are entirely outside his competence.'[15] On 3 April, together with Spaatz, Kuter and Brigadier-General Paul L. Williams (12th Air Support Command), he visited Patton who was wearing his 'fiercest scowl'. Patton told them he intended to make an issue of Coningham's outrageous telegram in which, 'he accused me of being a fool and lying.'[16] Patton was still 'very mad' as the delegation sat discussing the matter when, as Bradley recalled, 'along came four Me's about 300 feet high, machine-gunning the streets, jammed the back door so we couldn't get in or out when it [one of the aircraft] dropped a bomb.' 'Now how in hell did you ever manage to stage that?,' asked a shaken Spaatz. 'I'll be damned if I know,' shouted back Patton, 'but if I could find the sonsabitches who flew those planes, I'd mail them each a medal!'[17]

Next day, when Coningham appeared, both men were aware that some accord in this unholy row had to be reached and agreed that Coningham should send a message retracting his criticisms of the American ground troops, which he did the following morning. In public, Patton made handsome amends for his earlier signal, regretting what he called a 'misunderstanding' and accepting he was 'partially responsible.' Later however, he added a revealing comment. 'The sentence, "for which I was partially responsible," I put in – though a lie – to save his [Coningham's] face. I may need his help some day in another matter.'[18]

This incident laid bare the very bones of Anglo-American co-operation. Tedder thought Coningham's 'ill-judged signal' had created, 'grave danger of very serious political and international repercussions', but the long-term effects would probably be positive: 'Patton is now certainly a friend of ours and I think chance of bellyaching signals from Army greatly reduced.' The most disturbing aspect was to focus attention on the 'repeated failure of US troops', something which greatly worried Eisenhower because it might be used by W.R. Hearst's newspapers at home to support a campaign for confining American military effort to the Pacific theatre. 'We shall,' added Tedder, 'have be careful to avoid over-stressing British contribution to present campaign.'[19]

Patton thought this was exactly what was happening. If proof were required, new orders delivered on 3 April by a 'bird of ill-omen,' Brigadier Holmes of Alex's staff, confirmed it by downgrading II Corps and splitting up his forces.

While trying to advance on Kairouan, Ryder's 34th Infantry had been badly rebuffed in its approach to Djebel Haouareb by elements of Oberst Ernst-Günther Baade's 961st *Afrika* Rifle Regiment (999th Division), part of Kampfgruppe *Fullriede*.[20] Many Germans believed that US troops were not combat-worthy, as one officer's report stated: 'The American gives up the fight as soon as he is attacked. Our men feel superior to the enemy in every respect.'[21]

On the day he issued Patton's orders, Alexander told Brooke he had laid on for the Americans, 'what should have been a first class show', in the Gafsa–Maknassy area. 'In fact, I handed them a ready-made victory on a plate, but their hands were too weak to take it.' This was less than fair but Alexander had now decided that in the Fondouk sector, where a genuine offensive was now to be mounted, 34th Infantry should pass under command of Lieutenant-General Crocker's newly formed IX Corps. American objectives elsewhere were severely limited. At El Guettar, 1st and 9th Infantry were to resist any enemy advance up the Gabès road while merely threatening to attack. As soon as Montgomery broke through, the 9th was to be transferred to the north, on the British left, near the coast, while active reconnaissance at Maknassy was to establish that the enemy was retreating before 'the most aggressive action'[22] could be started.

Virtually excluded from participation in the final assault, Patton was as furious as might be expected: 'In this way the U.S. troops get wholly separated and all chance of being in at the kill and getting some natural credit is lost... I hope the Boches beat the complete life out of the 128th Brigade and 6th Armored [sic] Division. I am fed up with being treated like a moron by the British.'[23] Bradley was equally angry but, 'short of raising another disruptive furor [sic]', unthinkable so soon after the major row between Patton and Coningham, neither he nor Patton could do a thing.[24]

As part of the shake-up of American forces, Alexander told Eisenhower of his dismay at 1st Armored's performance and Ike, in turn, informed Patton. The real target was Ward; 'He is quite useless in my opinion,' wrote Alexander, adding that incompetents should not simply be removed and given jobs elsewhere in their senior rank, or even promoted – as happened to Fredendall.[25] Patton thought Ward too timid and was convinced already that he should be replaced. Nothing would have been done, however, without Alexander's instigation: 'I delayed removing General Ward in the hope that the Division would find itself,' Patton wrote soon afterwards.[26] 'Finally at the insistence of General Alexander and in consistence with my own judgement, Ward was relieved... .' But he hated doing it himself and despatched Bradley, who disagreed with the decision, to break the fateful news.

On 4 April Bradley arrived at Maknassy to tell Ward he was being sacked. 'Men devoted to Pinky – his personal loss will be irreparable,' observed Bradley's aide, Captain Chester B. Hansen, 'but situation demands a god [sic]... Germans playing a crafty game & we have not sufficient reserves to match him.'[27] A man of great integrity, Ward took his dismissal with characteristic dignity: 'Bradley gave me order for my relief. He much upset, more than I', and suspected Patton had knifed him: '[I have] been sacrificed to ego of the lion tamer. Brad most sympathetic.' Next day (7 April) after he had seen Eisenhower, who was 'most agreeable,' the penny dropped. 'I am not mean enough. The British think the 1st AD is not a good combat unit. Failure to take hills. HINDSIGHT ALEXANDER AND HIS C OF STAFF BEHIND IT ALL. They failed to give corps information of the enemy, who did not and could not tell me. Will be sent home... '[28]

Eisenhower agreed entirely with Patton's decision to remove Ward, believing him 'too sensitive, both to criticism from his immediate superiors and to the loss of his friends and subordinates on the battlefield', but arranged, through Marshall, that no stigma be attached to his relief.[29] Instead, like Fredendall, his return to the United States was put about as a, 'routine inter-exchange of officers.' But Ward never accepted for a moment that he had been anything but a sacrifice to British ambitions and there were many in 1st Armored who agreed. An ordinary soldier, 'feeling sort of funny writing my commanding officer,' sat down on 18 April and penned a heartfelt letter. 'I feel that I can speak for every person in the entire division both men and officers... there isn't a man in this division that wouldn't go through hell for you and know that they had the best guy behind them ever.'[30]

On his departure to what he termed, 'a big and interesting job', as commander of the Tank Destroyer Center at Camp Hood, Texas, Ward's staff was dispersed too. The new commander was Major-General Ernest Harmon who was called by Patton from 2nd Armored in Morocco. He arrived on 5 April to find Patton, in a foul temper: 'The party is all yours Harmon,' Ward told him at 1st Armored HQ.

That same day, a letter for Patton arrived from Eisenhower: 'General Alexander has told me that your Corps is <u>not</u> to be pinched out of the coming campaign. I therefore assume that when we have gotten 8th Army into the open, your entire Corps, less the 9th Division, will be given a definite sector and mission.'[31] This was no more than a sop to Patton's driving ambition but he had more immediate worries. The mepacrine swallowed against malaria always made him ill; he felt at present 'like hell.'[32]

***

Before the Axis troops facing Eighth Army were forced onto the Tunis plain one last natural barrier was defensible, the Wadi Akarit, cutting deeply inland for four of the 18 miles of the Gabès Gap between the coast and cliffs of Djebel Haidoudi to the west, standing sentinel over a metalled road linking Gabès to El Guettar and Gafsa. The far west of the Gap was anchored in the huge and desolate salt marshes of the Chott el Fedjadj, extending 120 miles inland. Allied intelligence had not grasped that these dried up quickly in April and might be by-passed. Close behind the western end of the Wadi, five miles inland, lay the saddleback of Djebel Roumana, running northwest roughly parallel to the coast road, from where the defenders, perched 500 feet up and unreachable by wheeled or tracked vehicle, had a perfect field of fire. Further west was Djebel Fatnassa, nearly 900 feet of shattered rock hewn into a labyrinth of gullies, pinnacles, chimneys and escarpments. A series of hills stretched onwards to Djebel Haidoudi, providing a natural obstacle to Eighth Army's progress. Anti-tank ditches guarded the approaches to Djebels Roumana and Fatnassa and in front was laid the usual tangle of wire and about 4,000 mines. In comparison with the Mareth Line, however, wire obstacles were thin, the position had little depth and could be contained and destroyed by artillery.[33]

On von Arnim's birthday (4 April) he entertained Kesselring and Messe to a sparse lunch, cauliflower cooked in oil and decent Tunisian red wine – most of the rougher stuff had been distilled into alcohol to supplement the desperately low stocks of fuel. Kesselring was optimistic that the Wadi Akarit could be held but von Arnim told him: 'I have confidence only in our German units... the badly armed Italian units are tired of war and have no longer much combat value.'[34] Equally doubtful, Ambrosio and Messe were determined to save First Italian Army from complete destruction by a timely withdrawal further north to Enfidaville if the Wadi Akarit was about to be breached. A message from von Arnim to Jodl (the operations chief at *OKW*) sent on 29 March revealed the precarious position of *Heeresgruppe Afrika*: 'Supplies shattering,' he signalled. 'Ammunition only available for 1–2 more days, no more stocks for some weapons such as the medium field howitzers. Fuel situation similar, large-scale movement no longer possible.'[35]

Owing to Allied bombing and, as some Germans claimed, the incompetence of Italian officials, much desperately needed supply tonnage could not be unloaded. On 1 April, the sinking of the supply ships *Nuoro* and *Crema* ended use of the route across the Sicilian Straits; thereafter only small craft that could complete the journey in one night ferried essential goods from Palermo, Marsala and Trapani.[36] Knowing the vehicle situation was now 'catastrophic,' having heard nothing from Jodl and convinced that the Wadi Akarit defences were 'nothing special,' von Arnim began secretly to prepare plans for withdrawing static units.

Word of this leaked out to the troops and, on 5 April, *Comando Supremo* warned First Italian Army that the position was to be held though it was common knowledge among 90th Light that a final defence line was being prepared further north.[37]

Facing the Wadi Akarit, Montgomery enjoyed enormous advantages. He intended using X and XXX Corps which pitched 44 battalions against the enemy's 38, 400 field and medium guns against his estimated 200 and, greatest disparity of all, 462 tanks against his 25.[38] In the skies, too, the Allies were close to obtaining absolute supremacy – the Luftwaffe could now muster only 178 serviceable aircraft out of 324 and the Italians about 65. The Ju-87 Stuka ground attack aircraft and equally obsolescent medium bombers had to be withdrawn and the Me-110s and Me-210s, used for escorting sea and air convoys, were no match for the Allied fighters.[39] Day after day, A-20B Bostons carried out intermediate altitude daylight attacks on enemy airfields, tank and motor transport formations – the famous 'Boston Tea Parties' – while B-25 Mitchells of the North African Strategic Air Force devastated enemy installations, airfields, bridges, marshalling yards, troop concentrations and the port areas of Sfax, Sousse, Tunis, La Goulette and Bizerte. By night Wellingtons maintained the assault.[40]

Montgomery planned his attack as an uninspired repetition of the way he had fought on the Mareth Line, using two infantry divisions from Leese's XXX Corps, 51st Highland on the right and 4th Indian on the left. Horrocks' X Corps was to be held in reserve ready to take advantage of a breakthrough. After learning that enemy forces were stronger than expected, Leese obtained Montgomery's permission to add a third infantry division, 50th Northumbrian, to attack the centre between Djebels Roumana and Fatnassa. The final plan hinged upon Tuker's enormous promise that 4th Indian could take the Fatnassa heights at night, including Djebels Rass ez Zouai and El Meida, before 51st Highland attacked Djebel Roumana. This was intended to outmanoeuvre the enemy's central defences and protect the exposed left flank of 50th and 51st Divisions.

Opposing them were the *Young Fascist* Division holding the most easterly positions from the coast along the Wadi Akarit, then two battalions of 90th Light, sitting astride the coast road. Next in line the *Trieste* and *Spezia* Divisions defended Djebel Roumana and as far west as Djebel Meida. On the western flank, XXI Corps' *Pistoia* Division protected Djebels Zouai and Fatnassa, a detachment of 15th Panzer Division was astride Haidoudi Pass on the Gabès–Gafsa road and, further still to the west, the remains of 164th Light were lodged in the hills, their commander, von Liebenstein, complaining to no effect that his forces were isolated and useless there. Of greatest concern to Eighth Army was the bulk of 15th Panzer, held in reserve behind XX Corps, 10th Panzer opposing American troops at Maknassy and 21st Panzer at El Guettar; they were within a night's travel of any part of the front. All in all, the strength of First Italian Army, including German elements, was about 106,000 troops.

Under a sickle moon on the night of 5 April, Tuker watched 7th Brigade, heavily laden, trudge forward through a slight ground mist. Stealthily, 1st Battalion, 2nd King Edward VII's Own Gurkha Rifles, infiltrated jagged cliffs. Stealing upon the unwary Italians, their *kukris* unsheathed, these superb mountain troops swarmed over the crests, smashing into the enemy's positions. There was some confusion on the approach to Djebel Zouai when a curtain of fire hit 7th Brigade HQ, wounding Brigadier Lovett and upsetting communications with his leading troops, but the pace never slackened.[41] Led by Subedar Lalbahadur Thapa, two sections of Gurkhas forced their way through a jagged ravine which carried them on a critical path between twin escarpments and over a narrow cleft commanding the outlying and dominant features of the Fatnassa massif.

The 2nd Battalion, 36th *Pistoia* Regiment, barred the way with anti-tank and machine-guns, mortars, grenades and small-arms fire but Subedar Thapa took out the machine-gun nests one by one and charged over the crest of the escarpment to attack a position covering the pathway. As two defenders fell under his *kukri* the others fled screaming. Immediately afterwards, Subedar Thapa was recommended for an immediate MC; on reading the citation, Montgomery raised the recommendation to a VC which was duly awarded.[42]

The way was now clear for Bateman's 5th Brigade to come up shortly before dawn, led by the wiry hillmen of Lieutenant-Colonel Roche's 1/9th Gurkhas. They penetrated 3,000 yards into the Fatnassa defences, storming ridge after ridge, taking over 2,000 Italian prisoners and only halting to allow Lieutenant-Colonel Scott's 4th Battalion, (Outram's) 6th Rajputana Rifle Regiment, to pass through and swing right, into the rear of the German forces facing 50th Division.

When 1/2nd Gurkhas cleared a way into the foothills of the Fatnassa complex, they had been closely followed by 1st Battalion, the Royal Sussex Regiment which attacked Djebel Meida. Many were hit by mortar fire from the 3rd Battalion, 125th Regiment. Within 1,000 yards of their objective, their adjutant wounded, the attack faltered but concentrated artillery fire from two divisions enabled the Sussexmen to capture Djebel Meida by daybreak, together with 600 yards of the left-hand end of the western anti-tank ditch at its foot, taking numerous prisoners and four 75mm guns which were immediately swung on the enemy.

While these hard-fought actions had been taking place, 4/16th Punjabis were held impatiently below the main ridges and when the crash of mortar and machine-gun fire was heard soon after midnight Lieutenant-Colonel Hughes released them to seize low ridges to the left of the main battle position. Throughout the night of 5/6 April could be heard the age-old cry, 'Allah Ho Akbar,' as the Punjabis fought their way over successive ridges, sweeping terrified defenders of the *Pistoia* Division before them and taking some 800 prisoners.[43] Watching the action from 4th Indian's artillery positions far below, Captain Jephson, one of the artillery officers, was startled when a small armour piercing shot passed clean between his legs, smashing a headlight on the vehicle behind.

At 0415 hours the attack by 50th and 51st Divisions jumped off, preceded by what Messe called, 'an apocalyptic hurricane of steel and fire', laid down on Djebel Roumana and the surrounding area by over 300 field and medium guns. 'Started barraging at 0400 and continued until 0540,' recorded Sergeant Caffell. 'During this time we are attacked in moonlight by enemy aircraft with butterfly bombs putting one of our guns out of action, killing Bombardier Neil ——, and wounding... others. A nasty interlude but we kept the other guns in action, and I was glad when daylight came. We hear that the Gurkhas and Camerons have taken their objectives. Thousands of POWs coming through this way.'[44]

On the right of the attack, 5th Queen's Own Cameron Highlanders and 5th Seaforth Highlanders (both of 152nd Brigade, 51st Highland Division) had begun to move forward early from their start tapes towards the Roumana ridge in order to cross minefields and an anti-tank ditch, hoping to catch the enemy by surprise. Watching them come up through the lines of 5/7th Gordon Highlanders, Private John Bain heard someone call out, 'Here they come. Poor bastards!' followed softly by, 'All the best mate!' One of the Seaforths answered, 'It's all right for you Jimmy... Lucky bastard!' but, as Bain remarked, 'the tone of his voice did not carry true resentment: it was rueful, resigned.'[45]

By full daylight the Camerons and 5th Seaforths had taken the ridge and 2nd Seaforths passed through, forcing a passage along the top. An hour later they had captured Point 112 at the north-eastern end while, at the base of the hills, two crossings on 152nd Brigade's front had been established through which rumbled Valentines of 50th RTR. Italian troops of 1st and 2nd Battalions, 126th *Spezia* Infantry Regiment, were reported dazed and surrendering in large numbers.

On the far right, 154th Brigade had made equally good progress. The 7th Argyll and Sutherland Highlanders advanced carefully through a minefield and crossed an offshoot of the Wadi Akarit. Finding their way barred by the eastern anti-tank ditch, but brilliantly led by their CO, Lieutenant-Colonel Lorne Campbell, they used rope ladders and the backs of captured Italians to scale its ten-foot sides. From there, 7th Battalion, the Black Watch, moved under shellfire left up the anti-tank ditch towards Roumana.

The only real setback was in the centre, where 69th Brigade of 50th Division was having a difficult time. The 7th Green Howards, on the right, managed to take an enemy outpost on Point 85 but in tandem with 5th East Yorkshires failed to reach an anti-tank ditch below the hog's back. Hit by concentrated artillery, mortar and small-arms fire from the Italian *Tobruk* and 39th Bersaglieri Regiments which wounded both COs, they dug in amidst mounting casualties. Private E. Anderson, a stretcher-bearer of the East Yorkshires, completely disregarding his own safety, carried back three wounded men and was killed attempting to bring in a fourth. He was awarded a posthumous VC. Following the stalled attack, 1/4th Essex, detached from 5th Indian Infantry Brigade for this operation, was ordered back again. Moving smartly, they marched along the line of battle, clambered over the escarpment at the western end of the anti-tank ditch and joined in the push on Roumana.

Apprehensive over these developments, early on 6 April Messe ordered 200th Panzer Grenadier Regiment to recapture the hill and 361st Panzer Grenadier Regiment, accompanied by a battalion from the *Pistoia* Division, to retake Djebel Zouai. Additionally, 15th Panzer and two batteries of 88mm guns were ordered into *Spezia* Division's sector. All First Italian Army's reserves were now committed and nearly 80 tanks were on their way to support from El Guettar.

Montgomery claimed later that the enemy's 'immense endeavours' prevented Horrocks punching through the hole torn in the Wadi Akarit defences until after dark on 6 April.[46] This is unconvincing and untrue. With his immense experience, versatile mind and intuitive understanding of the ebb and flow of battle, Tuker knew that the time had come to put through Horrocks' *corps de chasse*, either on the route established across the Wadi Akarit at its western end by his sappers, possibly on a line south-west of Roumana, or both. Accordingly, when Horrocks arrived at his HQ at 0845 hours that day Tuker had reports from all his units and urged him to pass X Corps through in pursuit of a broken enemy. He added that, 'immediate offensive action would finish the campaign in North Africa. Now was the time to get the whips out and spare neither men nor machines.'[47] Apparently convinced, Horrocks telephoned Montgomery for permission to put in X Corps, so retaining the momentum of his attack.

One of the problems about Monty's overweening personality was that, unless they were old and experienced hands like Tuker and Freyberg, it restricted the initiative of his subordinate commanders as Tuker's GSO2, Alfred Cocksedge, discovered. 'I think General Monty had, to all intents and purposes, handed over comd of the battle [of Akarit] to General Leese... The final plan was drawn up by Gen Leese in consultation with Div Commanders but he felt compelled to obtain Monty's approval before acting on it. In the same way, Gen Horrocks hesitated to commit his Corps without first consulting the Army Commander... '[48]

This proved fatal to the whole plan of cutting off Messe's army but at first Horrocks said he was going to put his armour through at once, using the routes made possible by 4th Division's rapid success. At 1045 hours, Leese ordered forward the New Zealand Division, which, nearly 30 minutes later, passed under command of X Corps. Freyberg seemed unsure whether he was to go east or west of Roumana. At noon he met Horrocks and shortly after the Staffordshire Yeomanry and 3rd RTR (both 8th Armoured Brigade) began to work their way through gaps at either end of the western anti-tank ditch. Very soon, however, the Staffordshires came under fire from German 88mm guns, cleverly sighted behind the lower slopes of Djebel Roumana and were badly held up by extensive minefields. The 3rd RTR met equally determined resistance from anti-tank guns at the exits from the Fatnassa massif.

On Djebel Roumana, a tremendous counterattack by 200th Panzer Grenadier Regiment, supported by tanks of 15th Panzer Division, shoved the Highlanders off the crest but 5th Seaforths clung on to the lower rocky slopes. They were joined in a bitter struggle to regain the ridge by 2nd Seaforths – driven off Point 112 – and by machine-gunners of D Company, 1/7th Battalion, the Middlesex Regiment. Throughout the day the fight continued unabated, sucking in 5th Black Watch, while, on the right, 154th Brigade battled to final objectives beyond the eastern anti-tank ditch but could not close the gap of just over a mile between its two battalions, 7th Argylls and 7th Black Watch. Lieutenant-Colonel Campbell, laboured throughout with grenade and bayonet to repel counter-attacks by two battalions (1st and 2nd) of 90th Light and tanks from 15th Panzer, winning a VC for his conspicuous bravery.

So fierce was the shelling that tank commanders of supporting Valentines from 40th RTR, some of them towing anti-tank guns, could not even put their heads out of their turrets. Once they crossed the anti-tank ditch they were all picked off by German 88s, their places filled by a squadron of Shermans from 4th County of London Yeomanry. Without full possession of Roumana, Leese's troops could do little more than hold on to their bridgehead, strengthened towards evening by the arrival of 1st Black Watch.

After a difficult start, the advance had picked up in 50th Division's sector. Sherman tanks got through the minefields west of Roumana and 6th Green Howards captured 400 Italians on the far side of the anti-tank ditch. They created space for the sappers to cut a path in order to bring up the anti-tank guns, but a group of German guns had ranged the ditch to a yard and was firing obliquely to the west from behind Roumana. At 1600 hours one shell struck a group of officers supervising the Indian engineers. Among them was the imperturbable Lieutenant-Colonel Blundell, who died later in a dressing station from his wounds. On the Green Howards' left the battle had ended for all but Lieutenant-Colonel Showers' 1/2nd Gurkhas who clung on to the crest and pinnacles of Djebel Zouai and outlying peaks of the Fatnassa complex.

'Crasher' Nichols, commanding 50th Division, was about to be replaced by Major-General Kirkman for his poor showing at the Mareth Line: 'He has no brains and is really stupid,' complained Montgomery.[49] But Nichols wasted no time in this battle and reported at 1225 hours that resistance on 50th Division's front was 'definitely broken.' Brigadier Bateman of 5th Indian Brigade also believed that the armour could have gone through immediately behind the 50th: 'About midday... I got reports that 4 Raj Rifles were operating down onto the plain... at one time we tried to shame the armour to action by offering to lead with our carriers!... As regards the subsequent "legends" of counter-attacks... not one materialised and 5 Brigade in its foremost positions overlooking the plain was never seriously threatened from the start. If the day had been one of... counter-attacks or heavy opposition, we would certainly have been the first to know all about it.'[50]

Others were equally adamant. 'When I got there [Point 152] with C Coy I could see a good deal of activity on the plain beyond,' wrote Lieutenant-Colonel Roche of the 1/9th Gurkhas, and 'the impression I had was of the enemy artillery hastily pulling out... I have no recollection of any heavy fighting on my right flank.'

Nor had Lieutenant-Colonel Scott of 4/6th Rajputs: 'I do not remember any heavy fighting at Wadi Akarit on our right flank during the daytime of 6 April. In fact, we were wondering at the time what was holding the armour up as things seemed fairly quiet and well in hand.'

Among those in 4th Indian who had a grandstand seat, Lieutenant-Colonel Noble of 1/4 Essex was at a loss to understand, 'why X Corps did not get on with the breakthrough... the only fighting I can recollect on our right was by 51

Division completing the job. My impression is that our armour sat back and provoked nothing but exasperation.'[51]

On the morning of 6 April there was therefore a fabulous opportunity to cut off much of First Italian Army. Montgomery signalled Alexander at noon that day, 'all main objectives captured according to plan. 10 Corps now in movement to pass through the hole blown by 30 Corps.'[52] Then why did Horrocks not put through the armour as expected? Humane but not a ruthless finisher, perhaps he was unwilling to sustain casualties on the scale which would have been required.[53] His failure, and Montgomery's, too – coupled with Alexander's, who had devised II Corps' faulty strategy and Patton's inability to complete part of it by breaking in from Maknassy – condemned the Allies to exactly another month of costly fighting with over 10,000 casualties.

Had 4th Indian Division possessed its third brigade, lost after El Alamein, and a reconnaissance unit, Tuker would undoubtedly have committed his troops to a thrust through 4/6 Rajputana Rifles, throwing the reconnaissance unit out to the Gabès–Sfax road and blocking the enemy's supply line and withdrawal. Pleased as he was at the division's prowess which had cost 400 casualties and put the Indian Army on the map again, he nevertheless reflected on the armour's failure to seize the initiative, delaying its thrust for 24 hours, unable to take open desert nor a large bag of prisoners: 'Here, in this spot, the whole of Rommel's [sic] army should have been destroyed and Tunis should have been ours for the taking. Again the final opportunity and the fruits of our victory have been lost.'[54]

Eighth Army HQ was given good notice by Y intelligence of the counter-attacks by 90th Light and 15th Panzer. Messe was unsure what was happening to his Italian troops and the Germans were fully occupied at Djebel Roumana. Their bitter criticism of the Italians' lack of resolve was confirmed at least by one battalion which lined up with its colonel to surrender, 'Saved both them and us a lot of trouble,' commented Leese.[55]

For over three hours on 6 April at HQ, First Italian Army, von Arnim, Gause (Arnim's chief of staff), Cramer (CO, *Deutsche Afrika Korps*), Messe and Bayerlein discussed the situation. Greatly pessimistic, von Arnim thought the time had come to retreat; Messe said he could hold until next evening and even longer if they were to throw, 'the last man into the furnace.'[56] In the meantime, reports were coming in that the *Spezia* and *Trieste* Divisions had been largely destroyed and that the enemy was advancing into their rear positions.[57]

By late afternoon the commanders of 15th Panzer and 90th Light Divisions were convinced that retreat was their only option in order to avoid annihilation next day. 'The enemy has captured all the commanding features of the Akarit Line and thus has brought about its collapse,' read a gloomy appreciation by 90th Light that evening. 'All the troops have been thrown into the Italian divisions' sectors and there are no more reserves. But the Army cannot make up its mind to retreat. By tomorrow this will be impossible.'[58] Within an hour Bayerlein received orders to move First Italian Army back behind a gun screen; Messe had already ordered the remnants of the *Trieste* and *Spezia* Divisions straight back to Enfidaville, 140 miles further north, and the *Young Fascist* Division to El Djem.

That morning Private Bain had climbed to Roumana past the bodies of Seaforth Highlanders, 'scattered like big broken dolls', on the hillside. When he reached the abandoned enemy slit-trenches there were many more corpses, littering the ground, their flesh beginning to turn waxy from a film of dust and sand and the, 'sly beginnings of decay', in which he smelt the fetid sweetness of the newly dead.

As the living began to strip them of their few possessions he shouldered his rifle and began walking steadily back down the hill. No one accosted him. There seemed to be no straggler line, no stop line. In a couple of days he reached Tripoli where he was arrested: 'I found the whole business of being in the ranks and in the infantry a brutalising business,' he explained years later. The battle had been, 'one almighty confusion and shambles', in which the ordinary soldier, as usual, had no idea of what was going on.[59] Reaching the end of his personal resources he deserted, becoming one of the Wadi Akarit's many casualties.

Notes to Chapter 14

[1] Alanbrooke Papers, 6/2/17.

[2] Tuker War Diary, entry for 26 March 1943.

[3] Patton to Marshall, 29 March 1943. Marshall Papers, Box 79, Folder 12.

[4] Knickerbocker, *et al.*, *Danger Forward*, p. 71.

[5] Message in G.2 Journal, 1st US Infantry Division, 29 March 1943; II Corps, Box 5684; World War II Operations Reports, USNA 301-2.2.

[6] General Charles W. Ryder interviewed by Dr George F. Howe (13 December 1950). OCMH Collection.

[7] Robinett to Harmon, 15 July, 1971; Robinett Papers, Box 5, Folder 29. Marshall Library.

[8] Jordan, *Jordan's Tunis Diary*, pp. 216–18, entry for 30 March 1943.

[9] Patton Diary, entry for 31 March 1943.

[10] For details of this incident see Bradley and Blair, *A General's Life*, p. 146. The matter is also mentioned by Patton and Hansen in their respective diaries for 1 April 1943; the latter in Hansen Papers, Box 1.

[11] Reproduced in Bradley, *A Soldier's Story*, pp. 62–3

[12] Spaatz Diary, entry for 2 April 1943. Spaatz Papers.

[13] Reproduced by Bradley, *A Soldier's Story*, pp. 62–3.

[14] Tedder, *With Prejudice*, p. 411.

[15] Two cables, Tedder to Eisenhower, 2 April 1943; Bedell Smith Papers, Box 14 and Tedder to Eisenhower, 3 April 1943; Eisenhower Papers, Box 115.

[16] Patton Diary, entry for 3 April 1943. Blumenson mistakenly dates this as 8 April.

[17] Recounted by Bradley in conversation with Hansen; Hansen Papers, Box 23 and in Bradley's *Soldier's Story*, pp. 63–4, in which he claimed the aircraft were Fw-190s.

[18] Blumenson, *Patton Papers, 1940–1945*, p. 209. Also Patton to Alexander and to Coningham, 5 April 1943. Eisenhower Papers, Box 115.

[19] Tedder to Portal, 17 April 1943. Eisenhower Papers, Box 115.

[20] Axis troops in the Fondouk area were 961st Infantry Regiment (999th Division); *Marsch* Battalions 27 and 34; Reconnaissance Unit 90; a mobile detachment of 334th Division; Italian II/91st Infantry Regiment; the locally raised *Algeria* Battalion; 2 troops of German artillery and 2 Italian. See Playfair, *Destruction of Axis Forces*, p. 379.

[21] Report by German troop inspector, 2 April 1943; quoted by Howe, *Seizing the Initiative in the West*, p. 582. Kampfgruppe *Fullriede* was formed on or about 26 February 1943, as a replacement for Grenadier Regiment 47 which had been sent to take part in von Arnim's Operation *Ochsenkopf* on 26 February.

[22] Alexander, 'Notes on Future Operations,' quoted by Blumenson, *Patton Papers*, p. 211.

[23] Patton Diary, entry for 3 April 1943.

[24] Bradley and Blair, *A General's Life*, p. 149.

[25] Alexander to Brooke, 3 April 1943. Interviewed by Howe after the war, Alexander denied absolutely having anything to do with Ward's dismissal and claimed he did not even know he had been removed. While it is true that he did not directly recommend Ward's relief, nor contact Patton about this, he would have known that Eisenhower would relay his misgivings to the II Corps Commander.

[26] Patton to Devers, 13 April 1943. Patton Papers, Box 25.

[27] Hansen Diary, entry for 4 April 1943.

[28] Ward Diary, entries for 4, 6 and 7 April 1943. Emphasis in original.

[29] Eisenhower's views were put to Ward when he returned home by Marshall; Marshall to Ward, 5 May 1943. Marshall Papers, Box 90, Folder 4.

[30] Combs to Ward, 18 April 1943; 1st Armored Division, 1942–1943, Box 2. Ward Papers.

[31] Eisenhower to Patton, 5 April 1943; Chandler, Eisenhower Papers, II, No.928. Emphasis in original.

[32] Patton Diary, entry for 6 April 1943.

[33] Kesselring, 'Final Commentaries on the Campaign in North Africa'.

[34] Von Arnim, 'Erinnerungen an Tunesien'. p. 87.

[35] Quoted by Playfair, *Destruction of Axis Forces*, p. 359.

[36] 'Kriegstagebuch der Heeresgruppe Afrika/O.Qu.'. entries for 1 and 2 April 1943; Feige, 'Relationship between Operations and Supply in Africa'; von Vaerst, 'Operations of the Fifth Panzer Army in Tunisia'.

[37] Playfair, *Destruction of Axis Forces*, p. 361.

[38] Direct comparisons are difficult; a typical German infantry battalion, at full strength, was 643 strong while there were 786 in a British rifle battalion. However, as von Arnim pointed out in his 'Recollections', in Tunisia the ratio was more like 1:4 since many German battalions were critically short of replacements.

[39] Anon., *The Rise and Fall of the German Air Force 1933–1945*, p. 253.

[40] 'Air Operations in Support of Ground Forces in North West Africa 15 March – 5 April 1943'; Spaatz Papers, Box 166.

[41] Brigadier Lovett was hit three times that day. Shot through the neck and suffering a smashed wrist he had to be ordered back, rebellious and indignant, Tuker, *Approach to Battle*, p. 328.

[42] Stevens, *Fourth Indian Division*, p. 223.

[43] Anon., *The Tiger Kills*, p. 274.

[44] Caffell Memoirs, diary entry for 6 April 1943.

[45] Scannell, *Argument of Kings*, pp. 19–20.

[46] Montgomery, *El Alamein to the River Sangro*, p. 58

[47] Stevens, *Fourth Indian Division*, p. 225, quoting Office Note [original long since vanished]. Corroborating evidence comes from 'Notes on conversation between Horrocks (Cmd 10 Corps) and Tuker (Cmd 4 Indian Division) at TAC HQ 4th Indian Division at about 0900 hours on 6 April 1943'; Tuker Papers, IWM 71/21/3.

[48] Cocksedge to Tuker, 29 July 1960. Tuker Papers.

[49] Montgomery to Alexander, 27 March 1943; quoted by Hamilton, *Monty: Master of the Battlefield*, p. 214. Brigadier Beak of 151 Brigade was also, unfairly, dismissed. Kirkman had been Monty's artillery chief and had recently been with First Army. Anderson remained in post since Alexander could not screw up the courage to sack him: 'All things considered I feel it best to leave alone,' he wrote on 29 March after Montgomery had offered Leese as a replacement. The only change was 'Cam' Nicholson instead of McNabb as Anderson's BGS.

[50] 'Statements from my File' in 'History of 4th Indian Division, Some Notes for its Wartime Commanders by Lt.General Sir Francis Tuker, late Comdr 4 Ind. Div'. (1958). Tuker Papers. The original comments by Bateman are in his Papers, 'Draft Narrative Account of 5 Indian Infantry Brigade, Tunisia 1943', (5 January, 1959).

[51] Roche, Scott and Noble all quoted by Tuker, 'History of 4th Indian Division: Some Statements from my File'. Tuker Papers.

[52] Playfair, *Destruction of Axis Forces*, p. 373.

[53] Warner, *Horrocks*, pp. 95–6.

[54] Tuker War Diary, entry for 7 April 1943.

[55] Leese to his wife, 6 April 1943. Leese Papers.

[56] Playfair, *Destruction of Axis Forces*, pp. 373–4.

[57] Report dated 6 April 1943; RH19-VIII/351.

[58] Quoted by Playfair, *Destruction of Axis Forces*, p. 374.

[59] Corporal Vernon Scannell. Sound archives recording, IWM 10009/4. Bain, who adopted his pen-name Scannell in 1945, was court-martialled and sentenced to three years' imprisonment for 'deserting in a forward area'. Sent to a harsh military prison in Alexandria his sentence was suspended for him to be released and take part in the Normandy landings in June 1944, when he was wounded.

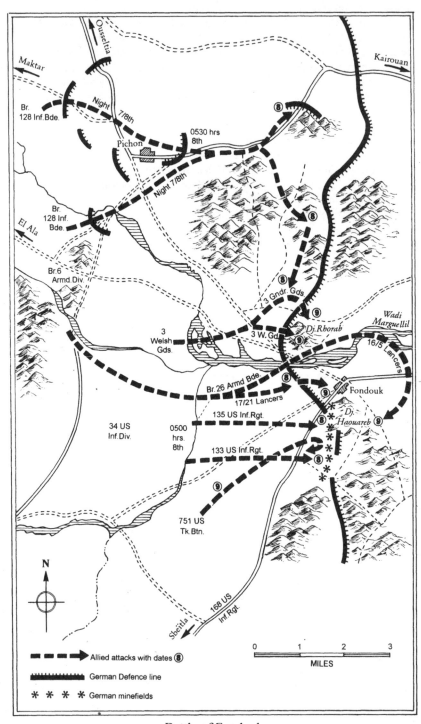

Ousseltia

Kairouan

Maktar

Br.
128 Inf. Bde.

Night 7/8th

Pichon

0530 hrs
8th

Night 7/8th

Br.
128 Inf.
Bde.

El Ala

Br. 6
Armd. Div.

3 Gndr. Gds.

Wadi
Marguellil

3
Welsh
Gds.

3 W. Gd.

Dj. Rhorab

16/5 Lancers

Br. 26 Armd Bde.

17/21 Lancers

Fondouk

135 US Inf. Rgt.

34 US
Inf. Div.

0500
hrs.
8th

Dj.
Haouareb

133 US Inf. Rgt.

751 US
Tk. Btn.

N

168 US Inf. Rgt.

Sbeitla

0   1   2   3

MILES

Allied attacks with dates ⑧

German Defence line

✳ ✳ ✳ ✳ German minefields

Battle of Fondouk
8 - 10 April 1943

Chapter 15

Go On At All Costs

'Where are you Eighth Army people going?'
'Tunis.'
'Where then?'
'Berlin.'

Exchange between Brigadier Kippenberger and a captured German officer at the Wadi Akarit, April 1943.[1]

Advancing through the Wadi Akarit position on 7 April, Sergeant Caffell saw for himself the grim cost of its capture: 'Some of our own dead infantry boys still lying unburied face down on the battlefield. I had to keep wrenching the steering wheel to avoid driving over them.'[2] Eighth Army's casualties had been higher than at any time since El Alamein. In 24 hours 1,289 men had been killed or wounded, 51st Highland Division suffering most heavily. Among them was Brigadier Kisch, Eighth Army's chief engineer, blown up when someone stepped on a mine. 'He had an eye like a hawk for mines and was our great anti-mine expert,' observed Leese, 'and would never have made a mistake. He is a terrible loss.'[3]

Air reconnaissance and Y Intelligence reported early on 7 April that, 'all elements' were withdrawing from the Wadi Akarit, as well as 10th and 21st Panzer from in front of Patton in the El Guettar–Maknassa area.[4] 'Violent enemy gunfire and bombing. The enemy is attacking and is beaten back,' recorded the Gefreiter for the last time (4–6 April) in the diary he had kept during the long retreat. Whether he was killed or was among the 125 Germans taken prisoner – together with 5,211 Italians – is not known. In all, First Italian Army had lost about six battalions.

That same morning Patton sent Benson's armoured column ahead from El Guettar, meeting with little resistance except some long-range fire. At about lunchtime, Patton moved up to join Benson and came upon his tanks held up in front of a minefield; ignoring the mortal danger he drove on while they followed and then told Benson, 'keep pushing for a fight or a bath [in the sea].' Turning back when only 40 miles from Gabès, Patton came across, 'quite a few prisoners, including Germans of a low type.' Shortly after, a British patrol met what Tuker termed, 'the Yanks... right hand tank'. Lieutenant Richardson's No. 5 Troop, B Squadron, 12th Lancers, came across Benson's armour south-west of Sebkret en Noual at 1530 hours and the junction between Eighth Army and II Corps had at last been accomplished. 'I am glad I was not there,' noted Patton, 'It would have been too spectacular.'[5]

The encounter was anything but that. 'Say, where's the booty?,' was the first question asked by the Americans.[6] Brisk and unemotional, representatives of two armies which had started out from opposite sides of a continent shook hands for the movie cameras. 'Seems to be end of [one] phase & start of another,' commented Hansen.[7] The meeting effectively ended the battles around El Guettar and Gafsa; much to Patton's annoyance he was ordered that evening by 18th Army Group to recall Benson's armour.

Alexander's intention now was to cut off the retreating Axis troops further north by striking eastwards with Crocker's IX Corps through the Fondouk Pass, between Djebels Haouareb and Rhorab. In the south the hunt was on as Eighth Army began to move forward over the network of roads dividing the great central Tunisian plain. Nearest the coast, 51st Highland Division was held up by the anti-tank ditch east of Roumana where Major Rainier saw a bulldozer burying heaps of enemy dead. On the Highlander's left, 7th Armoured raced ahead accompanied by the New Zealanders, with 8th Armoured Brigade under command spreading westward and linking with 1st British Armoured furthest inland.

Delaying actions were fought by 361st Panzer Grenadier Regiment, and tanks moving north-east from Gafsa and El Guettar, though they were heavily strafed by the Desert Air Force. Meanwhile, Bostons, Mitchells and Kittyhawks cratered the Luftwaffe's landing grounds. Fritz Bayerlein reported heavy casualties and unsettled morale. But, to general dismay, Eighth Army soon discovered that the great bulk of the enemy forces had carried out a remarkable retreat to new positions and that its own logistical difficulties prevented a rapid advance.

***

The last remnants of First Italian Army quickened their retreat on 8 April as Crocker ordered Brigadier James' 128th Infantry Brigade, whose Churchill tanks had arrived in a great hurry only 36 hours earlier, to attack across the Wadi Marguellil, which winds through the Fondouk Pass and stretches to the south-west of Pichon. Taking the village they advanced further eastwards to smash the enemy's *Algeria* Battalion and then, lacking any clear orders, they turned south towards Djebel Rhorab, four miles away, with a force consisting of 5th Hampshires and a squadron of tanks from 51st Battalion, RTR. They were stopped by increasing resistance from 1st Battalion, 961st Regiment.

Crocker's basic plan of attack at Fondouk was inept because Djebel Rhorab, threatening his right flank, was not included as a definite objective for 128th Brigade. Brigadier James had been told to deny its use to the enemy – not quite the same thing as capturing it. Meanwhile, 133rd and 135th Infantry Regiments (Ryder's 34th US Infantry Division, not yet fully trained), supported by Shermans of the 751st Tank Battalion and two companies of the 831st Tank Destroyer

Battalion, were to capture the heights south of Fondouk between Djebels Haouareb and el Jedira. 'Once more our infantry doggies went up against that damned saw-toothed ridge,' commented one officer.

Understandably anxious that Rhorab would not be taken by the time his troops left their start line, Ryder managed to get Crocker's agreement for his attack to go in at first light, after bombing and shelling had softened up the Germans. Crucially, he then changed his mind. Still overwhelmingly concerned about the danger on his right he ordered a night approach when the troops were already past the 2,000 yard bombline. Corps HQ cancelled the bombing for fear of hitting 135th Regiment as it advanced and, while the inexperienced troops milled about trying to find their bearings, the American artillery opened up on Djebel Haouareb. Far too soon, their shelling simply awakened the Germans and gave no cover to the infantry who had barely started to move forward.[8]

After further delay and asked to advance four miles over open ground in broad daylight against withering fire from the 961st's 2nd Battalion on their front and left flank, the attack units refused to leave their start line, dug shallow trenches, hid in the beds of dry wadis or lay full length behind sand hummocks. While their courage was not in doubt they lacked experience and leadership in such a daunting situation. Many had served mainly on line of communication duties and, when others had previously been committed to battle, their losses had been made up by replacements who, 'generally seemed to be below average in physical fitness, training and mentality. Quite a number of them had never had the benefit of a field manoeuvre and were not accustomed to overhead artillery fire which further decreased their efficiency temporarily. An excessive number of over-age and physically unfit men who could not stand the rigours of battle were received as replacements.'[9] These were men sent to assault units within 48 hours of arriving at the front.

Crocker was under great pressure to cut off First Italian Army as it streamed north but badly underestimated its strength at the Fondouk Pass. Intelligence sources had rightly located part of 999th Division and *Marsch* Bataillon 27, though estimates of their fighting potential – particularly of the ex-convicts – were low. As a tank expert, who fought in the battle of France and founded and trained 6th Armoured Division, John Crocker possessed a near-obsessive drive for perfection amongst his tank crews but demonstrated little understanding of infantry. Neither could operate successfully without the other but he believed that putting Keightley's armour through the Fondouk Pass and on 14 miles to Sidi Abdullah Mengoub – where 1st Guards Brigade would establish a solid base from which marauding tanks could cut off the retreating enemy – was relatively an easy task and one in which the infantry, on both sides, would play a minor rôle.

Keen to exploit as soon a possible he ordered Brigadier 'Pip' Roberts, switched from Eighth Army to command 26th Armoured Brigade, to send his Shermans off on a powerful reconnaissance. At about midday leading elements from 17/21st Lancers cut across the Americans at Fondouk just as they were beginning a re-organized attack, creating massive confusion and drawing more devastating fire which destroyed four tanks before the probing Lancers hastily withdrew. To their credit the shaken Americans sent in their own armour again which reached the foot of Djebel Haouareb. There, unsupported by infantry, they were easy meat for the cleverly sited German anti-tank guns and dual purpose 88s.

———•◆•——

Intensely frustrated by the previous day's events, Alexander told Crocker on 9 April to smash through with 6th Armoured and trap the Panzers hurrying towards Enfidaville, irrespective of whether or not the Americans had cleared the ridge south of Fondouk. Still unable to comprehend that the enemy held Djebel Rhorab in force, Crocker by-passed Keightley and ordered the capable and experienced Roberts to force the pass with 26th Armoured Brigade, whatever it cost. At the same time the Welsh Guards, from 1st Guards Brigade (transferred from 78th Division to 6th Armoured on 24 March), unsupported by prior artillery bombardment or tanks would attack up the steep slopes of Rhorab.

The colossal task of grinding through the enemy's double minefield and piercing his anti-tank screen was revealed to the squadron leaders of 17/21st Lancers at 0930 hours. 'Goodbye – I shall never see you again, we shall all be killed,' said young Major Nix to his tank commanders before leading the attack. Nevertheless, they advanced almost a mile over heavy sand before he radioed: 'There's a hell of a minefield in front. It looks about three hundred yards deep. Shall I go on?' 'Go on,' he was told. 'Go on at all costs.'[10]

Only a few advanced with the gallant Nix beyond the village of Fondouk where he was killed by a shell which punched into his Sherman. All but two of his squadron's tanks were disabled or destroyed and a second squadron, seeking a path through the deadly minefield, fared almost as badly, becoming bogged down and then shot to pieces.

Probing to the left of the pass, 16/5th Lancers at last discovered a safe route for the advance by running its tanks down into the bed of a wadi which was now firm enough to support their weight but had been too wet to allow the Germans to lay mines. Behind came 10th Rifle Brigade and 2nd Lothians, passing on either side derelict tanks, broken tracks hanging limply over top rollers, bogies and suspension units blown off.

The Welsh Guards had meanwhile suffered heavy casualties in their struggle to take Djebel Rhorab. After three hours all four rifle companies were pinned down and in intermittent wireless contact only; most of their senior officers and NCOs were dead or wounded. Just when everything seemed lost, the adjutant, Captain G.D. Rhys-Williams, rallied the shaken Guards and led them in a new attack at 1300 hours. As they closed in for the kill he was heard calling, 'Keep your distance, not too fast. Come on boys, we can do it.' Disappearing over a final crest he was discovered only minutes later, kneeling in the act of re-loading. He was quite dead, shot by a German sniper.[11] But his outstanding heroism drove home the attack: Rhorab was finally taken and down from the peak came over 100 dishevelled prisoners.

———•◆•——

Having reached a point from where they could break out beyond the Eastern Dorsale, 16/5th Lancers and the Lothians lay immobile during the hours of darkness on 9/10 April. This delay was crucial in allowing further units of Messe's army to retreat northwards; it resulted from a simple misunderstanding. Word had been received that 10th and 21st Panzer had left Eighth Army's front and were on their way to parry 26th Armoured Brigade's thrust. What had actually been sighted east of Fondouk, at about 1730 hours on the 9th, was Bayerlein's flank guard protecting the main German forces as they passed along the Kairouan plain, following the tracks of Italian elements left the previous evening. A few German tanks which approached Crocker's force were quickly seen off and four German self-propelled guns abandoned, but he remained worried about the enemy on Djebel Haouareb who had not been completely subdued.

As Crocker hesitated his opposite number, Oberstleutnant Fritz Fullriede, was reporting to *Heeresgruppe Afrika* that his right flank (where the Guards had broken through) had ceased to exist and his left was becoming very insecure as a result of a renewed attack by 34th Infantry Division and Coldstream Guards. At first light on the 10th 34th Division finally captured the Djebel Haouareb ridge. During the protracted fighting 34th Division's casualties, surprisingly, were not so heavy as in their previous action at Fondouk. Taking both together, however, the division lost 36 men and suffered 733 wounded – more than at any other time during the Tunisian campaign. Most of the casualties had shrapnel wounds and some senior officers fought on for hours in the front line after being hit. 'We had some British tank casualties,' reported the medical staff, 'the heroism of these boys was amazing. You couldn't make them complain even when you had to strip the burned skin off their hands and faces.'[12]

By morning on 10 April, when 'Pip' Roberts drove elements of 6th Armoured Brigade through heavy dust storms onto the Kairouan plain, most of the enemy had slipped away through the Fondouk Pass apart from a rearguard set to delay the pursuit, sometimes using captured Russian anti-tank guns. Late in the afternoon the Lothians and 16/5th Lancers were sweeping along the southern side of the main Fondouk–Kairouan highway when they caught up with the stragglers. In failing light they shot up an anti-tank screen, killing many of the gun crews and leaving the muzzles of four 88s and 16 lighter anti-tank guns pointing aimlessly skywards. Out on the vast plain glared the fiery torches of seven burning M13/40 Italian tanks.

Back at the Fondouk Pass, McQuillin arrived from the south with CC A, where he met units of the 168th US Infantry Regiment, both 24 hours too late to intercept the enemy's retreat which went on all next day. Following close behind under the cloudless sky, a scout car, two Jeeps and a photographer of 1st Derbyshire Yeomanry entered Kairouan unopposed at 1100 hours.

Seen from a distance the white velvet of the town's beautiful fluted domes seemingly floated over a scarlet carpet of poppies, but many Eighth Army troops were less than overwhelmed: 'Today we pass through the holy city of Kairouan, the City of a Hundred Mosques, but to us it looked just the usual wog town,' commented Sergeant Harris of a 22nd Armoured Brigade tank unit.[13] The last truck out was crammed with Italians. Before leaving the Germans systematically booby-trapped many buildings, blew up the water supply and destroyed an electric power station.

Earlier on the 11th, C Squadron of 1st Derbyshire Yeomanry, ranging 20 miles south-east of the town, met Lieutenant Richardson's troop of 12th Lancers, which seemed to specialize in these things. Again the encounter between First and Eighth Armies was downbeat, marked only by a few jokes and good-natured oaths on each side.

Advancing north and north-west the next day with orders to cut off the enemy on the Eastern Dorsale, Keightley's mass of tanks missed out until late that evening when the Lothians' B Squadron and 16/5th Lancers caught up with a fleeing column. 'Of the lorries all that remained was twisted metal, shattered windscreens, charred woodwork and tyres burnt to a fine ash. Both sides of the road and the road itself was littered with parts of vehicles, equipment, burnt-out ammunition cases and all the medley of burnt clothing, discarded arms, steel helmets and occasional dead that accompany a rout.' Beside the roadside were German prisoners. One badly-wounded youngster was, 'crying piteously behind his thick-lensed spectacles.'[14]

The failure to encircle and destroy First Italian Army before it settled behind the Enfidaville position exacerbated swelling resentment between the Allies. Opinion at 18th Army Group was extremely critical of the Americans' recent performance. Alexander talked about their 'Blah-Blah,' thought them 'crashing bores,' and, while their hospitality and generosity were boundless, considered their supposed business efficiency and hustle to be 'pure baloney.' Lieutenant-General McCreery dismissed the 'Fondouk fighters' who in a week would be claiming they had taken Fondouk and Kairouan whereas all they had done was retreat. 1st Armored consisted of 'Ward's Warriors' who had captured nothing.[15]

Such criticism was common throughout Eighth Army, from Montgomery down to the lowest ranks. Alan Moorehead, meeting the Eighth Army's vanguard, saw a sergeant lean from the turret of his sand-coloured armoured car: 'Who are you?' 'The First Army' 'Then you can go home now,' was the response.[16] More typical was a gunner's shouted comeback when passed by American troops giving the Eighth Army men a two-fingered salute: 'Going to fuck up another front, I suppose.'[17]

Unfortunately, when Crocker gave what he thought was a strictly private and off-the-record analysis of recent fighting and the part played by Ryder's division to a group of visiting Americans, his comments leaked out to press correspondents. The news soon got back to the United States and was magnified into blanket condemnation which accused the 34th of such poor training and inefficiency that its troops had been late on their start line and unable to take their objectives; indeed, they could only be trusted to clean up battlefields.

Ryder protested loudly that Crocker's plan had been badly flawed. Deeply suspicious of the British at Fondouk, he maintained his troops had not been expendable merely to allow 6th Armoured through the pass unscathed.[18] Having ordered that any criticism of his *own* performance was not to be suppressed, Eisenhower was enraged to discover his censors had extended this to *all* units and allowed Crocker's scathing indictment of the 34th's shortcomings to become public. Firing his chief 'fool censor' (General McClure) the C-in-C immediately began a publicity counter-offensive to restore to the public an image of Allied unity before the final push for Tunisia.

That could not be long delayed. In the north Koeltz's French XIX Corps had broken through the Eastern Dorsale after heavy fighting, losing the inspirational General Welvert, commander of the *Constantine* Division, killed on the last day (10 April) before the Germans withdrew. The French moved north-east from Pichon with the object of taking Djebel Mansour and dominating high ground around Pont du Fahs. On the 13th they linked up with the most westerly units of Horrocks' X Corps. By then Anderson had pressed forward on the front extending from Sedjenane southwards to the road running from Oued Zarga to Medjez. The task of forcing that road open as a preliminary to the final drive on Tunis fell to Evelegh's 78th Division.

Before undertaking that, however, Evelegh was also ordered to mount a limited offensive and regain Sedjenane. Brigadier Flavell's 1st Battalion (1st Parachute Brigade) had been left holding 'Bowler Hat', near Tamera. He was to help free the main coastal road axis running from Tabarka through Sedjenane to Mateur – and thence either to Bizerte or Tunis – by diverting attention from the attack put in by two of Evelegh's infantry brigades, the 36th and 138th, on his right, just south of the road. The whole of Freeman-Attwood's 46th (North Midland) Infantry Division's artillery and a *tabour* of Goums were in support.[19]

At 2200 hours on 27 March, a massive barrage of shells shrieked and moaned over the heads of the advancing paratroopers. 1st Battalion, passing 3rd Battalion on Bowler Hat, made good progress against moderate opposition from the 10th Bersaglieri Regiment, whom the Goums slaughtered in great numbers. An Italian colonel hastily surrendered, willingly handing over his sword but insisting on keeping his little dog.

On the left, 2nd Battalion advanced into an unsuspected minefield and ran into Witzig's Fallschirmjägers, who held high, wooded and rocky ground. Frost's men gradually worked their way onto a plateau, not far below the crest. An unfortunate German, blundering into their positions, screamed in pain when seized in a powerful arm-lock by Frost's signal sergeant. 'Put that man down will you Sergeant,' called Frost. Back came the instant reply: 'Oh, I can't do that sir, I've never had one before!'[20] When daylight came the paratroopers discovered they were on a false crest, well short of their objective. Clinging on to prevent the brigade's entire position being lost, they were plastered with concentrated machine-gun fire, artillery and mortar shells making it impossible to evacuate the wounded. Ordering fixed bayonets, Frost sounded a blast on his hunting horn. 'Waho Mohammed' they shouted as supporting guns and mortars suddenly poured fire into the enemy while the paratroopers broke cover. At the same moment B Company and part of 1st Battalion caught the Germans in a pincer-grip higher up the hill, just missing the redoubtable Major Witzig himself.

Doused by 'friendly' artillery fire, B Company suffered further casualties. Dazed and heavily depleted, the remaining 150 survivors had to be strengthened by a company from 3rd Battalion. That night, in pelting rain and pitch darkness, the 'Red Devils' clawed their way up again through a hail of fire while the Germans pulled back to their positions on Green and Bald Hills, which they had held in February. By 1145 hours next day, the Parachute Brigade was astride the main road near Tamera and 16 days later was relieved by troops of the 9th US Division.

They arrived to take over with much swagger and fuss. Inquiring if it were necessary for the Americans to wear helmets in what was now virtually a rest area, Lieutenant-Colonel Pearson of 1st Parachute Battalion was told by their CO: 'If George S. Patton says you wear your steel helmet, you wear it. If George S. Patton says attack, we attack, and that's where the goddamn fuck-up begins.' Pearson was inclined to agree.[21]

The corps commander, General Allfrey, came to see the paratroopers before they set off for Bou Farik, there to rest and re-organize before the invasion of Sicily. In five months, the brigade had suffered 1,700 wounded, killed and missing. As their train passed the biggest prisoner-of-war camp in North Africa there came flocking to the wire thousands of Germans who, seeing the red berets, cheered and cheered. 'It was our nicest tribute,' commented John Frost.[22]

These were few in number. Most paratroopers were furious at their treatment, used as infantry without adequate equipment and in the line continually since 26 January. Again and again they had fought off superior numbers and received no credit at all. Several war correspondents who knew the truth wrote to Alexander asking for the ban on reporting their activities to be lifted. The last thing the Army authorities wanted – or Churchill for that matter – was a decline in recruiting and questions in the House of Commons. The ban remained.

Resistance to the other prong of Evelegh's attack had been patchy. 'Swifty' Howlett's 36th Brigade, led by 5th Buffs, broke through the German defences to threaten the Fallschirmjäger left flank. On a wider sweep to the south, Brigadier G.P. Harding's 138th Brigade advanced behind 6th Lincolns until dense scrub became too thick even for the supporting Churchills from the North Irish Horse. Nothing daunted, a violent series of bayonet attacks by 6th Battalion, York and Lancs, resulted in the capture of the ore mine at Sedjenane. They became instant heroes in the British Press, including Lieutenant-Colonel Joe Kendrew, former England rugby forward, who got the first of his four DSOs- for outstanding leadership.

By the last day of March, 46th Reconnaissance Regiment (46th Infantry Division) had re-taken Sedjenane after 8th Argyll and Sutherland Highlanders battered their way to the outskirts of the village. Around them was a world of untidy and pitted earth, smashed and burned vehicles littering the roadside, thousands upon thousands of shell cases, petrol tins and mines in the growing fields of corn and over everything the heavy smell of dead flesh.[23]

———◦·◦———

Having recaptured the ground lost during Operation *Ausladung*, First Army was beginning to show its mettle. The 78th Division was concentrating at Teboursouk, ready to secure the second part of Anderson's limited objectives. Coming down from the north, 36th Brigade was united with 'Copper' Cass's 11th Brigade, which had been holding Oued Zarga, and the newly-arrived 38th Irish Brigade.[24] They were to attack ridges and peaks of the jumbled mass of high land running almost due east to west on the north side of the Béja–Medjez highway and take the villages of Toukabeur, Chaouach and Heidous as well as the hills, some of them rising to 3,000ft, including Djebels Ang, el Mahdi and Tanngoucha.

Evelegh used a model of the mountains to brief his COs with the First Army commander also present. 'The plan's all right but will the troops fight?,' asked Anderson. 'Well, sir,' replied Evelegh, 'one can only plan in the expectation that they will.'[25]

Major-General Hawkesworth's 4th Infantry (Mixed) Division[26] had recently arrived in North Africa and was sent straight to the front to relieve 46th Infantry Division at Hunt's Gap. Its task was to put in a noisy diversion while Evelegh's brigades pushed ahead in a 12-mile arc, supported by 184 guns extending over a five-mile front south of the Medjez road. At 0345 hours on 7 April they suddenly opened their barrage and as soon as this lifted, the infantry rose from their start lines and began climbing, on the left men of 38th Brigade, in the centre the 36th and 11th on the right.

The Irish Brigade's first objective was Djebel el Mahdi, a whale-backed ridge 1,400ft high, four miles long and liberally strewn with mines. By dawn the senior regiment, the Inniskillings, had driven the enemy off the southern end, losing their CO in the process. Following up in daylight, the Royal Irish got through unpleasant thorn scrub at the footings of Djebel Mahdi and discovered strewn bodies of 'Skins' who had charged straight over the top of a minefield in their preliminary attack. Carefully making their way through taped gaps they waited behind a boiling grey-black cloud of dust and flame as the gunners hit the crest of the ridge and, shortly after noon, went in with rifle and bayonet. Within three hours the Irish Fusiliers had cleared the rest of the hill. 'The sense and the emotive feelings of triumph with a flying enemy before one are like nothing I have known on any other occasion in this world,' remarked John Horsfall.[27] Four miles or so inside the enemy positions, with the opposition not yet cleared from their flanks, they dug in as the enemy hit back with self-propelled guns. Sweeping up in support, 2nd Hampshires and 16th Durham Light Infantry found the going difficult.

In the centre, 5th Buffs and 6th Queen's Own Royal West Kents were on their objectives by evening despite suffering casualties from enemy artillery and dive-bombing. To their right 1st East Surreys was making good progress towards the village of Toukabeur. Much was made possible by the startling climbing ability of the Churchills of the North Irish Horse. Advancing up seemingly impossible gullies and crevices in the limestone cliffs they covered the infantry who inched forward until they could hurl grenades into the enemy's gun positions. Next day they were crawling up 1,800 feet of Djebel Bech Chekaou while the infantry struggled to stay upright in a howling gale.

Ahead, to their left, in failing light and still lashed by raging winds, 5th Buffs managed to advance onto Point 667 (2,188ft) dominating the western range whose last several hundred feet were too precipitous even for the tanks. Already a message had flashed from the East Surreys: 'Touk is took' – they were in the village of Toukabeur. The following day, the West Kents forced a passage along the mountain ridges and Chaouach – 'Charwash' to the troops – was taken by a combination of East Surreys, Lancashire Fusiliers and tanks of 142nd Royal Armoured Corps.[28]

Outnumbered and poorly-supported the Germans hardly stood a chance in these western peaks but troops from 1st Battalion, 962nd Regiment, and 3rd Battalion, 756th Mountain Infantry, resisted with great courage, grudgingly giving space and fighting every step of the way.

Far away in the castle of Klessheim near Salzburg, their fate was being decided by Hitler, pale-faced with dark pockets of tiredness beneath his eyes, and Mussolini who was racked by stomach cramps. Between 7 and 10 April they agreed that Tunisia should be held at all costs.

Kesselring informed *Heeresgruppe Afrika* of this decision, taken in order to tie down Anglo-American forces by land, sea and air, bleed off tonnage which otherwise would be used in attacking southern Europe, maintain the blockade of the Straits of Sicily and force the enemy to ship supplies by routes open to U-boat attack. But on the matter of improving Axis supplies there was little apart from a few grandiose comments by Mussolini who promised, no matter what, to send his last ship to supply the hard-pressed troops.[29]

By mid-April, von Arnim was warning his men against defeatism and scare-mongering. They were pinned back in a final redoubt with the *von Manteuffel* Division in the far north, from the coast east of Sedjenane southwards to a junction with the 334th which, stiffened with a regiment of 999th Division, was holding north of Medjez. Next in line was the *Hermann Göring* Division, defending the south-western edge of von Vaerst's Fifth Panzer Army where it connected with Messe's First Italian Army on a boundary defined as running west of Bou Arada to the mouth of the River Miliane which flows past Pont du Fahs north-east to the coast in the Gulf of Tunis. The southern front was defended by Messe with 90th Light on the coast, astride the Enfidaville–Grombalia road, and the *Young Fascists* next inland (both XX Corps). In the centre, *Trieste* and *Pistoia* Divisions with 164th Light blocked the Pont du Fahs highway and, on the extreme right (or west), lay the *Spezia* Division. Mobile reserves consisted of 15th and 10th Panzer Divisions.

Where the coastal road from Sousse ran through to Bou Ficha and Hammamet it passed between the jaws of mountain ranges narrowing the rough, dark plain to no more than 7,000 yards. At the southern extremity is Djebel Takrouna, 500 feet of unrelenting rock and opposite, on the western side, Djebel Garci, an awful mass of jagged pinnacles and steep pitches, 1,000 feet high. Other obstacles combined to provide a truly formidable defensive position at Enfidaville. The Germans and Italians had given the area a cursory reconnaissance at the beginning of March and several construction staffs planned mine blocks and tank traps. Work began on a 60-mile front with labour provided mostly by the German-Arab *Lehrabteilung* assisted by some Italian troops. By 13 April an incomplete anti-tank ditch had been added and 3,000 mines sewn at the valley entrance. Positions had been selected on the map for artillery and heavy weapons which were to be manned as the retreating troops arrived.[30]

The strength of this position partly compensated for the Axis' lack of firepower. First Italian Army had only 260 guns (177 of them Italian) and the *Deutsche Afrika Korps* 104 (60 Italian); they were also deficient in tanks, fuel, ammunition and air cover but this did not always correspond to reduced morale, as one officer observed: 'On 11 April in the burning sun of mid-morning I saw eight men… marching along the Kairouan–Enfidaville road in full equipment carrying arms and extra ammunition. They had had no food and had already marched for 25 miles before I met them. They… refused my offer of a lift to any wounded saying that they would do the "little bit" of a march to Zaghouan. They arrived at battalion before nightfall.'[31]

Montgomery was in no doubt that he could crack open the position. In the popular press there was much speculation that he had shouldered the Americans out of the fight for North Africa and would have nothing to do with them. 'I suggest a certain modicum of truth [in this],' noted Major-General Penney, Alexander's signals chief, 'and illustrative of the disasters that may be caused by individuals and by speaking out too loudly and too soon.'[32]

Alexander outlined his plan on 27 March for the final offensive, punching here and there with only poorly-coordinated attacks by First Army; Montgomery contemptuously dismissed it as, 'a partridge drive.'[33] Early in April he certainly appeared to be thinking of his own thrust on Tunis though problems with Husky and the dangers of dissipating Allied energies in a two-pronged final attack prompted him to ask Alexander on 10 April whether Eighth or First Army was to carry it out.

The most suitable area for employment of armour lay west of Tunis and so Alexander required 1st Armoured Division and 1st King's Dragoon Guards armoured reconnaissance regiment to be sent from Eighth Army to join IX Corps. Meanwhile, Montgomery again told Alexander that he intended to 'gate crash' the Enfidaville position and asked for 6th Armoured Division to join his command. When it became clear, however, that First Army was to launch the main effort on

22 April he at once arranged for 1st Armoured and the King's Dragoon Guards to join Anderson.

From now on Eighth Army was to play only a minor part in Tunisia and Montgomery clearly lost interest in the whole affair. As Penney observed later in the month: 'Eighth Army attitude odd and a little childish. Trying to pull out and just pass the baby to someone else without fulfilling obligations [maintaining pressure in the south]. Impression gained was that as they were not going through to TUNIS they were tired of that battle and could go.'[34] Nevertheless, Montgomery told Alexander he would face up to the Enfidaville position and would make things, 'very unpleasant there for the Boche', so as to get him looking the wrong way when First Army went in. His colossal lack of tact, however, caused much friction between the Allies when 11th Hussars took the devastated town of Sfax on 10 April.

Flying into Gabès from Cairo five days later, Major Noble of the Cameron Highlanders saw a B-17 Flying Fortress taxi in, complete with American crew. They were on their way to Sfax, 'the Americans paying up their debts as he [Monty] had reached... [the town] when he said he would!'[35] A lighthearted bet had been struck by Bedell Smith and Montgomery, who boasted he would be in Sfax by mid-April. The wager was a Fortress for Monty's own use; to general amazement he took the matter literally so that his first act on getting there was to send off a message to Eisenhower: 'Captured SFAX early this morning. Please send Fortress to report for duty to Western Desert Air Force and the Captain to report personally to me.'[36]

Coming at a time of renewed criticism of American troops, this reminder of Eighth Army's success greatly embarrassed the C-in-C. Alan Brooke was in no doubt that Montgomery was wrong. Attempting to postpone or avoid the problem altogether, Eisenhower wired his sincere congratulations and suggested that, 'your Fortress will operate much better from landing fields at Tunis', still some weeks away.[37]

Montgomery typically would not allow the matter to rest. 'Am urgently in need of this Fortress,' he sent a signal to Eisenhower on the 15th, asking for the Flying Fortress to be flown directly to Gabès.[38] Eisenhower eventually informed Spaatz that, 'Bedell Smith had spoken out of turn in promising a B-17 to General Montgomery, but that the matter had become so complicated, with General Montgomery insisting that it was a more or less an official promise and the promise had been broadcast to the 8th Army.' Spaatz was instructed to, 'write a letter to Montgomery which would give the air-plane to him as a token from the NAAF.'[39] Furthermore, as Monty's superior officer and, 'in order to avoid professional jealousy', Alexander had to be offered a transport DC-3. Alexander had the good sense to refuse the offer realising, as he put it, 'the full military value of large aircraft cannot be fully exploited when they are assigned to individuals or for restrictive use... '[40]

Montgomery took possession of his Fortress and flew into Algiers on 19 April to pay his respects to Eisenhower, untroubled by having caused so much difficulty: 'He paid up willingly.' Meanwhile, the King's Dragoon Guards had entered the empty bomb-shattered port of Sousse (12 April) and, next day, the New Zealanders pushed in Messe's light rearguards and drove forward 30 miles to Enfidaville.

Hoping the enemy had not had time to get established, Freyberg ordered Kippenberger to take Djebel Garci and swing around eastwards into the village of Enfidaville. One look at the towering peaks before him convinced Kippenberger this was not on, and so he put in a cautious probing attack, led by 23rd Battalion along dusty tracks between high cactus hedges and olive trees. Finding Djebel Garci to be at least a divisional objective he went instead for the lower Djebel Takrouna. The division's artillery was strung out for miles when enemy fire began bursting among his trucks and, realizing there was no chance of his gamble paying off, Kippenberger turned about as a German self-propelled gun trundled down the road in front of Takrouna and began blazing away with high-velocity shells. At this moment the BBC announced that Enfidaville had fallen. Two brigade dispatch riders rode off to the village and returned from German captivity two years later. Also lost were the quartermaster of the divisional cavalry and two senior British sapper officers, misled by a careless radio correspondent.[41]

Garci and Takrouna were only to be won by some serious mountain fighting. Unfortunately the special skills required were not something which Eighth Army possessed. Apart from the Gurkhas there were few experienced hillmen and the difficulty of supplying mountain troops with mules was only slowly being solved. For men used to wide open desert spaces, Enfidaville was claustrophobic and filled with a brooding sense of trouble.

Many similar problems beset First Army which Anderson had ordered to advance again in mountainous country to reach a line from Sidi Nsir south-east to Heidous, squatting below the bulk of Djebel Tanngoucha. The West Kents opened this second phase on the night of 13/14 April by attacking Djebel Bou Diss, an outlying mass barring the way to the long ridge of Djebel Ang, beyond which a saddle connected to Tanngoucha. After cautious probing the previous day revealed the strength of the opposition, an artillery barrage preceded an infantry advance to the top of the hill under heavy mortar and machine-gun fire. Fierce hand-to-hand fighting drove off the enemy and the following afternoon a strong counter-attack was beaten back, inflicting severe casualties.

The 2nd Lancashire Fusiliers stormed Djebel Ang and took the heights where they were reinforced by the East Surreys. However, when a combined group of Fusiliers and 5th Northamptons tried to advance on Tanngoucha they were very badly knocked about.[42] A determined counter-attack by 1st Battalion, 962nd *Afrika* Regiment and *Brandenburg* Battalion (attached to 334th Division) wiped out the best part of two companies. Amid dank slabs and fissures of echoing rock a desperate struggle lasted throughout 15 April for Djebel Ang, pitting the East Surreys, Lancashire Fusiliers and Irish Brigade against 3rd Battalion, 756th Mountain Infantry and 1st Battalion, 962nd. The Irish had only just arrived after being relieved at Djebels Mahdi and Gerinat nearby by 6th Black Watch. Private

Framp of the Highlanders met their ghost-like figures trudging back covered in white dust, out on their feet with utter fatigue.[43]

A determined onslaught took the Irish Fusiliers back on to the ridge. They were assisted by Churchills and that evening went on to attack nearby Djebel Bettiour just as the Germans staged their own effort. The two sides passed in the dark until the Germans ran into a mixed bag of mule teams, cooks and the Irish Brigade HQ. In fierce fighting the Germans were beaten off with grenades and small arms, the wounded sent tumbling over 100 feet down the screes. Retreating, they stumbled unexpectedly into the main body of the Fusiliers who picked many of them off. This savage experience only hardened the resolve of the survivors for they fought on with great bravery, defying all logic.

At a critical stage in the battle for Djebel Ang, on 16 April, Brigadier Russell was badly shocked when a mortar killed his signals officer standing beside him which may explain some loss of control over the next few days in the brigade. The Inniskillings went in to attack Tanngoucha that night after the Buffs had mounted an attack on the prehistoric caves of Heidous and been bloodily repulsed. They took the peak but were forced to retreat by severe mortar and machine-gun fire which bolted the Arab drivers and their mules, carrying ammunition and 'beehive' charges – used to blast holes to build defences in the solid rock.

Hawkesworth's 4th Division was meanwhile struggling to advance from Sidi Nsir. On 12 April, 6th Black Watch was badly cut up by mortars and shells which killed the CO, adjutant, six other officers and over 50 men. Next day the division ground to a halt against implacable opposition and remained stuck for 72 hours. Then it advanced only eight miles, at very considerable cost to 2nd Battalion, Bedfordshire Regiment, before being relieved on 16 April by 1st US Infantry Division which had been cleaning up the battlefield around El Guettar. As 4th Division moved south-east to Medjez, 9th US Infantry also replaced Freeman-Attwood's 46th Division in the lush green wheatfields and rolling hills of the far northern sector.

These changes were part of a massive logistical switch on First Army's front, brilliantly executed preparatory to Anderson's final drive on Tunis. The decision to include II Corps was taken as much for political as military reasons. 'I have made Alexander agree as to the necessity of keeping all four American divisions together as a powerful Corps,' Eisenhower told Marshall, 'even if the logistical situation should make the arrangement seem somewhat unwise or risky.'[44] This was actually Bradley's brainchild following a visit by McCreery to Patton's CP, on 17 March, when McCreery explained Alexander's plans for the destruction of all Axis forces in Tunisia. When Patton and Bradley heard that the only American troops to be included were those of 9th Infantry – under British control – they were speechless with rage.

Sensibly, Patton maintained that battle experience was essential for American troops and then produced an argument, 'of great political significance', for retaining the 34th 'Red Bull' Infantry which Alexander wanted to send back for retraining. Ryder's was a National Guard Division of men from the Middle West where isolationism was deeply ingrained. Should they be left out in the cold, the whole National Guard system might be discredited and American public opinion swing further against the strategy of defeating Hitler before concentrating on Japan.

Armed with this, Bradley went to 18th Army Group at Haidra on the 13th, where he successfully pleaded the 34th's case. Against Alexander's wishes Eisenhower insisted on the vital importance of keeping II Corps together, with Bizerte as its objective, but Patton and Bradley would not be allowed to shift their forces from Anderson's command. Patton, still disgruntled, quickly accepted Eisenhower's suggestion that he should step aside and go to work on Husky thereby leaving Bradley commanding II Corps, and the order was written immediately.[45]

In order to smooth ruffled feathers Alexander, quite improperly, gave Bradley the right of appeal to him over Anderson's head on any order which he doubted. Fortunately, this worked out well enough because the eminently sensible Bradley only once used this device when questioning a demand for a US combat team when the British were badly held up, at the end of April, in trying to take Longstop Hill. The replacement of Patton by Bradley was kept secret in order to prevent the enemy suspecting anything about the Allies' future plans. While II Corps moved north, Patton and his staff drove back to Constantine. On the way, lunch with his friend Brigadier-General Everett Hughes, a staff officer in Algiers, provided an opportunity to let off steam: 'Says Ike is crazy. Too pro-British,' noted Hughes – who agreed.[46] Apart from this Patton was inclined to be positive about his spell at the front. 'I have been gone 43 days, fought several successful battles, commanded 95,800 men, lost about ten pounds, gained a third star and a hell of a lot of poise and confidence, and am otherwise the same.'

His replacement, who assumed command of II Corps on 16 April, was different in temperament and manner. Fifty years old, undemonstrative, almost diffident by nature, Omar N. Bradley habitually wore an old field jacket – in Tunisia a cast-off from one of Eisenhower's aides – earning him the title of the 'GI General'. This modest exterior, however, masked a rational and incisive mind. Before his briefing each morning by his G.2 ('Monk' Dickson) and G.3 (Bob Hewitt) he quietly called up his divisional commanders (Harmon, Allen, Ryder and Eddy), asking them precise questions. It was some time before his staff officers, ruled with a rod of iron by Bradley's chief of staff, Bill Kean (known behind his back as Captain Bligh), knew this information was why he was able to put them on the spot so easily.[47]

When the move order arrived II Corps HQ was under canvas on a hillside outside Béja – the town was largely destroyed and typhus was raging. In four days the corps' four divisions, well over 100,000 men, with guns, tanks, vehicles and supplies, had moved 200 miles and spread themselves northwards to Cap Serrat, crossing the lines of communication of the entire British First Army. For one force to move behind another like this demanded superlative planning and remarkably tight traffic control, though there were delays along the way, especially among the

British 1st Armoured Division and King's Dragoon Guards which had been inserted as stiffeners into IX Corps' sector.

The various units had been scheduled to move only at night but, as Bombardier Challoner, one of 1st Armoured Division's gunners, soon discovered, 'because the plan had been so frittered away... we were moving by fits and starts all day to reach the French town of Le Kef at dusk [on 16 April]... French and American Women's Services were about and we saw the first public cafés since Cairo. Most of the Americans were wearing their Egypt medal! More food for thought.'[48] To Monty's veterans their First Army comrades appeared at first sight 'neat and regimental... pale and earnest, as they sit bold upright, rifles in hand, in their new grey-camouflaged vehicles! And what a motley bunch we Desert Rats must look,' commented Private Crimp, 'tanned and weatherstained, sprawling over our sandblown trucks, brewcans bobbing on the side.'[49]

After four days' travelling around First Army's sector Oliver Leese was venomously angry: 'They are jealous as hell of us and our reputation and achievements. It's a pity but then... [Anderson] has no personality and puts nothing across – so what can you expect... I had the most extraordinary interview with... [him]... He was quite f——g about the 8th Army... I said nothing and listened in frank astonishment to a tirade of a mixture of jealousy and inferiority complex. It gave me no feeling of confidence – in fact only contempt... At one time, I hoped [Montgomery] would be merciful and considerate. I hope now he rams the 8th Army down their throat to the last drop. They are ignorant and untrustworthy in comparison and they must be forced to learn.'[50]

Alexander ought to have brought together Anderson and Montgomery to clear the air. Now it was truly poisonous and Leese took great offence at Anderson's recital of the difficulties faced by First Army and his dismissal of Eighth Army's easy achievements against 'mere' Italians. In addition, disaffection was rife among troops sent to join First Army: 'They all terribly miss [Montgomery] and his drive and decision and the confidence which he has inspired in us all.'[51] This was a big claim but newly-arrived Eighth Army units did openly consider themselves a cut above others. All men of 1st Armoured were warned by 18th Army Group HQ that the 6th British Armoured Division and the 46th Division had fought very hard and that formations within the First Army were very sensitive.

Settling in near the pretty village of Bou Arada, however, Bombardier Challoner heard widespread rumours that in recent fighting for high ground in the Oued Zarga–Medjez area the Hampshires, 'after having a bashing are reported to have given themselves up in droves and the DLIs [Durham Light Infantry] who put up a better show had heavy casualties.'[52] Such stories inspired little confidence in First Army's abilities.

Notes to Chapter 15

1 Kippenberger, *Infantry Brigadier*, p. 296.
2 Caffell Diary, entry for 7 April 1943.
3 Leese to his wife, 10 April 1942.
4 Hinsley, *British Intelligence*, II, p. 605. Enigma decrypts did not reveal the retreat until the next day, 8 April.
5 Patton Diary, entry for 7 April 1943; Tuker Diary, entry for same date. In fact, though claimed by Tuker, Richardson's patrol actually belonged to Briggs's 1st Armoured Division. The meeting is also recorded by Bradley in his War Diary, entry for same date; Bradley Papers, Box 4, War Diary, Part 1, June–July 1943. Also in Hughes's Diary on 8 April: 'What does that mean?,' he asked; Hughes Diary, Library of Congress.
6 Stewart, *History of the XII Royal Lancers*, pp. 414–15.
7 Hansen Diary, entry for 7 April 1943.
8 Colonel Robert Ward, former CO, 135th Infantry Regiment, interviewed on 30 November, 1950. OCMH Collection.
9 G.1 Report (30 June 1943); 34th Infantry Division, Operations Report 3 January – 13 May 1943; Box 9417; World War II Operations Reports USNA 334-0.3.
10 Moorehead, *African Trilogy*, p. 519.
11 Ellis, *Welsh Guards at War*, pp. 119–20.
12 34th Infantry Division, 'Narrative History, North Africa Tunisian Campaign'.
13 Sergeant J.R. Harris (4th County of London Yeomanry), Diary entry for 16 April 1943. IWM 86/5/1.
14 Antonio, *Driver Advance!*, pp. 29–30. The scene was witnessed by Antonio.
15 Alexander and McCreery both quoted in Penney Diary, entry for 14 April 1943.
16 Quoted by Pocock, *Alan Moorehead*, p. 147.
17 Macksey, *Crucible of Power*, p. 261.
18 Ryder interviewed by Howe.
19 About 1,000 Moroccan irregulars from the Atlas Mountains. Their speciality was vicious patrol work and it was rumoured they were paid 200 francs per prisoner, 50 for the ear of a dead German and not to be over-fussy whether the ear came from friend or foe. 'Our lads thought a lot of them and we certainly preferred to have them on our side,' commented Sergeant E.P. Danger (5th Battalion, Grenadier Guards, 24th Guards Brigade, 1st Armoured Division), Diary and Papers. IWM 82/37/1.
20 Frost in Arthur, *Men of the Red Beret*, p. 72.
21 *Ibid.*, p. 44.
22 Saunders, *Red Beret*, p. 119; Arthur, *Men of the Red Beret*, p. 75.
23 Guest, *Broken Images: A Journal*, pp. 118–19.
24 38th Irish Brigade was formerly of 6th Armoured and Y Division. It replaced 1st Guards which went in turn to 6th Armoured.
25 Quoted by Blaxland, *The Plain Cook*, p. 227.
26 A Mixed Division was an attempt to provide infantry with its own integral tank support. The concept was not pursued after Tunisia as command and control was considered too cumbersome.
27 Horsfall, *The Wild Geese are Flighting*, p. 108.
28 Ray, *Algiers to Austria*, p. 47; Chaplin, *The Queen's Own Royal West Kent Regiment 1920–1950*, p. 236.
29 Information Directive, 13 April 1943; RH19-VIII/351.
30 Von Vaerst, 'Operations of the Fifth Panzer Army', p. 15.
31 Quoted by Lucas, *Panzer Army Africa*, p. 180.

[32] Penney Diary, entry for 9 April 1943.

[33] Montgomery, 'The Final Phase in Tunisia. The Battle for Tunis', 14 May 1943. Montgomery Papers, BLM 35/1.

[34] Penney Diary, 21 April 1943.

[35] Colonel C.A.H.M. Noble (April–May 1943, Major, 5th Cameron Highlanders), Diary. IWM PP/MCR/181.

[36] Montgomery to Eisenhower, 10 April 1943. Eisenhower Papers, Box 83; copy in Bedell Smith Papers, Box 13.

[37] Eisenhower to Montgomery, 12 April 1943. Eisenhower Papers, Box 83.

[38] Montgomery to Eisenhower, 15 April 1943; Spaatz Papers, Box 12.

[39] Spaatz Diary, entry for 5 April 1943. *Ibid.*, Box 11.

[40] Alexander to Spaatz, 11 April 1943 and comment in Spaatz Diary, same day. *Ibid.*, Box 12.

[41] Kippenberger, *Infantry Brigadier*, p. 302.

[42] Jervois, *History of the Northamptonshire Regiment*, p. 142.

[43] Private C.T. Framp (6th Black Watch), 'The Littlest Victory'; TS Memoir. IWM 85/18/1.

[44] Eisenhower to Marshall, 16 April 1943; Chandler, Eisenhower Papers, II, No.946.

[45] Bradley, *A Soldier's Story*, p. 68; see also Bradley and Blair, *A General's Life*, pp. 144–5, 150; Bradley Memoir.

[46] Hughes Diary, entry for 17 April 1943.

[47] Bradley interviewed by Buhler.

[48] Bombardier L. Challoner, Journal 1942–43; IWM P479.

[49] Crimp, *Diary of a Desert Rat*, pp. 179–80; entry for 18 April 1943.

[50] Leese to his wife, 18 April 1943.

[51] Leese to his wife, 16, 18 and 20 April 1943.

[52] Bombardier L. Challoner, Journal 1942–43; IWM P479.

Chapter 16

Only a Question of Time

'I've had enough of this particular part of the world, you know I don't like hills, well I've been a bloody mountain goat lately.'

Lieutenant D.E. Brown, 17th Field Regiment RA, to his wife, 20 April 1943. Brown was shot through the head and killed in action on Longstop Hill on Good Friday, 27 April 1943.[1]

————————

The transfer of units from Eighth to First Army and II Corps' switch to the northern flank was possible only through total mastery of the air. In one spectacular raid on 22 March, 24 B-17s of the 301st US Bombardment Group blew up 30 acres of dock area at Palermo in an explosion whose shock waves buffeted the bombers at 24,000ft. Six ships were written off and two coasters lifted bodily onto the damaged pier.

Operation Flax began at 0600 hours on 5 April 1943, when 1st Fighter Group (North West Africa Strategic Air Force) sent out 26 P-38s on an independent fighter sweep of the Sicilian Straits. They shot down 16 enemy aircraft for the loss of two Lightnings while US Fortresses and Mitchells caused havoc amongst staging posts, transports and terminal airfields.

Repeated operations during the next two-and-a-half weeks culminated in two savage attacks, the first known as the 'Palm Sunday massacre' when four P-40 squadrons, with Spitfires flying top cover, caught a huge gaggle of enemy aircraft returning from a fleeting visit to the shrinking Tunisian bridgehead. Between 50 and 70 transport Ju-52s and 16 escorting aircraft were destroyed. 'The big thing in this… battle was to avoid collision,' reported a Spitfire pilot. 'The sky just above the sea was a mass of whirling propellers and burning aircraft.'[2] Allied losses were light; six P-40s and one Spitfire.

The second attack on 22 April brought the Axis system to the point of collapse. This time squadrons of Spitfires and Kittyhawks from the South African Air Force, Polish Flight, and 79th US Fighter Group pounced on 21 Me-323s, each capable of carrying 130 troops or ten tons of petrol (their cargo that fateful day). Over the Gulf of Tunis 16 fell like burning torches and ten escorting fighters were destroyed for the loss of only four Kittyhawks.[3] Göring immediately banned all transport flights to North Africa though, under pressure of events, he had to allow Ulrich Buchholz to resume night flights soon afterwards.

The daily average of arriving supplies now dropped to less than ten per cent of that needed to support two armies. Yet troop reinforcements kept arriving right up to the capitulation; 12,000 Germans by air in March, 9,000 in April and 300 in May. Others came by sea; in March 8,400 Germans and 11,000 Italians; in April 2,800 Germans and unknown numbers of Italians conveyed in destroyers pressed into service as troop-carriers, Siebel ferries, landing craft, barges and anything else which could float under the general command of Kapitän-zur-See Paul Meixner, an efficient Austrian and U-boat captain in the First World War. They ran the gauntlet of the Royal Navy, sweeping the seas with cruisers and destroyers operating out of Malta and Bône, and motor torpedo boats from an advanced base at Sousse. Heavily reinforced, the British 8th and 10th Submarine Flotillas intensified their patrols off the main ports of departure for Axis shipping despite serious casualties: the *Tigris*, *Thunderbolt* and *Turbulent* all lost with their valiant crews in March, the *Sahib* and *Splendid* in April.[4]

While the Axis supply position worsened daily, the Allies at last had adequate logistical reserves as troops and stores of every kind were sent from the main ports of arrival at Algiers, Oran and Tripoli to the front via Philippeville, Bougie and Bône. Transports sailing under the Levant Command between Alexandria and Tripoli were protected by Force H (commanded now by Vice-Admiral A.U. Willis) and ports in forward areas at Gabès, Sfax and Sousse were heavily exploited; 14,000 tons of army stores were landed at Sousse alone between its capture and the end of April.

The line of communication for II Corps shifted from Tébessa – supplied by road and rail from Constantine – to Bône, shared with First Army. Major-General Miller's (Major-General, Administration, at 18th Army Group) only anxiety was whether the enemy would stand and fight. 'Personally,' he wrote, 'I feel that the right course from his point of view would be to start now to evacuate his good personnel and best troops in anticipation of the final blow when it may be too late.'[5] The same idea had occurred to Kesselring and von Arnim, but time for a general withdrawal from Tunisia, possible earlier in the year and supported by Warlimont and Vice-Admiral Weichold, head of the German naval mission in Rome, had slipped away. Nevertheless, some thought was given to evacuating key personnel and, on 18 April, the Panzer Regiment *Hermann Göring* returned to Sicily, leaving behind its tanks.[6]

In Tunis, remaining families of the Frenchmen who had gone over to the Allies were ordered to France. Owing to heavy losses of shipping French officials vetoed any sort of movement by sea while the Italian Navy refused to take them on its destroyers. A first attempt to evacuate them by air nearly ended in disaster over Cap Bon when Allied fighters intercepted and shot down one aircraft before the others turned back. Most were eventually got away, Admiral Estèva among them.[7]

British intelligence estimated early in April that a number of jetties being constructed by the enemy along the eastern shore of Tunisia might be intended for evacuation purposes using self-propelled lighters, small coasters and light naval craft, such as E-boats. It was, remarked the British Chiefs of Staff, of 'capital importance' that any large-scale attempt to escape should be thwarted and, whatever naval and air forces might achieve, the best means of preventing this would be for First Army to storm Tunis and Bizerte at an early date.[8]

By mid-April von Vaerst knew the final offensive would not be long delayed but estimated it would fall either on First Italian Army around Enfidaville – because of the enemy's superior forces there – or Fifth Panzer Army in the Medjerda Valley where the terrain was more favourable. Their morale still high, having been told nothing about evacuation, the German troops' allegiance was reaffirmed by von Arnim in a sycophantic message to the Führer on his birthday (19 April). Von Arnim, however, had already written them off but no one had the courage to tell Hitler of the impending catastrophe.

Alexander's plans for the final attack on Tunis and Bizerte, approved by the Combined Chiefs of Staff and subsequently by Eisenhower, were issued from 18th Army Group HQ on 16 April. Operation Vulcan primarily involved First Army, which was scheduled to capture Tunis. II Corps, in Anderson's estimation capable of no more than a diversionary rôle, was ordered to cover the left flank while securing suitable positions to take Bizerte. In the meantime Alexander ordered Montgomery to distract enemy forces by exerting continuous pressure and advance on the route Enfidaville–Hammamet–Tunis while preventing the enemy scurrying into the Cap Bon peninsula.

Bradley's four divisions faced a stiff task in attacking well-defended enemy positions in a belt of rugged hill country stretching between 15 and 20 miles to Mateur, the key to unlocking the Bizerte area. He had trucks running day and night, lights blazing, to bring up ammunition: 'We're going to make it, General,' said Colonel Robert W. Wilson, Bradley's supply chief. 'You can definitely plan to go with the British on April 23.'[9]

From north of the Sidi Nsir–Mateur road to the coast near Cap Serrat, dense scrub in the valleys and on the lower slopes of a tumbling mass of hills and ridges made any movement difficult. Accordingly Bradley assigned a secondary role to Eddy's 9th Infantry, Colonel Magnan's three battalions of the Corps Franc d'Afrique, and 4th and 6th Tabors marocains commanded by Captain Verlet and Major Labataille in attacking along a 28 mile front. While Eddy's 39th RCT struck at enemy strongpoints around Djebel Ainchouna north of Jefna, 60th RCT and the Corps d'Afrique were to drive eastward along both sides of the Sedjenane River, wiping out German fortresses dominating the approach to Mateur through the Sedjenane Valley. Jefna itself was to be bypassed to the north while 47th RCT put in a holding attack against Bald and Green Hills, slightly to the west of Jefna, commanding the Mateur road.

In the nine-mile gap between 9th and 34th Division to the south, 91st Reconnaissance Troop was to mount vigorous patrols but Eddy was unhappy at this exposure on his right flank. 'Manton,' said Bradley when visiting his CP in the

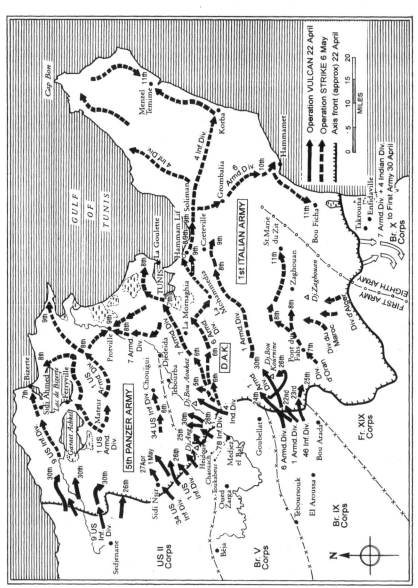

Operations Vulcan and Strike
April 1943

Sedjenane Valley, 'nothing's going to come through that gap. Why Bill Kean and I will go up with rifles to stop anything that might squeeze through.' Eddy smiled but remained unconvinced.[10]

Bradley planned his main attack in the southern zone, on a front of 13 miles generally devoid of natural ground cover. The Germans had built a comprehensive linked defence system, blocking narrow valleys with minefields, placing machine-gun and mortar posts on high ground and bringing artillery to bear upon natural approaches through which the Americans would have to advance. 'The enemy on his hill positions was constantly looking right down your throat,' remarked one officer.[11] The chief routes to Mateur ran through the Oued Tine and Djoumine Valleys, though the latter was entirely under enemy observation. An armoured force could be put through the broader Oued Tine but ran the risk of becoming confined in extensive minefields unless control of ridges and hills on both sides was assured. Consequently, 1st Infantry Division's three RCTs were detailed to clear hills north of this valley while 6th Armored Infantry (1st Armored Division) attacked high ground on the southern edge. North of the Béja–Mateur road the left flank was to be covered by a combat team from Ryder's 34th Infantry; the rest and parts of 1st Armored lay in support.

With a huge superiority in tanks, guns and shells (343,000 rounds were allotted to First Army) Anderson relied on strength rather than subtlety to shatter the enemy. He planned to attack the pivotal point of the Axis defence in the area bounded by Peter's Corner, a location eight miles east of Medjez on the road to Tunis, further along the same road to Massicault thence north to El Bathan, as well as driving the enemy from high ground in the south-west, including Longstop Hill, where over 200 enemy weapon pits had been entered on Allied battle maps. This task fell to Allfrey's V Corps; Evelegh's 78th Infantry was detailed to take Djebel Ang and Longstop Hill while Major-General Clutterbuck's 1st Infantry Division drove forward along the Medjerda River to Djebel bou Aoukaz and El Bathan. On the northern edge of the Goubellat Plain, Hawkesworth's 4th Infantry was to secure Peter's Corner and push into high hills beyond Ksar Tyr.

Entrances to the Goubellat plain were to be seized by Crocker's IX Corps, using Freeman-Attwood's 46th Infantry. When the initial break-in had been made, Briggs' 1st Armoured and Keightley's 6th Armoured were to swing north-east towards Massicault, smashing German armour which Anderson expected would be put in east of the Medjerda, and cut off any enemy still opposing V Corps' advance on a line from El Bathan to Massicault. Further south still around Pont du Fahs, Koeltz's XIX French Corps, with its three infantry divisions – Mathenet's *Maroc*, Conne's *d'Alger* and Boissau's *d'Oran* – together with Le Coulteux's Armoured Group and Lieutenant-Colonel Lindsay's 1st King's Dragoon Guards, was later to pinch out the enemy salient which bulged from Takrouna south-west towards Robaa before swinging north to the vicinity of Bou Arada.

———•◦•———

Before Anderson could deploy his forces, von Arnim put in a spoiling attack to assess their strength, code-named Operation *Fliederblüte* ('Lilac Blossom'), at

Banana Ridge, five miles east of Medjez overlooking German positions on the plain below – one of the jumping off points for 1st Division's 3rd Brigade – and nearby Djebel Djaffa, where 4th Infantry Division's 10th Brigade was lodged.

Under a cloudy sky and fitful moon on the night of 20/21 April, rapidly advancing armoured units of 10th Panzer, together with infantry from Generalmajor Schmid's *Hermann Göring* Division supported by 80 tanks, over-ran artillery positions on Banana Ridge.[12] At first light their main attack opened as Panzerabteilung 501's Tigers, supported by 88s, began a pincer movement. They ran straight onto guns brought up ready for the opening stages of Operation Vulcan. Firing over open sights, the gunners knew from intelligence reports all about the weakest point of the Tigers – the traverse ring attaching turret to body. Losing many of their tanks, surviving crews from 10th Panzer fought on foot in the light of burning hulks which lit up the countryside. Behind their armour, the infantry suffered terribly from concentrated artillery fire while machine-gun bursts destroyed most of those still on their feet. A bayonet charge, supported by Churchill tanks, re-took the whole ridge.

At Djebel Djaffa, south-east of Medjez, the attackers came within half a mile of 4th Division's HQ and neared Peter's Corner but here again the combined weight of Churchills supported by 17-pounder anti-tank guns repulsed them. There was some anxiety lest the troops, readying themselves for the forthcoming attack, might have taken too much of a beating and suffered serious disruption to their gun lines. In fact, German casualties were roughly equal but their loss of tanks much greater; proportionately they could ill-afford either.[13]

From press reports and signals traffic the Germans knew in detail of Montgomery's dispositions as he faced the task of squeezing through the Enfidaville bottleneck.[14] This was always going to be a very serious venture; the Germans' foreknowledge made it even more so and Montgomery's over-confidence ensured it. Acknowledging that there might be some 'tough fighting' ahead, Monty planned to burst through with Horrocks' X Corps and advance 12 miles on Bou Ficha at the northern end of the coastal corridor. Leese's HQ and 51st Division were to take no part since they were preparing for Husky.

Horrocks instructed 'Crasher' Nichols' successor, Major-General S.C. Kirkman, to hold and patrol the coastal sector of the Enfidaville front and Freyberg's New Zealanders to take Takrouna. Tuker's 4th Indian was to capture Djebel Garci and battle its way 12 miles north-east until it commanded the coast road. Erskine's 7th Armoured Division was to make a limited advance on the western flank while waiting for at least one brigade from Major-General E.G. Miles' 56th (London) Infantry Division to come up from Kirkuk (Iraq) to relieve them. Then an armoured attack along the coast road towards Hammamet would bring the decisive breakthrough.

Like Freyberg, Tuker was unimpressed with the plan, having been 'rushed up' on the left of the New Zealanders with a 'stiff job ahead' and placed back under X Corps – 'worse luck'. Horrocks' lack of imagination condemned the 4th Indian to

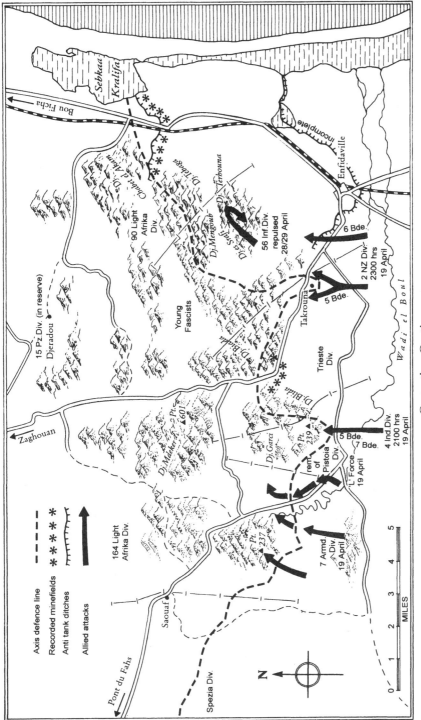

Operation Oration
April 1943

Axis defence line
Recorded minefields * * * * *
Anti tank ditches
Allied attacks

164 Light
Afrika Div.

15 Pz.Div. (in reserve)
Djeradou

Zaghouan

Pont du Fahs

Saouaf

Spezia Div.

N

0   1   2   3   4   5
MILES

7 Armd.
Div.
19 April

Pt.
237

L Force
19 April

Pt.
239

Djebel
Garci

Dj.Mdeker
Pt.
601

Pistoia
Div.

ment
of

Dj.Bliah

Dj.Biala

Young
Fascists

Trieste
Div.

Takrouna

5 Bde.

90 Light
Afrika
Div.

Dj.Mengoub

Dj.Srafi

Dj.Terhouna

56 Inf.Div.
repulsed
28/29 April

Dj.Tebaga

Dj.Arum

Sebkaa
Kralifa

Bou Ficha

Incomplete

Enfidaville

6 Bde.

2 NZ Div.
2300 hrs
19 April

Wadi el Boul

4 Ind.Div.
2100 hrs
19 April

5 Bde.
7 Bde.

capturing 'a few million sq miles of hills to make up for N.Z.'s lack of troops,' complained Tuker since Freyberg was insisting that he had put out all his strength in advancing 2,000 yards.[15] Freyberg had serious doubts about the enormity of climbing Takrouna though at the final conference before Operation Oration Horrocks was optimistic, seriously underestimating the enemy's strength and morale despite reports from patrols sent out by both divisions and other intelligence information. Few shared his confidence: 'That really was frightening,' commented Major Jephson about the planned advance up tangled rock to the virtually inaccessible pinnacle and remains of a Berber fort above Takrouna's ridge.

Tuker entrusted his Territorial battalion, 1/4th Essex with initial patrolling and the opening attack on Garci. Successive waves of 4/6th Rajputana Rifles and 1/9th Gurkhas were to follow, supported by a fierce artillery bombardment. Two miles away, across the plain, formations of New Zealanders prepared for another operation like Supercharge which had been so successful at the Tebaga Gap, where infantry would attempt to smash through behind a creeping barrage. But the topography was entirely different and what had worked in the desert was not automatically appropriate for the mountains. Still, there was an air of quiet optimism: Kippenberger told Horrocks that he thought the attack might be 'just on.' He planned to attack with 5th Brigade in two phases, first with 21st and 28th (Maori) Battalions advancing on the left and right of Takrouna and then with 23rd Battalion moving through the Maoris and advancing behind a barrage to take a second objective, Djebels Foukr and Cherachir. Meanwhile, on the right, Gentry's 6th Brigade was given the less demanding task of advancing north-east of Takrouna to capture several undulating ridges beyond Enfidaville.

Indians and New Zealanders were able to advance across the flat plain to their start positions with little trouble because von Sponeck (90th Light) and von Liebenstein (164th Light) had withdrawn their troops into the hills. '1 Italian Army hopelessly outnumbered,' noted von Arnim after a conference on 14 April, 'but held naturally strong defensive position which enormously valuable. Usual conflicts between Messe and Bayerlein but clear that now Messe really prepared to fight to [the] last.' For once these two agreed; 'Takrouna was the dominating point, flanking the enemy in both directions,' recorded the 90th Light's War Diary, 'and must be held as long as possible to keep up our OPs.'[16] Here the first attack was to be broken and diverted towards re-entrants in the coastal and central sectors.

—————

After a difficult approach to Djebel Garci, 4th Indian Division's attack was scheduled to jump off first. Forming up on their start lines on 19 April, faces puffed and bloated from the attentions of mosquitoes which swarmed about the region, the infantry awaited on a beautiful and serene day the coming of darkness. Beneath a bright moon, at precisely 2100 hours, 1/4th Essex troops arose and began wading through knee-high wet grass and spring crops as they approached their first objectives while the division's guns blasted enemy concentrations on the mountains. Far out in front a long-range Essex patrol, attempting to reach and mine the alternative road which ran behind Garci to Pont du Fahs, was nearly hit by this barrage. 'We continued until we came upon more enemy positions,' reported Corporal Thompson of the patrol. 'Lieut Hailes again ordered a frontal attack and while shots were being exchanged two enemy surrendered – we killed them.'[17]

The Essex battalion quickly secured a jumping-off position for the main assault by taking Djebel Blida, lying to the front of Garci itself and capturing 50 prisoners. At 2200 hours, 4/6th Rajputana Rifles began the steep ascent of Garci. Almost at once, the leading companies were hit by a blizzard of mortar and rifle fire from the *Pistoia* Division and German troops. For four hours, in which the bayonet and *kukri* were freely used, the Rajputans inched there way forward through dust and smoke in bitter hand-to-hand fighting. Following the loss of all company commanders, the attack wavered and halted until Havildar-Major Chhelu Ram, already wounded and with no regard for his personal safety, began reorganizing for a further advance.

Far below in the valley 1/9th Gurhkas could hear the sounds of battle but their own position was becoming increasingly uncomfortable as shells and mortars soared over the crest above, bursting among them. When Brigadier Bateman of 5th Brigade arrived at 0300 hours, he immediately gave permission for them to advance on the highest feature on the approaches to Garci. Scrambling up the rocky slopes, they were hit by concentrated machine-gun fire and in desperate clashes, during which two company commanders were wounded, they drove the defenders from a series of stone sangars. Then, with their *kukris* flickering in the darkness, they slashed the enemy who fled with wild cries through the night.

As they secured Point 330, the Rajputans suffered a savage counterattack. Out of ammunition, they waited until the enemy loomed out of the darkness and let fly with a volley of stones. This was followed by the bayonet and *kukri*; amid the screams, shouts, exploding shells and rifle-fire Chhelu Ram rallied his men: 'Jats and Mohammedans, no withdrawal! Forward! Forward!'[18] The line held but amongst the piles of huddled dead was the havildar-major. For his exceptional heroism he was awarded a posthumous VC, the second in the battalion. The Indian Order of Merit went to Jemadar Dwansing and there were many who thought he should also have received the supreme award.

While this frenzied struggle for Garci was taking place, the New Zealanders began their attack on Takrouna. Vast semicircles of light shimmered in the sky as the divisional artillery began its bombardment. At 2300 hours through the stubborn cactus groves went the troops, preceded by three Churchill tanks grinding forward on the front of each brigade, cutting through dense scrub. A planned advance of 100 yards in two minutes was much too fast, however, and threw out the whole programme. All three battalions on 5th Brigade front almost immediately began to take casualties.

On the west side of Takrouna, 21st Battalion failed to take its objectives and was in deep trouble on open ground. On the east flank, 23rd Battalion was badly cut up as it followed up the hard-pressed 28th Maoris. 'Sgts were promoting themselves to Platoon commanders,' recalled one NCO, 'Corporals to Sgts and so on and in many cases they no sooner promoted themselves than they were wounded, but everyone stood their ground and there was no panic.'[19] With one forward company reduced to 20 unwounded men and another to 17, the 23rd eventually linked up with the badly disorganized 28th Battalion beyond the rear of Takrouna. Despite their heavy casualties, the Maoris set about scaling the mountain before dawn from the east and south-west. They shot, bayoneted and grenaded their way through a hail of mortar bombs hurled by Germans and 1st Battalion, 66th *Valtellina* Infantry Regiment. A German voice was heard shouting, 'Let the bloody black bastards come.'

By breaking through a defensive pit system the Maoris secured a position above and behind the enemy and at daybreak some Italians began to surrender. There was still the problem of surmounting a perpendicular band of rock, too steep to climb, but this was solved by swarming hand-over-hand up telephone wires which had been strung by the enemy to the hovels sprawling down the western shoulder to the village of Takrouna near the road. Arriving at the pinnacle the Maoris threw grenades and after a wild firefight, killed 40 or 50 enemy and took 150 prisoners, among them an astonished German artillery observer and his radio operator. They were sent back down the hill while four survivors from the storming party, together with a few others who arrived later, set about defending the tiny garrison by blocking all approaches from the village. This was full of Italians, unaware of their presence until the Maoris began taking long-range pot shots.

By mid-morning on 20 April, 28th Battalion held the peak and had cleared nearby Djebel Bir, but nowhere was their hold secure and losses had been very heavy. Kippenberger decided to recall 21st Battalion which had also taken an awful hammering and put it into reserve to reinforce the fight for the eastern side of Takrouna. Under continuous mortar and small-arms fire the survivors struggled into battalion HQ while the most forward companies, out of contact, fought on for much of the day.

The disorganized companies of 23rd Battalion, though continuously mortared and shelled short of their final objectives, were well dug in beyond the road at the rear of Takrouna. They fought off repeated counter-attacks as a troop of Nottinghamshire Yeomanry tanks, which had lost touch with the infantry during the initial attack through the cactus hedges, withdrew and rejoined its squadron which was sent at first light to help force the enemy from the valley to the east. Gradually this was cleared, together with the hill's lower slopes and contact made with 6th Brigade which had enjoyed greater success.

Advancing on a relatively quiet front, 24th Battalion was on its objectives in good time. To the right, 26th Battalion found the Italians dazed from the opening barrage and without fight. Digging was difficult in the hard limestone and many men simply used the enemy's deep slit trenches which offered them good protection from much heavy shelling over the next four days. Meanwhile, on Djebel Garci, out of ammunition and having taken 30 per cent casualties in the night's fighting, two leading companies of Rajputans retreated. In the belief that the attack had foundered the enemy renewed his assault, throwing a counter-attack against 1/9th Gurkhas and the Essex battalion.

Brigadier Dimoline's (artillery commander of 4th Indian) response incorporated in his fire programme nearly 300 guns, capable of sending eight tons of shells onto a selected target within 60 seconds and able to switch to others in five minutes. 'FOO [Forward Observation Officer] reported that enemy infantry had got within 300 yards of him, when the full weight of the Divisional Artillery came down,' recorded Dimoline's log. 'The DF [defensive fire] he had called for fell slap amongst them. When the smoke and dust had cleared away nothing was seen of them afterwards. This was encouraging, and we hoped that Boche was getting a really bloody nose everywhere.'[20]

Despite this barrage, however, there was every possibility that the toehold on Garci might be lost and Tuker was worried by the situation on his right wing where the New Zealanders were having a desperately hard time on Takrouna. To prevent their isolation by a sudden enemy thrust he moved up 7th (Armoured) and 23rd (Motor) Brigades. Supported by 40th and 50th RTR, 7th Brigade's new commander, Brigadier Firth (who replaced Brigadier Lovett when he was wounded), was able to pass 4/16th Punjabis to Kippenberger. Shortly after midday on the 20th they were sent by 5th Brigade onto the plain south-west of Garci in full view of the enemy and took to the lower slopes of the mountain on their right. A boiling cloud of fire enveloped them but astonishingly, when the dust and smoke cleared, the Punjabis were still in impeccable formation, advancing steadily to relieve 1/9th Gurkhas.

Over on Takrouna, Kippenberger's 21st Battalion had relieved the Maoris on the pinnacle that same afternoon. In an exceptionally ferocious engagement the Italians lobbed grenades into buildings sheltering the Maori wounded, probably unaware they were there. Those still on their feet went berserk, bayoneting and shooting the attackers, many of whom tried without success to surrender, and throwing others over the cliffs.

Accurate shooting next day by one of the new 17-pounder anti-tank guns sent solid shot ricocheting through the stone buildings of Takrouna village. A concerted rush by a Maori platoon suddenly saw paratroopers of the *Folgore* Division, together with a few Germans of 104th Panzer Grenadiers, stumbling out of the ruins to surrender; only about 350 survived. This opened the way to take Djebel Takrouna, though not before Italian troops near the pinnacle recovered the body of Sergeant Bressaniniche, found still clutching his rifle. With his own blood he had written on a scrap of paper: 'Long live the King! Long live Italy! God save Italy!'[21]

'We Italians in Africa got better as the war went on,' observed Paolo Colacicchi, 'the Italians [were] very quick to learn, our units improved of course... The example of the Germans helped and by the time of Tunisia when the war in Africa as far as we were concerned [was] finished – I would have said we gave a pretty good account of ourselves... '[22] Tuker had witnessed their stubborn defensive abilities, both at Wadi Akarit and on Takrouna, and thought the sheer human cost of getting through the Enfidaville position too great. In two days' fighting his men suffered over 500 casualties and Freyberg's nearer 600. Some leading rifle companies of 5th Brigade on Garci lost nearly a third of their strength. No divisional commander could be expected to stand for such attrition in the cause of a faulty plan. Consequently, Tuker and Freyberg told Horrocks that further frontal attacks around Garci and Takrouna were simply not on.

Montgomery had still not written off Eighth Army's chances of rolling up the enemy along the coastal plane north of Enfidaville and being in at the kill. Under orders, Horrocks told Tuker and Freyberg that armour and lorried infantry would begin a push through the coastal plain on the night of 28/29 April while lower features on the western flank were occupied with light forces. They remained deeply worried and, as Horrocks admitted, 'in my heart of hearts I sympathised with them... [but] I could see no other way out than a direct attack, and our losses were bound to be heavy.'[23] He could have gone back to Eighth Army HQ and argued his case but Montgomery had chosen this unlikely instant to leave for Cairo, as the BBC soon revealed, to immerse himself in planning for Husky. 'Directly Monty realised he was really held up at Enfidaville... he rushed back to Cairo to plan for Sicily,' commented McCreery.[24] Brooke was equally caustic: 'It seems hardly a suitable moment for him to be absent from his Army,' he told Alexander.[25]

While Monty was away, plans for the new attack went ahead but divisional commanders were uneasy and their staffs quarrelsome as a general edginess spread throughout Eighth Army. Meanwhile, the relief of Tuker's men on Garci was carried out as planned on the night of 22/23 April by Brigadier Graham's 153rd Brigade. The battered Essex, Rajputans and Gurkhas moved to a well-earned rest in a reserve area south-west of Enfidaville. The 'old hands,' wrote Signalman Bradshaw (serving with 4th Indian's artillery), 'thought the attack on Garci to be the toughest in two-and-half years of fighting.'[26]

On the following night (23/24 April) 5th Seaforth Highlanders relieved the Maoris on Takrouna and took turns with another battalion of Brigadier George Murray's 152nd Brigade, 5th Queen's Own Cameron Highlanders, in holding what the troops soon nicknamed 'Edinburgh Castle.' Murray told Kippenberger, rather gloomily, that his men would have to stop taking their bagpipes into battle. Why, Kippenberger asked? Well, explained Murray, since the pipers were continually shot to pieces the British Army could not afford £80 to replace each set of pipes.[27]

The brunt of attacking the high, crescent-shaped ridge of Djebels es Srafi and Terhouna, overlooking 4th Indian's advance towards Tebaga five miles to the north of Enfidaville, fell upon the New Zealander's 26th Battalion flanked by 201st Guards Brigade. They managed to take Terhouna, against stiff resistance, by daylight on 25 April but those trying to capture Djebel Srafi were caught in savage gun and mortar fire and could make no progress. In the afternoon a second attack developed into a series of sharp, individual engagements as the Italians' machine-gun posts were gradually annihilated with bayonet and rifle. By evening the New Zealanders had dug in on Srafi ridge and, anticipating a counter-attack, asked battalion HQ for urgent tank support. 'Brewers [tanks] on their way,' was the reply. Under intense enemy mortar and shell fire next morning another request went to HQ. Back came the curt response, 'Brewers haven't got wings.' This was too much for the troops waiting anxiously on the ridge. 'If Brewers haven't we may soon have,' they signalled.[28]

An hour later the tanks arrived and the difficult task began of recovering the wounded, lying out in the open. Matters then quietened down until the night of 26/27 April when the New Zealanders were being relieved by Brigadier Lyne's 169th Brigade (2/5th, 2/6th, 2/7th Queen's Royal Regiment). This was the first of two brigades to arrive from Major-General Miles' 56th Infantry which had covered 3,200 miles in 32 days from Kirkuk. As the changeover took place enemy gunners again ranged on Djebel Srafi, killing and wounding troops of 26th Battalion which lost one-third of those taking part in this small-scale operation.

Montgomery reappeared on 26 April, unwell with tonsillitis and in a foul temper. Horrocks was told to, 'Stop bellyaching', and get on with the battle. To Freyberg, who estimated a successful attack towards Hamammet along the coast could cost his division 4,000 casualties and a failure 1,000, he said, 'the big issues are so vital that we have got to force this through here.'[29] Horrocks also thought Operation Accomplish would involve excessive casualties and claimed he told Monty at the time: 'We will break through but I doubt whether at the end there will be very much left of the 8th Army.'[30] Nevertheless, preparations went ahead for the offensive – whose success depended on First Army's attack which, if successful, would make it redundant.

There was, however, small evidence of any advance in the north. Although Operation Vulcan was not delayed by Generalmajor Schmid's spoiling effort, Anderson's troops who attacked early in the morning of 22 April found the going hard everywhere.

In the southern sector Crocker's IX Corps sent in 46th Division to strike at high ground west of the Sebkret el Kourzia (Sugar Lake) under cover of a very heavy artillery bombardment by over 200 guns. Behind waited 6th Armoured, ready to exploit deeper into the Goubellat Plain towards the tall twin peaks ('Twin Tits' to the troops) of Djebel bou Kournine. 2/4th King's Own Yorkshire Light Infantry, badly disorganized by the earlier enemy assault, asked for the attack to be postponed but were committed nonetheless; a shell then grievously wounded their CO and killed the COs of 152nd Field Regiment and 6th Lincolns.[31]

Supported by Churchills from A and B Squadrons of 51st RTR, 138th Brigade was on its objectives before noon. On the right 128th Brigade, supported by C Squadron, could make little headway against an enemy well positioned on and around Two Tree Hill. Not until daybreak next morning (24 April) did they discover the defenders had slipped away in the night.

6th Armoured Division moved forward later than anticipated and was slowed by a maze of deep wadis, but 26th Armoured Brigade, led by 16/5th Queen's Royal Lancers, scattered and destroyed the battalion HQs of 9th Battalion, 69th Panzer

Grenadier Regiment, and 14th (Panzer Jäger) Battalion, 104th Panzer Grenadier Regiment, in successive days. During the attack's second day, 17/21st Lancers ran into 7th Panzer Regiment and Panzerabteilung 501 and was unable to gain a major advantage in the horribly difficult terrain, under accurate gunfire and strafed by newly-introduced but unwieldy Henschel Hs-129Bs. On their left flank desert veterans of Briggs' 1st Armoured moved across the green symmetry of the Goubellat Plain but quickly discovered a deadly profusion of mines amid the growing corn. Well-sited German 88s shot up the Shermans and Crusaders of the Queen's Bays and 9th Lancers (both 2nd Armoured Brigade) as they groped their way among innumerable small wadis. Hours later burning tanks still littered the area.

Unable to make real progress, Crocker began to switch 6th Armoured for 1st Armoured on the night of 24/25 April and the following day, while the 1st pushed hard forward, 6th Armoured swung south and attacked towards the summits of Djebel Kournine. This double-headed thrust on a narrow front against clever interlocking defensive fire from 10th Panzer and *Hermann Göring* Divisions failed to penetrate but fixed 10th Panzer and worsened the parlous ammunition and fuel situation of Fifth Panzer Army.[32] Subsequently, Anderson ordered Crocker to send 6th Armoured into Army reserve and grind on with 46th Infantry (less 139th Infantry Brigade, also into reserve) and 1st Armoured Divisions.

In the meantime, in Allfrey's V Corps sector, 78th Division had sent in two brigades, 36th against Longstop Hill – which could not be by-passed because from there the Germans could shell the two roads running into Tunis – and 38th against Heidous and Tanngoucha. Following a spectacular dry electric storm on 22 April, the opening barrage at 0100 hours from over 400 guns deluged Longstop's crests and sloping ridges with 50,000 pounds of high explosive inside the first five minutes. Following up were the 6th West Kents – cooks, storemen and administrative troops pressed into the front line – accompanied on their right by 5th Buffs.

Before reaching the base of Longstop they were in trouble from mines, barbed wire and enemy machine-guns but fought their way up through boiling clouds of fumes and dust. German troops of the 756th Mountain Infantry Regiment (334th Infantry Division) were waiting, dug deep into their trenches. Safe here they waited until the barrage lifted and then rose up, checking the West Kent's advance until after dawn, though the Buffs managed to clamber higher up the western shoulder. It was in broad daylight that 'Swifty' Howlett, commanding 36th Infantry Brigade, sent forward 8th Argyll and Sutherland Highlanders to storm the crest. They had been meant to pass through and capture the adjoining peak of Djebel el Rhar but the slowness of the original advance rendered this impossible. Advancing on that warm, sultry morning – the troops strung out in wheatfields to minimise casualties for the rifle companies were only about 50 strong – battalion HQ was suddenly swamped by shells, killing the CO, Colin McNabb, and key members of his staff.

Into the breach stepped young Major Jack Anderson. In an outstanding feat of leadership he shot and bayoneted his way to the top, supported by several tanks of the North Irish Horse. Of some 300 Argylls who had started out, only four officers and 30 men stood with him on the summit. For this feat of arms Anderson was awarded a VC and Bill Wilberforce the DSO for bringing up his 1st East Surreys (11th Brigade), in order to maintain a precarious hold on the mountain.[33] To reinforce the Argylls and East Surreys, Howlett sent the West Kents and next morning (24 April) 6th Battalion was ordered to take Djebel el Rhar, separated from Djebel el Ahmera by a deep gully. The troops had trouble forming up in the face of devastating mortaring from Heidous and fell short of their objective. When Howlett called off the attack only 80 men were left in four rifle companies and these had to be hastily re-organized into two, both pitifully under-strength.

The troops on Longstop held on under continuous mortar and artillery fire until mid-day on 26 April when the Buffs swept round the right flank of Djebel el Rhar and, supported by a squadron of North Irish Horse, drove off the enemy, capturing more than 300 Germans. At last the mountain was in British hands and the door to the Medjerda valley, where the final attack would be launched, lay ajar. Directly ahead was the prize of Tunis, barely 30 miles away. Profoundly moved by the feat Evelegh announced the award of an immediate DSO to Howlett, who celebrated in style with the battered remnants of the 6th West Kents as they rested and refitted at Chassart Teffana.

Not far away to the north-west, 38th Irish Brigade had somewhat recovered from the hard fighting of 16 April on Djebel Ang and Tanngoucha despite having to endure six days' continuous mortaring, sniping and shelling. Then, in intermittent drizzle during the night of 22/23 April, the Royal Irish Fusiliers struggled through intense shelling to swarm up the solid slab of rock wall on Point 622, while the Inniskillings had another crack at Tanngoucha and the London Irish the village of Heidous. Despite reaching the ridge at both ends the Fusiliers failed to take the whole of their objective. Heidous and Tanngoucha were resolutely defended and it took a superhuman effort by the Northern Irish Horse to get three Churchills over Djebel Ang and hull down on The Kefs by 24 April. Next day, as von Arnim was rearranging his forces, the Fusiliers attacked with three tanks in support and crawled onto the crest of Point 622 which they held despite heavy casualties.

The defences on Heidous and Tanngoucha now began to crumble and it was on the latter that the Inniskillings came across the body of Lance-Corporal James Given of the Fusiliers who, a week earlier, had been treated by the MO for a splinter gash across his forehead. Having raided the medical rum rations, Given got fighting drunk and staggered off to wage a one-man-war. 'He was a true Faugh, with simple tastes,' commented a Fusilier, 'rum and the regiment.'[34]

Other formations from V Corps worked up from Medjez el Bab to villages on the right of the Medjerda as far as Crich el Oued (soon dubbed 'Cricklewood' by the troops) and, east of Peter's Corner, Sidi Abdallah. To ease the path of 4th Division towards Tunis, Major-General Clutterbuck's 1st Infantry attacked on 23

April towards the hills abandoned before Christmas. Opposition from 754th Infantry Regiment (334th Infantry) was stiff as ever. The defenders had turned some ancient dry wells into barracks and dug nearly two miles of trenches. Brigadier Colvin's 24th Guards Brigade was forced to storm them in an old-fashioned infantry charge under cover of heavy artillery. Beyond was high ground above Crich el Oued which had to be taken against blistering counter-attacks; in hand-to-hand fighting both sides suffered heavy casualties but Grenadier, Scots and Irish Guards held their ground.

On their right flank Brigadier Moore's 2nd Infantry Brigade also took severe losses. 2nd Battalion, North Staffordshire Regiment and 1st Battalion, the Loyal Regiment supported by field, medium and heavy artillery were on their objectives quickly but could not dig in soon enough to prevent being thrown back by a sharp counter-attack. For hours the fighting swayed backwards and forwards in a series of brutal individual skirmishes in which Lieutenant Sandys-Clarke, a Loyals' platoon commander, won a posthumous VC when he took out several machine-gun nests and died within touching distance of another. By the end of this first day, 2nd Brigade's attack had faltered with just over 500 casualties. In support, 142nd Regiment, Royal Armoured Corps, (25th Brigade, 4th Division) had sustained damage to 29 of its 45 tanks caused by unremitting fire from Tigers of Panzerabteilung 501.

Next day (24th April) Brigadier Matthews' 3rd Brigade, leading with 1st King's Shropshire Light Infantry and 2nd Sherwood Foresters, managed to crack open the ridge position but lost over 300 casualties. Among the dead was the Foresters' much-loved Lieutenant-Colonel J.D. Player, whose will stipulated that £3,000 should be given to the Beaufort Hunt and that the incumbent of the living in his gift should be a 'man who approves of hunting, shooting, and all manly sports, which are the backbone of the nation.'[35]

As soon as Longstop was taken the Guards were able to advance on the 26th over 2,000 yards through the Gab-Gab Gap towards Djebels Asoud and Bou Aoukaz, dominating the approaches to Tébourba from the east bank of the Medjerda. Confident orders were received that a daylight attack on two long ridges leading to Bou Aoukaz had been fixed for the afternoon of 27 April. Every man was appalled by the timing; unlike divisional HQ they knew the cost of such a suicidal assault.

At first relatively free from harassing fire, 1st Irish on the right and 5th Grenadiers on the left were stepping out in their long, steady pace on the approach when they were saturated by shell and mortar fire from The Bou. Said one Irish Guardsman, 'They threw everything but their cap badges at us.' Grimly they stuck to their task, platoons spread out in open order in the burning cornfields, lines of rifle butts pointing from the broken earth to mark the dead. 'Thank God for drill, it keeps you going,' remarked one man.[36] What was left of the Irish battalion – only 173 men out of four rifle companies and advanced HQ – clung on to their ridge for the next three days, mortared and shot at more or less non-stop by Kampfgruppe *Irkens*, formed on 24 April by von Arnim who brought together all his remaining armoured units into one composite force.[37] On May Day just 80 survivors were relieved by 6th Gordon Highlanders; they left behind over 700 German dead.

To the west, 5th Grenadiers, also badly cut up, got on their objectives while 1st Scots Guards scaled The Bou's left flank, losing Captain Lord Lyell, killed while bayoneting the crew of a particularly troublesome 88 and awarded a posthumous VC. Muddled staff work immediately handed the hill mass back to the enemy and another attack next day by desperately tired Scots Guards could not quite regain the whole position. A prolonged and bloody struggle continued in which, on 29 April, Lance-Corporal Kenneally (1st Irish Guards) won a VC for charging German infantry who were preparing to counter-attack, scattering them in all directions and then returning nonchalantly to his platoon.[38]

On the right of 1st Infantry Division, 12th Infantry Brigade (4th Division) attacked on 24 April towards Peter's Corner with the object of carving an opening for 10th Brigade supported by 21st Tank Brigade. Brigadier Dick Hull, earlier in command of Blade Force and now promoted, sent his 2nd Royal Fusiliers on a strenuous night march south of the Massicault–Medjez road towards a series of small hills and, behind Peter's corner to the south-east, a high, bare ridge at the foot of which sheltered the village of Ksar Tyr.

The Fusiliers were stopped in their tracks by troops of the *Hermann Göring* Jäger Regiment, losing the greatly-admired Lieutenant-Colonel Maurice Brandon who had risen to command from the ranks.[39] The next night, 25/26 April, the Fusiliers tried again, this time in conjunction with 6th Black Watch. Neither could make headway through well-positioned enemy minefields and 12th RTR lost ten of its Churchills which had been committed in support.

Brigadier Hull then called up 1st West Kents from Banana Ridge to assault three features, Sidi Abdallah, Cactus Farm and Point 133. During confused and hard fighting over the next four days (27–30 April) in which the Germans used flame-throwing tanks for the first time in the campaign, the battalion took over 300 casualties and was forced to retreat. Regular bombing by flights of Bostons on Ksar Tyr and heavy shelling destroyed most of the village without winkling out the defenders. Nor could repeated attacks by 12th Brigade shift them even when Hawkesworth called in from 10th Brigade the 2nd Battalion, Duke of Cornwall's Light Infantry, which had been waiting to drive on Tunis.

Decimated and exhausted, 12th Brigade could do no more. On the night of 30 April it was relieved by Cass's 11th Brigade from 78th Division. Next day the Germans sent a captured American officer carrying specific map references of an area where they sought a 24-hour armistice in which to bury their dead who were piled in heaps along the front. Other than daylong pulverizing attacks by bombers and artillery on those exact locations there was no reply. The British thought it was simply a ruse whereby the enemy could bring up reinforcements and supplies.[40]

This blood-letting forced von Arnim to shift General der Panzertruppe Hans Cramer's *DAK* to new positions at Pont du Fahs, stripping First Italian Army of its armour, while some of its units were sent to Fifth Panzer Army. Such changes inevitably caused some confusion, as one officer reported: 'Here the situation changes hourly. An order is followed by a counter order. Since 11th [April] the fighting has entered its final stages and the task of maintaining the bridgehead is really only a question of time. With men alone we could hold the front but materially we are in an inferior position. The Luftwaffe cannot supply us and that which comes by sea is a drop in the ocean... we are on the defensive because we cannot fight tanks with the bodies of men and with shot guns... '[41]

As the Divisions *du Maroc* and *d'Alger* of the French XIX Corps moved towards Pont du Fahs, von Arnim and von Vaerst agreed on 27 April that the situation was very serious. From Y intelligence the British knew that all enemy units were reduced in strength and hard-pressed by Crocker's IX Corps. Alexander thought Crocker had, 'started off very well... in this recent battle', but he was accidentally wounded in the chest by an unfortunate demonstration of the PIAT (anti-tank) weapon on 27 April.[42] Nevertheless, calamitous damage done to its 334th Infantry Division by the British 1st and 78th Infantry Divisions in V Corps' sector, together with advances by the French and Americans against the *von Manteuffel* Division, greatly disturbed Fifth Panzer Army HQ.

In the far north the Corps Franc d'Afrique and Tabors marocains were fighting a separate battle all their own. A motley force of Free French escapees from Vichy France, political refugees, Berber tribesmen and Spanish Loyalists who had sought asylum, they were commanded by, amongst others, a Jewish doctor and a Spanish admiral. The *tabour* of Goums in particular was extending its terror with the knife and, it was said, without expenditure of ammunition.

Next to them 3rd Battalion, 47th RCT (9th Infantry Division) moved towards Jefna on 23 April, bumping up against Manteuffel's right wing, which offered only light opposition, and sent powerful patrols in the direction of Green Hill, north of the Mateur road. Opposite, 1st Battalion pushed through a series of ridges behind strong artillery support to within a mile of Bald Hill. Supported by active patrols, 39th RCT (which had relieved 1st Para Brigade at Tamera) put in its 1st and 3rd Battalions to take the commanding height of Djebel Ainchouna, to the north-west of Jefna. They had to fight their way through scrub and waist-high underbrush, scrambling through minefields and up rocky slopes against mortars, grenades, rifle and machine-gun fire. 1st Battalion, in particular, was badly cut up, losing its CO and most of his staff.

On 25 April, the 39th finally took Ainchouna's four miles of peaks and ridges. Newly committed, its 2nd Battalion took four days to capture one particularly well defended position (Hill 382) but by 30 April all three battalions had swept the crests and could dominate the enemy's installations, routes and supply dumps around Jefna. Over 4,000 rounds of high explosive fired off in a single day by 26th Field Artillery Battalion forced 160th Panzer Grenadier Regiment to begin a hurried withdrawal to the north-east on 1 May, shortly before 39th's forward patrols entered the town. Two days later 47th RCT occupied Green and Bald Hills

– made untenable for the enemy by the Americans' outflanking northern movement – and opened the Jefna–Mateur road.

Further north still, 9th Division's 60th RCT and the Corps Franc attacked on 23 April, Americans along the hills on both sides of the Sedjenane Valley and the French towards Bizerte. Having just replaced Italians who had little stomach for the fight, 962nd *Afrika* Rifle Regiment held up the 60th's three battalions, struggling through deep scrub to avoid the few roads which were invariably mined. In such rugged country attacking units often outran their artillery support but there was now a growing professionalism and determination about the American infantry. 'We learned that to live we must take to the ridges and advance along them, avoiding the natural "avenues" of approach up the valleys,' explained one officer. 'Heads of valleys were always strongly defended and heavily-mined – to advance along the valleys was disastrous. Taking to the ridges was tedious, strenuous business but it saved hundreds of lives and gave physical possession of the high ground.'[43]

With ammunition, weapons and supplies carried by mule train, they drove over the heights towards Kef en Nsour which 3rd Battalion captured on 2 May, and consolidated their positions overlooking the Mateur plain. As its wounded were evacuated, 962nd Regiment turned at bay, but despite much individual bravery could not resist indefinitely. Southwards as well, the right flank of Generalmajor Fritz Krause's 334th Infantry[44] and Fallschirmjäger Regiment *Barenthin* on the left wing of the *von Manteuffel* Division were bent back by a vigorous American assault which followed several days of ground reconnaissance.[45]

Between the Oued Tine and Sidi Nsir–Tébourba road stands a belt of smooth round-topped hills and it was into this area that 1st US Infantry struck behind an artillery barrage on 23 April with three RCTs, the 16th, 18th and 26th. Detachments of 1st Engineers had to clear 1,800 mines buried in wheatfields before the 26th could make much progress. The 16th also encountered mortar and artillery fire as it advanced from the southeast.

On the division's right flank, 18th RCT's 2nd Battalion ran into determined counter-attacks by 10th Panzer. It advanced only at the cost of heavy casualties, supported by a company from Lieutenant-Colonel Carr's 1st Battalion, 13th Armored Regiment. After grim fighting the Germans began to retreat eastwards on the morning of 25 April, away from many of the heights which overlooked, from the north, the entrance to 'The Mousetrap' (the small north-eastern exit from the upper Tine Valley).

In the south, 6th Armored Infantry Regiment (1st Armored) protected the right flank of Allen's 1st Infantry and secured the left of 38th Irish Brigade's attempt on Heidous. The rest of 1st Armored (less 13th Armored Regiment) was held in reserve until infantry cleared the Tine Valley for its tanks to drive through on Mateur. One of Harmon's first actions on taking over from 'Pinky' Ward at Lessouda, where the division had been resting and refitting after the fighting near Maknassy and El Guettar, was to call together every officer. Reprimanding and fining those who turned up late, he lambasted them for their lack of aggression and fighting record. The 1st Armored was, he told them, carried by First Army as non-combat-worthy.

This was deeply resented for over 300 had been killed during March and early April. Robinett thought it demonstrated a definite lack of judgement by Harmon who later admitted he had miscalculated the effect of what was intended as a fighting speech.[46] Others were upset by his replacement of Brigadier-General McQuillin from CC A by Colonel Kent Lambert on 13 April. Yet Harmon could do no other for Patton, in a fit of temper, had instantly relieved McQuillin. He was a, 'fine and cooperative officer', thought Harmon, who sent him on rotation back to the United States, 'with no derogatory remarks on his ability.'[47]

Most of 1st Armored arrived in the Béja area on 22 April due to the inspired efforts of Harmon to pass off his division as a single combat command – he had no authority to transfer more. Keen to assert his independence, Robinett (commanding CC B) had privately asked Eisenhower on 11 April if he could return to British V Corps and participate in the final drive on Tunis from Medjez el Bab since, 'officers and men felt they have a score to settle with the Germans in that area.'[48] Wisely, Eisenhower ignored this and CC B was now reconnoitring towards the Mousetrap with 18th RCT.

South of the Oued Tine, Colonel Robert Stack drove his 6th Armoured Infantry Regiment across a series of hills and during heavy fighting on 28 April, as 1st Battalion attacked over one of the many ridges running from Djebel Ang to the Tine Valley, Private Nicholas Minue stalked at least ten enemy gunners through the high grass, bayoneting them and seeking out more enemy positions until he was killed.[49] His supreme courage earned him a posthumous Medal of Honor and helped his regiment spring the Mousetrap by forcing a German withdrawal (after the British had taken Heidous) to a second line of defence on the edge of the Tine Valley, though further to the north-west the enemy still held strongly to an area near Sidi Nsir.

Later, Bradley took Anderson on a personal reconnaissance of the Mousetrap and explained the minelaying tactics of Major Wiltz's engineer battalion. Pointing toward the German positions, Anderson said, 'Oh, yes, Major Wiltz, the stout fellow, I knew him well before the war.' This angered Bradley. 'To us Wiltz was a German s.o.b.,' he said.[50]

Progress eastwards by 1st Infantry to open up the Tine Valley had exposed it to counter-attacks on the left flank and Robinett's CC B was forced into a muddy night march on 23/24 April to provide protection. Bradley decided therefore, on 26 April, to revise II Corps' plan of attack. Allen's front was narrowed and 34th Infantry Division readied to attack on his left, into the hills east and west of Sidi Nsir.

Due to Harmon's insistent urging, 1st Armored took over the whole of the southern flank that connected with First Army. Visited by Anderson, he was asked what he expected to do with his tanks in the difficult terrain ahead. Patiently Harmon explained the plan, agreed with Bradley, to put them through to Mateur. 'Just a childish fancy,' commented Anderson, waving his swagger stick vaguely,

'Just a childish fancy,' and strode away. 'I'll make that son of a bitch eat those words,' mouthed Harmon.[51]

At the centre of II Corps' sector between 26 April and 2 May, operations focussed on Hill 609 (Djebel Tahent), the last commanding height west of Mateur, whose white cliffs towered above surrounding hills on which the 334th Infantry and *Barenthin* Regiment had organized interlocking defensive support positions. 'Doc' Ryder's men had little experience of attack but a surfeit of retreats; his 168th Infantry had been very badly mauled at Sidi bou Zid. 'Get me that hill,' Bradley told Ryder, 'and you'll break up the enemy's defences clear across our front. Take it and no one will ever again doubt the toughness of your division.'[52] After Fondouk, the 34th had been able to get in some real training before moving to the vicinity of Béja and the troops assembling along the Sidi Nsir–Chouïgui road were confident.

On the left, 1st and 3rd Battalions of 168th RCT began the assault behind a heavy barrage by 175th Field Artillery Battalion and the corps artillery. For three days they struggled against strong opposition through undulating hills. Meanwhile, under machine-gun, mortar and artillery fire Colonel Robert Ward's 135th RCT fought to take Hill 490, directly barring the way to Hill 609. Totally ignoring its strategic character, Anderson suggested bypassing it through the valleys but Bradley disregarded this certain commitment to disaster. All day on 28 April, the air was heavy with the crack and rumble of American artillery pounding Hill 609 as 1st and 2nd Battalions of the 135th prepared to attack enemy outposts. Concurrently, 3rd Battalion was to distract the defenders with a feint at the south-western end and 2nd Battalion of 168th to carry its line to the north.

At 0500 hours on 29 April the troops set off through the ripening corn. 1st and 2nd Battalions were soon held up by increasing enemy resistance and 3rd Battalion, forsaking its holding operation, had to go it alone in an unsupported frontal attack. Through intermittent mortaring and gunfire one unit managed to reach a village of stone huts in the last deep fold of the hill, beneath a barren precipice 200 feet above. The rest of the battalion struggled half a mile up steep slopes and settled for the night.

Aided by an assault over the north-west shoulder by 1st Battalion, 133rd RCT and 17 of 1st Armored Regiment's Shermans, they attacked again next morning. Two tanks were soon lost to accurate gunfire but others shot up signalled targets and blinded the enemy on the hill; meanwhile the plateau above was plastered from end to end by artillery while sappers lifted mines from village paths. Swarming up the broken face of the cliff, the infantry, 'grabbed and hung on to the tails of their tanks'. At the same time, troops of 2nd Battalion, 168th RCT, attacked the northern tip of Hill 609 and by late afternoon, with 1st Battalion of the 133rd, controlled most of the plateau. Its capture proved to be an outstanding and much-needed American success, providing a springboard to further victories. When the Germans counter-attacked on the 31st from the north-eastern slopes in great force they were driven back by devastating fire from a company of 2nd

Battalion, 168th RCT (which had relieved the 135th). Throughout the rest of the day Ryder's men held on though dive-bombed and plastered with artillery fire, as the Germans fought to regain this bastion which was so important to their overall strategy.

In the Tine Valley Harmon's mobile armoured elements were on half-hour alert, the men eating at their tanks. Engineers had been out, marking two mine-free corridors part way along the valley while from Mateur came the sound of explosions and a spreading glow of fires as the enemy got ready to abandon the town. Further north 9th Division had smashed the enemy's control of Jefna, leaving him clinging to the last remnants of high ground on the edge of the Mateur Plain.

Intended only to protect First Army's flank, II Corps had done much better than the British expected while what Montgomery had dismissively termed Anderson's 'partridge drive' on the bigger objective of Tunis itself had stalled. But so had Montgomery's Enfidaville attack.

At II Corps HQ on 1 May, Bradley considered the distinct possibility of driving all the way to Bizerte and might have taken the gamble with another division to throw into the line. An unsuccessful exploitation, however, could have resulted in the Germans shifting additional forces to the American front, helping First Army to break through but stalemating his own effort. 'This campaign is too important to the prestige of the American army to take such risks,' he told assembled officers.[53] In no mood to pull British chestnuts out of the fire, Anderson's request on 28 April for a RCT to relieve one of his brigades was coolly received: 'he was told that we could ill spare it but would study the matter. Looks like start of old game of piecemealing US units.'[54]

Bradley then got Eisenhower's agreement that American and British units should not be intermingled and used his right of appeal to Alexander, who backed his decision not to send assistance. Clearly, Anderson – and Montgomery – would have to find their own solutions.

Notes to Chapter 16

[1] Lieutenant D.E. Brown, Papers. IWM 83/16/1.

[2] Wisdom, *Triumph Over Tunisia*, p. 173.

[3] Craven and Kate, *Torch to Pointblank*, pp. 188–9; Playfair, *Destruction of Axis Forces*, pp. 413–16; Memorandum, 14 April 1943, 'The Battle Story of Flax', Spaatz Papers, Box 19.

[4] Roskill, *The Navy at War*, pp. 281–2; Cunningham, *A Sailor's Odyssey*, pp. 523–7.

[5] Miller Diary, entry for 15 April 1943.

[6] Report, 18 April 1943. RH19-VIII/351.

[7] Von Arnim, 'Erinnerungen an Tunesien', p. 99.

[8] British Chiefs of Staff to Joint Staff Mission in Washington, for Combined Chiefs of Staff – copy to Eisenhower, 7 April 1943. Eisenhower Papers, Box 60.

[9] Bradley, *A Soldier's Story*, p.80.

[10] *Ibid.*

[11] To Bizerte With the II Corps, 23 April – 13 May 1943, Historical Division, US War Department, 1943; republished by Center of Military History, United States Army, p. 9.

[12] Schmid had been promoted from Oberst on 1 March 1943. He commanded only the *Hermann Göring* units still in North Africa and his staff was no more than an advance HQ. In the attack on 20/21 April, the following units were engaged: Kampfgruppe *Audorff* (i.e. one battalion Grenadier Regiment *Hermann Göring* and 754th Grenadier Regiment [334th Division]); 1st and 3rd Battalions, Jäger-Regiment *Hermann Göring*; 7th Panzer Regiment (10th Panzer Division); Panzerabteilung 501 (13 Tiger tanks operational on 20 April).

[13] The Germans lost some 300 men taken captive, the British 'several hundred'; von Vaerst, 'Operations of Fifth Panzer Army', p. 19.

[14] 'Assessment of the Enemy', Report, 18 April 1943. RH19VIII/364.

[15] Tuker Diary, entries for 15 and 18 April 1943.

[16] Quoted by Stevens, *Bardia to Enfidaville*, p. 310.

[17] Report by Corporal Thompson (1/4th Essex); Bateman Papers.

[18] Stevens, *4th Indian Division*, p. 237.

[19] Quoted by Ross, *23 Battalion*, p. 259.

[20] Quoted by Stevens, *4th Indian Division*, p. 243.

[21] Quoted by Cody, *28 (Maori) Battalion*, pp. 310–11.

[22] Thames Television series. IWM 002951/02.

[23] Horrocks, *A Full Life*, p. 164. See also Lewin, *Montgomery as Military Commander*, pp. 139–40. Lewin fought at Enfidaville and was critical of the attempt to break through there.

[24] McCreery to Tuker, 17 August 1959. Tuker Papers, 71/21/6.

[25] Brooke to Alexander, 28 April 1943. Alanbrooke Papers, 6/2/17.

[26] Signalman C.H. Bradshaw, 'War Reminiscences of the Middle East Campaign'; IWM PP/MCR/203. The author was a telephonist and line signaller with 1st Field Regiment RA, 4th Indian Division.

[27] Kippenberger, *Infantry Brigadier*, p. 314.

[28] Norton, *26 Battalion*, p. 275.

[29] GOC's (Freyberg) Diary 26 April 1943; quoted by Stevens, *Bardia to Enfidaville*, p. 352.

[30] Horrocks letter, 14 February 1951; *ibid*. Also *A Full Life*, p. 164.

[31] Ellenberger, *History of the King's Own Yorkshire Light Infantry*, Vol. VI, p. 33–4.

[32] Von Vaerst, 'Operations of Fifth Panzer Army', p. 20.

[33] Major Anderson was also decorated with the DSO as the result of earlier bravery. He was killed six months later in Italy by so-called 'friendly fire' from British 25-pounders. Wilberforce was killed by a shell on 6 May, the same day that he heard he had been awarded the DSO.

[34] Horsfall, *The Wild Geese are Flighting*, p. 144.

[35] From a note made by Keith Douglas on one of his manuscripts; see Graham, *Keith Douglas 1920–1944: A Biography*, p. 199.

[36] Verney, *The Micks*, p. 113.

[37] Kampfgruppe *Irkens* was commanded by Oberst Irkens under the personal supervision of von Vaerst. It comprised: 5th Panzer Regiment (21st Panzer); 7th Panzer Regiment (10th Panzer); 8th Panzer Regiment (15th Panzer); Panzer Abteilung (Tiger) 501; 47th Grenadier Regiment; Artillerie Abteilung; Italienische Artillerie Abteilung; two Flak Abteilungen; Gruppe *Audorff* i.e. 754th Grenadier Regiment; 1st Battalion *Hermann Göring* Division. See Bender and Law, *Uniforms, Organization and History of the Afrikakorps*, p. 109.

[38] Kenneally's war record was bizarre, recounted by John Patrick Kenneally, *Kenneally VC*.

[39] Brandon achieved the unique distinction of becoming CO of the 2nd Royal Fusiliers in which he had been RSM and then Quartermaster only two years before. See Parkinson, *Always a Fusilier*, pp. 117–18.

[40] D'Arcy Dawson, *Tunisian Battle*, p. 224–5; Jordan, *Jordan's Tunis Diary*, p. 246, entry for 1 May 1943.

[41] Quoted by Lucas, *Panzer Army Africa*, p. 183.

[42] Alexander to Brooke, 19 May 1943. Alanbrooke Papers, 6/2/17. The PIAT – Projector Infantry Anti-Tank – replaced the obsolete Boys anti-tank rifle.

[43] HQ 9th Infantry Division, 'Report on Combat Experience and Battle Lessons – Tunisia', 21 June 1943; II Corps, Box 7327; World War II Operations Reports, USNA 309-0.4.

[44] Krause replaced Generalmajor Friedrich Weber, former commander of 334th Division, who had fallen ill, on 15 April 1943.

[45] The *von Manteuffel* Division was commanded by Generalleutnant Bülowius as from 31 March 1943 but there was no change in the unit designation, just as there was no adjustment when Oberst Barenthin was wounded and evacuated. Command of his Fallschirmjäger Regiment was taken by Major Baier who had jumped at Crete with the German invasion and had badly broken his leg. As a result he wore an iron brace and was frequently in severe pain but this did not stop him leading his men from the front and they had the highest regard for him. His identification tags allotted him to a *Stammrolle* – a fictitious German unit used to list certain Luftwaffe officers for identification in Berlin while concealing their actual field units.

[46] Robinett, *Armor Command*, pp. 214–15.

[47] Harmon to Bedell Smith, 12 April 1943; Chief of Staff, Official Correspondence File. Bedell Smith Papers, Box 15.

[48] Robinett to Eisenhower, 11 April 1943. Robinett Papers Box 12; Marshall Library.

[49] Howe, *Battle History of 1st Armored*, p. 232.

[50] Bradley Commentary. Hansen Papers.

[51] Harmon, *Combat Commander*, p. 130.

[52] Bradley, *A Soldier's Story*, p. 85.

[53] Hansen Diary, entry for 1 May 1943. 'Is this the beginning of the end... ?,' noted Hansen at the head of this entry.

[54] Bradley War Diary, entry for 28 April 1943. Bradley Papers, Box 4.

Chapter 17

Smash Through to Tunis

'The greatest and most formidable attack yet made by the British armies in this war, will begin to-morrow... We ought to do it now; God help us if we can't.'

War correspondent Philip Jordan in his diary, 5 May 1943.[1]

The Americans were confident. 'Let's radio Monty,' suggested Bradley to his chief of staff, 'and ask if he wants us to send him a few American advisers to show his desert fighters how to get through those hills.'[2] The Eighth Army was stuck at Enfidaville; neither it nor First Army was being pushed in for the kill. 'Ike says Alex isn't so good as he thinks he is. He is up against some real fighting now,' noted Everett Hughes.[3]

Plans had gone ahead for Operation Accomplish against the wishes of Freyberg and Tuker although years later Dick McCreery told the latter: 'I always wanted to move troops round from the Eighth Army front to the First Army area sooner than we did but Alex was always reluctant to take a strong line with Monty!'[4] 18th Army Group never intended the final attack on Tunis to be made other than by First Army but relied on Monty's prestige and the threat posed by Eighth Army to convince the enemy that the assault would come from the south. Supposing this to have been an ingenious feint, someone forgot to tell Montgomery since Horrocks ordered 56th Division to take Djebels Srafi and Terhouna on the night of 28/29 April. Brigadier Lyne's 169th Brigade had been at the front for less than 48 hours. His inexperienced troops were from London's southern outskirts – clerks, shop assistants, small tradesmen. The whole tenor of their lives had been respect for the law: not to trespass, steal and above all, not to kill. 'It is a great personal shock to a man with this background and upbringing,' commented Lyne, 'when he realises that not only must Germans be killed, but he is the man to do it.'[5]

An initial attack carried well but a sharp counter-attack on the morning of 29 April threw the attackers off Srafi and they retreated in disorder after their CO had been killed, stampeding through their own gun lines and men waiting to follow up. 'It was only the second time I had seen our infantry running,' commented Ronald Lewin, 'the first was at Mareth when they came back through my gun position. At this stage in the African campaign it was a horrible sight... '[6] This incident, insignificant in itself, finally convinced Montgomery that Eighth Army could not break through the Enfidaville position without taking unacceptable casualties which might have damaging repercussions on planning for Husky. His views were not well received at 18th Army Group HQ, as Miller reported: 'A wire from Monty to say he can't attack making inexperience of 56 Div as excuse. We feel Monty is not playing the game and suspect him of really being a little man who has been playing big. He will not risk failure after success – will not co-operate and is thinking of himself alone... What is clear is that we must smash up the Hun here and clear Tunisia and do it quickly. If Monty won't do it, then someone else must.'[7]

On 30 April Alexander breakfasted with McCreery and Broadhurst at Monty's forward Tactical HQ. Afterwards, Montgomery pushed the case for First Army to put in the final blow while Eighth Army held south of Enfidaville. Alexander confirmed that he proposed to attack all along First Army's front with Freyberg commanding IX Corps in place of the wounded Crocker. Montgomery dismissed this at once – Freyberg was, 'a nice old boy, but... a bit stupid. You'd better have Jorrocks. Jorrocks – he's the chap.'[8] Consequently, he summoned Horrocks to the meeting and told him: 'You will go off to-day, taking with you the 4th Indian Division, 7th Armoured Division, and 201st Guards Brigade, and you will assume command of the 9 Corps in General Anderson's army. You will then smash through to Tunis and finish the war in North Africa.'[9]

Although Montgomery claimed that, 'the plan for the final phase of the Tunisian war was given out by me,' he never entirely abandoned the idea of Eighth Army blitzing through the Enfidaville position until Lyne's attack failed.[10] Opposition from Freyberg, and especially Tuker, eventually persuaded him to change his ideas. 'There is no doubt in my mind,' wrote Tuker, 'that Monty's intention was to attack in full force towards Hammamet and that this intention was selfish and simply aimed at wiping 1st Army's eye... I prevented... [him] from doing so and constantly urged the Medjez attack.'[11] While Montgomery undoubtedly played a part in changing the Allies' plans he was not the only one behind Operation Strike which, early in May, brought about a sudden end to the war in Tunisia.

———◆◆———

'My heart leapt,' commented Horrocks on hearing he was to command IX Corps in the final attack on Tunis. 'This was the real art of generalship – a quick switch, then a knock-out blow.' Tuker was delighted to leave Enfidaville – 'We were now to stick a feather in First Army's cap and very glad indeed we were to do so.' Horrocks was replaced by Freyberg at X Corps and Kippenberger, putting up the insignia of a (temporary) Major-General, acquired an ADC and the New Zealand Division.[12]

The transfer of 4th Indian, 7th Armoured and 201st Guards Brigade took place in an unending procession of vehicles, driven hard by night over 200 miles to Medjez el Bab, without hindrance from the enemy. Their landing grounds under remorseless attack, the Germans had removed their ageing and vulnerable Stukas to Sicily; only fighters now defended Tunis and Bizerte and these could not be spared to attack this great convoy.[13] When Eighth Army's trucks swept into the ordered echelons of First Army, bemusement and disbelief greeted the scratched and rusty vehicles in what was left of their desert paintwork. The veterans' arrogant self-confidence, 'did not make us very popular', remarked Captain Edney of 7th Armoured Division, 'who the hell were these swaggering dirty looking soldiers who had come out of the desert and thought themselves the answer to everything?'[14]

Until 2 May, Kesselring's intelligence staff believed the main weight of attack would come from the direction of Pont du Fahs but, in the meantime, traffic movements and radio intercepts enabled von Arnim to forecast accurately that the assault would be mounted against Fifth Panzer Army through the Medjerda Valley. This persuaded *Heeresgruppe Afrika* to attach strong forces from First Italian to Fifth Panzer. At the beginning of the month, heavy armour was brought up and placed in position in the Medjerda Valley followed by remnants of 8th Panzer Regiment, detached from 15th Panzer, which reached a point south-west of Tunis about 4 May. The rest of the division which could be moved, together with all Messe's tanks, 88mm guns and most of his artillery, was also sent north to Fifth Panzer Army but plans to transfer other units from the *Afrika Korps* foundered on lack of petrol and the devastating effect their withdrawal would have on Italian morale. If the army group – which had moved its CP to the Cap Bon peninsula – was split by enemy attack, Fifth Panzer was to take command of the north and First Italian Army the south. The struggle was to be continued to the last round.

Arrangements to protect the expected vital area of Fifth Panzer Army's front on the Medjerda Plain included placing the motorcycle battalion of 10th Panzer, equipped with anti-aircraft guns, behind the first line of defence as flak protection for the port of Tunis and siting 88mm flak batteries southwest of the city. 10th Panzer, less its tanks, was left at Goubellat. In the Medjerda Valley, on 2/3 May, it attacked just south of the river in order to throw off balance British V Corps' infantry who had penetrated there and afterwards was held in readiness for further action near Massicault.[15] Little else could be done for the Axis forces were virtually out of fuel and ammunition. The Allies learned from intercepts of the German naval command's wireless traffic in Tunisia that *Heeresgruppe Afrika* expected, 'a complete supply breakdown', at the end of April if matters did not improve and units had so little fuel that their movements were restricted to between six and 37 miles. So catastrophic was the situation that the Luftwaffe could no longer find even the 35 gallons of fuel needed each day to operate its radar and by 4 May supplies of rations, water and ammunition could not be guaranteed to the troops.

Heroic efforts to alleviate the supply problem included a despairing request from Kapitän Meixner to use two supply U-boats, normally deployed in the North Atlantic, in four trips each month, ferrying 72,000 cubic metres of fuel into Tunisia.[16] The last two merchantmen to attempt the hazardous run had both been sunk and their 3,500 tons of supplies totally lost.[17]

Every last man was drafted into the defence line, including even medical personnel. Mindful of the fast-approaching ruin *Heeresgruppe Afrika* ordered some intelligence staff and Luftwaffe technicians, together with secret direction-finding indicators and microwave radio sets, back to Europe. Instruments that could not be saved were destroyed. Among the returning troops was Ernst Küstner who left by sea for Trapani military base and felt, he said, like a rat leaving a sinking ship.[18] Bayerlein, who was ill, and von Manteuffel who had collapsed from exhaustion, were evacuated, the latter in the last hospital ship to leave Tunis which was severely bombed *en route*. Getting up from his sickbed, he quelled the panic and helped put out the flames, eventually arriving safely on the Italian coast.[19]

Using the pretext of ill health, von Arnim invalided Generalmajor Weber of 334th Division out of North Africa as well. Others who departed were von Arnim's long-time adjutant and his only daughter's fiancée, Major von Kathen, who had to be hauled bodily onto an aircraft, and two generals who had not come up to scratch but were offered new appointments in Europe, Hildebrandt (21st Panzer) and Ziegler (*DAK*).[20] Their replacements, Generalmajor Heinrich-Hermann von Hülsen and General der Panzertruppe Hans Cramer had little time in which to assert their authority before they were captured.

Also leaving North Africa for good was Generalleutnant Gause, recalled to a conference in Italy, and Oberleutnant Heinz Werner Schmidt, formerly an aide to Rommel. Summoned from Sonderverband 288, he arrived exhausted and caked in mud at First Italian Army HQ, to be told he had been granted 14 days' leave to get married. When he tried to arrange for his faithful driver to accompany him, the old soldier said: 'First, Herr Oberleutnant, I must pay a visit to the hospital. I shall be back soon.' Schmidt never saw him again.[21]

Replacements for Weber, von Manteuffel and Bayerlein were Krause, Bülowius and Oberst Markert. Others were offered the chance to flee but refused, including General der Panzertruppe von Vaerst and his chief of staff, Generalmajor von Quast, Oberst Pomtow (Fifth Panzer Army's operations officer), von Liebenstein (164th Light) von Broich (10th Panzer), von Sponeck (90th Light) and Borowietz (15th Panzer). For all of them, time was fast running out.

———————

The main feature of Operation Strike was an overwhelming onslaught on a 3,500-yard front by Horrocks' IX Corps. Lining up on the right of the Medjez–Tunis road, 4th British Infantry Division and, opposite, 4th Indian were to make the initial break-in; 6th and 7th Armoured Divisions would then pass through the same day in a dash for Tunis. As protection on the right flank the French XIX Corps was to take Djebel Zaghouan while on the left flank, V Corps was to capture Djebel Bou Aoukaz and be ready to support the main thrust. Further north, II Corps was to win high ground around Chouïgui and the river crossings at Djedeïda and Tébourba.

Horrocks knew that the best chance of a successful armoured thrust would carry straight across the single bridge at Medjez el Bab, up the Medjerda Valley to

Massicault, on to St Cyprien and so to Tunis. His divisional commanders generally agreed this axis but there was argument about the actual methods to be employed. Tuker wanted a night attack, supported by concentrated artillery; Hawkesworth and Horrocks himself favoured the more traditional daylight assault behind a general barrage.

Some very straight talking by Tuker convinced the corps commander that a daylight attack into hills overlooking 4th Indian's area, with no real chance of tank support until the infantry could deal with the 88s, 'like all other 1st Army attacks, would just peter out on the enemy's forward positions and the battle would have to be fought again from further back.'[22] Moreover, 4th Indian was low in strength and extensive casualties might have a very serious effect on its capabilities in a daytime offensive. These points were not carried easily; Tuker even asked to be relieved of his command if such an assault were ordered and remarked to Horrocks at one point, 'Well, I'm off! You don't want me here, but they need good commanders in Burma.'[23]

In order to conceal his intentions, Anderson had 18th Army Group camouflage section erect 70 dummy tanks near Bou Arada, hoping to persuade von Arnim that the main thrust would be on the Goubellat plain, to the right of 1st Armoured Division, or that he had divided his armour. Radio traffic appropriate to two armoured divisions and a corps HQ was broadcast, with a few plausible security lapses, and German intelligence provided with agents' reports which indicated strong Allied armour in the area. Although the dummies were painfully obvious these distractions kept part of 21st Panzer tied to the Pont du Fahs area and left only a weakened 15th Panzer opposite the main British thrust line.

Set to jump off in dark moonless conditions at 0300 hours on 6 May, Horrocks' attack was supported by 442 guns (652 if V Corps is included) with 350 rounds apiece. In comparison, von Arnim's men were down to an average of 25–30 rounds per gun and there were virtually no reserve shells in the dumps for field and anti-tank guns.[24] Nor could he rely on his armour. The few remnants in Kampfgruppe *Irkens* were out of fuel and totally immobilised near Djebel Bou Aoukaz as were most surviving Tigers of Panzerabteilung 501 on the Cap Bon peninsula. Horrocks had some 400 tanks; 7th Armoured alone possessed 72 Shermans, 21 Grants and 47 Crusaders while 21st and 25th Army Tank Brigades from 4th Infantry Division were entirely equipped with Churchills.

Harmon's tanks, meanwhile, were already in Mateur. American successes in the north around Jefna and the Tine Valley had forced the Germans to withdraw on the night of 1/2 May behind the Tine sector. Against light opposition, 1st Armored rolled forward 30 miles through the Mousetrap and entered the town at about 1100 hours on 3 May. By piercing the German main defence line in the north, the Americans prevented von Arnim from effectively concentrating more forces in the Medjerda Valley. On the 4th, Harmon ordered Robinett to see if CC B could inflict further damage while Lambert's CC A came up on the opposite (northern) flank. Engineers built river crossings near Mateur as the division consolidated its strength for an attack which Harmon intended would punch a hole clean through to the coast.

1st Armored's advance was confined by the terrain to a double-headed thrust along two roads leading to the Tunis plain: one force (CC A) via the naval arsenal of Ferryville in the north to strike the main Tunis–Bizerte highway while the other (CC B) swung south-east by way of Djedeïda to block any retreat by the enemy on Tunis itself. Both were ranged by German artillery and anti-tank guns on Djebel Achkel, 1,600 feet above the Ferryville road, and on a hill mass stretching from there south to the Djedeïda route.

'Can you do it?,' Bradley asked Harmon. 'Yes, but it's going to be expensive.' 'How much?' A shrug of the shoulders. 'I'd guess fifty tanks to finish the job.' Bradley took the hard decision. 'Go ahead,' he said. 'It'll cost less in the long run if we cut him to pieces quickly.'[25]

Tentative probes into hills separating the Mateur plateau from the coastal plain confirmed the enemy had holed up there behind strongly-maintained defences. When 91st Reconnaissance Squadron from CC A launched a preliminary attack against Djebel Achkel on 4 May it met ferocious opposition from elements of Gruppe *Witzig* and battled for many hours to advance a third of the way up the steep western slopes, capturing about 80 prisoners. A few hundred others fighting on with unshakeable determination had to be blasted out of stone buildings by tank destroyers.

While grey skies grounded aircraft of the North-West African Tactical Air Force – though 242 Group RAF remained operational – Robinett suffered repeated air attacks *en route* to Mateur as Me-109s bombed the new bridge into the town from the south. After this he seemed less keen to push south-east along the Mateur–Djedeïda road skirting the five mile belt of hills where the remnants of the *Hermann Göring* Division lay in wait. He was further dismayed when Captain Dwight S. Varner's company, flanking 13th Armored Infantry, was hit by intense artillery fire, losing nine of its tanks.

At the division's HQ in the afternoon of 5 May, Harmon urged aggressive attack but was gloomily received by his unit commanders who had pessimistic views on likely losses. Part of the division was still equipped with 51 M3 Lee tanks brought from the United Kingdom; they were falling to pieces from long use. Even Harmon later admitted it was 'criminal' to send his men into action so badly equipped.[26]

As Robinett returned to CC B Harmon came to a sudden conclusion: 'Hell, that fellow isn't going to fight for me tomorrow,' he yelled and started off intending to replace him with Benson. At that moment a sudden strafing attack blew Robinett's vehicle apart, wounding the driver and driving a shell fragment into Robinett's left thigh where it tore through the sciatic nerve. Harmon realised at once that he would be out of action for some time and so Benson, 'aggressive and brave,' took over without Robinett being bounced.[27] The metal was removed from Robinett's crotch, with a hunk of his overalls still wrapped round it, but there was delay in suturing the nerve and Robinett spent eight months back home in the Walter Reed

Hospital, never again to be afforded more than limited status as commandant of an armor school. Through this misfortune Harmon now had the two forceful combat command leaders he wanted and the 'cold-blooded fighter' Lieutenant-Colonel Howze, temporarily in command of 2nd Battalion, 13th Armored Regiment (CCB), who was to distinguish himself in the coming fighting.

Coupled with 1st Armored's drive north-eastwards from Djebel Achkel and along the southern edge of Lac de Bizerte to seal off any retreat towards Tunis, north of the lakes two RCTs from 9th Infantry and Corps Franc D'Afrique were to advance on Djebel Cheniti. On this peak the enemy had anchored the northern part of his new defensive line which ran south-east around the shoreline of Garaet Achkel (where one German regiment, out of fuel, had only partly withdrawn), through Ferryville to Djebel Achkel and its associated hill mass. An interlocking attack ensured that should the defenders be pushed off Djebel Cheniti those north of Garaet Achkel would have to fall back on Bizerte or risk running into 1st Armored coming up from Mateur to Ferryville.

On 1st Armored's right the enemy's defensive line now ran from just east of the Oued Tine at Kef en Nosour, a hill mass south-east of Mateur, to good defensive positions ten miles to the south, between Eddekhila and Chouïgui, in hills rising between 600 and 1,000 feet above the plain. These might be outflanked if Benson managed to push his CC B along the Mateur–Djedeïda road. Beyond was Tébourba and the approach to Tunis. To breach this line 1st Infantry was scheduled to attack across the Tine into the northern hills while 34th Division moved directly east on Eddekhila and Chouïgui.

Preliminary moves began on 3 May when 168th RCT (34th Infantry) started out for Chouïgui, supported by 175th Field Artillery Battalion. Patrols advanced easily across the Oued Tine plain and reached towards Eddekhila next day, where they met the first German opposition. Ryder's men took to the high ground instead of simply boring in across open country; on 5 May they swung into hills south-west of the town and after a day spent scrambling across broken, rocky ground and steep slopes they captured it. Northwards was the Chouïgui Pass, the 168th's next objective. Meanwhile, Terry Allen had sent the Big Red One into hills west of the Tine facing Djebel Douimiss. On 6 May they faced the daunting prospect of attacking the *Barenthin* Regiment, well lodged on this hill mass. Sure of their aggressive intent, Allen was about to make the fundamental mistake of over-committing his men.

In the far north, the Corps Franc worked its way into three hills to the west of Djebel Cheniti on 4 May and a poorly-supported enemy infantry attack down the peak's western slope was smashed by US artillery. Next day, 47th RCT (9th Infantry) began an outflanking march from Jefna which took it into the hills on the left. By 6 March Eddy's men were due north of Cheniti and threatening to cut the Mateur–Bizerte road.

In First Army's sector, Djebel Bou Aoukaz was wreathed in smoke and flame as over 600 guns saturated it with high explosive on the afternoon of 5 May. A series of grim rushes carried troops of the 1st Battalion, Duke of Wellington's Regiment, and 1st King's Shropshire Light Infantry, forward on the left and right of the long-suffering 5th Grenadier Guards. This combination proved too much for elements of Kampfgruppe *Irkens* who were driven off as the Guards watched the struggle with interest from their grandstand seat. As the main attack passed beneath his lofty perch next day, Sergeant Danger of the Guards was on Bou Aoukaz identifying dead bodies: 'the smell of death haunted me for weeks afterwards,' he wrote. 'In one case, we picked up a body by the legs to put it in the grave and the leg came off in my hand because it was so decomposed.'[28]

Signs of preparation for the great assault were everywhere on First Army's front. The sappers had driven roads, put up new steel bridges and opened cuttings through solid rock. Passages had been cleared across minefields, start tapes laid, guns sited and shells stockpiled. Troops of Scorpions stood ready to sweep through mines still unlocated and spigot mortar groups assembled to meet counter-attacks. Wellingtons and Bisleys struck at roads and transport, Fortresses hit Tunis and La Goulette while the Strategic and Tactical Air Forces preyed on enemy shipping. At night Bisleys, Wellingtons and French Leos softened up enemy strongholds and smashed troop concentrations in the Medjerda Valley. From 700 miles away Truscott's 3rd Infantry Division was hurrying to join II Corps' 1st Infantry south-east of Mateur.

Provided that infantry from 4th British and 4th Indian Divisions had torn a hole in the enemy's defences by 0700 hours on 6 May, tanks were to be released on either flank, 7th Armoured towards St Cyprien and 6th Armoured into the hills south of La Mornaghia. 'If by tomorrow night the infantry objectives have been gained and the tanks level or a little beyond them on each flank, we shall have done very well,' said Horrocks.[29] In the light of what was to happen this cautious comment was to assume considerable interest.

⸻

Right on cue, one field gun on every seven yards of front poured tons of high explosive into the funnel of the Medjerda Valley. At first light the first of 2,000 sorties to be flown that day took off; concentrated bombing of a 'box,' four by three and a half miles in size, by the Tactical Air Force delivered a creeping barrage behind which the infantry advanced. Before 0900 hours on 6 May pilots were reporting they had nothing to bomb. The enemy had dragged his aircraft from the airfields and taken his vehicles off the roads. He had gone to ground, dug into trenches and heavily camouflaged gun pits. British and Indian infantry waited briefly while sappers cut a path through barbed wire and probed for mines; then above the aroma of crushed corn and wild thyme arose the acrid smell of cordite as 1/9th Gurkhas and 4/6th Rajputana Rifles swept uphill. Their first rush took them deep into the German defences; prisoners were shot or left behind to be collected later, along with the wounded. Whole chains of enemy machine-gun posts, firing target-indicating white tracer, were wiped out.

By the time 1/4th Essex followed up burial parties were already out collecting the sprawled dead. Some Indian troops, now two miles beyond their start line, were busy with brew cans as others slept despite the continuous roar of fighter and tank-buster aircraft. Veering to the right across the front of 4th Infantry Division the Essex men, closely supported by 30 Churchills of 25th Tank Brigade, moved towards their final objective (Point 165) while one company raced off to Frendj where a car full of Germans was captured. A battery of *Nebelwerfers*, ranged on 4th British Division, was overrun with its crews and ammunition, the first time these fearsome weapons had been captured. Casualties were light; at a cost of 137 killed and wounded a gap had been prised open, towards which 7th Armoured began to move. By 0845 hours their tanks were abreast of 4th Indian Division's objectives.

On the right of the Medjez–Tunis road, 1/6th Surreys and 2nd Duke of Cornwall's Light Infantry (10th Brigade) were supported by Brigadier Ivor Moore's 21st Tank Brigade and a massive weight of artillery firing over 16,000 shells in two hours. By 0700 hours they had smashed their way onto the Massicault ridge. 'From the top of the turret,' wrote Lance-Corporal Cook of 48th RTR, 'the sight was most remarkable – behind us the spectacle of a long line of flashes which lit up the sky away into the distance, casting eerie shadows as we moved slowly past them towards the German positions: in front, tracer shells and bullets criss-crossed the wide valley... we all seemed to be quite exhilarated by the sight and by the occasion – there was a fine sense of drama and we had our small part to play in it.'[30]

On the receiving end of this massive onslaught 15th Panzer cracked and collapsed. Command and communications broke down and Germans were seen, very unusually, running away or trying hastily to surrender – not always successfully as Cook witnessed: 'About 200 yards from our tank, a German climbed from a slit-trench with hands held above his head. An approaching infantryman, armed with a Bren gun, stopped and waved to the German to come forward. The latter must have understood the gesture, but he didn't move; he seemed to be pointing down into the trench. Again the British soldier motioned, but again the German refused to move, his hands still above his head in the position of surrender. I can imagine that the infantryman was scared... that a trap lay ahead and that he could walk forward into it so easily. With a final gesture to the German which, once more, remained unacknowledged except by his hand again pointing downwards, the infantryman swung his Bren at the hip and sent a burst at the German, killing him instantly. Then two British soldiers ran up and I saw them go down into the trench and lift out a wounded man. The one who had died had obviously been trying to protect his comrade by drawing attention to him and, in doing so, had given his life for him.'[31]

Alexander had left Horrocks in no doubt that *speed* and refusal to be thrown off a direct line to Tunis were essential.[32] Yet when Tuker told him, as early as 0940 hours, that the enemy's defences seemed to have collapsed and 7th Armoured could, 'go as fast and as far as it liked,' 6th and 7th Armoured were not driven on and instead made only slow progress throughout the rest of the day.

This was in part due to the fact that 15th Panzer, now in full retreat, was hurriedly recalled and sent north of the Medjerda where elements of 334th Infantry Division were located around Djebel Lanserine. The distinct impression at IX Corps' HQ shortly before 1300 hours that, 'the enemy [are] not aware of direction of our attacks and are now pulling out as fast as they can', made no difference either to Keightley or Erskine. Both wished to establish a firm base before committing their tanks to a further advance and neither wanted to disturb the complicated order of vehicles in each division extending in a 30-mile-long procession, other than to bring up 201st Guards Brigade (6th Armoured) and 131st Lorried Infantry Brigade (7th Armoured) which took time.

Brigadier Bateman (5th Indian Brigade) was at a loss to know why the breakout was progressing so slowly. 'By first light we had certainly reported success (i.e. Brigade final objectives gained) and so far as we could tell there was nothing to stop the Armour going through from then on.'[33] Tuker thought it 'pretty feeble' that 7th Armoured could push ahead only eight miles beyond the infantry by the evening, when it pulled up just north of Massicault, and that 6th Armoured took three hours longer to reach a position two miles to the east. They then halted for maintenance when a swift dash might have cut off the enemy streaming away towards the north and east.

A breathing space had again been provided but this time it did not matter for *Heeresgruppe Afrika* was already at its last gasp, its command structure rapidly disintegrating: 'Between the Medjerda and the Medjez–St Cyprien road the enemy has achieved his decisive breakthrough to Tunis,' it reported. 'This sector was heroically defended by 15th Panzer Division... but these troops could not survive an assault mounted by numerically far superior infantry and armoured formations with massed artillery support, and accompanied by air attacks of an intensity not hitherto experienced. The bulk of 15th Panzer Division must be deemed to have been destroyed... There can be no doubt that on 7th May the road to Tunis will be open to the enemy, and that the fall of the city of Bizerte is only a question of time... '[34] Non-combatants and administrative personnel were hurriedly making their way to the Cap Bon peninsula.

Nothing was now coming into Tunis or Bizerte by sea though remarkably 53 men arrived on the 6th by air, accompanied by 25 tons of fuel and several tons of *Feldpost*. At the same time commanders of the various German units were informed that Tunis was to be evacuated by 1700 hours the next day, the Army Group's *Oberquartiermeister* warning, however, that this depended on the tactical and fuel situation.[35]

The Americans had apparently ground to a halt after their main attack opened in parallel with First Army. Too confident that Regiment *Barenthin* was about to come apart, 1st Infantry ran into severe trouble after Allen committed 18th and 26th RCTs, supported by a company of 1st Armored Regiment, across the Tine. Badly held up, first by minefields and then by the collapse of a bridge across a deep wadi, the 18th was left exposed in the Chouïgui foothills on Djebel Douimiss, where it suffered heavy losses. Both RCTs were forced to retreat back across the Tine and for the rest of the campaign were motionless, simply preventing any westward movement by the enemy. Bradley was annoyed: 'The gesture was a foolish one and undertaken without authorization. For Allen's path of attack led nowhere... A commander attacks, I reminded him, to take objectives, not to waste his strength in occupying useless ground.'[36]

South of 1st Division, Ryder's 168th RCT had also encountered severe resistance as it attempted to turn northwards along the hills towards the Chouïgui Pass. In the north, while 47th RCT was outflanking the enemy, Eddy's 60th RCT passed through the Corps Franc and attacked Djebel Cheniti but throughout 6 May could not drive him off the south-western slopes.

In 1st Armored's sector, Colonel Robert Stack's 6th Armored Infantry Regiment (CC A) drove into the hill mass of Djebel el Messeftine, south-east of Djebel Achkel where 91st Reconnaissance Squadron was stalled. They were met by determined opposition from infantry and tanks and it was not until 1630 hours that the Messeftine ridge had been cleared. A co-ordinated attack by two companies of 13th Armored Regiment to drive the Germans from a secondary ridge was halted by intense artillery fire. Amid a stiff counterattack and confused fighting, the enemy regained the ridge by 2100 hours apart from one point where 3rd Battalion, 6th Armored Infantry, tenaciously held on.

About the only success was that of CC B (13th Armored Regiment and attached units). Most of the day Benson's men struggled to knock out many anti-tank guns concealed on the lower slopes of hills along the Mateur–Djedeïda road, losing 12 tanks, 15 battle-damaged and suffering 60 casualties. Rallying his 2nd Battalion at critical moments, by evening Colonel Howze had pushed it to the junction with a road leading due north, six miles east of Mateur, from where he could cut off the enemy's direct access from the rear of the Djebel Achkel hill mass to Tunis via Djedeïda. From there he was set to charge eastwards at daybreak on 7 May.

In the hills a little to the north of the Medjerda, 78th Division was stationary. Far to the south, around Bou Kournine, 1st Armoured and 46th Infantry Divisions remained static in a holding operation as were the New Zealanders and 56th Division at Enfidaville. Keeping on the pressure, however, did not eliminate some vicious fighting at The Bou, 'unnatural, forbidding and repellent', where 1st Armoured lay under the watchful eye of a German observation post which brought down artillery fire on every forward movement.

Here, burial parties were overrun by the flood of death. Arriving at a nearby wadi on 26 April, Bombardier Challoner of 2nd Regiment RHA (1st Armoured Division), witnessed the aftermath of a recent violent tank engagement: 'One Mark IV special... had been burnt out while running down from the crest of the hill. Inside there were at least three dead bodies; one, the driver, turned with his knee up on his seat as if to clamber out when the heat had overcome him. His clothes, skin and features were entirely gone, only shreds of flesh and sinew clung to the blackened bones and the boiling brain had blown the top off his head. And yet still very recognisable as a man.'[37] Considerably shaken by what they saw,

Challoner and his comrades buried the remains of the bodies in the shadow of the ruined tank.

During a lull in the action, on or about 6 May, von Arnim managed a brief visit to the 65 men and two artillery observers, all who were left to defend The Bou. They could not hope to mount any kind of offensive but were ordered to delay the enemy as long as possible.

------◆◆◆------

At Enfidaville there was no chance of blitzing through the German defences with only two British divisions (50th and 56th), 2nd New Zealand, and one French division exerting any pressure after Montgomery recalled the 51st Highland into reserve. 'As far as the world is concerned,' he told Alexander, 'and particularly the enemy, Eighth Army is still controlling the battle in this corner of the world.'[38]

It did not seem so to the men who faced up to 90th Light in the hills around. Every night the high ground turned into a resounding inferno of bursting shells and bombs; on 2 May, as they cheered bombers unloading onto targets beyond the hills, Lieutenant McCallum's battalion was suddenly attacked by several aircraft: 'My sergeant was buried. He had to be dug out. My batman was punctured in the base of the spine and was taken away on a stretcher. Another man died in a short time. The rest of us escaped. Some time later someone came up from the battalion HQ. He said the airfield had been on the telephone with apologies and the pilots were to be court-martialled. Said someone, "If they court-martial all the pilots who have ever bombed their own troops there won't be any bloody air force left."'[39] Three days later the New Zealand 5th Brigade was mistakenly bombed by the Americans while relieving John Currie's 8th Armoured Brigade at night on the western side of Djebel Garci,. The rest of the division, Gentry's 6th Brigade, was well behind the front at Sidi bou Ali, expecting daily to be sent up again. Visiting them, the New Zealand Minister of Defence was soundly barracked after trying to enthuse the troops to more fighting for which warning orders had just been received. In the event, none of the brigade was put back into the line.

This unwelcome development fell to Ralf Harding's 5th New Zealanders who were given the task of pinching out the Garci massif by Freyberg. On the night of 6/7 May 23rd Battalion, supported by the 28th, attacked an area 15 miles west of Takrouna in a drizzle which gave way to heavy rain accompanied by thunder, lightning and a gale force wind. Initial gains were encouraging with few casualties but, throughout the next day, intense shelling gave little respite. Even so, a sudden and fierce enemy attack on the night of 8/9 May was very unexpected because the German collapse on First Army's front had by then assumed catastrophic proportions.

------◆◆◆------

Horrocks' failure to capitalise on the breakthrough along the Medjez–St Cyprien road on 6 May, puzzled von Arnim. 'A Rommel on their side,' he declared, 'would have said, "On to the sea!"'[40] In the evening von Arnim ordered his forces to retreat step-by-step into the 'fortress area' at Enfidaville, Zaghouan and Hammam

Lif. The centre and left of Fifth Panzer Army was to pull back to a line running from Tébourba to Djebel Oust, overlooking the road roughly half-way between Pont du Fahs and La Mohammedia. At a last meeting in von Arnim's bunker on the Bellevue Heights with von Vaerst they decided not to defend Tunis and Bizerte, for which there was neither the strength nor means, since both would needlessly be destroyed without changing the fate of the army. As for the guns in the forts at Bizerte, they pointed out to sea and could not be trained inland.

The *DAK* was also ordered to draw in its right wing to a line from Zaghouan to Djebel Oust and later assume command of the *Hermann Göring* and 10th Panzer Divisions. On the Cap Bon peninsula First Italian Army was to take control of the defences and hold its positions. The fortuitous discovery of an undamaged drum of fuel on the beach enabled von Arnim to move his HQ south to Sainte Marie du Zit, just east of Djebel Zaghouan; as he left, von Vaerst's troops were busy destroying port installations at Bizerte and Ferryville.

Notes to Chapter 17

1 Jordan, *Jordan's Tunis Diary*, p. 251.
3 Bradley, Soldier's Story, p. 90.
3 Everett S. Hughes Diary, entry for 1 May 1943.
4 McCreery to Tuker, 17 August 1959. Tuker Papers, 71/21/6.
5 Major-General L.O. Lyne, 'Autobiography,' (unpub. TS). 71/2/4.
6 Quoted by Macksey, *Crucible of Power*, p. 288
7 Miller Diary, entry for 29 April 1943.
8 Broadhurst's recollections of the meeting, quoted by Hamilton, *Monty: Master of the Battlefield*, p. 238.
9 Horrocks, *A Full Life*, p. 166.
10 In Sicily on 1 June 1943, Captain Patrick Mayhew attended a ceremonial parade addressed by Montgomery: '... [he] ends with a five-minute talk on how pleased he is to get 78th Division and 5th Northamptons in particular into "my" Eighth Army. If he had had the 78th Division, he could have taken Tunis and Bizerta by himself.' Mayhew, *One Family's War*, p. 191.
11 'Some Notes by General Tuker'.
12 Freyberg complained to his wife on 1st May that he had had, 'a pistol placed at my head and been selected to command the X Corps.' Quoted by Paul Freyberg, *Freyberg V.C.*, pp. 432–3.
13 Generalmajor Hans Seidemann, commander of *Fliegerkorps Tunis*, Kesselring's representative in North Africa, also left for a safer haven.
14 Captain J.E. Edney (of 1/5th Queen's Royal Regiment but serving on the staff of 131st Brigade, 7th Armoured Division) TS Account; IWM 85/6/1. Also Bradshaw, 'War Reminiscences.'
15 Von Vaerst, 'Operations of the Fifth Panzer Army,' p. 22.
16 Kapitän-zur-See Meixner to *Oberquartiermeister i.G.* Brand, 3 May 1943; *Kriegstagebuch der Heeresgruppe Afrika* – O.Qu., 3–6 May 1943; RH19-VIII/243. BA-MA.
17 Report to *Oberquartiermeister* 5 May 1943.
18 Ernst Küstner, 'Von Paris bis Frauenreuth', diary entry for 26 April 1943; *Die Oase*, March 1971, p. 11.

[19] Franz Kurowski, 'Division Manteuffel im Brükenkopf Tunesien', *Die Oase*, August 1968, pp. 9–10.

[20] Samuel W. Mitcham, 'Arnim', in Barnett, ed., *Hitler's Generals*, p. 351.

[21] Schmidt, *With Rommel in the Desert*, p. 191.

[22] 'Some Notes by General Tuker'.

[23] Quoted by Macksey, *Crucible of Power*, p. 295.

[24] In May 1947 Alexander claimed enemy ammunition depots were found to be well stocked and photographs widely circulated apparently supported his claim. Careful examination of them shows, however, that the 'ammunition' consists almost entirely of spent cases.

[25] Bradley, *Soldier's Story*, p. 92.

[26] Harmon to Eisenhower, 21 May 1943; Harmon Papers, Box 1. Harmon argued strongly that his M3-equipped battalion should be given the M4 Sherman.

[27] Harmon interviewed by Howe.

[28] Danger Diary, entry for 6 May 1943.

[29] D'Arcy-Dawson, *Tunisian Battle*, p. 231.

[30] Lance-Corporal Edmund Cook (48th RTR), 'Another War, Another Corporal'. IWM (not catalogued when consulted).

[31] *Ibid*.

[32] Horrocks, *A Full Life*, pp. 170–1.

[33] Tuker, 'Some Notes'.

[34] Lewin, *Afrika Korps*, pp. 247–8; Playfair, *Destruction of Axis Forces*, p. 451.

[35] Message from *Oberquartiermeister Heeresgruppe Afrika* 6 May 1943; RH19-VIII/243; also Lucas, *Panzer Army Africa*, p. 185.

[36] Bradley, *A Soldier's Story*, p. 93.

[37] Challoner, MS Journal.

[38] Montgomery to Alexander, 5 May 1943. Montgomery Papers, BLM 36/4.

[39] McCallum, *Journey with a Pistol*, p. 126.

[40] Von Arnim, 'Erinnerungen an Tunesien', p. 110–1.

Chapter 18

We Shall Fight to the Last

'The war in Africa, as far as we are concerned, is over and everyone is enjoying the peace and quiet. It is sort of an anti-climax however and not at all like we thought it would be; the guns have stopped shooting – that's about all.'

Entry in War Diary, 68th Armored Field Artillery Battalion (1st Armored Division), 10 May 1943.[1]

'That's the end of the Tunisian episode.'

Major-General Tuker, entry in his diary for 15 May 1943.[2]

As tanks of 6th and 7th Armoured and 201st Guards Brigade began to roll out of their overnight laagers on 7 May, signs of the enemy's widespread confusion and collapse were everywhere. Through the Medjerda Valley rumbled the artillery, anti-tank guns, fuel and ammunition wagons, workshops and recovery vehicles. Ahead were the tanks, visors down, flattening the ripening wheat as they worked past empty gun pits and abandoned trenches. At La Mornaghia German notices warned of typhus in the village but leading tanks of 1st RTR (22nd Brigade), accompanied by 5th RTR on the left and 1st Guards Brigade on the right, were intent on reaching the shallow semi-circle of hills around the city of Tunis. It was here that the last few *Hermann Göring* Panzers, supported by a dozen or so 88mm guns, made their final stand.

The contest was one-sided as Brigadier Carver's tanks and medium artillery smashed the opposition; manned only by anti-aircraft defence crews, the 88s were not as deadly as usual. From the ridge could be seen the whole wide sweep of the bay and Tunis itself, grey under sullen, leaden clouds and a spreading canopy of black smoke rising from a burning dump on the race-course airfield. Finding no more than scattered resistance, Erskine ordered in his troops at 1430 hours. On the edge of the city, a patrol of B Squadron, 11th Hussars, met another from C Squadron, 1st Derbyshire Yeomanry, and decided to share the honour of entering.

In fact, the Derbyshire Yeomanry just headed the Hussars who were delayed by madly rejoicing crowds, as their Signal Log revealed: '"B" Squadron... report right patrol now seems to be right in town itself. Can 1st Royal Tanks send something forward to help? It is raining steadily, the Troop is surrounded by surprised Germans firing at the cars, hundreds of others surrendering, wildly excited civilians blocking way, showering flowers and pressing wine and other offerings.'[3]

Nevertheless, in a BBC broadcast on 9 May, Frank Gillard presented the capture of Tunis as, 'another example of Monty's left hook', and the next day headlines in newspapers from the London *Daily Sketch* to the *Tunis Telegraph* credited Eighth Army with entering the city and winning single-handed the North African campaign – to Anderson's intense annoyance. This was, 'in very bad taste and likely to have the most unfortunate effect on First Army', complained the Deputy CIGS, General Nye, who asked why Monty's army could not be kept in its place and how Eisenhower's censors failed to suppress such harmful reports.[4]

Close behind the leading patrols came tanks from 1st RTR and infantry of 1/7th Queen's Royals (131st Brigade) mopping up. For the most part enemy troops offered little resistance; one collection was ferried away to captivity in a Bren Gun carrier. Mistaking them for British the crowds threw flowers which the Germans caught and sat back stiffly, each man clutching a small posy in his hand. Two self-important Italian officers demanded to be driven to their quarters to collect waterproofs. They were hustled away, still protesting.

In the harbour of La Goulette the Italian steamer *Belluno* was crammed with 650 British and American POWs. A bombing attack the previous day which smashed her rudder persuaded some Italian guards to jump overboard and swim to safety but the Germans methodically swung out the last of her boats as she settled in shallow water and took the wounded ashore. One of the first acts as Tunis was liberated was to take them to hospital and bring the others to safety.

Further along the coast, Hans-Georg Moschallski of the *Hermann Göring* Division heard from the BBC that events were hastening to a conclusion. Disgusted at the sudden collapse of the German command structure, his unit quickly surrendered and on the eight-day journey by rail to Casablanca they came face-to-face with the realities of war against the Allies: 'When I saw the miles of war supplies parked along the railway lines – millions of barrels of fuel, tanks, guns and lorries – my heart sank to my boots,' he remarked.[5]

As the French population of Tunis celebrated, Anderson ordered 6th Armoured to drive south-east towards Soliman and Grombalia in order to prevent the enemy setting up positions in defence of the Cap Bon peninsula. After a night of much confusion as the 1/7th Queen's Royals sought out the last pockets of resistance, into Tunis the next day came dog-tired infantry from 78th Division, lorried there on Anderson's orders to receive some of their due for their magnificent and exhausting fighting in the hills.

By a happy coincidence – it was not planned that way – Americans entered Bizerte at about the same time as the British took Tunis. There had been no slackening of the enemy's resistance on the 6th but when 47th and 60th RCTs (9th Infantry), advancing on both sides of Djebel Cheniti, finally took the hill and cut the Mateur–Bizerte road the Germans were forced into a full retreat. Bradley was keen to get troops into Bizerte before the Germans demolished the port and called Eddy, who was not aggressive enough for his liking: 'But the road to Bizerte is lousy with mines, Omar. We can't even put a jeep over it until the engineers clear it.' 'Well then, get off your trucks and begin walking, but get the hell to Bizerte,' he ordered.[6]

Stung into action, Eddy sent 47th RCT marching on the town and whipped his armour ahead of 3rd Battalion, 60th RCT. Crossing a ford constructed by 15th Engineer Battalion over Oued Douimiss on the Bizerte road, 9th Reconnaissance Troop lifted scores of mines. When the way was clear they were passed by Company A, 751st Tank Battalion supported by two companies of 894th Tank Destroyer Battalion which entered Bizerte at 1615 hours, followed shortly by 9th Reconnaissance.

The town was dead, deserted by its civilian population which had fled to Tindja or Ferryville. Only the Germans remained. In a church tower a machine-gun nest was active and their tanks and gunners were on gentle slopes, hardly a quarter of a mile away to the south, across the narrow sheet of water which leads to the sea out of Bizerte lake. From here they pumped shells at the tank destroyers when they ventured into any street running on a north–south axis. The Americans, firing back, knocked out two artillery pieces. Despite the presence of US tanks bivouacked in the central section of Bizerte airport the doughboys of 47th RCT, entering the town very early on the following morning (8 May), encountered continuous sniper fire. Nevertheless, Bradley had succeeded in blocking all routes. Elements of the 47th also controlled ground to the north-west, ready to repel any counter-attack, with 60th RCT on the hills commanding the Ferryville–Bizerte road.

To the south, an early morning attack on 7 May by 168th RCT (34th Infantry) finally broke German resistance to an advance on the Chouïgui Pass; as they withdrew Ryder's men entered Chouïgui itself in the afternoon, where they made contact with units from V Corps. Meanwhile, 1st Armored put out three columns which wrecked the enemy's defences on the line Ferryville–Mateur. At the northern end, CC A got 91st Armored Reconnaissance Squadron and 2nd Battalion, 39th Infantry Regiment (temporarily transferred from 9th Division) into Ferryville soon after noon. The town was undamaged but precision bombing had blasted a square mile of workshops, warehouses, power-plants, torpedo-sheds and assembly plants at the naval arsenal.[7]

In the heights around Messeftine Ridge the second prong of 1st Armored shattered the enemy with concentrated artillery fire as 6th Armored Infantry Battalion cleaned out any survivors. At the same time, Crosby's 3rd Battalion, 13th Armored Regiment, thrust northward beyond the area cleared by Howze the previous day and hunted down enemy concentrations. A detachment reached the road from Ferryville which loops round the southern shore of Lac de Bizerte to join the Tunis–Bizerte highway but by then elements of 1st Armored Regiment and 6th Armored Infantry had already advanced from Mateur to cut this route. Fighting their way past tanks and artillery they swung north-eastwards, driving the enemy onto the flats south of Lac de Bizerte and moving to entrap armour sited in the hills south-east of Bizerte. On the right, CC B was pushing the third prong of 1st Armored's attack along the Mateur–Djedeïda road. Howze's 2nd Battalion, 13th Armored Regiment, seized a crossroads six miles east of Mateur and during the day moved further towards Protville. At Pont du Fahs, elements of Koeltz's XIX Corps entered the town.

⟫•⟪

From Bou Arada to Tunis, First Army had driven a mighty wedge between Fifth Panzer Army in the north and First Italian Army in the south. All von Vaerst's forces were threatened with piecemeal destruction by 1st Armored's drive eastwards and northward from Mateur and Ferryville just as Messe stood in danger of immediate extinction from the encircling movement of the British 6th Armoured Division.

On 30 April Mussolini had telegraphed the Führer pointing out that unless more supplies and aircraft were sent urgently to counteract the Allies', 'shattering air superiority', then the troops, 'fighting splendidly,' would have their fate sealed.[8] Hitler, beyond ordering unyielding resistance to the last man, could do nothing while Mussolini revealed to the Japanese Ambassador in Rome that a general evacuation was impossible. Knowing that the Germans regarded Tunisia as lost, the Duce and Kesselring were, however, still talking of reinforcing Tunisia on 4 May. Kesselring received instructions from Keitel that units were to be amalgamated and spare staff, what the Italians called the *mangiatori* (best translated as 'useless mouths'), evacuated. *Comando Supremo* sent von Arnim and Messe similar orders but these may never have reached them.

In the rapidly shrinking band of territory still controlled by Axis forces, the *Oberquartiermeister der Heeresgruppe Afrika* had lost contact with the northern half of the front. Oberstleutnant Brand was still trying to supply units wherever they could be reached. One plan was to use landing craft and *Sturmboote* (rubber boats) to ferry goods from ship to such harbours as were left in German hands. Another was to use 'Dunkirk piers' (vehicles driven into the water to form a chain from ship to shore).[9]

Such desperate measures were never attempted because the Italo-German machine began to shrink and collapse in upon itself with fearful speed. On 8 May, CC A of 1st Armored struck again in the north with tanks and assault guns, breaking up a final attack by remnants of 15th Panzer around Djebel Kechabta and driving the enemy from Djebel Sidi Mansour, four miles east of Ferryville, taking over 200 prisoners. From the crest of the hill troops of 3rd Battalion, 1st Armored Regiment, and 2nd Battalion, 6th Armoured Infantry, observed Germans in full retreat, scurrying across the Tunis–Bizerte road towards the village of El Alia. Next day, when 15th Panzer had completely exhausted its artillery ammunition, 3rd Battalion captured the village without difficulty other than that posed by, 'the determination of several thousands of Germans to surrender.'[10]

While one arm of 1st Armored was involved at El Alia, another was reaching around the southern shore of Lac de Bizerte towards the village of El Azib, astride the Tunis–Bizerte highway. This involved Carr's 1st Battalion, 13th Armored Regiment, which was forced to cross perilously open ground. Two companies of light tanks were therefore ordered to, 'drive like hell, pray, and rally in a wooded area a mile south of El Azib.' Flat out, they ran the gauntlet of enemy guns for eight minutes. Six were hit but the enemy was forced to retreat, which opened a corridor for the remainder of the battalion, 91st Reconnaissance Squadron and 3rd Battalion, 6th Armoured Infantry.

In the hills south of Lac de Bizerte, CC B's advance was held up by the craggy terrain but a determined push by Howze brought his 40 tanks to high ground from which they were able to cut the Tunis–Bizerte road at the Oued Medjerda crossing. From their vantage point they could see, on the coastal flats, hundreds of trapped enemy vehicles turn to fiery torches and the sky lit by tracer bullets as the Germans shot off the last of their ammunition. As sniping and shelling died down in Bizerte, 47th RCT withdrew so that the Corps Franc could make a symbolic entry. 'All the nice suburban houses were empty,' noted Master Sergeant Tommy Riggs, 'with marks of shell and bullet on the plaster. Arabs were in the road carrying gilt-framed pierglasses and fine chairs, and having no luck looking like the owners.'[11] A few locals still around gave the troops a wildly exuberant welcome. 'Where are the Gaullists?,' was the question heard time and again, and 'Who is Giraud?'

'The legend of de Gaulle is more powerful here than anywhere else in North Africa: it would be a political error not to cash in on it and thereby redeem the mistakes of last November,' commented Philip Jordan. 'Giraud's regime is as reactionary as ever it was; and will continue that way, with the open support of the [US] State Department and the silent backing of Whitehall.'[12] But despite Giraud's efforts to shed much of his anti-semitic and extremist following he was being steadily out-manoeuvred by de Gaulle, of whom Harold Macmillan observed: 'he is a more powerful character than any other Frenchman with whom one has yet been in contact.'[13]

While political matters were being decided at Tunis and Bizerte, Koeltz's XIX Corps was advancing on Djebel Zaghouan. Generals Boissau and Le Coulteux, travelling fast to the north-east from Pont du Fahs with the Division *d'Oran* and the armoured group, struck unexpectedly strong opposition but Generals Conne and Mathenet put the *d'Alger* and *du Maroc* Divisions beyond the Pont du Fahs–Takrouna road and set them toiling up Zaghouan's formidable lower pitches.

In the adjoining IX Corps sector, Horrocks replaced 7th Armoured with 1st Armoured Division which had at last pushed beyond Bou Kournine when the Germans melted away on the night of 6/7 May. A small patrol sent to bury recent casualties discovered a horrible sight, with the slopes and summits littered with bodies of men mown down in successive assaults. The burial party had to tread carefully and six were wounded on a mine when someone's boot fouled a tripwire.

Crossing the Oued Miliane, 1st Armoured moved on 8/9 May past small villages *en fête* to Créteville. Veering south-eastwards on the 9th, the division entered hills on either side of the Grombalia–Tunis road and was forced to run the gauntlet of artillery and mortar shells on its way to prevent the enemy moving into or out of the Cap Bon peninsula. In the meantime, 7th Armoured swung north from Tunis, one prong along the road to Bizerte and another parallel to the Oued Medjerda where fierce clashes took place on the 8th. Many Germans and Italians who had given up the fight made for the river where enterprising Arabs offered them a ferry service on horseback to the west bank – at 50 francs a crossing.

West of Protville elements of 6th Armoured linked up with 1st Battalion, 1st US Armored Regiment on 9 May. As the 1st Battalion turned north on the Bizerte road, passing thousands of prisoners and great mounds of discarded arms and equipment, 3rd Battalion, 13th Armored Regiment, and 11th Hussars took the road to Porto Farina. Their arrival saved many enemy troops, busy trying to lash together rafts, from certain death since, on 8 May, Admiral Cunningham had set up Operation Retribution – so named after the agonies suffered by British troops while evacuating Greece and Crete in 1941. Moving in every available destroyer for close patrol work by day and night off the Cap Bon peninsula he signalled: 'Sink, burn and destroy. Let nothing pass.'

The 'Kelibia Regatta' as destroyer captains termed it, took place in heavily-mined waters outside an exclusion zone covered by Allied aircraft and shore batteries. On the night of 8/9 May, IIMS *Tartar* with two other destroyers, the *Laforey* and *Loyal*, sank two ships with their cargoes of ammunition and tanks. On the *Tartar*, Lieutenant-Commander Hay could hear the shouts of men in the water. 'We circled round once more... but it would have been useless to try and pick them up then. I was glad to see the davits and falls on one of the ships were empty and two or three large black shapes were, no doubt, the ship's lifeboats.'[14]

Conflicting evidence had been assembled by Allied intelligence but air reconnaissance over the whole area detected no signs of evacuation even though German radio broadcast on 8 May that the African campaign was over and troops would be taken off in small boats. At the last moment some did manage to escape like 18-year-old W. Jüttner, conveyed from hospital to a ship about to sail. However, sunken and damaged vessels littering the harbour prevented it putting out and so, accompanied by 12 other wounded comrades, he was rushed to El Aouina airfield where, at 1600 hours on 8 May, the last Ju-52 took off for Palermo, only minutes before the Germans blew up the airstrip. Surviving an attack by British fighters and a forced landing to repair the damage, the aircraft arrived at its destination the next day.[15]

On 10 May another hospital ship, the Italian *Virgilio*, sailed from Korbons; on board was Hauptmann Reutter carrying secret reports for the *Heeresgruppe Afrika* War Diary. Shortly before 0900 hours the ship was stopped by three British destroyers; as she was boarded Reutter quickly destroyed all his orders and papers. Ordered back to Tunis at first, the ship was allowed to continue her passage to Naples later that afternoon.[16] A few others escaped, like the tank repair company from Panzerabteilung 501 pushed back to Cap Bon, which took a pioneer landing boat and made off for Sicily. Without water or provisions of any kind 18 men suffered terrible privations, eventually drifting ashore on Sardinia totally exhausted. Officially, only 632 officers and men were evacuated from Tunisia: about another 1,000 were rescued by the Royal Navy during the first two weeks in May from rowing and sailing boats, rubber dinghies, rafts, clinging to empty fuel drums and even driftwood.

Had there been any intention to fight to the death on the Cap Bon peninsula in order to cover a last-minute wholesale evacuation, 6th Armoured would have prevented it. Ordered to Soliman, Grombalia and Hammamet by Anderson, on 8 May the division approached Hammam Lif where a narrow defile bars the way at the only northern entrance to the Cap Bon peninsula and Djebel el Rorouf runs down in precipitous falls to within 1,000 yards of the sea.

The stopper in the neck of the bottle was the town itself through which 6th Armoured had to pass since the beach was intersected by a wadi, considered impassable for tanks. The town and heights around were infested by a hastily formed German outfit, Gruppe *Franz*, consisting of a Panzerjäger unit and artillery. They had tanks hull-down behind the breakwaters, over 30 guns of various calibres covering the approach, a strong armament of anti-tank guns in the town backed up by mortars and *Nebelwerfers*, machine-guns on the hills and heavier artillery on the summits.

A simple head-on attack was obviously suicidal unless the heights dominating the town could be captured. About midday the 2nd Lothians' armour on its approach was hit by anti-tank guns firing straight down the road. There was a pause while the Welsh Guards, nearly three miles back, were brought up to take the dominating narrow, crescent-shaped ridge of Djebel el Rorouf. That afternoon, as 3rd Grenadier Guards moved smoothly inland against light resistance, taking 400 Italians prisoner, 3rd Welsh Guards attacked towards the crest, 750 feet above. Watched by crowds of interested civilians on the road below, and supported by Lothians and Border Horse tanks, they were swept by mortar and machine-gun fire. Not until nightfall was the battalion able to take out a troublesome German mortar located in a nearby cement works and even then could do no more than consolidate its hard-earned gains having lost 24 killed and 50 wounded. But the fight had been knocked out of the defenders and when the Coldstream Guards came up they were able to clear the remainder of the ridge fairly easily.[17]

The way was now open for 26th Armoured Brigade to attack frontally. This was still a very formidable task. Arriving in time to see the last of the enemy cleared from Djebel el Rorouf, Horrocks witnessed the blunting of the first probing attack by Lothians' tanks on the morning of 9 May and, anxious about the speed of his thrust, ordered the town to be taken without further delay. Other 'red hats' visiting the Lothians' regimental HQ included Keightley, Roberts and Anderson himself: '… their reactions to Nebelwerfer fire were much as ours,' commented one tank driver, 'and they hastily jumped or crawled for cover under our tanks.'[18]

At 1500 hours three squadrons of Lothians' tanks went in again, one of them with infantry riding on their hulls. Deadly fire from well-sited 88s led to a series of bloody engagements as they fought their way into the town's six parallel streets. Once there, infantry cleaned up house by house, driving snipers out of one six-storey building in vicious hand-to-hand fighting. Meanwhile, two tank troops had forced their way across the beach, rounding the wadi where it falls into the sea by driving through the surf and running a gauntlet of anti-tank guns.

In immediate danger of becoming surrounded the Germans hastily withdrew towards Grombalia and the pursuit was on, across the base of the Cap Bon peninsula. The remarkable capture of Hammam Lif wrecked 22 Shermans but opened a gap through which the armour surged forward. This breakthrough amazed von Broich (of 10th Panzer) who thought it the most remarkable event of the campaign.[19] As dusk fell leading tanks were three miles short of Soliman from where 6th Armoured was to swing south-east and then south, towards Bou Ficha and Enfidaville.

On this same day (9 May), the Americans completed their destruction of the remains of Fifth Panzer Army in the north. Some 300 officers and men of the *Hermann Göring* Division still held out on Djebel Achkel but everywhere else resistance collapsed as von Vaerst's forces were sliced into smaller and smaller pieces. Generalmajor Josef Schmid had lost contact with his troops on the mountain several days previously; now he showed von Arnim a signal received from Göring himself ordering him back to Italy. The contempt in which von Arnim held the Reichsmarschall deepened. From the last heights under German control near Porto Farina, von Vaerst was still holding on with a couple of Tiger tanks and a handful of infantry. At 0930 hours he sent a final situation report to *Heeresgruppe Afrika*: 'Our armour and artillery have been destroyed; without ammunition and fuel; we shall fight to the last.'[20]

German units resisted until they had expended all their ammunition and then quietly surrendered. They had done their duty; indeed, some went beyond it, like the crews of the last seven tanks of 10th Panzer which dug in when completely out of fuel and carried on until they had no more shells and bullets. Then, like other units, they blew up their vehicles and destroyed their weapons.

At 1000 hours Generalmajor Fritz Krause and his aides arrived at Harmon's HQ to seek an end to the fighting. Harmon radioed Bradley, seeking advice, and was told bluntly: '... we have no terms. It must be unconditional surrender.' While Bradley ordered a halt to avoid unnecessary casualties, Krause, his face stone-hard and betraying no emotion, negotiated a surrender at noon on II Corps' front. Maurice Rose, Harmon's young chief of staff, was sent back with the German delegation carrying a set of explicit instructions. 'They are to collect their guns in ordnance piles and run their vehicles into pools. Tell them,' ordered Bradley, 'that if we catch them trying to destroy their stuff the armistice is off. We'll shoot the hell out of them.'[21]

Later that afternoon the generals and their staffs arrived in Mercedes-Benz staff cars. Formally clad in their crisp dress uniforms, stiffly they presented themselves to Harmon who, in utter contrast, was in his creased and sweat-stained working uniform. 'You would have thought the bastards were going to a wedding,' he said. Last to arrive was von Vaerst who signed off in a final signal at 1523 hours from his HQ to *OKW* and von Arnim.[22] II Corps had netted six German generals, von Vaerst, Krause, newly-promoted Borowietz, Bülowius, Kurt Bassenge and Georg Neuffer (commander, Luftwaffe 20th Flak Division). Refusing to have anything to do with them, Bradley had them locked in a German hospital overnight with an ordinary sack of K-rations and a picture of Adolf Hitler, hung on a wall by one of their aides. Next day, 'Chet' Hansen handed the generals over to the British authorities where they were saluted and invited to lunch. The only people not fed were Hansen and his driver. 'We were annoyed,' commented a justifiably aggrieved Bradley.[23]

In the meantime, tens of thousands of prisoners were entering the barbed wire cage, erected by American engineers north of the heavily used road west of Mateur, on the sandy plain stretching towards Djebel Achkel. Sitting atop his carrier, Lieutenant Royle, a 78th Division gunner, looked at the streams of Germans passing by, 'and thought that up to a few hours ago we had been trying to kill each other. And now it was all over.'[24]

The way in which the Germans suddenly caved in seemed to show that individuals lacked initiative in an unanticipated crisis; remove the immediate command structure, said some observers, and the body will rapidly fall apart. There was some truth in this; the speed and weight of the Allied attack broke the Axis positions and made prolonged resistance useless. But the prisoners were, wrote Major-General Penney, 'disciplined and not demoralised.'[25] Commanders of all units had their men well in hand until the close of fighting: as von Vaerst observed, 'The German soldier went into captivity with the sense of not having been defeated on the field of battle but of having been a victim of the collapse of the supply system.'[26] This was especially true of the remnants of Rommel's *Afrika Korps*.

Ralf Harding's 5th Brigade was still under determined attack in the hills west of Takrouna. During the night of 8/9 May, 23rd and 28th Battalions were hit by 88mm and 210mm guns firing haphazardly and *Nebelwerfers* loosing off four at a time. 'This was a puzzling affair,' commented Kippenberger, 'the Germans had never before attacked at night in our experience, and it was hard to understand their reasons for now doing so.'[27]

Freyberg had not expected any notable results from the probing attacks he had been ordered to mount between 4 and 9 May in which the New Zealand Division lost 16 killed and 36 wounded. There had been no signs of a general collapse and on the coastal sector Messe had appeared even to strengthen his defences. Nevertheless, that was where 56th Division – commanded by Major-General Graham who had taken over from Miles on 5 May – was ordered by X Corps to advance on the night of 10/11 May.

A battalion of Brigadier Birch's newly-arrived 167th Brigade had successfully attacked the *Young Fascist* outposts 24 hours earlier, whereupon the brigade was ordered to take the foothills on the left of the sector before being relieved by 6th New Zealand Brigade which was to attempt a decisive breakthrough. It fared just as badly as had its unfortunate sister brigade, the 169th, on the night of 28/29 April. Fierce opposition sent the 167th reeling back, losing 63 killed, 104 missing and 221 wounded. Messe's troops might be awaiting their inevitable fate but they could still sting, even though, like the *DAK*, they were completely immobilised through lack of fuel: 'In effect the Corps was waiting for the end and was mainly preoccupied in ensuring its long service in Africa be brought to an honourable conclusion,' Messe observed.[28]

The failure of 167th Brigade deterred X Corps from putting in Gentry's New Zealanders; they at least had the consolation of knowing that greatly increased shelling revealed an enemy who knew the end was in sight and was no longer trying to husband his dwindling stocks. With the end of the campaign imminent, however, there was, as Kippenberger noted, a certain amount of 'gun shyness' among his troops.

⊷◈⊶

Riding down from Cap Bon on 10–11 May, 6th Armoured was held up at the white-walled Arab town of Soliman by a screen of anti-tank guns and so, leaving a force to contain it until 4th Infantry Division arrived, Keightley turned south-east towards Grombalia. An advanced patrol of the Rifle Brigade reported little resistance while another from the Derbyshire Yeomanry, travelling fast beyond Soliman, surprised a German mess at dinner. 'Dinner excellent, champagne sweet' they signalled to division. 'German now sampling bully-beef.'[29]

Still holding on 11 May, *Armeegruppe von Arnim* and *Armeegruppe Messe* were hastily formed and within hours lost touch as Mathenet's Division *du Maroc* destroyed much of what was left of 21st Panzer. Le Coulteux's armoured group swept beyond Djebel Zaghouan reaching Sainte Marie du Zit that evening and Boissau's Division *d'Oran* moved forward parallel with Bateman's 5th Brigade in the hills north of Zaghouan. Sandwiched between French and Indian troops, Germans began to surrender in droves, great pillars of smoke arising from their burning dumps and transport. Throughout the night of 11/12 May, units reported to von Arnim's HQ for the last time: 'Ammunition used up, tanks and artillery pieces destroyed.' Fighting patrols from 1/9th Gurkhas and 4/6th Rajputana Rifles brought in 2,000 POWs and next morning (12 May) one of the latter's carrier patrols accepted the surrender of the entire Italian *Superga* Division. Not to be outdone, even company cooks of 1/4th Essex seized transport and brought in their own prisoners.

By then 6th Armoured had reached the last remaining stronghold of enemy resistance, Bou Ficha, immediately north of Enfidaville, where 90th Light was dug-in. Freyberg had called on von Sponeck to surrender on the 10th, repeating his demand early next day, but received no answer. At about 1000 hours 26th Armoured Brigade came into radio contact with the wearied leading units of 56th

Infantry Division, three miles to the south, thus menacing 90th Light from both sides. Shells from German 210mm guns on the heights kept leading elements of 26th Armoured Brigade at bay and some vehicles were lost to accurate anti-tank fire. As the defenders began deliberately using up their ammunition there was much indiscriminate firing and this furious barrage of artillery, anti-tank, machine-gun and small arms fire from the heights continued with renewed ferocity on the morning of 12 May, 'a perfectly crazy day', thought Kippenberger. At about 1330 hours concentrated artillery of 6th Armoured, joined by the combined fire of 144 guns of the New Zealand Division, ranged the Germans' HQ. Bou Ficha disappeared under a great cloud of dust and smoke as three waves of Bostons pattern-bombed the enemy's positions; soon after, the tanks advanced.

From every gun-site, slit trench and dugout came a frantic waving of white flags. Down from the hills, late in the afternoon, came von Sponeck's men, white faced and shocked by the pulverizing display of Allied power. Keightley received von Sponeck's capitulation and sent him on to Freyberg, who had come forward through 56th Infantry Division, to whom he repeated his unconditional surrender. Going out next day with Freyberg and Graham to a gap in a minefield on the 56th's front, Brigadier Lyne came across a, 'nasty scene when some Italians, apparently put off by the sight of so many senior officers, tried to take a short cut through their own minefield and got blown up. Some of the British spectators were also wounded.'[30]

In orders issued on 12 May, Anderson demanded complete maps of minefields before surrenders were accepted and enemy units were ordered not to destroy militarily valuable material. The men of 6th Armoured were, however, disappointed to find that troops of 90th Light had systematically smashed all their highly-prized binoculars and anything else which might have been taken for souvenirs.

Away in the hills to the north of Sainte Marie du Zit, Cramer and von Arnim prepared to close down their operations. At 0040 hours on the 12th, Cramer radioed his last defiant message to the *OKW*: 'Ammunition shot off. Arms and equipment destroyed. In accordance with orders received *DAK* has fought itself to the condition where it can fight no more. The *Deutsche Afrika Korps* must rise again. *Heia Safari*.'[31]

Later the same day, von Arnim sent off his last report to *OKW* and a few private signals from staff to their families at home. Then all communications with the outside world were severed as radio installations were destroyed together with Rommel's caravan, which von Arnim set on fire with his own hand, having vowed that no enemy would ever lay claim to it. Slowly, the sounds of battle from the surrounding heights ebbed away, 'as if', wrote von Arnim, 'nature itself was holding its breath.' By this time troops of Lieutenant-Colonel Glennie's 1st Royal Sussex had worked their way onto the heights around von Arnim's HQ. Knowing a reconnaissance unit was nearing his position, von Arnim arranged for three officers to carry a letter to Glennie's HQ offering his surrender together with that of his staff and Hans Cramer. The delegation was headed by, 'a small, bullet-headed, fair-haired, closely cropped German colonel,'[32] Oberst Nolte, *Stabschef* (chief of staff) of *DAK*.

While Tuker prepared for formal negotiations with Nolte, 1/2nd Gurkhas intervened. Mopping up south of Sainte Marie du Zit, Lieutenant-Colonel Showers climbed a ridge to reconnoitre his position when he spotted a German staff car, parked in a nearby hollow, with an officer waving a white flag beside it. Clambering down, he found himself in von Arnim's HQ where 1,000 Germans had been drawn up on parade. He was told that Nolte had already left to arrange a surrender and so, accompanied by an English-speaking German officer, Showers returned to brigade HQ. On the way, he met Glennie who was about to post guards around the camp. Hearing what had happened, Tuker contacted Allfrey and the two generals with Nolte, interpreters, the intrepid Showers and an escort, arrived at von Arnim's HQ, now guarded by men of the 1st Royal Sussex.

Both von Arnim and Cramer had turned out in their dress uniforms, strung about with decorations and Iron Crosses. 'They gave an impression of green, scarlet and gold,' remarked Tuker. He was wearing a pair of much-worn drill trousers, a threadbare battledress jacket without medal ribbons and the usual reverse-hide desert boots; Allfrey was equally plainly dressed and Showers, 'an extremely dirty officer and most unshaven', completed the scene. Walking straight past von Arnim's proffered handshake, Tuker led the way to his caravan where negotiations began.[33] From the start, von Arnim was difficult; he could not surrender his units because contact with them had been destroyed and refused to do so even when offered an Allied radio link. At this, Tuker threatened to move his division and attack 90th Light (which had not, at that time, surrendered) from the rear. Their lives, he told von Arnim bluntly, were on his head.

At this von Arnim agreed to surrender his own staff and that of Cramer, petulantly threw his revolver on the table with a clatter, followed by his penknife. In the meantime, his staff were lining up outside to say goodbye. 'Arnim was very red in the face and extremely peevish on the whole,' noted Tuker, 'while Kram [Cramer] was most ingratiating, talked a little English and tried to be friendly.' Guarded by a Gurkha officer and Royal Sussex detachment, von Arnim and Cramer were driven through the lines of their saluting troops to meet Alexander – inadvertently making their way through one of their own minefields – von Arnim standing up, gesticulating angrily at his driver. 'I... was cold and brusque at this meeting,' observed Tuker. 'As a plain soldier and no diplomat, I could not in those circumstances have brought myself to be a whit more cordial to the German commanders.'[34]

Alexander, however, was his usual polished self at 18th Army HQ, near Le Kef, where von Arnim arrived on 13 May, hospitably offering him supper and a tent for the night. Major-General Miller thought the German, 'looked a decent sort of man. He said they never had any intention of withdrawal.'[35] Other than that the interview was not very productive observed an HQ intelligence officer, David Hunt, and von Arnim appeared bewildered by the suddenness of the collapse. Eisenhower absolutely refused to meet him or receive his sword in surrender.[36]

Meanwhile, Bradley and his lieutenants dealt brusquely with remnants of the *Hermann Göring* Division still clinging to Djebel Achkel. 'Monk' Dickson was instructed, on 11 May, to see that their resistance was brought to a speedy conclusion and ordered von Vaerst to scribble a note to whomever was now in charge of the division. Delivered under a flag of truce, this summoned them – and the rest of Fifth Panzer Army – to lay down their arms. Back came the American officer and an Oberleutnant, his wounded arm in a sling. Before surrendering the Germans wanted to verify the message from von Vaerst. 'Tell him to go to hell,' said the battalion commander whose men surrounded the hill. Then the division would surrender, replied the Oberleutnant, if they could receive a document verifying that they were the last to lay down their arms on this front. 'Brother,' was the blunt response, 'either you'll come down right now and cut out this monkey business or we'll carve that certificate on your headstone.' A rapid attack killed some of the defenders and word soon got around. From the heights appeared several hundred men claiming unconditional surrender.[37]

This left only Generale di Armata Messe, commanding the greatly weakened *Young Fascist*, *Trieste* and 164th Light Divisions, in touch with the *OKW* and *Comando Supremo*. On the morning of 12 May Messe received permission from Mussolini to negotiate an 'honourable surrender' and sent a message at about 1300 hours to Eighth Army offering to cease hostilities. This was picked up by the New Zealanders and X Corps alerted. At 2030 hours Freyberg sent this uncompromising reply: 'Hostilities will not cease until all troops lay down their arms and surrender to the nearest Allied unit.'[38]

Late in the evening New Zealand signals picked up another message from Maresciallo d'Italia Messe – he had been promoted field marshal that day – whose representatives had left to meet those of X Corps. Travelling by a difficult route, General Mancinelli, Oberst Markert and Major Boscardi, arrived at Freyberg's HQ at 0830 hours on the 13th. There they attempted to open negotiations but were told that only an unconditional surrender would be accepted; failing that hostilities would resume soon after noon. Lacking the necessary authority to accept these terms, Mancinelli returned with a British officer to Messe's HQ where a message had been received from Freyberg of what had taken place. At 1220 hours Messe issued orders for the surrender of all his German and Italian troops and, later in the day, together with von Liebenstein, surrendered in person to Freyberg.

On low ground between the sea and positions occupied by 90th Light, Ronald Lewin had seen the white flags of surrender go up, 'first in small clusters, turning into larger groups as platoons merged with companies. White everywhere, as if butterflies were dancing over the hills.'[39]

'The Hun has jagged in,' reported Private Crimp. Alexander sent an altogether more grandiose message on Thursday, 13 May, to Winston Churchill who was in Washington for the Trident Conference: 'Sir, it is my duty to report that the Tunisian campaign is over. All enemy resistance has ceased. We are masters of the North African shores.'[40]

In Berlin next day, Goebbels confided to his diary: 'In Tunis[ia] the fight is ended. I write this with a heavy heart. I simply cannot read the exaggerated Anglo-American accounts. They are full of insults to our soldiers, who fought with legendary heroism to their last round of ammunition.'[41]

For once, the master of lies was telling something like the unvarnished truth.

Notes to Chapter 18

[1] 68th Armored Field Artillery Battalion, History (TS), Diary entry for 10 May 1943; 1st Armored Division WWII Survey, Box 1. USAMHI.

[2] Tuker's War Diary, entry for 15 May 1943.

[3] Quoted by Verney, *The Desert Rats*, pp. 158–9.

[4] Lieutenant-General Sir Archibald Nye to Eisenhower, 12 May 1943; AFHQ Cable Log, Bedell Smith Papers, Box 3.

[5] Quoted by Sullivan, *Thresholds of Peace*, p. 6.

[6] Bradley, *A Soldier's Story*, p. 93; Bradley Commentary, Hansen Papers.

[7] Clifford, *Three Against Rommel*, p. 406.

[8] Deakin, *The Brutal Friendship*, pp. 281–2.

[9] *Oberquartiermeister i.G.* Brand, 7 May 1943; *Kriegstagebuch der Heeresgruppe Afrika – O.Qu.*, 7–8 May 1943; RH19-VIII/244. BA-HA.

[10] Anon., *To Bizerte with the II Corps*, p. 48.

[11] Master Sergeant T. Riggs, 'Notes on Campaign', 25 June 1943; Robinett Papers, Box 4. Library of Congress.

[12] *Jordan's Tunis Diary*, p. 255, entry for 7 May 1943. The same point was made at the time by other war correspondents including John D'Arcy Dawson and A.B. Austin.

[13] Macmillan, *War Diaries*, p. 101, 'Record of Conversation, 1 June 1943'. Late in June, de Gaulle visited Tunis in a 'brief but spectacular' procession, receiving an ecstatic welcome. Lieutenant M.W. Bowley, 'A Junior officer in the Mediterranean Theatre', TS Memoir. IWM 85/9/1.

[14] Lieutenant-Commander P.R. Hay, Journal, entry for 8 May 1943. IWM 83/13/1.

[15] W. Jüttner, *Die Oase*, No. 5, May 1981, p. 12.

[16] *Kriegstagebuch der Heeresgruppe Afrika – O.Qu.*, 7–8 May 1943.

[17] Ellis, *Welsh Guards at War*, pp. 123–8.

[18] Antonio, *Driver Advance!*, p. 49.

[19] D'Arcy Dawson, *Tunisian Battle*, pp. 243–4.

[20] Quoted by Howe, *Northwest Africa*, p. 662.

[21] Bradley, *A Soldier's Story*, p. 97.

[22] 'Unterlagen und Gerät vernichtet. Auf Wiedersehen, es lebe Grossdeutschland und sein Führer'; Schramm, *Kriegstagebuch*, Vol. V, p. 452, entry for 9 May 1943.

[23] Bradley Commentary. Hansen Papers.

[24] Lieutenant Royle, Memoir.

[25] Penney Diary, entry for 10 May 1943.

[26] Von Vaerst, 'Operations of the Fifth Panzer Army', p. 25

[27] Kippenberger, *Infantry Brigadier*, p. 319.

[28] Quoted by Playfair, *Destruction of Axis Forces*, p. 454.

[29] D'Arcy Dawson, *Tunisian Battle*, p. 244.

[30] Lyne, 'Autobiography'.

[31] Schramm, *Kriegstagebuch*, V, p. 465, entry for 12 May 1943.

[32] Tuker, 'The Taking of General Oberst von Arnim and General Kram' [Cramer, Cmdr. DAK], TS Account, 22 November 1946. Tuker Papers, 71/21/3.

[33] Tuker later claimed von Arnim's caravan on behalf of 4th Indian Division. It was subsequently displayed in various parts of India in aid of military charities. See Stevens, *Fourth Indian Division*, ftn. p. 255.

[34] Tuker, *Approach to Battle*, p. 378.

[35] Miller Diary, entry for 13 May 1943. Brigadier Strong saw von Arnim in a different light, finding him, 'a typical overbearing Prussian, with little apparent understanding of the position in which he found himself', and still believing Germany would win the war. Strong, *Intelligence at the Top*, p. 91.

[36] Eisenhower refused to see any of his defeated foes until the end of the war; see *Crusade in Europe*, pp. 172–4.

[37] Bradley, *A Soldier's Story*, p. 99; 'Surrender of *Hermann Göring* Division', Commentary, Hansen Papers.

[38] Quoted by Playfair, p. 458.

[39] Lewin, *Life and Death of the Afrika Korps*, p. 248.

[40] Alexander to Churchill, 13 May 1943. Alexander Papers.

[41] Lochner ed., *The Goebbels Diaries*, p. 297; entry for 14 May 1943.

Epilogue

'Altogether I feel rather stupidly and unreasonably depressed... I think it is the reaction, more than anything, and the loss of so many people one has known and liked... War is horrid, messy, bloody.'

Officer of the Royal Fusiliers (City of London Regiment), May 1943.[1]

'Some did not complete the show and some will never see their homes again but the best of the people I have known in the service have been in the desert.'

Flight Lieutenant E. Chadwick, RAF, in a letter home, 24 May 1943.[2]

'Cut any stress on good morale of German POWs or troops which would support enemy propaganda of gallant troops who were overwhelmed or accepted inevitable,' read a message from the British Chiefs of Staff to Eisenhower's HQ on 13 May 1943.[3] This was, however, precisely what had happened.

Flowing back from Cap Bon towards Tunis and Bizerte and out of the mountains around Enfidaville, thousands upon thousands of troops made their way into captivity, German officers driving themselves in blunt-nosed open Volkswagen staff cars and a few Mercedes-Benz, Italians in Toppolino Fiats and Lancias, carrying great mounds of personal kit, very few of them accompanied by guards. Two trains passed each other, prisoners riding in one lot of trucks and British Tommies in the other: 'British Army no good,' called out a German soldier. A Tommy shouted back, 'Who put you in the f·····g cattle truck?'[4]

Major-General Strong admitted that the total number of prisoners taken, 'far exceeded our estimates', and there was much difficulty in finding accommodation for them.[5] Allied intelligence thought provision would have to be made for 150,000 – failing to take into account the number of extra administrative troops and civil and military officials in Tripolitania who had nothing to do with the final battle but headed back into the last bridgehead waiting to be picked up.[6] The Italians were put to work under fixed bayonets: 'Very disorderly and dirty in their habits,' recorded Lieutenant-Colonel Shirley Smith, 'unlike the Germans.'[7] In the open barbed-wire enclosure at Le Bardo, a suburb of Tunis, the Germans methodically buttoned together their groundsheets to provide tent-like shelters but had to be kept in separate compounds from the Italians because of mutual ill-feeling. The latter were, observed Sergeant Danger, allowed to roam around at will, while the Germans remained closely guarded.[8]

Tragedy was only narrowly averted in one US compound when the grass was accidentally set alight, but it was the French who demonstrated least concern for the welfare of their prisoners. Major-General Penney saw them ill-fed and, contrary to the Geneva Convention, forced to clear minefields. At Grombalia, where a huge compound had been established, the entire band of 10th Panzer turned up carrying their instruments. They were put on parole and played for battalions of Evelegh's 78th Division. Food was not a problem after the first massive influx of POWs because the enemy's ration dumps, unlike his fuel and ammunition stores, were well stocked. The civilian population in towns, however, had little to eat and the Allies had to ship in sufficient supplies to prevent outright starvation.

In due course most of the prisoners were sent to Britain, America and Canada, roughly a quarter of a million of them, which is about the closest one can get to any final reckoning.[9] Messe and his staff had two floors at their disposal in the high security quarters of the White House, at Wilton Park in south Buckinghamshire. They enjoyed six months' croquet and tennis with two Italian admirals until the Italian capitulation when they were sent home to help the Allied cause. Messe became Army Chief of Staff in Marshal Badoglio's government, surviving the change to Ivanoe Bonomi in 1944 but losing his post the following year.

The German generals were held in closer detention not far away, at Cockfosters, where they joined Generalleutnant Ludwig Crüwell and General-leutnant Wilhelm Ritter von Thoma, captured earlier in the desert war.[10] Their rooms were bugged and von Arnim made little attempt to hide his outrage at never having received a clear plan of operations in Tunisia, at the contradictory orders issued by both German and Italian High Commands, and the failure of promised supplies.

For the victors there were the usual plaudits. Only in First Army were there any serious misgivings. In a less than frank letter, Eisenhower thanked Anderson on 10 May for his 'perfect team play.' Anderson was quick to reply, not through Alexander as propriety dictated, but in a personal letter two days later. 'I don't know what our future relations will be after this show is cleaned up...,' wrote Anderson, 'but I do hope it will not mean a complete severance of our paths, and that I may still have a close relationship in one form or another with you and the US Army.' Not long after he wrote again, this time in a spirit of misgiving and confusion: 'As First Army seems to be disappearing I would appreciate being able to help my bewildered Commanders and men. Please send a senior officer urgently to help throw light on the darkness. Of course I will do all I can to help in a spirit of utmost co-operation if only some information is vouchsafed me.'[11] Eisenhower merely passed the letter on to his staff. First Army was dying, dismembered and despatched to other formations, its only job to oversee the reorganization of Allied control in Tunisia into four subordinate sectors along the coast as the French assumed responsibility for internal security.

On 22 May de Gaulle arrived at Algiers to open negotiations with Giraud. After much hard bargaining a French Committee of National Liberation was formed and recognised by the US, British and Russians as the *de facto* French government. Many difficulties remained, which were not resolved by the complicated system of dual control which was set up. Within a year, however, de Gaulle's authority was complete.

Allied morale plummeted once the Tunisian campaign was over, especially among troops who thought they would be going home after the fighting. This affected all units apart from the New Zealand Division where 6,000 of those with the longest service were to return on furlough. Eighth Army men who had fought throughout the desert campaign were scheduled for Husky and there was much discontent when it was realized there was to be no home leave.

Many American troops were livid at news of POWs being shipped to the United States while they had no chance of seeing home. Rarely disciplined by Allen and Roosevelt, men of the Big Red One left their mark in rioting and brawling all the way from Arzeu. 'We all play by the same ground rules,' Bradley told Allen, 'whatever the patch we wear on our sleeve.' This had no discernible effect and Allen was ordered to get his troops out of Oran, back to their dreary tented bivouacs and strenuous training. Part of the problem had been caused by a complete lack of imagination on the part of the US Army authorities who had rushed the division back to such miserable conditions.

Harmon, a much stricter disciplinarian, explained the need for regulations to 1st Armored and reported that, after the first rush of excitement had died away, his men were, 'settling down to soldiering in a good fashion. Our number of disciplinary cases in town', he added, 'has dropped from around 50 to 70 a day to an average of about 10 and some days [we] only have one or two.'[12] Manton Eddy's 9th Infantry fetched up at Magenta, dusty, fly-ridden and sun-baked, 50 miles south of Sidi-bel-Abbes, the French Foreign Legion HQ. Before going into bivouac, however, an advance camp on the water's edge was occupied at Nemours in French Morocco, where officers and men swam and filled themselves on decent rations and a truckload of beer, exchanged in an enterprising transaction with a merchantman for a load of souvenirs.

Similar efforts were made by the British authorities to keep the troops occupied. Passes were issued for First Army men to visit Tunis, though there was little to see until Basil Dean arrived on 7 May to begin organising an ENSA show, John Berryman's 'Laughter for Tonight.' The company flew in from Gibraltar and performed to packed audiences, first at Bougie and then at the Théâtre Municipal, fronting one side of the main square in Tunis, where Anderson strode on to the stage and declared open, amidst tumultuous cheers, the first garrison theatre in North Africa.[13] Otherwise, the city offered little apart from rough local wine:

'Tunis itself is rather marred by the drunkenness of British and American soldiers,' noted the Rev. Gough Quinn of the Coldstream Guards. 'It was a disappointing sight and I fear must do us harm.'[14] Captain Edney of 131st Brigade witnessed bitter clashes between men of the First and Eighth Armies, a result of widespread ill-feeling between them.

At Gueriat el Atach tragedy struck suddenly on 26 May when a party visiting Longstop, to see what lessons might be drawn, touched off an anti-personnel mine. Eight were killed; Brigadier Maxwell and Lieutenant-Colonel Robertson, CO 7th Battalion, the Suffolk Regiment, were badly injured.[15]

Most men spent their time sunbathing on areas of beach specially cleared of mines and swimming in the translucent, warm sea. Easing down, slackening off, was something which all who had been in the front-line needed, as the recently promoted Captain Royle made clear in a letter home on 11 May: 'Looking back on the last six months it seems as if one has been holding one's breath and you have just let it go for the first time. What I mean is I can now completely relax whereas before you always knew that a shell might come over and were always on the look out for one. It has been a hell of a strain on us and some of the men have cracked up. I am afraid my nerves are in a rather poor state as if an explosion takes place anywhere near me I jump feet in the air and go cold all over! I suppose it's only natural as I have had a good bit of shit flung at me since I became a Captain but a few weeks rest will see me O.K. again.'[16] Thirty years later, however, Royle admitted he was still badly affected by any loud or sudden noise. Another officer, grievously distressed at the loss of a corporal in his platoon while carrying out a hurried order wrote: 'I dare not trust myself to feel his death at the time, but my rage and grief at it fermented in the bottling up and were not purged for years after the war.'[17]

Another effect on men who found themselves thousands of miles from home was a dulling of the conventions that ruled their civilian lives. Noticeable was an indifference, quickly acquired, to sudden death. 'A very young private lounged up to our car and started chatting,' recorded an American war artist, George Biddle, who was sketching at Bizerte: 'He... talked of the fighting on [Hill] 609. He said: "The Jerries are good mountain fighters. They dig in and you can't dig 'em out. But once you get 'em on the plain and show 'em the bayonet they stick up their hands and come right to you. They got my buddy just two weeks back. I seen four or five of 'em stick up their hands but I give it to 'em. I said: 'Fuck you, you god damn bloody Germans'; and I give it to the bastards, bam, bam, bam."'[18]

At about the same time, Captain Royle was writing home: 'I never thought I would see men blown to pieces and eat food with dead lying a few feet away unburied, but one took it as a matter of course. Its awful how callous one becomes but it's the only way.'[19] Like many others he found a hard emotional shell was essential to survive the heartrending loss of so many good comrades. Victory in the Tunisian campaign was purchased with men's lives, 10,290 of them, with a further 21,363 missing and 38,688 wounded – in total 70,341 Allied casualties.

The dead were scattered in groups, nearest to where they fell. Sentries were mounted to shoot packs of marauding dogs and drive off Arabs who dug up the bodies. To discourage grave-robbers, caps were removed from hand-grenades before they were placed carefully in the pockets of the dead; anyone attempting to disinter a corpse received the full effect.[20] Of German and Italian troops wounded, missing or killed there were less exact figures. Later assessments by German and Italian authorities give their dead as 8,563 and 3,727 respectively, to whom have to be added the missing and those wounded and evacuated before the surrender. All that can safely be said is that Axis losses were much higher than those of the Allies.

Eisenhower hated the idea of a vainglorious parade, preferring a combination of celebration and commemoration of those who had sacrificed their lives. Nevertheless, 'it turned out to be just a Victory Parade',[21] noted Butcher, held under a sweltering sun through the streets of Tunis on 20 May. Roars of cheers and applause greeted the Zouaves, Tirailleurs, Moroccans, Algerians and Foreign Legionaries, led by a detachment of Spahis in red cloaks with drawn swords, astride their white horses. There followed Goums in their burnouses, carrying long-barrelled desert rifles and murderous knives in their belts. A French detachment led by Koeltz, 'poor in physique and general appearance', still impressed Macmillan because, 'one felt it a sort of resurrection of France, and because one realised what a brave show they had put up all these months with such poor equipment and material.'[22]

Two American regiments followed, superbly turned out in finest quality uniforms and equipment, led by a brass band. Yet many of them still looked like raw recruits: besides, it was impossible to make a dramatic impact while marching in the US Army's standard rubber soled boots. What was to come, therefore, was even more effective.

In the distance was heard the faint sound of pipes then, marching in slow time, came the massed pipers of the Scots and Grenadier Guards and such Highland Regiments as were available. To *Flowers of the Forest* they marched and counter-marched with perfect precision; there then followed a long procession of British units, the divisional generals, brigadiers, colonels leading their formations, stepping out with representatives of the RAF and Leclerc's men (who had refused to march with the French). Apart from the Highland pipers and a few detachments from the 11th Hussars, Derbyshire Yeomanry and Gurkhas, the entire British march-past was First Army; the Eighth was considered to have had its own affair at Tripoli in February.

At Mostagenem, II Corps HQ was disbanding, as was Alexander's 18th Army Group HQ. Major-General Penney thought it was, 'like the end of term break up at School – clearing up all day and saying Goodbye to those who were not joining Force 141, the planning HQ for HUSKY.'[23]

First Army was already dead and gone. 'Now that the break up of First Army is complete and General George Clark assumes command of all troops in Tunisia...

it is obvious that I cannot continue here without any responsibilities or occupation,' Anderson wrote plaintively to Eisenhower at the end of May. Early next month he was again complaining that he had received no orders: 'I wrote to the CIGS [Brooke], who promised to let me know soon after he gets home what I am to do, so I hope it won't be long before I get some definite offers.'[24] Despite polite letters of praise to Anderson, which went on well after the end of the war, it was obvious that Eisenhower was quite ruthless in casting off someone without the driving aggressiveness of Patton nor the limitless self-confidence of Montgomery.

By Anderson's own admission it was his quiet, withdrawn personality which prevented him from making a greater mark. Writing to Eisenhower in 1948 he confessed that, 'I have always had to fight against a queer sort of inhibition, or shyness, which prevents me coming out of my shell except with very intimate friends or a few naturally sympathetic acquaintances. Often I would like to expand, but find it very difficult; a queer thing human nature.'[25]

When neither Roosevelt nor Churchill could spare their closest military advisers, Marshall and Brooke, Eisenhower became the compromise choice for Husky and later his known administrative and conciliatory skills marked him out as Supreme Allied Commander for Northwest Europe. 'With that tremendous personality of his he could say "no" and make you feel better about it than a lot of people who said "yes",' remarked Ira Eaker.[26] What threatened to undermine Eisenhower's efforts was the, 'back-biting and trivial, parochial, intramural competition that was going on,' said a leading USAAF commander Brigadier-General Quesada, which placed a question mark over how far AFHQ at Algiers really operated as a genuinely coherent Allied command.[27] But the fact that it did not fall apart was undoubtedly due to Eisenhower's leadership.

Judged by its original objectives, the Allied campaign in Tunisia was a failure. Eisenhower's early expectations were to be in Tunis by Christmas 1942, and trap Rommel in Libya. Due to a combination of Allied mistakes and determined German resistance, neither proved possible. Had the proportion of troops assigned to capture and hold harbours and bases in the Torch invasion forces been reduced, particularly the Algiers contingent, in favour of a more mobile strike force, the initial move eastwards on 10 November might have proceeded with greater dash than it did.

Anderson was not best suited to direct this, nor to mollifying the Americans who remained prickly when told by British officers – often deliberately or unintentionally supercilious – how to do their job. A potent source of trouble, never quite resolved, was the proper application of airpower and the campaign in Sicily would reveal quite conclusively that channels of control, basic allegiance and differences in national aims could still cause problems.

As it was, the failure to wind up the North African campaign until some months later than Eisenhower expected led to unforeseen advantages. By pouring scarce resources into Tunisia in order to keep Italy in the war, Hitler was forced to divert them away from the hard-pressed Eastern Front and ensured that in the end the Allies captured far more men and *matériel*.[28] This was not what the Allies had thought would happen though much virtue was made out of necessity at the time as if it had been planned that way.

Had two very big 'ifs' been resolved – that is, had Tunis been taken within six weeks of the TORCH landings and Montgomery been able to cut off and destroy the best part of the retreating German and Italian armies – it is possible, as Eisenhower suggested, that the Italian mainland might have been attacked in early summer 1943 and units firmly established in the Po Valley far to the north before the onset of winter. The timing of the Tunisian campaign was always under severe pressure because of the contingency of other plans waiting upon it; as it turned out, the Allies kept to their revised schedule in North Africa with just two days to spare.

In the process, Americans became battle-hardened and sorted out some of the worst of their training problems. Pitted against them had been German troops, especially the *Afrika Korps*, whom Bradley considered the best fighters they met in the whole war, 'young men, early twenties, seasoned veterans... good physical condition. Never knew they were beaten.' As late as August 1943 some were still being captured, coming down out of the hills, having refused to give in until completely out of food and ammunition.[29]

Now the fighting was over the peoples of Tunisia were returning to their homes, laden with possessions. Soon the victorious troops would have to give up looted treasures, as one harassed postal officer reported: 'Individuals insisted upon sending captured enemy material home and consequently base censor returned numerous packages containing hand grenades, helmets, bayonets and even rifles.'[30]

In Britain the bells pealed out again for the Tunisian victory, the second time inside six months that a beleaguered people heard good news. In America people had, as Bradley said, 'concrete evidence that things were beginning to pay off. Here was a victory we could see and recognize. [It] rubbed the taste of Kasserine out of the mouths of our people.'[31] But the price paid for that victory lay heavily on mourning families and was witnessed at first hand by the concentration and grave registration units that undertook the grim task of gathering the dead into eight large cemeteries on ground later donated in perpetuity by the post-war Tunisian government.

Returning briefly to Tunisia early in 1944, Patton remarked: 'It is strange how completely the big battlefields have been cleared up, particularly the big dump near Tébessa and the dump at El Guettar. There is absolutely no sign they ever existed.'[32] Fearful that Arab nationalists might repair derelict weapons and vehicles and turn upon them, the French authorities had carefully swept most of the battle areas clean of debris.

In February 1949, when Leese visited British cemeteries, they had no stone headstones or centre cross. Though well-weeded they were bare of grass or trees because no irrigation had been laid on. In Tunis church there were many memorials and on the site of all the main battles a simple column about ten feet high had been erected, bearing a plaque commemorating the men who fought there – at Wadi Akarit, Mareth, Takrouna, Wadi Zigzaou (where destroyed Valentine tanks had been left as rusting memorials) and at El Hamma. On the heights of El Rhorab, looking out through the Fondouk Gap, and on the rocky crest overlooking Hammam Lif two stones were raised, bearing the names of those who fell in the battle, The Welsh Guards' Regimental crest and the motto, *Cymru am byth* – 'Wales for ever.' On Bou Aoukaz a white marble cross bore the inscription: 'To the Memory of the Officers, W.O.s, N.C.O.s and Guardsmen of the 1st Battalion, Irish Guards, who died on and around this hill April 27th–30th, 1943. *Quis separabit?*'

Near Carthage the Americans and French had laid out cemeteries for their dead while the Free French had been interred together at Takrouna, Eighth Army men at Enfidaville and the Germans on a hill near Hammam Lif. Only the Italians reclaimed their fallen for burial in their native soil. On pergolas flanking the graves in the British cemetery near Medjez were carved the names of 1,956 men who had no known resting place, in Keith Douglas's words, 'the dead men whom the wind powders till they are like dolls'.

'My husband was very precious to me. It was a terrible shock to hear of his death; a most bitter blow,' wrote the widow of a soldier, killed in action.[33] There, too, was the true cost of victory.

Notes to Epilogue

[1] Quoted by Parkinson, *Always a Fusilier*, p. 126.

[2] Chadwick Papers.

[3] 'Troopers' to 'Freedom', 13 May 1943; AFHQ Cable Log.

[4] Shirley Smith Diary, entry for 14 May 1943

[5] Strong, *Intelligence at the Top*, p. 91.

[6] Hunt, *A Don at War*, p. 182. AFHQ Intelligence estimated 150,000 not 200,000 as Hunt later reported and commented: 'it is evident that the enemy's supply and administrative services were more elaborate and numerous than had been calculated.' AFHQ G.2 Weekly Summary – Intelligence 15 May 1943; II Corps, Box 3157; World War II, Operations Reports, USNA 202-2.6.

[7] Shirley Smith Diary, entries for 15 and 22 May 1943.

[8] Sergeant E.P. Danger Diary, entry for 11 May 1943; IWM 82/37/1.

[9] No final tally was ever made of those who surrendered in Tunisia. Unwounded prisoners in Allied hands on 25 May numbered 238,243; Howe, in his US Official History, mentions 275,000 and 18th Army Group estimated 244,500 prisoners taken between 20 March and 13 May.

[10] Sullivan, *Thresholds of Peace*, pp. 221–3.

[11] Anderson to Eisenhower, 12 and 17 May 1943. Eisenhower Papers, Box 5. Anderson was not told of the fate of First Army until the very morning of official celebrations in Tunis.

[12] Harmon to Clark, 25 June 1943 in response to letter from Clark, 20 June 1943; 'Correspondence (Personal (CG)) (April December 1943)', Harmon Papers.

[13] Dean, *The Theatre at War*, p. 351. Dean was the Founder and Director of ENSA – the Entertainments National Service Association.

[14] Quinn Diary, entry for 12 May 1943.

[15] Nicholson, *The Suffolk Regiment 1928 to 1946*, p. 274.

[16] Royle, letter home 11 May 1943. Memoir.

[17] Second-Lieutenant John Clark (6th Lincolns), 'Battle Honour in Tunisia', in Moynihan, ed., *People at War*.

[18] George Biddle Diary, 11 April – 19 November 1943; Biddle Papers, Box 2. See also his *Artist at War*, which contains some of his diary comments but omits significant material that reflects adversely on American troops. The passage quoted is only to be read in the original manuscript diary.

[19] Royle, Memoir.

[20] Biddle Diary, entry for 17 May 1943. Burial was normally carried out within 48 hours after a man had been killed and isolated burials removed to slightly larger cemeteries during lulls in the fighting.

[21] Butcher, *Three Years with Eisenhower*, p. 263.

[22] Macmillan, *War Diaries*, p. 89, entry for 20 May 1943.

[23] Penney Diary, entry for 15 May 1943.

[24] Anderson to Eisenhower, 4 June 1943. Eisenhower Papers, Box 5.

[25] Anderson to Eisenhower, 23 December 1948. Eisenhower Papers, Box 5.

[26] Ira C. Eaker, interviewed by Lieutenant-Colonel Joe B. Green, April 1972; MHRC.

[27] Elwood R. Quesada (Deputy Commander, North West African Coastal Air Force Command) interviewed by Lieutenant-Colonel Steve Long and Lieutenant-Colonel Ralph Stephenson, 12/13 May 1975; MHRC.

[28] Brigadier-General Davis to James C. Cook (Office of Secretary of War, Washington), 28 May 1943. Thomas Jefferson Davis Papers, Box 1. Eisenhower Library. But see Ellis who cautions against simplistic comparisons of German losses at Stalingrad and 'Tunisgrad' in his *Brute Force*, p. 306.

[29] Harmon, 'Report on Combat Experience and Battle Lessons for Training Purposes', 13 June 1943; US Army Records, 1941–50, 1st Armored Division; Eisenhower Papers, Box 18; Bradley Commentary, Hansen Papers.

[30] Office of Postal Officer, Operations Report, part of G.1 Report (30 June 1943); 34th Infantry Division, Operations Report, 3 January – 13 May 1943.

[31] 'Tunisian Lessons'. Hansen Papers, Box 23.

[32] Patton to Allen, 13 January 1944; Allen Papers, Box 3.

[33] Letter to the Rev. F.J. Brabyn, TS Account. IWM 87/59/1.

Order of Battle
Allied Ground Forces

ALLIED FORCES NORTH AFRICA

Commander-in-Chief:	*General Dwight D. Eisenhower*
Deputy Commander-in-Chief:	*Lieutenant-General Mark W. Clark*
	(to 19 February)
Chief of Staff:	*Major-General Walter Bedell Smith*

18TH ARMY GROUP:

	General Sir Harold R.L.G. Alexander
	(appointed 19 February)
Chief of Staff:	*Major-General R.L. McCreery*

FIRST ARMY

	Lieutenant-General K.A.N. Anderson
Brigadier General Staff:	*Brigadier C.V.O'N. McNabb*
	Brigadier C.G.G. Nicholson
	(from 1 April)

Army Troops

1st Independent Parachute Brigade
(Bgde attached 78 Div from 11 Dec 1942, to 6th Armd Div from 28 Jan 1943, and 46 Div from 24 March)
1/2/3rd Parachute Battalions
1st Parachute Squadron, RE

1st Commando 6th Commando

V Corps *Lieutenant-General C.W. Allfrey*

78th Infantry Division *Major-General V. Evelegh*
(Acted as Initial Task Force then under V Corps from 6 December)

11th Infantry Brigade
2nd Lancashire Fusiliers
1st East Surreys
5th Northamptons

36th Infantry Brigade
5th Buffs
6th Queen's Own Royal West Kents
8th Argyll & Sutherland Highlanders

1st Guards Brigade
(Attached to 11th Brigade from 25 November, independent from 4 December, operational from 6 December; attached to 6 Armd Div from 2 February, transferred 24 March)
3rd Grenadiers 2nd Coldstreams
2nd Hampshires*
* *Replaced by 3rd Welsh Guards, 1 March*

Divisional Troops
56th Reconnaissance Regiment, RAC
17/132nd/138th Field Regiments, RA
49th Light AA Regiment, RA

214/237th/256th Field Companies, RE
64th Anti-Tank Regiment, RA
281st Field Park Company, RE

Blade Force
(See also Chapter 3, p. 39, footnote 21)

17th/21st Lancers

C Battery, 72nd Anti-Tank Regiment

Troop of 5th Field Squadron RE

B Squadron, 1st Derbyshire Yeomanry

G Troop, 51st Light Anti-Tank Regiment

B Company, 10th Rifle Brigade

6th Armoured Division   *Major-General C.F. Keightley*
(Joined IX Corps, 12 March 1943)

26th Armoured Brigade
16/5th Queen's Royal Lancers

17/21st Lancers

2nd Lothians & Border Horse

10th Rifle Bde

38th Irish Infantry Brigade
6th Royal Inniskilling Fusiliers

2nd London Irish Rifles

1st Royal Irish Fusiliers

*(Bgde attached to Y Div Feb, joined
78 Div 14 Mar; transferred 24 Mar)*

Divisional Troops
1st Derbyshire Yeomanry

152nd Field Regiment, RA

51st Light AA Regiment, RA

144th Field Park Squadron, RE

12th Royal Horse Artillery

72nd Anti-Tank Regiment, RA

5/8/625th Field Park Squadrons, RE

46th (North Midlands) Infantry Division
         Major-General H.A. Freeman-Attwood

(Operational late January – joined IX Corps 14 April)

128th Infantry Brigade
1/4th Hampshires

2/4th Hampshires

5th Hampshires

138th Infantry Brigade
6th Lincolns

2/4th King's Own Yorks LI

6th Yorks and Lancs

139th Infantry Brigade
2/5th Leicesters

5th Sherwood Foresters

16th Durham Light Infantry

Divisional Troops
58th Anti-Tank Regiment, RA

70/71/172nd Field Regiments, RA

273rd Field Park Company, RE

115th Light AA Regiment, RA

270/271/272nd Field Companies, RE

1st Infantry Division   *Major-General W.E. Clutterbuck*
(Operational mid-March)

24th Guards Infantry Brigade
5th Grenadier Guards

1st Scots Guards

1st Irish Guards

2nd Infantry Brigade
1st Loyals

2nd North Staffs

6th Gordon Highlanders

3rd Infantry Brigade
1st Duke of Wellington's

2nd Sherwood Foresters

1st King's Shropshire Light Infantry

Divisional Troops
81st Anti-Tank Regiment, RA

2/19/67th Field Regiments, RA

6th Field Park Company, RE

90th Light AA Regiment, RA

23/238/248 Field Companies, RE

4th Infantry (Mixed) Division
Major-General J.L.I. Hawkesworth
(Operational from early April 1943; joined IX Corps 3 May)

10th Infantry Brigade
2nd Beds and Herts
1/6th East Surreys
2nd Duke of Cornwall's LI

12th Infantry Brigade
2nd Royal Fusiliers
6th Black Watch
1st Queen's Own Royal West Kents

21st Army Tank Brigade
12/48th Royal Tank Regiment
145th Regiment, Royal Armoured Corps

Divisional Troops
22/30/77th Field Regiments, RA
91st Light AA Regiment, RA
18th Field Park Company, RE

14th Anti-Tank Regiment, RA
7/59/225th Field Companies, RE

Army and Corps Troops

25th Army Tank Brigade
51st Royal Tank Regiment
Northern Irish Horse
142nd Regiment, Royal Armoured Corps

Artillery
23/102/140/166th Field Regiments, RA
54th* and 56th Heavy Regiments, RA
87/93rd Anti-Tank Regiments, RA
11/17/105/117th Light AA Regiments, RA
* *with French XIX Corps*

4/5/58 and 74th Medium Regiments, RA
5/8th Survey Regiments, RA
58/80th Heavy AA Regiments, RA

IX Corps
Lieutenant-General J.T. Crocker
Lieutenant-General B.G. Horrocks
(from 30 April)
(Corps operational as Army Group Reserve 24 March; under First Army from 12 April)

6th Armoured Division
(from 12 March)

1st Armoured Division
(from 15 April)

46th Infantry Division
(from 14 April)

4th Infantry (Mixed) Division
(from 3 May)

7th Armoured Division

4th Indian Division

201st Guards Motor Brigade *(from 30 April)*

United States II Corps
Major-General Lloyd R. Fredendall
Major-General George S. Patton
(from 6 March)
Lieutenant-General Omar N. Bradley
(from 14 April)

Corps Troops
202nd Military Police Company
53rd Signal Battalion (with att. units)
19/20th Engineer Regiments
2nd Platoon, 470th Engineer Coy (and other units)
2618th Provisional Quartermaster Truck Battalion (and other units)
Provisional Ordnance Group

2642nd Armored Replacement Battalion
51st Medical Battalion (with att. units)
188th Ordnance Battalion (and att. units)

Medical Detachment

1st Armored Division

Major-General Orlando Ward
Major-General Ernest N. Harmon
(from 4 April)

Tank Regiments
1st Armored Regiment
13th Armored Regiment
6th Armored Infantry Regiment

Divisional Artillery
27th Armored Field Artillery Battalion
68th Armored Field Artillery Battalion
91st Armored Field Artillery Battalion

Special Troops
81st Armored Reconnaissance Battalion
141st Armored Signal Company
1st Armored Maintenance Battalion

16th Armored Engineer Battalion
1st Armored Supply Battalion
47th Armored Medical Battalion

Attached
91st Reconnaissance Squadron
443rd Coast Artillery (AA) Battalion

776th Tank Destroyer Battalion
Air Support Party

1st Infantry Division

Major-General Terry de la Mesa Allen

Infantry Regiments
16th Infantry
18th Infantry
26th Infantry

Divisional Artillery
5th Field Artillery Battalion
7th Field Artillery Battalion
32nd Field Artillery Battalion
33rd Field Artillery Battalion

Special Troops
1st Engineer Battalion
1st Medical Battalion
1st Signal Company

1st Quartermaster Company
1st Cavalry Reconnaissance Troop
701st Ordnance Company

Attached
701st Tank Destroyer Battalion
Det., 2624th Signal Service Regt

105th Coast Artillery (AA) Battalion
Air Support Party

9th Infantry Division

Major-General Manton S. Eddy

Infantry Regiments
39th Infantry
47th Infantry
60th Infantry

Divisional Artillery
26th Field Artillery Battalion
34th Field Artillery Battalion
60th Field Artillery Battalion
84th Field Artillery Battalion

Special Troops
15th Engineer Battalion
9th Medical Battalion
9th Signal Company

9th Quartermaster Company
9th Cavalry Reconnaissance Troop
709th Ordnance Company

Attached
62nd Armored Field Artillery Battalion
Battery II, 67th Coast Artillery (AA)

434th Coast Artillery (AA) Battalion
Air Support Party

34th Infantry Division

Major-General Charles W. Ryder

Infantry Regiments
133rd (less 2nd Btn) Infantry
135th Infantry
168th Infantry

Divisional Artillery
125th Field Artillery Battalion
151st Field Artillery Battalion
175th Field Artillery Battalion
185th Field Artillery Battalion

Special Troops
109th Engineer Battalion
109th Medical Battalion
34th Signal Company

109th Quartermaster Battalion
34th Cavalry Reconnaissance Troop
734th Ordnance Company

Attached
813th Tank Destroyer Battalion
107th Coast Artillery (AA) Battalion

751st Tank Battalion
Air Support Party

Also operational:

13th Field Artillery Brigade
1st Field Artillery Observation Battalion

17/36/178th Field Artillery Regiments

Attached
106th Coast Artillery (AA) Battalion
Battery E, 67th Coast Artillery (AA)
65th Armored Field Artillery Battalion
1st Batt, 213th Coast Artillery Regiment
(less Batteries C and D)

HQ, 5th Armored Artillery Group
58th Armored Field Artillery Battalion
601st Tank Destroyer Battalion

2626th Coast Artillery Brigade (AA)
Batteries C and D, 213th Coast Artillery
690/692/694th Coast Artillery Batts
67th Coast Artillery Regiment
(less Batts E and H and 1st/3rd Batts)

3rd Battalion, 213th Coast Artillery
436th Coast Artillery Battalion

French XIX Corps   *General Louis-Marie Koeltz*
(From 3 February 1943)

Division *d'Alger*   *General Conne*

Division *du Maroc*   *General Mathenet*

Division *d'Oran*   *General Boissau*

Division *Tunisie*   *General Barré*

Division *du Constantine*   *General Welvert to 10 April*
        General Schwarz
(Division withdrawn and replaced by Division d'Oran*)*

Other French Forces in Tunisia
Bataillon de Marche 1
Bataillon de Marche 4
Bataillon de Marche 7
15 Regiment des Tirailleurs Sénégalais
4th and 6th Tabors Marocains

Bataillon de Marche 2
Bataillon de Marche 5
13 Regiment des Tirailleurs Sénégalais
43 Régiment d'Infanterie Coloniales

Armoured Group (General Le Coulteux)

1st/2nd/3rd Battalions, Corps Franc d'Afrique (Colonel Magnan)

EIGHTH ARMY
General Bernard L. Montgomery

Brigadier General Staff: *Brigadier F.W. de Guingand*

Under Command

1st Army Tank Brigade
42nd Royal Tank Regiment
44th Royal Tank Regiment

Squadron, SAS Regiment

2nd AA Brigade
2nd Light AA Regiment, RA
69th Heavy AA Regiment, RA

12th AA Brigade
14/16/27th Light AA Regiments, RA
88/94th Heavy AA Regiments, RA

X Corps
Lieutenant-General B.G. Horrocks
Lieutenant-General Sir Bernard Freyberg
(from 30 April)

1st Armoured Division
Major-General R. Briggs

2nd Armoured Brigade
Queen's Bays
9th Queen's Royal Lancers
10th Royal Hussars
Yorkshire Dragoons

7th Motor Brigade
2nd King's Royal Rifle Corps
2nd Rifle Brigade
7th Rifle Brigade

Divisional Troops
12th Royal Lancers
2/4/11th Regiments, RHA
76th Anti-Tank Regiment, RA

42nd Light AA Regiment, RA
1/7th Field Squadrons, RE
1st Field Park Squadron, RE

7th Armoured Division
Major-General A.F. Harding
Major-General G.W.E.J. Erskine

(Joined X Corps 2 November; to XXX Corps 26 November; returned to X Corps 18 March; joined IX Corps 30 April)

22nd Armoured Brigade
1st Royal Tank Regiments
5th Royal Tank Regiment
4th County of London Yeomanry
1st Rifle Brigade

131st Lorried Infantry Brigade
1/5th Queen's Royal Surrey Regiment
1/6th Queen's Royal Surrey Regiment
1/7th Queen's Royal Surrey Regiment

4th Armoured Brigade Group
(To NZ division 12 December)
1st King's Royal Rifle Corps
1st King's Dragoon Guards
1st Royal Dragoons

Divisional Troops
11th Hussars
3rd Royal Horse Artillery
4/97th Field Regiments, RA
65th Anti-Tank Regiment, RA

15th Light AA Regiment, RA
4/21st Field Squadrons, RE
143rd Field Park Squadron, RE

50th (Northumbrian) Infantry Division

Major-General J.S. Nichols
Major-General S.C. Kirkman
(from 14 April 1943)

(Joined XXX Corps, 2 January)

69th Infantry Brigade
5th East Yorks
6th Green Howards
7th Green Howards

151st Infantry Brigade
6th Durham Light Infantry
8th Durham Light Infantry
9th Durham Light Infantry

Divisional Troops
65/74/111/124th Field Regiments, RA
102nd (NH) Anti-Tank Regiment, RA
34th Light AA Regiment, RA

233/505th Field Companies, RE
235th Field Park Company, RE
2nd Cheshires (MG)

XXX Corps
Lieutenant-General Sir Oliver Leese

Corps Troops
7/64/69th Medium Regiments, RA

8th Armoured Brigade
(Joined XXX Corps 26 November, and New Zealand Division 14 March)
3rd Royal Tank Regiment
Staffs Yeomanry

Notts Yeomanry (Sherwood Rangers)
1st Buffs

201st Guards Motor Brigade Group
(Joined XXX Corps 26 February, and IX Corps, First Army, 1 May)
6th Grenadiers
2nd Scots Guards

3rd Coldstreams

23rd Armoured Brigade Group
40/46/50th Royal Tank Regiments
121st Field Regiment, RA

11th King's Royal Rifle Corps

General Leclerc's Force
(Joined from Lake Chad January 1943, incorporated as L Force)

51st (Highland) Infantry Division

Major-General D.N. Wimberley

152nd Infantry Brigade
2nd Seaforths
5th Seaforths
5th Cameron Highlanders

153rd Infantry Brigade
5th Black Watch
1st Gordon Highlanders
5/7th Gordon Highlanders

154th Infantry Brigade
1st Black Watch
7th Black Watch
7th Argyll and Sutherland Highlanders

Divisional Troops
51st Reconnaissance Regiment
126/127/128th Field Regiments, RA
61st Anti-Tank Regiment, RA
1/7th Middlesex (MG)

274/275/276th Field Companies, RE
239th Field Park Company, RE
40th Light AA Regiment, RA

56th (London) Infantry Division

Major-General E.G. Miles
Major-General D.A.H. Graham
(from 5 May)

(Joined X Corps 20 April)

167th (London) Infantry Brigade
8th Royal Fusiliers
9th Royal Fusiliers
7th Ox and Bucks LI

Divisional Troops
220/221/501st Field Companies, RE
100th Light AA Regiment, RA
563rd Field Park Company, RE

169th (London) Infantry Brigade
2/5th Queen's Royal Surrey Regiment
2/6th Queen's Royal Surrey Regiment
2/7th Queen's Royal Surrey Regiment

64/90/113th Field Regiments, RA
67th Anti-Tank Regiment, RA

4th Indian Division
Major-General F.I.S. Tuker
(Joined IX Corps, First Army, 30 April)

5th Brigade
1/4th Essex
4/6th Rajputana Rifles
3/10th Baluch*
1/9th Gurkha Rifles
* *Until February 1943*

7th Brigade
1st Royal Sussex
4/16th Punjabis
1/2nd Gurkha Rifles

Divisional Troops
1/11/32nd Field Regiments, RA
149th Anti-Tank Regiment, RA
11th Madras Field Park Company, IE

2/4th Bengal/12th Madras Field Coys., IE
57th Light AA Regiment, RA
6th Rajputana Rifles (MG)

2nd New Zealand Division
Lieutenant-General Sir Bernard Freyberg
Major-General H.K. Kippenberger
(from 30 April)

5th NZ Infantry Brigade
21st Battalion
23rd Battalion
28th (Maori) Battalion

6th NZ Infantry Brigade
24th Battalion
25th Battalion
26th Battalion

4th Light Armoured Brigade Group
(Joined NZ Div 12 December; joined XX Corps, replaced by 8th Armoured Brigade, 14 March)
1st King's Dragoon Guards
1st The Royal Dragoons

Divisional Troops
2nd NZ Divisional Cavalry Regiment
7th Anti-Tank Regiment, NZA
6/7/8th Field Company, NZE
27th NZ Battalion (MG)

4/5/6th Field Regiments, NZA
14th Light AA Regiment, NZA
5th Field Park Company, NZE

Order of Battle
Axis Ground Forces

HEERESGRUPPE AFRIKA

Army Group Commander:	Generalfeldmarschall Erwin Rommel
	(23 February – 9 March)
	Generaloberst Hans-Jürgen von Arnim
	(9 March – 13 May)
Chief of Staff:	Oberst i.G. Fritz Bayerlein
	Generalleutnant Heinz Ziegler

PANZERARMEE AFRIKA/FIRST ITALIAN ARMY*
* From 23 February

Army Commander:	Generalfeldmarschall Erwin Rommel
	(until 23 February)
	Generale di Armata Giovanni Messe
Chief of Staff:	Generalmajor Alfred Gause
	Oberst i.G. Fritz Bayerlein
	Oberst i.G. Markert
	Oberst i.G. Siegfried Westphal
	Oberst i.G. Fritz Bayerlein

Deutsches Afrika Korps	Oberst Fritz Bayerlein
	(until 19 November)
	General der Panzertruppe Gustav Fehn
	(wounded 16 January)
	Generalmajor Kurt von Liebenstein
	(wounded 17 February)
	Generalleutnant Heinz Ziegler
	(temporary to 5 March)
	General der Panzertruppe Hans Cramer
Chief of Staff:	Oberst i.G. Bayerlein
	Oberst i.G. H.W. Nolte
21st Panzer Division	Generalmajor Heinz von Randow
	(killed 21 December)
	Oberst Hans Georg Hildebrandt
	(sick leave 25 April)
	Generalmajor Heinrich-Hermann v. Hülsen

100th Panzer Regiment	125th Panzer Grenadier Regiment
155th Panzer Artillery Regiment	192nd Panzer Grenadier Regiment
21st Reconnaissance Battalion	200th Anti-Tank Battalion
200th Panzer Engineer Battalion	200th Panzer Signal Battalion

15th Panzer Division	*Generalleutnant Gustav von Vaerst* *(sick leave)* *Oberst Eduard Crasemann* *(temporary to December 1942)* *Generalleutnant Gustav von Vaerst* *Oberst Willibald Borowietz* *(from 12 December)*

8th Panzer Regiment   115th Panzer Grenadier Regiment
33rd Panzer Artillery Regiment   33rd Panzer Reconnaissance Battalion
33rd Panzer Anti-Tank Battalion   33rd Panzer Engineer Battalion
78th Panzer Signal Battalion

90th Light *Afrika* Division   *Generalleutnant Theodor Graf v. Sponeck*
(Not under DAK command)

155th Motorised Grenadier Regiment   200th Motorised Grenadier Regiment
361st Motorised Grenadier Regiment   190th Panzer Battalion
190th Motorised Signal Battalion   190th Motorised Artillery Regiment
580th Panzer Reconnaissance Battalion   190th Panzer Anti-Tank Battalion
190th Motorised Engineer Battalion

164th Light *Afrika* Division *(Not under DAK command)*	*Generalmajor Karl-Hans Lungershausen* *Oberst Siegfried Westphal* *(temporary from 6 December 1942)* *Generalmajor Kurt Freiherr v. Liebenstein* *(from 1 January 1943)* *Oberst Becker* *(temporary from 16 January)* *Generalmajor Fritz Krause* *(temporary from 17 February)* *Generalmajor Kurt Freiherr v. Liebenstein* *(from 13 March 1943)*

125th Panzer Grenadier Regiment   382nd Panzer Grenadier Regiment
433rd Panzer Grenadier Regiment   220th Artillery Regiment
220th Panzer Reconnaissance Battalion   220th Motorised Engineer Battalion
220th Motorised Signal Battalion

Ramcke (2nd) Parachute Brigade

                  Generalmajor Hermann Bernard Ramcke
Four battalions arrived North Africa, July/August 1942, placed with other divisional units under direct command of *Panzerarmee Afrika*. After inadvertently being left behind in retreat from El Alamein, November 1942, rejoined Rommel's forces. Thereafter various units used until remnants of brigade evacuated – apart from some elements which surrendered, May 1943.

Corpo d'Armata XX   *Generale di Corpo d'Armata Giuseppe de Stefanis*

132nd *Ariete* Armoured Division

                  Generale di Divisione Francesco Arena
(Largely destroyed at El Alamein; reconstituted as Light Armoured Division)
8th Montebello Armoured Car Regiment   10th *Vittorio Emanuele II* Arm'd Car Regt
16th Lucca Armoured Car Regiment   135th Armoured Artillery Regiment

101st *Trieste* Semi-Motorised Division
Generale di Divisione Francesco La Ferla
(Remnants only escaped destruction at El Alamein)

65th Valtellina Infantry Regiment	66th Valtellina Infantry Regiment
9th Bersaglieri Regiment	21st Po Artillery Regiment
146th Anti-Aircraft Battery	411th Anti-Aircraft Battery
101st Anti-Tank Battalion	

Folgore Parachute Division   *Generale di Divisione Enrico Frattini*
(Only remnants after retreat from El Alamein)

Corpo d'Armata XXI   *Generale di Corpo d'Armata Enea Navarini*

80th *La Spezia* Airborne Division
Generale di Divisione Gavino Pizzolato

125th *La Spezia* Infantry Regiment	126th *La Spezia* Infantry Regiment
80th Artillery Regiment	80th Anti-Tank Battalion
80th Engineer Battalion	70th Machine-Gun Battalion
39th Bersaglieri Battalion (attached to 126th Infantry)	

16th *Pistoia* Motorized Division
Generale di Divisione Guglielmo Falugi
(Absorbed remnants of Generale Calvi di Bergolo's Centauro *Division by April)*

35th Pistoia Infantry Regiment	36th Pistoia Infantry Regiment
3rd Fossalta Artillery Regiment	16th Anti-Tank Battalion
16th Mortar Battalion	51st Engineer Battalion

136th *Giovani Fascisti* Infantry Division
Generale di Divisione Nino Sozzani

136th *Giovani Fascisti* Infantry Regt	136th Artillery Regiment
25th Engineer Battalion	

FIFTH PANZER ARMY*   *General der Panzertruppe Walther Nehring*
* XC KORPS until 9 December 1942   *(to 9 December)*

Generaloberst Hans-Jürgen von Arnim
(to 9 March)

General der Panzertruppe Gustav v. Vaerst

Chief of Staff: *Generalleutnant Heinz Ziegler*
Generalmajor von Quast

10th Panzer Division   *Generalleutnant Wolfgang Fischer*
(killed 1 February)

Generalmajor Freiherr von Broich
(from 5 February)

7th Panzer Regiment	90th Anti-Tank Battalion
69th Panzer Grenadier Regiment	86th Panzer Grenadier Regiment
Sturmregiment *Hermannn Göring*	A4 Panzer Grenadier Battalion
90th Artillery Regiment	Flak Group *Böhmer* (Luftwaffe)
10th Motorcycle Battalion	90th Panzer Reconnaissance Battalion
49th Panzer Engineer Battalion	90th Signal Battalion

21st Panzer Division

Generalmajor Heinz von Randow
(killed 21 December)
Generalmajor Hans-Georg Hildebrandt
(1 January – 25 April)
Generalmajor Heinrich-Hermann v. Hülsen

5th Panzer Regiment	200th Anti-Tank Battalion
104th Panzer Grenadier Regiment	155th Artillery Regiment
590th Reconnaissance Battalion	200th Panzer Signal Battalion
200th Panzer Engineer Battalion	

334th Infantry Division

Oberst Friedrich Weber
(promoted Generalmajor 1 January)
Generalmajor Fritz Krause
(from 15 April)

754th Panzer Grenadier Regiment	755th Panzer Grenadier Regiment
756th Mountain Infantry Regiment	334th Anti-Tank Battalion
334th Artillery Regiment	334th Engineer Battalion
334th Signal Company	334th Mobile Battalion

999th Light *Afrika* Division

Generalleutnant Kurt Thoma
(23 December – 1 April; missing)
Oberst Ernst-Günther Baade
(from 2 April)

961st *Afrika* Rifle Regiment	962nd *Afrika* Rifle Regiment
963rd *Afrika* Rifle Regiment	999th Artillery Regiment

Division von Broich
(Div von Manteuffel, 7 Feb)

Oberst Fritz Freiherr von Broich
(18 November – 5 February)
Generalmajor Hasso von Manteuffel
(7 February – 31 March)
Generalleutnant Karl Bülowius

Barenthin Parachute Regiment	T3 Infantry Battalion
2nd Artillery Regt (4th/12th Battalions)	190th Artillery Regiment (4th Battalion)
11th Parachute Engineer Battalion	10th Bersaglieri Regiment

Division *Hermann Göring*

Generalmajor Josef Schmid
(March – 9 May)

(Elements in Tunisia arrived from November 1942 and known as Kampfgruppe Schmid *– advance party of Division* Hermann Göring *– until other units arrived February 1943)*

Panzer Regt *H Göring* (1st Battalion)	1st Gren Regt *H Göring* (2nd/3rd Batts)
1st, 3rd Regt *H Göring* (1st/2nd Batts)	69th Pz Grenadier Regt (9th Battalion)
104th Pz Grenadier Regt (14th Battalion)	90th Artillery Regiment (2nd Battalion)
1st Flak Regiment *H Göring*	

1st *Superga* (Assault and Landing) Division
(Under DAK command, 13 April)

Generale di Divisione Dante Lorenzelli
Generale di Divisione Conte Fernando Gelich

91st *Basilicata* Infantry Regiment	92nd *Basilicata* Infantry Regiment
5th *Superga* Artillery Regiment	1st, 101st, 136th Anti-Tank Battalions 1st,
101st Engineer Battalions	T5, A22, A25, A26 Field Replacement Batts

Imperiali Brigade

Generale di Brigata Imperiali de Francavilla

6th Battalion (composite)	15/M41 Armoured Battalion
557th Anti-Tank Battalion	35th, 58th, 77th Artillery Battalions

Allied Battle Casualties
November 1942 – May 1943

British	*First Army*	*Eighth Army*
Killed in Action	4,439	2,036
Wounded	12,575	9,055
Captured/Missing	6,531	1,304

US/French	*II Corps*	*French*
Killed in Action	2,311	1,100
Wounded	8,555	8,080
Captured/Missing	5,355	7,000

Source: Howe, *Northwest Africa*, p. 675.

Bibliography

Unpublished Sources

Imperial War Museum, London

Major-General D.R.E.R. Bateman, Papers.

Lieutenant M.W. Bowley, Memoir.

Signalman C.H. Bradshaw, Memoir.

Lieutenant D.E. Brown, Papers.

Sergeant (later Lt) E.W. Caffell, Memoirs.

Bombardier L. Challenor, Journal 1942–43.

Sergeant E.P. Danger, Diary and Papers.

Captain J.E. Edney, Account.

Private C.T. Framp, Memoir.

Lt-Cdr P.R. Hay, Midshipman's Journal.

Lieutenant R.F. Kinden, Memoir.

Maj-Gen D.L. Lloyd Owen, Notes on LRDG.

Gen Sir Gordon Macmillan, Papers.

Signalman J.W. Beaumont, Diary and Papers.

The Reverend F.J. Brabyn, Diary.

Bombardier J.E. Brooks, Letters.

Brig C.G. Buttenshaw, 'Blade Force' War Diary.

Flight-Lieutenant E. Chadwick, Papers.

Lance-Corporal E. Cook, Account.

Brigadier H.K. Dimoline, Papers.

Lieutenant-Colonel G.Y. Feggetter, Memoir.

Sergeant J.R. Harris, Diary.

Major-General J.C. Haydon, Torch Diary.

Lieutenant-General Sir Oliver Leese, Papers.

Maj-Gen L.O. Lyne, Autobiography (unpub.).

Major-General C.H. Miller, Papers.

Field Marshal Viscount Montgomery of Alamein, Diary and Papers

The relevant sections of these papers which I consulted have since been published in an edition edited by Stephen Brooks, *Montgomery and the Eighth Army: A Selection from the Diaries, Correspondence and other Papers of Field Marshal the Viscount Montgomery of Alamein, August 1942 to December 1943*, The Bodley Head for the Army Records Society, 1991.

Colonel C.A.H.M. Noble, Papers.

R. Priestley, Memoir.

Lieutenant P. Royle, Memoir.

Lt-Gen Sir Francis Tuker, Papers.

Signalman A. Parker, Memoir.

The Reverend J.E.G. Quinn, Diaries.

Lieutenant-Colonel K. Shirley Smith, Diary.

Brig (later Maj-Gen) G.P. Walsh, Papers.

IWM Sound Archives

'The World at War': interviews with David Brown; Paolo Colacicchi; Colonel Hugh Daniel; A.H. McGee; Harry Mitchell. IWM Sound Archives: Gunner Greenwood; Major Francis Jephson; Corporal Vernon Scannell.

Liddell Hart Centre for Military Archives, King's College, London

Field Marshal Viscount Alanbrooke, Diary and Papers.

Captain B.H. Liddell Hart, Memoranda.

Major-General Sir (William) Rowell Campbell Penney, Diary.

Captain G.C. Wynne, Papers.

Public Record Office, Kew, London

Field Marshal Viscount Alexander of Tunis, Papers WO/214.

First Army HQ, War Diary WO/175.

First Army Command Post, War Diary WO/175.

Middle East Forces WO/201.

Churchill Archives Centre, Churchill College, Cambridge

Admiral of the Fleet Viscount Cunningham of Hyndhope, Papers.

Eisenhower Library, Abilene, Kansas
Lieutenant-General Walter Bedell Smith, Papers and Collection of WW II Documents.
Captain Harry C. Butcher, USN, Papers and Diary.
Brigadier-General Thomas Jefferson Davis, Papers.
General Dwight D. Eisenhower, Papers, Pre-Presidential 1916–1952.
Brigadier-General Lauris Norstad, Papers 1930–1987.
Captain James R. Webb, Diary and Papers.
US War Department, Operations Division, Diary 1941–46.
1st Armored Division, US Army Unit Records, 1941–50.

Manuscript Division, Library of Congress, Washington D.C.
Colonel George S. Biddle, Diary and Papers.
General James H. Doolittle, Operations File, 1942–43.
Colonel (later Brigadier-General) Everett S. Hughes, Diary.
General George S. Patton, Diary and Papers.
Brigadier-General Paul M. Robinett, Papers (part).
General Carl A. Spaatz, Diary and Papers.

George C. Marshall Research Library, Lexington, Virginia
General George C. Marshall, Papers.
Brigadier-General Paul M. Robinett, Orders and Letters.
Brigadier-General (later Lieutenant-General) Lucian K. Truscott, Papers (part) and aide's
    Diary.

Modern Military Field Branch, US National Archives, Suitland, Maryland
World War II Operations Records 1940–48: i) II Corps; ii) 1st Infantry Division; iii) 3rd Infantry
    Division; iv) 34th Infantry Division.

United States Military History Institute, Carlisle Barracks, Pennsylvania
Office of the Chief of Military History, World War II, Supreme Command Papers: includes
    interviews with Alexander, Bedell Smith, Coningham, Cunningham, Curtis, Dickson,
    Harmon, Ismay, Kenner, Marshall, Portal, Ryder, Colonel R. Ward and the Major-General
    Ernest Nason Harmon Papers, George F. Howe Papers and Stanley Matthews Collection.
Military History Research Collection; World War II, Mediterranean: includes interviews with
    Bradley, Clark, Conway, Eaker, Howze, Kerwin, Porter, Quesada, Rosson, Sloan, Waters,
    Yarborough.
Major-General Terry de la Mesa Allen, Papers.
Colonel William S. Biddle, Papers.
General Omar N. Bradley, Papers including War Diaries, 1943, and Memoir 1893–1945
    (unpub.).
Captain Chester B. Hansen, Diary and Papers.
Lieutenant-Colonel Hamilton H. Howze, Correspondence 1908–1945.
Lieutenant-Colonel Oscar W. Koch, Draft for 'Intelligence in Combat' (unpub., 1954).
General Sir Frederick Morgan, Papers.
Major Martin M. Philipsborn, Papers.
William M. Stokes, Papers 1942–45.
Major-General Orlando Ward, Papers – includes various interviews by Russell Gugeler with
    Howze, etc., Diaries of Ward and Captain E.C. Hatfield, lengthy biography of Ward by
    Russell A. Gugeler (unpub.) and 1st Armored Division Papers 1942–43.
US Army Ground Forces (Observer Board): Mediterranean Theater of Operations, Papers.
1st Armored Division, WW II Survey, Papers.
HQ, 9th Infantry Division, Papers.
Foreign Military Series (second copies of those held in National Archives) – some in
    translation, others in German original – titles as given in Detwiler, *et al.*, *German Military
    Studies*: MS C-075; MS C-098; MS D-001; MS D-008; MS D-017; MS D-040; MS D-067; MS
    D-071; MS D-086; MS D-098; MS D-120; MS D-147; MS D-166; MS D-173; MS D-174.

Bundesarchiv-Militärarchiv, Freiburg i Br.
Translated from original:
RH19-VIII/31 Battle Reports, German-Italian Panzer Army.
RH19-VIII/32 ditto.
RH19-VIII/39 Supporting Documentation to Battle Reports.
RH19-VIII/40 ditto.
RH19-VIII/41 ditto.
RH19-VIII/242 *Kriegstagebuch der Heeresgruppe Afrika/O.Qu.*
RH19-VIII/243 ditto.
RH19-VIII/244 ditto.
RH19-VIII/322 Rommel's Personal Files 1940–43 (copies).
RH19-VIII/351 'War in Tunisia,' Reports, March-April 1943.
RH19-VIII/352 ditto, March 1943.
RH19-VIII/355 ditto, January 1943.
RH19-VIII/357 Military-Political Situation in Tunis.
RH19-VIII/358 ditto – various reports.
RH19-VIII/359 ditto.
RH19-VIII/364 Enemy Situation Reports – various units.
RH24-200/78 Supplement to *Kriegstagebuch Nr.9, DAK.*
RH24-200/80 ditto – Incoming messages, orders, etc.
RH24-200/81 ditto.
RH24-200/82 ditto – Outgoing messages, orders, etc.
RH24-200/83 ditto.
RH24-200/84 ditto.
RH24-200/88 Activity Reports, *DAK* IIa Department.
RH24-200/117 Article: 'The Story behind the Story' (in English).
RH24-200/118 Report by Rommel on African Campaign, 19 January 1943.

Published Sources
Country of publication is UK, unless otherwise indicated.

i: Memoirs and Papers

Alexander of Tunis, Earl, *The Alexander Memoirs 1940–1945*, Cassell, 1962.
Barré, Georges, *Tunisie, 1942–1943*, Berger-Levrault, Paris, 1950.
Biddle, George, *Artist At War*, Viking Press, N.Y., 1944.
Blomfield-Smith, Denis, ed., *Fourth Indian Reflections: Memoirs of a Great Company*, Privately printed, 1987.
Blumenson, Martin, ed., *The Patton Papers 1940–1945*, Houghton Mifflin, Boston, 1974.
Bradley, Omar N., *A Soldier's Story*, Henry Holt, N.Y., 1951.
    and Blair, Clay, *A General's Life*, Sidgwick and Jackson, 1983.
Bryant, Arthur, *The Turn of the Tide 1939–1943: A Study Based on the Diaries and Autobiographical Notes of Field Marshal the Viscount Alanbrooke*, Collins, 1957.
Butcher, Harry C., *Three Years With Eisenhower*, Heinemann, 1946.
Cavallero, Ugo, *Comando supremo; diario 1940–43 del capo di S.M.G.*, Cappelli, Bologna, 1948.
Chandler, Alfred D., *et al.*, eds., *The Papers of Dwight David Eisenhower, The War Years*: II, John Hopkins Press, Baltimore, 1970.
Churchill, Winston S., *The Second World War*, IV, *The Hinge of Fate*, Cassell, 1951.
Clark, Mark, *Calculated Risk: His Story of the War in North Africa and Italy*, Harrap, 1951.
Coon, Carlton S., *The Anthropologist as OSS Agent 1941–1943*, Gambit, Ipswich, Mass., 1980.
Crimp, R.L., *The Diary of a Desert Rat*, Leo Cooper, 1971.
Cunningham of Hyndhope, Viscount, *A Sailor's Odyssey*, Hutchinson, 1951.
Detwiler, Donald S., Burdick, Charles B., and Rohwer, Jürgen, eds., *World War II German Military Studies: A collection of 213 special reports on the Second World War prepared by former officers of the Wehrmacht for the United States Army*, Garland, N.Y., 24 volumes, 1979.

Eade, Charles, ed., *Onwards to Victory: War Speeches by the Right Hon. Winston S. Churchill C.H., M.P., 1943*, Cassell, 2nd edn., June, 1945.

Eisenhower, Dwight D., *At Ease: Stories I tell to Friends*, Doubleday & Co., N.Y., 1967.
   Crusade in Europe, Heinemann, 1948.

Ferrell, Robert H., ed., *The Eisenhower Diaries*, W.W. Norton, N.Y., 1981.

Gardiner, Henry E., 'We Fought at Kasserine,' *Armored Cavalry Journal*, March–April, 1948.

Lochner, Louis P., ed., *The Goebbels Diaries*, Hamish Hamilton, 1948.

Guest, John, *Broken Images: A Journal*, Longmans, 1949.

de Guingand, Sir Francis, *Operation Victory*, Hodder and Stoughton, 1947.

Harmon, E.N., with MacKaye, Milton, and MacKaye, William Ross, *Combat Commander: Autobiography of a Soldier*, Prentice-Hall, Englewood Cliffs, NJ, 1970.

Harvey, John, ed., *The War Diaries of Oliver Harvey 1941–1945*, Collins, 1978.

Sherwood, Robert E., ed., *The White House Papers of Harry L. Hopkins*, II, *January 1942–July 1945*, Eyre & Spottiswoode, 1949.

Horrocks, Brian, *A Full Life*, Collins, 1960.

Hunt, David, *A Don at War*, William Kimber, 1966.

Ismay, Lord, *The Memoirs of General the Lord Ismay*, Heinemann, 1960.

Kenneally, John Patrick, *Kenneally VC*, Kenwood, Huddersfield, 1991.

Kesselring, Albrecht, *The Memoirs of Field-Marshal Kesselring*, Greenhill Books edn., 1988.

Kippenberger, Sir Howard, *Infantry Brigadier*, OUP, 1949.

Leahy, William D., *I Was There: the Personal Story of the Chief of Staff to Presidents Roosevelt and Truman based on his Notes and Diaries made at the time*, Gollancz, 1950.

Liddell Hart, B.H., *The Memoirs*, Cassell, 1965.
   The Rommel Papers, Hamlyn edn., 1984.

Lloyd Owen, David, *The Desert My Dwelling Place*, Arms and Armour Press edn., 1986.

Lloyd Owen, David, *Providence Their Guide: A Personal Account of the Long Range Desert Group 1940–45*, Harrap, 1980.

Loewenheim, Francis L., Langley, Harold D., and Jones, Manfred, eds., *Roosevelt and Churchill: their Secret Wartime Correspondence*, Barrie & Jenkins, 1975.

Maclean, Fitzroy, Obituary of David Stirling, *Independent* newspaper, 6 November 1990.

Macmillan, Harold, *War Diaries: Politics and War in the Mediterranean, January 1943 – May 1945*, Macmillan, 1984.

Mayhew, Patrick, ed., *One Family's War*, Futura edn., 1985.

Muggeridge, Malcolm, ed., *Ciano's Diary 1939–1943*, Heinemann, 1947.

McCallum, Neil, *Journey with a Pistol: A Diary of War*, Gollancz, 1959.

Messe, Giovanni, *La mia armata in Tunisia: come finì la guerra in Africa*, Rizzoli, Milan, rev. edn., 1960.

Montgomery, B.L., *The Memoirs of Field Marshal the Viscount Montgomery of Alamein*, Collins, 1958.
   El Alamein to the River Sangro, Hutchinson, n.d. (1948).

Peniakoff, Vladimir, *Popski's Private Army*, Mayflower edn., 1975.

Potter, F.E., *Tebessa? Wherever's That?*, Merlin Books, Braunton, Devon, 1987.

Richardson, Charles, *From Churchill's Secret Circle to the BBC: the Biography of Lieutenant General Sir Ian Jacob*, Brassey's (U.K.), 1991.

Roberts, G.P.B. (Pip), *From the Desert to the Baltic*, William Kimber, 1987.

Robinett, Paul McDonald, *Armor Command: the personal story of a commander of the 13th Armored Regiment of CC B, 1st Armored Division and of the Armored School during World War II*, US Armor Association, Washington DC, 1958.

Scannell, Vernon, (pseud.), *Argument of Kings*, Robson Books, 1987.

Schmidt, Heinz Werner, *With Rommel in the Desert*, Panther edn., 1960.

Schramm, Percy E., ed., *Kriegstagebuch des Oberkommandos der Wehrmacht*, 6 vols., Bernard and Graefe, Munich, 1982 edn..

Stainforth, Peter, *Wings of the Wind*, Falcon Press, 1952.

Stimpson, Henry L., and Bundy, McGeorge, *On Active Service in Peace and War*, Harper & Brothers, New York, 1948.

Strong, Sir Kenneth, *Intelligence at the Top: The Recollections of an Intelligence Officer*, Cassell, 1968.
Tedder, Lord, *With Prejudice*, Cassell, 1966.
Truscott, Lucian K., Jr., *Command Missions: A Personal Story*, E.P. Dutton, N.Y., 1954; Arno Press reprint edn., N.Y., 1979.
Tuker, Sir Francis, *Approach to Battle: A Commentary Eighth Army, November 1941 to May 1943*, Cassell, 1963.
Warlimont, Walter, *Inside Hitler's Headquarters 1939–45*, Weidenfeld and Nicolson, 1964.

ii: Contemporary Accounts
Anon., *To Bizerte With the II Corps, 23 April – 13 May 1943*, Historical Division, US War Department, 1943; republished by Center of Military History, United States Army, Washington, DC, 1990.
Anon., *The Tiger Kills: India's Fight in the Middle East and North Africa*, G. Claridge & Co., Fort, Bombay, 1944.
Austin, A.B., *Birth Of An Army*, Gollancz, 1943.
Clifford, Alexander, *Three Against Rommel: The Campaigns of Wavell, Auchinleck and Alexander*, Harrap, 1943.
    The Conquest of North Africa, Burke Publishing Co., n.d. (*c.*1943).
D'Arcy Dawson, John, *Tunisian Battle*, Macdonald, n.d. (1943).
Hill, Russell, *Desert Conquest*, Alfred A. Knopf, N.Y., 1943.
Ingersoll, Ralph, *The Battle is the Pay-Off*, Harcourt, Brace, N.Y., 1943.
Jordan, Philip, *Jordan's Tunis Diary*, Collins, 1943.
Kennedy Shaw, W.B., *Long Range Desert Group 1940–43*, Collins, 1945.
Liebling, A.J., 'Profiles: Find 'Em, Fix 'Em, and Fight 'Em,' *New Yorker*, 24 April, 1943.
MacVane, John, *War and Diplomacy in North Africa*, Robert Hale, 1944.
Marshall, Howard, *Over to Tunis: The Complete Story of the North African Campaign*, Eyre and Spottiswoode, 1943.
Information, Ministry of, *The Army at War: Tunisia*, HMSO, 1944.
Moorehead, Alan, *African Trilogy*, Hamish Hamilton, 1944.
Oliver, Lunsford E., 'In the Mud and Blood of Tunisia,' *Colliers Magazine*, 17 April, 1943.
Pyle, Ernie, *Here is Your War*, Peoples Book Club edn., Consolidated Book Publishers, Chicago, 1944.
Rainier, Peter W., *Pipeline to Battle*, William Heinemann, 1944.
Ramsay, Guy, *One Continent Redeemed*, Harrap, 1943.
Talbot, Godfrey, *Speaking from the Desert: A Record of the Eighth Army in Africa*, Hutchinson, n.d. (1944).
Wisdom, T.H., *Triumph Over Tunisia: Being the story of the part of the Royal Air Force in the African Victory*, George Allen & Unwin, 1944.
Zanuck, Darryl F., *Tunis Expedition*, Random House, N.Y., 1943.

iii: Secondary Published Works
Anon., *The Rise and Fall of the German Air Force 1933–1945*, Arms and Armour Press, 1983. A facsimile reprint of a 1948 official publication.
Ambrose, Stephen E., *The Supreme Commander: The War Years of General Dwight D. Eisenhower*, Doubleday, N.Y., 1970.
Antonio, D.G., *Driver Advance!: being a short account of the 2nd Lothians and Border Horse 1939–1946*, Lothian and Border Regimental Association, Edinburgh, 1947.
Arthur, Max, *Men of the Red Beret: Airborne Forces 1940–1990*, Hutchinson, 1990.
Azéma, Jean-Pierre, *From Munich to the Liberation, 1938–1944*, CUP, 1984.
Barber, Laurie, and Tonkin-Covell, John, *Freyberg: Churchill's Salamander*, Hutchinson, 1990.
Barclay, C.N., *The History of the Royal Northumberland Fusiliers in the Second World War*, William Clowes for Regimental History Committee, Royal Northumberland Fusiliers, 1952.
Barnett, Correlli, *The Desert Generals*, William Kimber, 1960; 2nd edn., Pan Books, 1983.
    ed., *Hitler's Generals*, Weidenfeld and Nicolson, 1989.

Bartimeus, pseud, *The Turn of the Road: being the story of the part played by the Royal Navy and Merchant Navy in the landings in Algeria and French Morocco of combined British and United States forces on 8th November, 1942, and the final destruction of the axis forces in North Africa*, Chatto and Windus, 1946.

Behrendt, Hans-Otto, *Rommel's Intelligence in the Desert Campaign*, William Kimber, 1985.

Bellis, Malcolm A., *US Divisions: North Africa & Europe*, compiled and published by the author, 1989.

de Belot, Raymond, *The Struggle for the Mediterranean 1939–1945*, Princeton UP, New Jersey, 1951.

Bender, Roger James, and Law, Richard D., *Uniforms, Organization and History of the Afrikakorps*, James Bender Publishing, San Jose, Ca., 1973.

Bennett, Ralph, *Ultra and Mediterranean Strategy 1941–1945*, Hamish Hamilton, 1989.

Bentwich, Norman, and Kisch, Michael, *Brigadier Frederick Kisch: Soldier and Zionist*, Vallentine, Mitchell, 1966.

Blaxland, Gregory, *The Plain Cook and the Great Showman: The First and Eighth Armies in North Africa*, William Kimber, 1977.

Blumenson, Martin, *Rommel's Last Victory: The Battle of Kasserine Pass*, Allen & Unwin, 1966.

Brett-James, Antony, *Conversations with Montgomery*, William Kimber, 1984.

Breuer, William B., *Operation Torch: The Allied Gamble to Invade North Africa*, St. Martin's Press, N.Y., 1985.

The British Army in World War II: A Handbook on the Organisation, Armament, Equipment, Ranks, Uniforms, etc, 1942, Greenhill Books edn., 1990.

Burdon, R.M., *24 Battalion: Official History of New Zealand in the Second World War 1939–45*, War History Branch, Department of Internal Affairs, Wellington, NZ, 1953.

Burk, Robert F., *Dwight D. Eisenhower: Hero and Politician*, Twayne Publishers, Boston, 1986.

Carell, Paul, *The Foxes of the Desert*, MacDonald, 1960.

Carver, Michael, *Dilemmas of the Desert War: A New Look at the Libyan Campaign 1940–1942*, Batsford, 1986.

Calvocoressi, Peter, *Top Secret Ultra*, Cassell, 1980.

Chalfont, Alun, *Montgomery of Alamein*, Weidenfeld and Nicolson, 1976.

Chalmers, W.S., *Full Cycle, The Biography of Sir Bertram Home Ramsay*, Hodder & Stoughton, 1959.

Chaplin, H.D., *The Queen's Own Royal West Kent Regiment 1920–1950*, Michael Joseph, 1954.

Childs, Marquis, *Eisenhower: Captive Hero: A Critical Study of the General and the President*, Hammond and Hammond, 1959.

Clay, Ewart W., *The Path of the 50th: The Story of the 50th (Northumberland) Division in the Second World War 1939–1945*, Gale & Polden, Aldershot, 1950.

Cody, J.F., *28 (Maori) Battalion: Official History of New Zealand in the Second World War 1939–45*, War History Branch, Department of Internal Affairs, Wellington, NZ, 1956.

Cowles, Virginia, *Who Dares, Wins: the story of the Phantom Major – David Stirling and his Desert Command*, Ballantine Books edn., N.Y., 1959.

Craven, Wesley Frank, and Cate, James Lea, eds., *The Army Air Forces in World War II*, Volume Two, *Europe: Torch to Pointblank. August 1942 to December 1943*, University of Chicago Press, 1949.

Daniell, David Scott, *History of the East Surrey Regiment*, Vol. IV, 1920–1957, Ernest Benn, 1957.

Regimental History: The Royal Hampshire Regiment, Vol. 3, 1918–1954, Gale and Polden, Aldershot, 1955.

Davies, W.J.K., *German Army Handbook 1939–1945*, Ian Allan, 1973.

Deakin, F.W., *The Brutal Friendship: Mussolini, Hitler and the Fall of Italian Fascism*, Weidenfeld and Nicolson, 1962.

Dean, Basil, *The Theatre at War*, Harrap, 1956.

D'Este, Carlo, *Patton: A Genius for War*, HarperCollins, 1995.

Die Oase, Journal of the *Deutsches Afrika-Korps* Association – various dates and authors.

Ellenberger, G.F., *History of the King's Own Yorkshire Light Infantry, Vol. VI, 1939–1948*, Gale & Polden, Aldershot, 1961.

Ellis, John, *Brute Force: Allied Strategy and Tactics in the Second World War*, Andre Deutsch, 1990.

Ellis, L.F., *Welsh Guards at War*, London Stamp Exchange edn., 1990.

Essame, Hubert, *Patton the Commander*, Batsford, 1974.

Forty, George, *Afrika Korps at War: 2. The Long Road Back*, Ian Allan, 1978.
    The Armies of Rommel, Arms & Armour, 1997.
    US Army Handbook 1939–1945, Allan Sutton Publishing, 1995.

Foster, R.C.G., *History of the Queen's Royal Regiment*, Vol. VIII, 1924–1948, Gale & Polden, Aldershot, 1953.

Fox, Sir Frank, *The Royal Inniskilling Fusiliers in the Second World War*, Gale & Polden, Aldershot, 1951.

ffrench-Blake, Lt.-Col., *A History of the 17/21st Lancers 1922–1959*, Macmillan, 1962.

Freyberg, Paul, *Bernard Freyberg, V.C.: Soldier of Two Nations*, Hodder & Stoughton, 1991.

Gelb, Norman, *Desperate Venture: The Story of Operation Torch, The Allied Invasion of North Africa*, Hodder & Stoughton, 1992.

Gilbert, Martin, *Winston S. Churchill*, Volume VII, *Road to Victory 1941–1945*, Heinemann, 1986.

Graham, Desmond, *Keith Douglas 1920–1944: A Biography*, OUP pbk edn., 1988.

Hamilton, Nigel, *Monty: The Making of a General 1887–1942*, Hamish Hamilton, 1981.
    Monty: Master of the Battlefield 1942–1944, Hamish Hamilton, 1983.
    Monty: The Field-Marshal 1944–1976, Hamish Hamilton, 1986.

Hezlet, Sir Arthur, *The Submarine and Sea Power*, Peter Davies, 1967.

Hinsley, F.H., *British Intelligence in the Second World War*, II, *Its Influence on Strategy and Operations*, HMSO, 1981.

Horsfall, John, *The Wild Geese are Flighting*, Roundwood Press, Kineton, 1976.

Howarth, T.E.B., ed., *Monty at Close Quarters: Recollections of the Man*, Leo Cooper, 1985.

Howe, George F., *The Battle History of the 1st Armored Division*, Combat Forces Press, Washington, 1954; repr. The Battery Press, Nashville, Tennessee, 1979.
    Northwest Africa: Seizing the Initiative in the West, United States Army in World War II, the Mediterranean Theater of Operations, Department of the Army, Washington, 1957.

Howard, Michael, *The Mediterranean Strategy in the Second World War*, Weidenfeld and Nicolson, 1968.

Hurstfield, Julian G., *America and the French Nation 1939–1945*, University of North Carolina Press, 1986.

Jackson, W.G.F., *Alexander of Tunis as Military Commander*, Batsford, 1971.
    The North African Campaign 1940–43, Batsford, 1975.

Jervois, W.J., *The History of the Northamptonshire Regiment: 1934–1948*, The Northamptonshire Regimental Committee, Northampton, 1953.

Jones, Matthew, *Britain, the United States and the Mediterranean War; 1942–44*, Macmillan, 1996.

Jones, Vincent, *Operation Torch: Anglo-American Invasion of North Africa*, Pan/Ballantine, 1973.

Joslen, H.F., *Orders of Battle: U.K., and Colonial Formations and Units in the 2nd World War; 1939–1945*, 2 vols., HMSO, 1960; repr. London Stamp Exchange, 1990.

Keegan, John, ed., *Churchill's Generals*, Weidenfeld and Nicolson, 1991.

Knickerbocker, H.R., *et al.*, *Danger Forward: The Story of the First Division in World War II*, Albert Lowe Enterprises, Atlanta, Georgia, 1947; repr. The Battery Press, Nashville, Tennessee, 1980.

Knight, C.R.B., *Historical Records of the Buffs: Royal East Kent Regiment (3rd Foot), 1919–1948*, The Medici Society, 1951.

Knightly, Phillip, *The First Casualty: From the Crimea to Vietnam: the War Correspondent as Hero, Propagandist and Myth Maker*, Harcourt Brace Jovanovich, N.Y., 1975.

Kurowski, Franz, *Endkampf in Afrika: Opfergang der Heeresgruppe Rommel in Tunesien 1942/43*, Druffel, Leoni am Starnberger See, 1983.

Langer, William L., *Our Vichy Gamble*, Knopf, N.Y., 1947.

Lawler, Nancy Ellen, *Soldiers of Misfortune: Ivoirien Tirailleurs of World War II*, Ohio University Press, 1992.

Lewin, Ronald, *The Life and Death of the Afrika Korps*, Corgi edn., 1979.
   Montgomery as Military Commander, Batsford, 1971.
   Rommel as Military Commander, Batsford, 1968.
   Ultra Goes to War: the Secret Story, Hutchinson, 1978.
Lucas, James, *Panzer Army Africa*, Macdonald and Jane's, 1977.
Macksey, Kenneth, *Crucible of Power: The Fight for Tunisia 1942–1943*, Hutchinson, 1969.
Madeja, W. Victor, ed., *The Italian Army Order of Battle 1940 to 1944: Between Fascism and Monarchy*, Valor, Allentown, Penn., rev. edn., 1990.
Martin, T.A., *The Essex Regiment 1929–1950*, The Essex Regiment Association, Warley Barracks, Brentwood, 1952.
Matloff, Maurice, and Snell, Edwin M., *United States Army in World War II: Strategic Planning for Coalition Warfare 1941–1942*, Department of the Army, Washington, D.C., 1953.
Maule, Henry, *Out of the Sand*, Corgi edn., 1967.
Mayer, Leo J., 'The Decision to Invade North Africa (TORCH), 1942,' in *Command Decisions*, ed. Greenfield, Kent Roberts, Methuen, 1960.
Messenger, Charles, *The Tunisian Campaign*, Ian Allan, 1982.
Mitcham, Samuel W., *Hitler's Field Marshals and their Battles*, Grafton Books edn., 1989.
   Hitler's Legions: The German Army Order of Battle, World War II, Dorset Press, N.Y., 1985.
Moorehead, Alan, *Montgomery: A Biography*, Hamish Hamilton, 1946.
Morison, Samuel Eliot, *History of United States Naval Operations in World War II*, Volume 2, *Operations in North African Waters, October 1942 – June 1943*, OUP, 1947.
Moynihan, Michael, ed., *People At War*, David & Charles edn., 1989.
Nafziger, George F., *The German Order of Battle: Panzers and Artillery in World War II* Greenhill, 1999.
Neillands, Robert, *The Raiders: The Army Commandos 1940–1946*, Weidenfeld and Nicolson, 1989.
Nicholson, W.N., *The Suffolk Regiment 1928 to 1946*, East Anglian Magazine, Ipswich, 1948.
Nicolson, Nigel, *Alex: The Life of Field Marshal Earl Alexander of Tunis*, Weidenfeld and Nicolson, 1973.
Norton, Frazer D., *26 Battalion: Official History of New Zealand in the Second World War 1939–45*, War History Branch, Department of Internal Affairs, Wellington, NZ, 1952.
Onslow, Earl of, *Men and Sand*, Saint Catherine Press, 1961.
Orange, Vincent, *Coningham: A Biography of Air Marshal Sir Arthur Coningham*, Methuen, 1990.
Pack, S.W.C., *Invasion North Africa 1942*, Charles Scribner's Sons, N.Y., 1978.
Parkinson, C. Northcote, *Always a Fusilier: The War History of the Royal Fusiliers (City of London Regiment), 1939–1945*, Sampson Low, 1949.
Pawle, Gerald, *The War and Colonel Warden*, White Lion edn., 1974.
Pendar, Kenneth, *Adventure in Diplomacy: Our French Dilemma*, Dodd, Mead & Company, N.Y., 1945; De Capo edn., N.Y., 1976.
Perrett, Bryan, *Allied Tanks North Africa: World War Two*, Arms and Armour Press, 1986.
Pierre-Gosset, Renée, *Algiers 1941–1943: A Temporary Expedient*, Cape, 1945.
Playfair, I.S.O., *et al.*, *The Mediterranean and Middle East*, Vol. IV, *The Destruction of the Axis Forces in Africa*; History of the Second World War United Kingdom Military Series, HMSO, 1966.
Pocock, Tom, *Alan Moorehead*, Pimlico edn., 1991.
Ray, Cyril, *Algiers to Austria: A History of 78 Division in the Second World War*, Eyre & Spottiswoode, 1952.
Richards, Denis, and Saunders, Hilary St. George, *Royal Air Force 1939–1945*, Volume 2, *The Fight Avails*, pbk edn., HMSO, 1975.
Roskill, S.W., *The Navy at War 1939–1945*, OUP, 1960.
   The War at Sea, 1939–1945, Vol. II, *The Period of Balance*; History of the Second World War United Kingdom Military Series, ed. J.R.M. Butler, HMSO, 1956.
Ross, Angus, *23 Battalion: Official History of New Zealand in the Second World War 1939–45*, War History Branch, Department of Internal Affairs, Wellington, NZ, 1959.

Ruppenthal, Roland G., *United States Army in World War II: The European Theater of Operations, Logistical Support of the Armies*, Vol. I, *May 1941 – September 1944*, Department of the Army, Washington D.C., 1953.

Rutherford, Ward, *Kasserine: Baptism of Fire*, Macdonald, 1971.

Saunders, Hilary St. George, *The Green Beret: The Story of the Commandos 1940–1945*, New English Library edn., 1975.

> *The Red Beret: The Story of the Parachute Regiment at War 1940–1945*, Michael Joseph, 1950.

Sainsbury, Keith, *The North African Landings 1942: a Strategic Decision*, Davis-Poynter, 1976.

Sixsmith, E.K.G., *Eisenhower as Military Commander*, Batsford, 1973.

Smithers, A.J., *Rude Mechanicals: An Account of Tank Maturity during the Second World War*, Grafton edn., 1989.

Stanton, Shelby L., *Order of Battle: US Army, World War II*, Presidio, Novato, Ca., 1984.

Stevens, G.R., *Fourth Indian Division*, McLaren, Toronto, Ontario, 1948.

Stevens, W.G., *Bardia to Enfidaville: Official History of New Zealand in the Second World War 1939–45*, War History Branch, Department of Internal Affairs, Wellington, NZ, 1962.

Stewart, P.F., *The History of the XII Royal Lancers*, OUP, 1959.

Strawson, John, *General Sir Richard McCreery: A Portrait*, Privately published, 1973.

Sullivan, Matthew Barry, *Thresholds of Peace: Four Hundred Thousand German Prisoners and the People of Britain 1944–1948*, Hamish Hamilton, 1979.

Terraine, John, *Business in Great Waters: The U-Boat Wars 1916–1945*, Leo Cooper, 1989.

> *A Time for Courage: the Royal Air Force in the European War, 1939–1945*, Macmillan, N.Y., 1985. Published in the UK by Hodder & Stoughton as *The Right of the Line: the Royal Air Force in the European War, 1939–1945*.

Thomas, R.T., *Britain and Vichy: The Dilemma of Anglo-French Relations 1940–42*, Macmillan, 1979.

Tomkins, Peter, *The Murder of Darlan: A Study in Conspiracy*, Simon and Schuster, N.Y., 1965.

Vanderveen, Bart H., ed., *The Observer's Fighting Vehicles Directory, World War II*, Frederick Warne, 1969.

Verney, G.L., *The Desert Rats: The History of the 7th Armoured Division 1938 to 1945*, Greenhill Books edn., 1990.

Verney, Peter, *The Micks: the Story of the Irish Guards*, Peter Davies, 1970.

Verrier, Anthony, *Assassination in Algiers: Churchill, Roosevelt, de Gaulle, and the Murder of Admiral Darlan*, Macmillan, 1990.

Ward, S.G.P., *Faithful: The Story of the Durham Light Infantry*, Nelson, 1963.

Warner, Philip, *Horrocks: The General Who Led from the Front*, Sphere Books edn., 1985.

Watson, Bruce Allen, *Exit Rommel: The Tunisian Campaign, 1942–1943*, Praeger, Westport, Connecticut, 1999.

Wellard, James, *The Man in the Helmet: The Life of General Patton*, Eyre and Spottiswoode, 1947.

Winterbotham, F.W., *The Ultra Secret*, Weidenfeld and Nicolson, 1974.

Yarborough, William Pelham, *Bail Out Over North Africa: America's First Combat Missions 1942*, Philipps Publications, Williamstown, NJ, 1979.

Young, Desmond, *Rommel*, Collins, 1950.

Index

Index